Columbia University

Contributions to Education

Teachers College Series

No. 814

AMS PRESS
NEW YORK

THEORIES OF 146926

SECONDARY EDUCATION

IN THE UNITED STATES

By JOSEPH JUSTMAN, Ph.D.

TEACHERS COLLEGE, COLUMBIA UNIVERSITY

CONTRIBUTIONS TO EDUCATION, NO. 814

Bureau of Publications

TEACHERS COLLEGE, COLUMBIA UNIVERSITY

New York · 1940

Library of Congress Cataloging in Publication Data

Justman, Joseph, 1909-
    Theories of secondary education in the United States.

    Reprint of the 1940 ed., issued in series: Teachers
College, Columbia University. Contributions to edu-
cation, no. 814.
    Originally presented as the author's thesis, Columbia.
    Bibliography: p.
    1. Education, Secondary--United States. 2. Edu-
cation--Philosophy. I. Title. II. Series: Columbia
University. Teachers College. Contributions to edu-
cation, no. 814.
LB1607.J85 1972   373.73   70-176923
ISBN 0-404-55814-3

Reprinted by Special Arrangement with Teachers
College Press, New York, New York

From the edition of 1940, New York
First AMS edition published in 1972
Manufactured in the United States

AMS PRESS, INC.
NEW YORK, N. Y.   10003

Acknowledgments

GRATEFUL acknowledgment is made to those who by their advice and encouragement helped this work to its completion. In particular, the writer is under deepest obligation to his teacher and the sponsor of this study, Professor Thomas H. Briggs. For his wise counsel and personal encouragement throughout the study as well as for the lasting personal and professional values gained in the course of several years' association with him, the writer is very grateful. He is greatly appreciative of the help he received from Professor Isaac L. Kandel, whose generously given advice and friendly professional interest were a constant source of great support. To Professor Irving Lorge the writer is indebted for invaluable suggestions for dealing with the problems of method that arose at the study's inception. Finally, the writer welcomes this opportunity to express to the Advanced School of Education of Teachers College his appreciation of the understanding and considerate way in which it extended to him every opportunity and every means to carry on and to complete this work of research.

JOSEPH JUSTMAN

Contents

Theories of Secondary Education
in the United States

Introduction

IT IS THE OBJECT of this study to present for comparative and critical examination several of the main currents of theory evident in contemporary secondary education. The need for such a study does not at this time require much justification. Great social events have brought in their train great educational problems. Ours is an age of unusual educational accomplishment; but accomplishment is rarely without its perplexities, doubts, misgivings. Nowhere have both accomplishment and attendant perplexities been more strikingly evident than in secondary education. The secondary school has grown amazingly under our very eyes, so quickly, indeed, that we have not had the time to develop very much concern about it. Problems arising out of sheer physical growth have commanded most of the attention of practical schoolmen, and for a time left little room for less immediately pressing but more important considerations—considerations of purpose and direction, and of fundamental method. But at present the contemplation of achievement is marred somewhat by the realization that we have left unsolved many problems. We cannot very long avoid facing the issues that have been created, and recent literature bears increasing testimony that we are aware of this fact. But there is danger even in facing issues squarely, danger that we shall be tempted by the magnitude of our problem to sacrifice the comprehensive view for greater piecemeal thoroughness. An issue, however inclusive it may be, cannot be entirely adjudicated on the merits alone of its opposing alternatives. Its contending alternatives are like links in separate chains that have happened to interlock: one cannot disengage the links without disturbing also the larger chains. If we are ever to resolve our present perplexities, we shall

1

do so only by retaining a careful perspective of education as a whole. And the maintenance of one's perspective becomes more likely when one has considered and consciously chosen from the various alternatives that present themselves, each apparent in its comprehensive relationships. The outcome may be eclecticism, but it is an eclecticism that is itself a synthesis of what is best in each alternative possibility.

The emphasis in this study is on the broad but distinctive points of view discernible in secondary education. The final effect may be, unfortunately, to give a somewhat over-simplified view of the current situation, as if comprehensiveness and consistency in thinking were the rule in contemporary education. The purpose is, however, to reveal the main lines of educational controversy rather than faithfully to represent the whole of it. The points of view which are thus to be presented have been drawn from the literature of education.

Meaning of Secondary Education.—Secondary education, as here used, is a term of convenience for referring to a certain period in the systematic educational experience of the child, the limits of which will be more exactly described below. Secondary is not used at this point in any technical sense. The study agrees fully with the principle stated by the Committee on the Orientation of Secondary Education [1] that education is a "gradual, continuous, unitary process," and that secondary education is a stage in that process. There is no such thing as a theory of secondary education per se. Essentially, a theory of secondary education is a *theory of education applied to the secondary period,* though this period may differ in particular emphases given to it from the periods that precede and follow. The theories presented are first and foremost theories of education in their bearing upon the secondary period.

The secondary period is here defined as that period in the life of youth beginning approximately at the age of 12 and extending until such a time as the youth is ready to take leave of the school or of some comparable social agency set up for his guidance, supervision, and instruction, in order to make his own way in society and to continue his education independently (and, as defined, the secondary period would include the period of the continuation school, of other types of part-time schools

---

[1] Committee on the Orientation of Secondary Education, *Functions of Secondary Education,* p. 15. Department of Secondary School Principals, National Education Association. 1937.

for youth, of the government-regulated C. C. C. camps), or until he is ready to enter an institution of higher education.[2] Where, in more precise terms of chronological age or of particular institution, this period terminates, will be indicated in course by each of the theories; on the approximate beginning of this period, practically all theories agree.

A working definition of secondary education such as this, formulated in terms of a time-unit rather than in terms of educational technique, and postulating, moreover, a very extensive time-unit, has the following advantages: It provides a common ground upon which theories that differ with respect to fundamental conceptions may meet; it does not at the outset exclude any theory; it is comprehensive in scope, ruling out no part of what any theory may legitimately hold to be *secondary* education, and allowing for consideration of recent developments, near to what was traditionally the close of the secondary-school period, which have not yet been incorporated into the regular scheme of education;[3] it is flexible, allowing for the easy adjustments of its limits to fit the varying definitions of the secondary period. On the other hand, such an inclusive definition of secondary education results in sizable discrepancies in the use of the term *secondary*: not all theories are willing to agree that secondary education is co-extensive with all of post-primary education of any kind up to what is definitely the higher collegiate or university level.[4]

[2] It is not proposed, in this study, to deal with theories of higher education. The dividing line between secondary and higher education could not, however, be set arbitrarily. In the survey of the literature it was found that a number of writers hold that secondary education extends as far as the end of the second college year. This is therefore accepted as the boundary line between secondary and higher education beyond which the study will not go. According to some theories, of course, secondary education should not extend that far.

[3] See, for example, the suggestions made by the Committee on the Orientation of Secondary Education in its first Report, *Issues of Secondary Education,* Issue II, pp. 113 ff. 1936. Similar consideration of new developments is to be found in the writings of Douglass, Hutchins, Judd, Spaulding, and others, and will be indicated in the appropriate place.

[4] Hutchins, for instance, uses the terms secondary education and general education to indicate respectively the educational periods from ages 12 to 16 and 16 to 20. (R. M. Hutchins, *No Friendly Voice,* pp. 109–110. 1936.) Similarly, in the Report of the Orientation Committee, *Issues of Secondary Education,* pp. 79–128, a distinction is made between the secondary school and a new social agency that must be established for students for whom the present secondary school is not appropriate. In accordance with the comprehensive definition of secondary

This study seeks to compare theories of education as they are to operate in the period outlined, regardless of the nomenclature used to identify this period by the adherents of any particular theory. The term secondary is a convenient one, being already in use by all theories for the larger part of this period. Therefore, to avoid the irritation to the reader and possibly the confusion that might result from any discrepancy in the later use of terms, the following definite declaration must be made: The term secondary education will be used in this study to refer to the education throughout the entire period as defined; whatever proposals are advanced by any theory of education for all parts of this period will be considered as constituting *its* theory of secondary education, regardless of how a particular theory may choose to restrict its use of the word secondary. Whenever it is necessary to use the word secondary in the sense to which it is restricted by the theory under discussion, as, for example, in describing the series of schools proposed for this period, the word will be enclosed in quotation marks.

Meaning of "Theory."—When does a series of principles, presented together, constitute a theory, and how is a *theory* of secondary education to be identified? This study proposes to deal with logically related sequences of educational principles, based on the one hand upon fundamental conceptions regarding man and society and the nature of human development (that is, psychology) stemming in turn from some understandable theory of values, and pointing on the other hand toward a program of secondary education at least the outlines of which are clearly described. Such a definition is essential in trying to steer a steady course between the Scylla of generality and vagueness and the Charybdis of concrete proposals based upon no clearly evidenced understanding of the larger factors involved. This definition served therefore as the standard of relevance throughout the survey of the literature in the selection of the source materials. It is perhaps to be regretted that this study could not undertake to deal with contributions to educational theory in which no direct application was made to the secondary period; the problem of formulating a theory of secondary education from such materials would have been a problem of dealing with inferences. The data obtained in this way, were the magnitude of the task itself not an

---

education used in this study, consideration of the nature and purposes of this agency will be included.

important obstacle, would not have been of the same order of reliability as the other data obtained from explicitly formulated theories of secondary education, and the two sets of data would not easily have lent themselves to integration and comparison. The magnitude of the problem, however, even as here delimited, made such a venture out of the question.

General Method.—The progression has been from an indefinite general through the specific to a definite general. To define the problem in concrete terms and to provide a tentative framework of procedure, certain general theories of secondary education were at the beginning assumed. As the study progressed and the nature of the actual data was revealed, the original assumptions were greatly modified (and, in fact, new categories emerged). The procedure was as follows: With the definitions furnishing general guidance and with additional criteria (to be described below) serving further to narrow the field, there were assembled from the literature of education such writings, of individuals and of groups possessing a common or single point of view, as seemed best to meet the requirements. These writings offered specific theories of secondary education—the raw materials of the study. The next step was to group these specific theories, on the basis of fundamental identities or similarities, into *systems* of cognate theory. The theories of secondary education presented in the following chapters are not specific theories, but *generalized systems of theory* within which specific theories have been integrated. Social Evolutionism, for example, is a composite of the theories of Bagley, Judd, and Morrison rather than a faithful representation of the theory advanced by any one of the three. The systems approach homogeneity in different degrees, depending upon the nature of their specific components. Thus, Humanism is considerably further from being a homogeneous system than is, for example, Social Realism. Following the work of synthesis, the last general step in the procedure was, treating each system (as far as possible) as a unit theory of secondary education, to analyze it for comparative presentation.

It is necessary to describe on what basis the specific writings which furnish the raw material of the study were chosen. It was decided at the outset that a single study such as this would have to address itself primarily to those writings which, so far as could be judged by a reader, represent an earnest and sustained effort to deal in a fundamental and comprehensive way with the problems of secondary education. Another consideration was a desire to have as many differing points of view represented as were found to have systematic, constructive expression in educational literature. These two considerations were combined, and in a way modified each other (that is, in some cases comprehensiveness was sacrificed so that the study might gain in representativeness). These two criteria—comprehensiveness and representativeness—served in the selection of the writings that contribute the framework of the study. A third criterion was developed in course after the outlines of the framework had become apparent. It was judged well to include such writings as, though less comprehensive than the others and fundamentally not original, yet contributed important and original ideas within the constructed framework. With the more comprehensive writings to furnish the framework of the systems, these could very well be used to show variations within a system—whether in emphasis, in direction, or in other respects. These three criteria were formulated with a view toward making it possible to achieve within the scope of a single study the ends both of integration and of comparison. The criteria were applied, not with any kind of mechanical objectivity, but in the best judgment of the writer conscious of the ends he was trying to achieve.

In the contributions to the literature of modern education, an increasingly important role is being played by productions of cooperative effort—society publications and yearbooks, reports of commissions and investigating groups, cooperative studies centering around a single theme, and the like. Insofar as such writings were in theory of secondary education as here defined, and insofar as, when evaluated by the criteria described above, they seemed to be suitable, they were used as source material. The contributions were of course less extensive than those of individual writers, but in every case they allied themselves with some more general and comprehensive framework already present, and supplied additional data of an important and sometimes distinctive nature.

Sources of Data.—The specific data upon which the generalized theories of secondary education are based have, accordingly, been drawn from the writings of Bagley, Briggs, Butler, P. W. L. Cox, H. R. Douglass, Norman Foerster, L. T. Hopkins, Hutchins, Judd, Kandel, Learned,

H. C. Morrison, F. T. Spaulding, and V. T. Thayer; and from the following group contributions, each of which is allied in point of view with some one person already mentioned or with the general educational theory of Experimentalism as elaborated by Dewey, Kilpatrick, Bode, Childs, Counts, and others: *A Challenge to Secondary Education, Democracy and the Curriculum, Functions of Secondary Education, Issues of Secondary Education, Reorganizing Secondary Education,* Reports of the Pennsylvania Study of the Carnegie Foundation, Reports of the Regents' Inquiry into the Character and Cost of Public Education in the State of New York, *Science in General Education, The Changing Curriculum, The Community School,* and *Youth Serves the Community.* These writings comprise the materials finally chosen from a much wider field originally surveyed. An attempt was made to draw from them the implications for educational theory of the major current social-economic-political problems, of the development of science and its application to practical living, as well as of certain new movements or developments within the field of education itself (such as the formation of the Civilian Conservation Corps for youth, and the various "youth" studies of the American Youth Commission and their practical consequences).

Applicability of the Findings.—It must be pointed out that this study does not pretend to speak for "all" theory of secondary education. In the realm of educational theorizing, completeness of investigation is not possible, nor is there any such thing as perfect representativeness of the findings. *The materials that were chosen must be regarded as speaking, first of all, for themselves,* rather than as samplings from which inferences are to be drawn regarding the nature of a much broader universe. The selection was dictated by what promised to yield fruitful material for a comparative study. Much more could have been chosen as suitable, but the material had to be kept within limits that would allow careful treatment. In the writer's judgment, the sources listed above contain main distinct trends of thought at present prominent in the thinking about secondary education. This was a condition necessary to make possible the interplay of ideas essential for the realization of the purposes of the study.

That the theories of secondary education here elicited are more than merely the expression of their authors is hardly to be doubted. It is impossible, however, to establish definitely to what degree these theories are representative of the thought now circulating in the large realm of secondary education. A theory of education does not proceed in the rigid pattern of a geometric demonstration. A number of educational theories may possess common or similar basic premises, but they may veer away from each other as they proceed from these premises. When, for example, they deal with the solution of a specific problem of secondary-school curriculum, they may be in thorough disagreement with each other. As a result of working through a much larger area of the literature than is here specified, and of becoming somewhat familiar with the vagaries of educational theory, the writer feels that he can make the following generalizations as to the applicability of his data with a reasonable degree of confidence: It is probable that most of the systematically thought-through theories relating to *public* secondary education [5] can in every case be associated in their basic premises with some one of the theories here presented. The underlying assumptions made, the principal values held, most of the governing educational principles therefore, would be largely similar to, though probably not completely identical with, those of one of the four systems of theory discovered in this investigation. In the remaining respects the outside theories might not always coincide with the theories here given. Finally, it is certain that an extension of this study to include more writings would have extended the intellectual area covered by each system, and increased internal differences. Were this extension continued indefinitely, a good part of the framework of this study would be broken down. Theorists, to the extent that they build on foundations originated by others, tend toward eclecticism; some, however, cross the bounds of sound eclecticism and indulge in an indiscriminate accumulation of often incompatible principles which is really a contradiction of theory.

Anatomy of Theory.—The procedure for integrating the specific theories into systems developed out of a recognition of the nature of

[5] It is necessary here explicitly to note that, for several reasons, the very important Catholic theory or theories of education have not been included for consideration in this study. Catholic theory does not lend itself to ready comparison with secular theories of education, and cannot be evaluated on the same terms as the others. It is not, moreover, intended for general application to non-Catholic students.

theory that grew in the course of the work. As the definition of theory of secondary education indicates,[6] it was assumed that a theory, to be adequate, must possess as its two indispensable elements (1) a conception of the Good Life, and (2) a systematic account of how the Good Life can be gained or approached through a process of education. (As will be seen later, these two are not unrelated.) In the course of a growing familiarity with the literature, it became possible to identify each of these elements in much smaller and more precise units; that is, there were revealed those *pivotal concepts* which, when systematically organized, form what may be called a conception of the Good Life, and distinguish it from all other conceptions (concepts, for example, that may be expressed in such terms as "the relation of the individual to society," "the nature of the good society," "the concept of democracy," "the method of social progress," "the meaning of freedom"), and those pivotal concepts which go to make up what may be called a system of psychology (namely, "the nature of intelligence," "the method of human development," "individual differences," "heredity and environment," etc.). The smaller units were valuable in that they made it easier to match theories (therefore to integrate them, to compare them) and to trace each to its value-sources. Each specific theory was analyzed in terms of these pivotal concepts, and made to reveal its basic values. It was noted that what gave these theories consistency, what held each together as a theory of secondary education, was a theory of values. The theory of values was then subjected to close scrutiny and compared with the others. Ultimately the specific theories were grouped in terms of a common theory of values. Each of the systems of educational theory, the exposition of which follows in these pages, possesses a more or less common theory of values.

The Four Theories.—In this manner, four systems (or theories of secondary education as used in this study) were obtained. Their validity once established, it is intended to compare the systems as integral units rather than to compare the constituent elements within each system. The emphasis in the study is, therefore, on the differences *among* systems rather than on the internal variations *within* systems, though the latter will not be unjustifiably minimized. Each system is analyzed and presented under the following headings: The Social Dynamics of

[6] *Supra*, page 4.

Secondary Education, The Psychological Foundations of Secondary Education, The Meaning of Secondary Education, The Method of Secondary Education. A critical review of each of the systems of theory, taken as a whole, concludes the study.

A brief account needs to be given of the manner in which the four theory-names were determined. The purpose of the names used is to provide a handy means of reference to the theories themselves; it is important to remember that in themselves the names neither add to nor detract from the validity of the categories they represent. The names were in fact not chosen until the study was all but completed. In choosing them, it was not especially desired to invent new terms if appropriate old terms were available; yet, not in all cases was it possible to discover terms already in use that were both appropriate and significant. The result was a compromise arrangement, the names ultimately chosen being: Humanism, Social Evolutionism, Social Realism, and Experimentalism. It is important to remember that, as here used, the names refer to theories of secondary education as totalities, not merely to the philosophical bases or positions of these theories. (There is, for example, no such philosophy as Social Realism; the name here refers to the entire theory of secondary education.)

In Part II of this Introduction, each theory of secondary education is described as a system of thought and identified in terms of its theory of values. Here also an attempt is made to indicate some of the internal differences that characterize each theory. Before turning to that, however, it is necessary to make clear in what manner the terms "values" and "theory of values" are understood and used.[7]

Theory of Values.—Educational theories differ essentially with regard to the values that they accept and that they hold out as ends of the educative process. Such values may be intelligence or faith, reason or experience, individuality or conformity, social need or individual right, self-restraint or self-expression, the familiar, the regular, the permanent, or the novel, the sudden, the changing. One's conception of the Good

[7] Axiology or the study of values is a rather recent branch of philosophy, and there is still considerable confusion in the use of terms. The writer will therefore be pardoned for formulating and adhering to his own definitions. For a brief discussion of the meaning of values and a survey of theories of value, see J. S. Mackenzie, *Ultimate Values,* pp. 91–186. London: Hodder and Stoughton Ltd., 1924.

Life for man is a summation of such values; a conception of the educative process is an explanation of how these values may be achieved, and involves the establishment of values that are minor, less permanent, auxiliary—in short, instrumental values.

A value is, defined roughly, a "good," an object or action or quality or idea that one esteems highly, and that, in the conduct of living, one would prefer to other things as "worthy to be achieved." [8] To valuate is to place an estimate upon objects or actions or qualities or ideas occurrent in one's experience for the guidance of one's living. The purpose of valuation is practical: a value motivates human action, affects human decisions, results in the doing of one thing rather than another. An estimate is placed on all things of which the human being becomes aware as affecting his living in some way. The conscious purpose in living then becomes to realize those things upon which a high valuation has been placed (the valued things, or the values) and correspondingly to avoid or to fail to realize those things upon which a low or a negative valuation has been placed (the non-valued things, or the non-values). Values are of various orders, some being logically antecedent to others.

Values are for the most part not intellectual ultimates; they are rather the immediate bases upon which judgments having practical bearing are made. To know that an educational theory values adaptability to change, creativeness, self-expression, economic security, etc., is not sufficient: it is necessary to know in what way these values are determined. More basic than values are certain postulates regarding the nature of the world we live in and our method of knowing it. Collectively these may be called *a source of values*. A theory of values must include some understandable account of its value-sources. It is quite possible to argue that any intellectual postulate is itself a value, and that the only true source of value therefore is some affective element in personality or some psychological state that prompts an individual in the direction of some things rather than of others.[9] Conceding the admissibility of this

---

[8] Mackenzie, *op. cit.*, p. 97.

[9] For example, if "tender-mindedness" is associated with an inclination toward Rationalism and "tough-mindedness" toward Empiricism (W. James, *Pragmatism*, pp. 11-12. New York: Longmans, Green and Company, 1907.), it may be argued that these elements in personality, "tender-mindedness" and "tough-mindedness," are the ultimate source to which values may be traced. This is merely an illustration. This writer does not know whether James would have so argued.

argument and affirming further that *some sources of value are themselves set up as values* (for example, mind, experience, God), it is still
necessary to distinguish between the fundamental value or the value of
the first order and those which are subsequently derived from it. A
source of values is here conceived as consisting of those fundamental
postulates that help to explain how people arrive at the ends toward
which their practical living, and, of course, their theory of education, are
directed. It answers the significant question, "How do these people account for what they want?"

The important values that characterize each of the several theories of
secondary education here presented will be made clear in the course of
the study's development. In Part II of this Introduction they are indicated in a summary manner; in the main, however, emphasis in this
part is on the sources of value of each theory and on the manner in
which its values are to operate in human living.

PART II: **THEORIES OF SECONDARY EDUCATION**

HUMANISM

General Characteristics.—The term Humanism is used to refer to
that system of educational theory which incorporates the individual
theories of Butler, Foerster, Hutchins, Kandel, and Learned. As a
general point of view in education, the theory represented as Humanism
may be traced back in history in an unbroken line to the early
Renaissance, and beyond that, in Western thought, to the educational
theories of Aristotle and Plato; the present theory is a continuation of
that historic tradition, addressing itself in modern terms to the educational needs of the modern world. The historic Humanism is not a
unity, a single philosophy either of life or of education; rather it is a
general point of view which allows great latitude for individual variation. The historic Humanism, defined broadly, is an aggregate of
individual theories that are proximate rather than homogeneous. What
is true of the historic is true also of the modern Humanism. It cannot
be called a closely-knit system of educational theory: there exist within
it important variations among individuals. The most important variation involves a disagreement on the meaning of mind or the source of

values. So vital a disagreement, of course, would warrant the division of this single category into two different categories of educational theory, were there not good reasons why the various theories might well be presented together. Such consequences for secondary education as arise from this disagreement, and from others existent among the individual theories, will not be overlooked in this discussion.

What justifies the inclusion of the various individual theories within a single category is that, with respect to most of their educational values and *general* means of realizing these values, the theories are very much alike. Individuals may differ on the theoretical sources of value, yet agree on the values themselves: this, generally speaking, even the two most conflicting individual theories within Humanism do. Humanist theories possess a common criterion of values: a conception of humanness as something distinct from and above the rest of nature. They exhibit a highly developed sense of the fitness of things in their relation to man. A common idealism enables them to encourage mind to act in independence of nature. A common regard for tradition gives them a large ground in which their values, though entering from different directions, meet and flow along in a single channel. As theories of education the individual Humanist theories are much closer to each other than their basic philosophical differences would indicate.

The major division within Humanism is with respect to the meaning of mind (that is, the source of values) and the manner in which values are to be regarded. Butler, Kandel, and Learned are essentially rationalists. To Foerster, however, mind is primarily disposition for ethical living guided by meanings intuitively apprehended; only secondarily is it a value-creating instrument.[10] A large consequence for education of this disagreement is a difference in conception of method of mental training: the second theory lends itself more readily to formal discipline. But many other conflicts in educational theory that might have arisen from so fundamental a difference are cancelled by the fact that the individuals on both sides are Humanists. It must be remembered that Rationalist-Humanists are Humanists first and Rationalists

---

[10] This writer is not clear as to where, between the two, Hutchins belongs. Hutchins is inclined to class himself as a rationalist, but at a certain point in his thinking he allies himself with the opponents of rationalism. The writer is inclined to place him with Foerster. It is a fact that in the alignment of sides within Humanism, Hutchins and Foerster are frequently to be found together.

afterwards, and so in their way are the Intuitionist-Humanists. In the following account of the theory of values of Humanism, a more detailed statement of the nature of the disagreement will be presented, and, in the chapters that follow, the implications of the disagreement for secondary education.

Common Basic Premises.—A convenient starting point is the characteristic principle of Humanism of viewing man as apart from and superior to the rest of nature. It is empirically evident (to Humanism) that human life differs from the rest of living nature to an extent that justifies a dualistic view of human and non-human life. It is in the *differentness* between man and nature that the meaning of humanness is to be sought, and in seeking to account for this differentness, Humanism ascribes it to the presence in man of mind or soul. The meaning of humanness is to be found, therefore, in the possibilities and accomplishments of mind or soul, and human values (1) arise out of mind or through the instrumentality of mind, and (2) in the course of their progress, tend to increase and extend the differentness between human and non-human life.

Through the instrumentality of mind, man has been able to achieve for himself greater security in living and greater control of the direction of existence. Progressively he has freed himself from many of the conditions that nature exacts from other living things as the price of survival, and to an extent has created his own conditions that seem better to provide for his material needs, in the process re-creating nature to insure the permanence or at least the continuance of these conditions. Viewing it in this way, mind has enabled man to entrench himself in nature, but, what is much more important, in a way of which man is himself conscious, which he has conceived, which he intends.

It is in this latter respect that the true significance of mind lies, raising human living above the level of "existence" or even "adjustment to nature." Human living in nature is in accordance with ends conceived by man himself and in a manner deliberately calculated to realize them. These ends are of course limited by the fact that man is a biological being, and, in essential processes, must abide by those conditions that maintain life everywhere; but within these limits man is able to create a way of life that seems to himself better to express the meaning of humanness than does the "way of nature." Discovering in himself certain natural impulses which he judged unworthy, man has succeeded to a considerable extent in checking these impulses, refining them, sublimating them, replacing them with new and more worthy conduct-motivations. In the process, man has created for himself a moral and ethical life that is without parallel elsewhere in nature. The principles which govern this living are the outcome of man's possession of mind. It is this fact that makes the possibilities of human living unique, and human values like no other in nature. Mind has achieved a "human" life for man, and it is in the direction of living more and more this life that human progress lies.

Rationalist-Humanism.—The manner in which such a life is achieved depends, of course, upon the manner in which the human mind is conceived, and it is here that the division among Humanists occurs. It is the theory of the Rationalist-Humanists [11] that mind is in essence the capacity to convert into meaningfulness the raw data of perceptual experience; that man discovers his own purpose by reference to the meanings that he thus establishes; that values are a function of understanding the world, and vary qualitatively with the degree of understanding that man has achieved; that all ethical conduct has a rational basis, that it grows out of man's belief that the ideas he has point the way to the fulfillment of his destiny, that ideas exercise their own compulsion; that "freedom of the will" is simply the power that comes to human beings from a knowledge of "things-as-they-are" to guide their living within the limits of nature that man has extended.

To the Rationalist-Humanists [12] man's standing in the world comes solely by virtue of his being able to "know" it. The world of matter exists independently of mind, but it is mind that gives meaning to matter. The sensible world of experience is a world of "things"; mind translates the meaning*less* objects of experience into meaning*ful*

[11] The reader has probably already noted that the difference in theory of mind here referred to (within Humanism) is a difference not only of theories of knowledge but also of theories of reality, that is, different types of Idealism are involved. The writer has chosen to consider both these types of differences under only the epistemological categories, Rationalism and Intuitionism. The names themselves are used purely for the purpose of making a general distinction. The writer has for this the precedent of William James who constantly used the term Rationalism when he was referring to much more than just a theory of knowledge.

[12] As opposed to the Intuitionist-Humanists.

objects. Literally, the mind *lends* meanings to things. The meaningful aspect of reality is therefore created in mind. A meaning may thus be defined as an assumption that mind makes regarding the nature of a sensed fact, which, as long as it stands, serves mind as its representation of that fact. Mind interprets the meaning of a thing in its own terms and in terms of recognized relations of things to each other. Successive views of concrete reality influence mind to retain its meanings or to change them. Mind tends to unify, to systematize, and to extend meanings thus drawn from experience. By such a process mind builds up a meaningful pattern of world which corresponds to what it sees or thinks it sees outside itself. Mind does not necessarily assume an a priori relatedness or unity among things. Such a unity as mind gives to world is a unity which its external subject-matter, coupled with its own unifying tendencies, makes possible. Mind assumes that the world exists and that it can be known; it seeks, thereupon, to know what the world is like—to understand it in its permanent and in its changing aspects, to know it in all its manifestations, whether they are singular or regularly recurrent. As mind is successful in creating "responsible" meanings and in arranging them in more inclusive and cohering patterns, man is able to design for himself the kind of life with which his meanings seem to be in harmony. Human values are created by mind in terms of a growing world-picture; they represent to man his purpose in the world as he knows it.

Intuitionist-Humanism.—Intuitionist-Humanism agrees that mind includes capacity to give meaning to the data of sensory experience, that man's control in nature is a result of this capacity, that the mastery of *things* is primarily dependent upon our understanding of them. But it denies that the highest *human values* grow primarily out of man's capacity to attach meanings to sense-data and through laborious synthesis of these meanings. Meanings occur in mind not solely as a result of its authorship. Man does create meanings, but meanings are also *communicated* to man directly, not necessarily via sense-perceptions. The meanings thus communicated are higher meanings; they deal with an ethical rather than a material content. With respect to them, reason serves in a subordinate capacity: it clarifies and regulates, but it does not oppose or disprove. The conception of reality here implied is rather different from the Rationalist-Humanist: it assumes a world responding to a prime mover, operating according to a definite plan. The mind of man (or soul, as it should perhaps more properly be called) is more than capacity for reasoning. It is primarily capacity for "goodness," for a high order of ethical living that is denied to all non-human living things. But to have capacity for goodness is not at once to realize it. In man there is a struggle between an ethical and a temperamental self, and goodness is realized only as the ethical self gains control, as man learns to live by principles that are not necessarily natural or instinctive. The highest principles are the meanings, not created by mind out of piecemeal investigation of its own experience, but communicated to it whole. To capture such meanings, man's whole being reaches out in a supreme effort to "know," and the result of such outgoing of experience is a direct, subjective, intuitive insight into the meaning of humanness as expressed through ethical conduct. By such means, only the highest, the guiding values, have been obtained. Reason must still operate in interpreting, applying, extending, in building up a whole realm of subordinate ethical concepts, and in conceptualizing a world of things. But with regard to the highest values the function of reason is regulative and not creative. These values are not subject to validation by cognitive processes, but the commonness of their existence in human experience is an objective affirmation of their reality.

Implications of the Differences between Rationalist-Humanism and Intuitionist-Humanism.—It is evident that from these differences in conceptions of nature of mind and origin of values, there follows another essential difference with regard to status of values. Revealed values of accepted supernatural origin [18] possess an authority that cannot be matched by values of admittedly human origination. Such values tend to be absolute, non-evolutionary, and unchallengeable by those who accept them. Reason harmonizes, interprets, extends, but does not really disturb. Human progress means progress toward a realization of these values rather than a progress of them. This much must be said in explanation of the undeniable mutual hostility existent between rationalists and those in whom reason must harmonize with a higher faith. On the other hand, bitter quarrels concerning the origin

[18] It will be recognized that Foerster is here presenting the philosophic basis of traditional Christianity.

and status of values must not disguise the fact that the values themselves are very largely similar—because their criterion is the same. Also, the great truths for which divine origin is claimed are few in number and general in meaning. The Intuitionist-Humanists deny the final authority of reason rather than disclaim its use: indeed their very many subsidiary values are rational in origin and subjected to validation by ordinary human processes, and they undergo revision and development in the process of continuous application.

While, in the following paragraphs, the statements regarding the growth and validation of values represent more accurately the point of view of Rationalist-Humanism than of Intuitionist-Humanism (that is, the point of view of Butler, Kandel, and Learned rather than of Foester and Hutchins), the reader will be able to make for himself the modifications that are necessary to render these statements appropriate to the latter.

The Values of Humanism.—It follows from what has been said that principles for the guidance of human living cannot be drawn by reference to natural law operative in non-human species. Man is more than a biological organism. His values are the outcome of mind operating in awareness, it is true, of the limitations of man as biological organism, but sensitive also to its special human mission and possibilities. For production of its values, mind can seek no precedent in nature, and for validation of its values it has only itself to fall back upon; "science," for example, will not do, because it is itself a creation of mind and determined by its values. Fortunately the mind of man is an instrument that labors not merely for man, but for all humanity. Man, everywhere, regardless of his time and place, works to achieve an understanding of himself, a knowledge of the human function. The achievements of individual minds merge and become the common collective property of all humanity. The effect is that of a universal mind, in terms of which values are created and with reference to which they are verified. The making of values becomes the continuous cumulative enterprise of all humanity, and human living is based upon a continuity of values. By the same logic, the verification of values is in terms of the total background of human experience. We do not begin anew with each generation; we take over what man has previously learned and we build upon it. In this we have no option, for we are born into a world which has been remade in accordance with previous human values. To be in ignorance of previous values is not to understand the world we live in; to discard values previously tried and verified in human experience is to court disaster. The Good Life is the life that, basing itself on the continuity of human tradition, seeks to harmonize its own experience with the accredited values of the past.

The heritage of value is of a mixed character. Values differ among themselves with respect to their degree of verification, and therefore with respect to the degree of authority to which they are entitled. Certain principles of conduct have, by their repeated occurrence in mind and by their consistent validation, earned the status of truths, as authoritative in their own way as are the "laws" of nature. To repudiate them is to fly in the face of the collective wisdom of mankind. To develop as a human being means to take over these values and to use them in the guidance of living—to extend them, to refine them, perhaps even to revise them when conditions warrant and the best available intelligence so dictates, but never lightly and without misgivings. Such values must be not only transmitted from generation to generation but deeply inculcated in every individual of each succeeding generation, not merely as objects of knowledge but as ideals authorizing conduct. But not all inherited values are in the category of truths; indeed, in the nature of things, most of them are not. The world-picture is not a finished thing. The world of our experience has elements of change as well as elements of permanence. Inherited values are not always in agreement. And we, by building on the achievements of our predecessors, are constantly learning more about ourselves and the world. Most of the values that the past has made available to us, therefore, are not to serve as fixed controls of conduct. They serve rather as starting points for our thinking, as means of orientation to the world about us. We test them, use them, change them; but the final decision with respect to them rests with us. It is indispensable for continuous civilized living that they be transmitted, but their function is in that they supply mental content rather than rules of order.

It must not be inferred that the availability of proved values thereby relieves the individual of the necessity of working out for himself the Good Life. To come into the rich inheritance of the past is not to be relieved of the necessity of using mind in an original, creative way.

To cherish trusted values is to be assured of going at least part of the way in the right direction. But the prime task of the human being in every generation is still to "know himself" in the world he lives in. Man uses values in self-guidance; he does not merely follow values. Only as he can apply values to the understanding and control of his situation, as he can deal with them in an independent, knowing way, can he live the Good Life. In addition to realizing a rich content of value to serve both as ideals of conduct and as basic material for thought, the development of the individual must include the cultivation of skill in independent use of values.

Inherited values differ also with respect to intrinsic worth, and their rank order of merit is not necessarily a function of the degree to which they have been accepted. The aspiring minds of men do not all reach the same heights. The meanings available and possible for the guidance of human living may be arranged in a hierarchic order, ranging from those which have suggested themselves to the common sense of all humanity to those which have taken shape only in minds of translucent vision. The latter lack the popular confirmation in human experience that makes values common. Undoubtedly some of the highest meanings that convey to man a sense of his humanness have been accepted by mankind only after persistent persuasion (and even compulsion), and some have undoubtedly even yet received little trial in human experience. The heritage of values includes all these. And limiting or rejecting the alternative of using pressure or force in inculcating values, the fact remains that an individual is potentially capable of realizing a degree of humanness in proportion as he possesses mind or the capacity for apprehending, comprehending, or creating values. Human beings differ, therefore, in this most important of all things—their capacity to be human. And any assertion about human equality must be within the limitations of this fact. Human beings are basically unequal, and each person is potentially capable of development to the degree that he possesses mind. The Good Life is, in essence, an individual life; society, principles of social arrangement, must be founded on that fact. And so, indeed, must education.

Summary.—The principal values of Humanism center around the human capacity for mind or soul, a capacity in which is summed up the essential distinction between human and non-human life. Values for human living are created (Rationalist-Humanism) or apprehended as well as created (Intuitionist-Humanism) by mind. The Good Life is increasingly the life of the mind which is inclusive of, but also in a sense opposed to, the naturalistic living of non-mental beings. This Good Life cannot be validated against merely "natural" processes because man has long since consciously broken with "natural" processes as being unworthy of himself. In man, new "natural" processes, peculiar to himself, are created. The Good Life can be validated, except negatively, only by its appeal to mind itself, and the most reliable criterion of validation is the collective mind of humanity as expressed by the great meanings (and intuitions) that have been collected. The direction toward human certainty is in human agreement. We must seek help in the past for knowledge of ourselves just as we must rely on the past for a knowledge of the world we are born into. The human present is continuous with the human past; tradition is a guide of which we must avail ourselves if we would not go wrong. Traditional values merit our respectful regard, even when we do not accept them completely.

Universally accepted values are not, however, the highest values; they cannot be, for human minds rise to unequal heights. Great values may be transferred to mediocre minds, but they do not originate there. Although a certain degree of humanness may be attained by all, the capacity for humanness varies with the capacity for mind. That considerable differences in such capacity exist, both experience and science affirm. With each individual, therefore, his outlook on things, his conception of the Good Life and the degree to which he can attain it, must be peculiarly his own. The unit of living is the individual life. The individual precedes society in importance.[14] This principle must be taken into account in working out arrangements of a political and an economic sort. But there is no need to fear any conflict between the good man and the good society; the good man is bound to be social, that is, to conduct himself in conscious awareness of his obligations as a participant in communal living. Man attains goodness by applying in his own living the values which humanity has judged most worthy,

[14] In this respect, Kandel is at variance with the general tendency of Humanism. In his emphasis upon the social (although not in his conception of society) Kandel closely approaches both Social Evolutionism and Social Realism.

and in building upon these values. These values do not express "natural" inclinations; they sometimes go counter to them. To maintain himself upon his high level of humanness, therefore, man must be self-disciplined. Self-discipline must be accounted as one of the great human values; through it man maintains his resolution to live the life of his soul rather than the life of "nature." Self-discipline is hardly possible without understanding, without that quality of mind which appreciates the significance of what it is trying to do. Nor is further building upon proved and accepted values possible without the development of mind. As mind is central in the conception of the Good Life, so the training or development of mind is central in the educative process directed toward achieving the Good Life.

SOCIAL EVOLUTIONISM

General Characteristics.—The system of educational theory here offered as Social Evolutionism—based upon the writings of Bagley, Judd, and Morrison—comes closer than does Humanism toward representing a sustained common intellectual attitude and point of view. There is, in general, agreement on basic values, how they are derived, how they are to be used. The differences are mainly (though not altogether— see immediately below) differences in the emphasis that is placed upon certain values as against others, and sometimes reflect more the special interests or areas of work of the individual contributors than they do an intrinsic disagreement in basic thought.[15] The most serious division within the system centers on the conception of the precise manner in which psychological development takes place, and brings together

---

[15] In addition, however, a number of personal differences must be noted:

With respect to social theory, Morrison is the most conservative of the three. He is inclined to think that we have an exaggerated notion of the social changes that have taken place in our time.

Judd is more the scientist than the other two. He is more willing to depart from tradition, and put new values to the test. He is not as critical of some of the products of recent educational science (e.g., the intelligence test) as are the other two.

Bagley is the most conservative with respect to curriculum. He shows, at times, a strong leaning toward formal discipline and the formal-disciplinary studies.

Bagley and Judd on one side as against Morrison on the other.[16] So serious a division is bound to have important implications for educational method—curriculum, organization of subject-matter, method of instruction—and these will, in the proper place, be indicated.

As an intellectual system with its own philosophical basis, Social Evolutionism is traceable in the recent past back to Herbert Spencer,[17] who on the basis of the biological principles of Darwin developed a broad world-view with large implications for ethical theory. The present Social Evolutionism, however, in certain important respects follows not the rather mechanistic evolutionary theory of Spencer but the more vitalistic theory of "emergent evolution" as recently developed by Lloyd Morgan[18] and others.

Starting Point: Theory of Evolution.—Social Evolutionism draws its values fundamentally from its conception of the world-process, and especially as that process is exemplified in human history. The world, or nature, is in evolution. The evolving process is not in a continuous, determinate direction, moving in regular and understandable progression from lower to higher forms. The evolutionary process is saltatory, the direction of its course indeterminate, the consequences of its "leaps" unpredictable. Together with continuity of structure there is discontinuity of function. Simpler elements are continuously combining to form higher and more complex structures with new functions, and every once in a while such a structure will "leap out" to exhibit a property or function, not only new, but strikingly different *in kind* from anything previously exhibited by its simpler predecessors. Such structures with their new qualities are emergents, and each emergent has to some extent deflected or altered the course of evolution. The history of the world is essentially a history of the appearance of these striking emergents and the manner in which they have affected the cosmic process. And, as if nature were being propelled by some great inner force, each change has been a step forward, a move toward a higher level. Nature in evolution seems to be aiming at certain values,

[16] *Vide* Chapter II, pp. 159 ff.
[17] Herbert Spencer, *First Principles*. New York: D. Appleton and Company, 1868 (second edition).
[18] C. Lloyd Morgan, *Emergent Evolution*. New York: Henry Holt and Company, 1927.

and, while these values are not in advance ascertainable, the concrete realization of them is to be accounted as progress, and that is the only kind of progress that nature can make.

Man in Evolution.—The emergence of man has been the highest in the long series of organic changes (beginning with the emergence, out of inorganic matter, of life itself) that has marked the course of cosmic evolution. In its effect, this emergent has been the greatest of all: the emergence of man has served to introduce into cosmic evolution a new kind of method of progress—a method that can insure the practically permanent survival of mankind and progress through its own unaided efforts. The long series of structural integrations that culminated in the formation of the human nervous organization has made possible in man the development of a new function—the "mind" function. Through this function, the life-process for man has been made different from the life-process of all other organic things included within nature. A chance for survival has been replaced by a large degree of assurance of survival; and to a degree, also, continuous and controlled progress has modified the saltatory and unpredictable "progress" of evolution that in many cases involves the elimination of the organism itself.

Prior to the emergence of the "mind" function, living things "struggled for survival" in nature, with the outcome decided by accidental possession of adjustive equipment rather than by voluntary activity on the part of the organism. The formula for evolution was variation within the species, inheritance of variant traits, and survival or extermination according as inherited traits were suited to the conditions of environment or served advantageously in the struggle for existence. This was the "law" of survival by "natural selection," and it was a "law" that was prodigal of life. The emergence of the "mind" function has, for man, changed chance adaptation into deliberate adjustment, possibility of survival through struggle into assurance of survival through cooperation, dependence upon the bounty of nature for the maintenance of life itself into a large degree of independence.

Mind an Outcome of Evolutionary Learnings.—Like other living things in nature, man is dependent for his existence upon successful adaptation to his surroundings. But in him adaptation as an impersonal process of nature gives way to an adaptation of an intentional, self-directed kind. Man is a consciously adjusting organism. The object of man's adjustment is to establish himself more securely in his world, to obtain the things required to maintain life in the most desired way. The capacity which man exhibits in making adjustment is called *mind*. Mind is made possible by a highly developed nervous organization which has its center in the brain, but mind itself is not brain, nor is it an intangible but definite property with which man is endowed at birth. Mind is a function, a resultant capacity of organism for continuously making successful self-adaptation; and this is developed progressively in the course of adaptation-seeking activity. Mind is not inherited. What is inherited is a nervous structure that enables man to develop mind. People differ with respect to inherited nervous structure, and with respect to the limits to which they can ultimately attain mind; but whether they actually differ with respect to mind depends upon the adjustive process they have been through. Mind is a capacity which is created in process, and this capacity has tremendous possibilities for being extended. Man has in the course of his history greatly extended his adjustive capacity. What started probably as mere sentience or consciousness or capacity for awareness of things has in the course of time become capacity to utilize and to control nature. As products (and concrete evidence) of this capacity have come the instruments which now serve man in adjustment—mechanical tools to do his work, ways of organization, ways of communication, ways of social cooperation, ideals by which he guides his conduct along lines known to be desirable. One of the characteristics of mind is its capacity for growth. Mind is continuously developing, and, as it develops, it enables man to conceive and to reach continuously higher levels of adjustment.

The essence of mind is in the ability to make adaptations, to create the behavior that results in successful adjustment. To a degree, animals below man are adaptable, too: animals can "learn" or "profit" from experience. But "man's supremacy in the animal series is due to his ability to profit not only by his own experiences, but also by the experiences of others." [19] Man is able to assimilate learnings distilled from experience, to store them, to hold them "on tap," and to release them in making the proper responses required by a situation. Adaptability is

[19] W. C. Bagley, *The Educative Process*, p. 14. 1905. Quoted with permission of The Macmillan Company, publishers.

an extensible product. A large degree of adaptability is inherent in the organism that man inherits: even without training, in the course of natural experiencing man would be able to make adaptive responses impossible for any other living things. But adaptability—that is, the capacity to make the responses serving the ends of human adjustment— can be tremendously extended by training. Man becomes increasingly adaptable as he takes over unto himself the learnings of previous human experience and finds out how to use them. In the process, man is made over: within "the human cerebrum, a new world is created." [20] The learnings distilled from previous human experience become not only the means of realizing established ends of living, but the means on the basis of which new ends are created. In order to facilitate adjustment, to extend human adaptability, to make possible the easier getting, exchanging, storing, using, and transmitting of learnings, man invented society and the societal way of life. Society is the greatest achievement of mind.

Importance of Society.—Originating in the course of man's efforts to secure a better adjustment, society has become not only a means but one of the ends of human living. It serves as the great repository from which man draws an inexhaustible supply of learnings distilled from the past experience of the race. The cooperative and harmonious utilization of these learnings to further the ends of individual adjustment has become the indispensable *manner* of living. Living in society with others is also a pleasurable end in itself. With society also has come a new way by which man may make progress—the method of *social evolution.* Social evolution has for practical purposes displaced organic evolution or "nature's" way of making progress. "The unique fact in human life is that a method has been evolved which makes it possible to take over into the individual's nervous system a vast body of experience which has been accumulated through racial experiences and is too complex to be transmitted through physical inheritance." [21] By accumulating a reservoir of learnings and by ensuring the continuous transmission of these learnings, society makes possible a continuous improvement in the quality of human living. By extending these learnings

[20] C. H. Judd, *Psychology of Social Institutions,* p. 12. 1926. Quoted with permission of The Macmillan Company, publishers.
[21] *Ibid.,* p. 327.

to every individual member of the group through techniques that it has itself devised, and by fostering cooperation by individuals in the application of these learnings to the solution of the various problems of life, society succeeds in humanizing the law of nature: what was "the survival of the fittest" becomes cooperative effort to ensure the survival of all.

The process of cosmic evolution did not of course terminate with the emergence of man. Nature is still in evolution, and undoubtedly even man is in process of organic evolution. But measured in terms of human life, organic evolution is a slow (to human vision, almost a motionless) process. As far as can be determined there has been little fundamental change in the organic structure of the body in the last half million years.[22] But within the relatively short period of society's existence, there has been a tremendous improvement in human life. "The societal evolution of the last 6,000 years has probably covered as much ground as did organic evolution from the first appearance of mammals to homo sapiens."[23] The individual owes his comparative success in living to the efficacy of the process of social evolution.

Nature of Human Values.—What has been said so far establishes the basis upon which Social Evolutionism constructs its value-system. Insofar as it regards all human living as conducted essentially in terms of adjustive processes, the world-view of Social Evolutionism is naturalistic. Human values are developed with reference to the end of obtaining better adjustment in nature. There is nothing about human beings that dissociates them in this respect from other living things. Human values are not of otherworldly or supernatural origin. Morality, appreciation of beauty, ideals of truth and justice, of self-abnegation and altruism, arise out of no human illusions of superiority, but from discovery by man that they serve better his ends of adjustment. Religion itself is naturalistic in origin: it is a sanctification of values that have so utterly proved themselves in human experience that man has surrounded them with supernatural sanctions to lessen the risk of losing them. The values for human living that we accept are simply the learnings distilled from experience that have in the course of time

---

[22] Bagley, *op. cit.*, p. 17.
[23] H. C. Morrison, *Basic Principles of Education*, p. 82. 1934.

proved their worth in human living. These are added up for us, kept
and transmitted to us by society. Possessing them, we do not need to
begin all over the arduous task of learning from our own experience,
of suffering again from elementary mistakes that our ancestors have
long since discovered and catalogued, of renewing bit by bit the stock
of positive wisdom that would aid us in our attack upon nature. Out
of the experience of the past, society makes available to us, for the
guidance of our living, trusted learnings that ensure at least a partial
degree of success in meeting the problems of adjustment which we may
encounter.

But adjustment, in human beings, is an evolving, progressive concept. The goal of adjustment is no final, stationary goal; man, using
trusted values to guide him, is continuously creating new ends for his
living. (The greatness of mind lies in its power of pushing back goals,
of seeing new ends.) This truth has a twofold consequence for the
nature of values. In the first place, human values must be considered
with reference to an evolving criterion. Since it is true that certain
basic conditions of living are duplicated on several levels of adjustment,
it is true also that certain basic values are thus duplicated. The chances
are that what was considered an act of cowardice by primitive man
would still be so considered today. But in moving from one level of
living to another, values quite commonly undergo alteration. What
was moral behavior on one level of living is not necessarily that on a
higher level. In the process of social evolution, values undergo cumulative growth, refinement, modification, or dissolution. In the second
place, transmitted values never serve fully to solve for man his problems of adjustment. Accredited values, properly assimilated by the individual organism, help that organism to become adaptable. In a
positive way, such values provide the mental content in terms of which
the individual can interpret situations for himself: even new ends of
living must be conceived in terms of familiar values. In a negative
way, they provide mental ballast: even when conceiving new ends, the
intelligent person takes care not to go counter to established values.
But in either case application of trusted values is no guarantee of success in new ventures of living. Each effort at finding a new way of life
is bound to be in the nature of an experiment, and man must wait and
see whether it works. Applying the results of previous experience

serves to enhance the probability of success; ignoring them or departing from them increases the chances of failure in solving new problems of adjustment.

Discovering Values.—Values do not exist merely as "furniture of the mind." To realize human ends is to remake nature in the process; values serve as bases of action. In his upward evolution, man has continuously remade nature in accordance with values that he has developed. At the same time, however, he has not always been careful to realize in his concrete living all the highest values available to him. To discover values for the guidance of modern life, it is not advisable to seek them either in the naïve world of nature, on the one hand, or in the most recent phase of societal evolution, on the other. In the one case, man has advanced so far in continuously redefining his ends of living, and to such an extent re-created nature, that neither his ends nor his conditions of living are likely to be reproduced anywhere in a simpler state of nature. Certainly, to remain alive or to "exist" is no longer a satisfactory end, nor are the problems of adjustment today in the simple terms that confronted primitive man. In the second case, societies in periods of rapid development do overlook or disregard certain values that are essential to their existence.[24] Fairly well-advanced societies have slipped back and disappeared because they disregarded the learnings of earlier experience. At any particular time, the values by which a society must be guided are to be sought in the total experience of mankind, using the last phase of societal development as the object of valuation as well as the base from which measurement is taken.

Values are verified empirically, in terms of both individual and of race experience. There are no extra-experiential standards. Values are judged to be valid when the consensus of mankind is that they further and do not set back human beings in their efforts to provide a more secure and better life for all. Negatively, values are valid when they do not go contrary to the learnings that man has previously established as being essential in his adjustment. It goes without saying that, in human experience, there is room for difference of opinion about values. Only time can tell. In the meantime, it may be assumed that the collective

[24] This is the criticism that Social Evolutionism strongly makes of contemporary American society.

experience of a group is a better instrument of validation than is the judgment of a single individual, and, by the same token, the accumulated experience of several generations or of a large segment of total race experience is a far better measure than is the judgment of a single generation (unless conditions have altered so fundamentally that no comparison is possible). History affords the best judgment of what is right and wrong. The highest values for present living are those learnings which history shows to have accounted for man's present climb to the top, and, negatively, those learnings without which he cannot remain where he is.

For the most part these values exist in our present conscious experience; they are part of the social heritage to which we have become heir. But not all, or even enough, of these highest values have been so handed down. What *is* the social heritage has always been decided in a rather crude, inexact way, without systematic identification and cataloguing of elements. Certain values that have obtruded themselves upon our consciousness by virtue of their force or their cruciality we have incorporated into this consciously-transmitted heritage; other more subtle values have eluded us. Also, there have crept into the social heritage, as we know it, what only purport to be, but are not truly, values (as, for example, certain aristocratic "values" serving the interests of a special small group). Recently man has invented a new instrument which may serve the purpose of identifying with greater precision the learnings that have in the past benefited mankind and that promise to do so in the future. This new instrument is the science of society—anthropology, ecology, sociology—through which it will be possible to explore society in all its dimensions and add greatly to man's store of crucial values. If then, with the aid of another new instrument of society's—the universal school—these learnings are effectively transmitted to and lodged with all, man's dream of being able through the instrumentality of the social heritage to assure security of present gains and continuous evolution to a better life for all, will be possible of realization.

Summary.—The end of human living is to establish all human beings securely and happily in nature—to ensure, in other words, their satisfactory adjustment. Man is not particularly "unique," a creature of destiny, with *super*natural aspirations. He is rather a highly developed organism with a nervous system that makes it possible for him to develop this genius that we call mind for guiding and securing his own adjustment in nature. In a way, that is sufficient to set him apart from other living things so that their observed modes of conduct cannot qualify to serve him as values. But his own values are no more than means for facilitating his own adjustment in nature. Mind is not a "prize" that was given to him; it is a capacity which he acquires through the continuous assimilation of learnings serving the ends of adjustment.

What precisely constitutes human adjustment can never be finally and absolutely defined; man is constantly formulating new meanings of adjustment and in the process raising himself to new levels of living. These new levels may be regarded as higher levels if, in time, they are actually shown to have extended human material effectiveness in nature. It has become certain that whatever ends man will continue to set for himself will be within and attainable only through a societal culture. These ends will be defined in terms of social living and will be attained through cooperative effort. Society is the source from which can be obtained values for the guidance of human living; as such its importance is secondary only to life itself. Whatever arrangements man makes for preserving himself must also preserve and strengthen society. The good, whatever the special aspect in which it reveals its goodness, must also be the social: this holds true of the good life, the good man, the good law, or the good education. Democracy, while in essence a guarantee of certain rights of the individual, must be conceived in a way that will strengthen, not weaken, the integrity of the social organism.

Society, however, is not to be identified with that segment of it that faces us immediately in the present; to do that is to identify the part with the whole. The "present social order" may be good or bad, depending on whether or not it exemplifies in its life-behavior the most important learnings that have been distilled out of the accumulated experience of the past. The past itself is an important accessory to our present living; it presents us with tremendously important values which, if they cannot by themselves indicate what our present living shall be, can help to guide us in our living and at least to avoid disaster. To make skillful use of past experience is mind's chief contribution to man, and it is, in fact, what has made possible man's evolution through social rather than biological means. But what is important in the experience of the past are the actual learnings that have served man in his adjustment, not the supposed "learnings," and not "values" that a dominant and exclusive aristocracy has handed down on the pretext that they were values for all. Soon, with the help of science applied to the study of society, we shall be able to identify these values exactly, which, by their special pertinence to our situation, have the greatest bearing upon our living.

In the meantime, as we explore the total history of mankind, certain learnings reveal themselves as reliable values. There becomes apparent, in the first place, the importance of what we may call self-discipline, or self-control, or volitional maturity—the consistent ability to act from higher impulses than those merely "natural," to persist in the face of difficulties, to subordinate means to ends, to sacrifice lower to higher values, and so on. Another value, closely allied with this, is the necessity for strong social attitudes and socialized conduct, that is, for unselfishness, for regard for the rights of others, for respect for law and order, for temperance of one's own desires when they encroach upon the desires of others. A review of history shows that no society that has ignored or trifled with these values has survived, however high an eminence it once occupied.

The essence of humanness and the achievement upon which the greatest valuation in human living must be placed is adaptability. The higher the level of adjustment, the greater is the need for adaptability. But as was said before, adaptability is not the gift of heredity nor can it even be guaranteed by training. The best way to achieve adaptability in a particular environment is to assimilate the learnings that have gone into the making of that environment and those that past experience has proved should go into it. But adaptability does not imply changeability and disdain of loyalties; nor does it connote self-centeredness. The traits that make for adaptability are common traits, and most of them are traits that have long since proved their value. The Good Life, in its individual and societal aspects, is a function of the thoroughness and effectiveness with which society succeeds in inculcating in all its individuals the significant learnings to which it has access through its long continuous experience.

SOCIAL REALISM

General Characteristics.—More than any of the other systems, Social Realism [25] endorses the general trend that American education has followed within most of the present century. The system carries to their logical conclusions in educational theory the implications of a realistic-pragmatic [26] attitude, characteristic in large of the American temper, that received vigorous philosophic confirmation and support in the writings of William James. [27] Constructed primarily from the point of view of the secondary school, Social Realism naturally offers a program of secondary education more complete as to essential details than those of the other systems. Social Realists are in agreement on a general theory of values and on the body of sociological and psychological principles emerging from it; their differences, as yet, are comparatively minor differences in the manner in which certain of the general principles are being construed. [28] To a greater extent than any other systems of thought here presented, Social Realism speaks as a single theory of secondary education.

Fundamental Postulates.—The fundamental values of Social Realism arise out of an attitude toward the world and the problem of knowing it. Typical of this attitude is a feeling that man is a rather humble character in the universe which he inhabits; and, although the future

[25] Based upon Briggs, H. R. Douglass, Spaulding, and the earlier writings of Cox. The more recent work of Cox definitely places him with the Experimentalists. Under the category of Social Realism are also included the two Reports of the Committee on the Orientation of Secondary Education of the Department of Secondary School Principals, *Issues of Secondary Education* (1936), and *Functions of Secondary Education* (1937), and Spaulding's volume, *High School and Life* (1938), a Report of the Regents' Inquiry into the Character and Cost of Public Education in the State of New York.

[26] Social Realism does not fall entirely within Realism or within Pragmatism, as these categories are generally understood. In its thinking are revealed strong tendencies of both.

[27] See especially James's *Pragmatism* (1907), *The Will to Believe* (1897), pp. 1–32, *Some Problems of Philosophy* (1911), *Essays in Radical Empiricism* (1912), all published by Longmans, Green and Company, New York; also the "Philosophy of William James," in R. B. Perry's *Present Philosophical Tendencies*, pp. 349–378. New York: Longmans, Green and Company, 1912.

[28] This statement regarding disagreement is more fully discussed in the critical review of Social Realism in the concluding chapter.

may be viewed with confidence, it is necessary that man move with caution and investigate the foundations on which he builds his living. Just as Humanism tends to exalt man (at least in relation to nature), Social Realism tends to put him into his proper (human) place. The position of Social Realism assumes as self-evident the fact that the world exists and acts and moves and is altogether real, independently of man as knower. The problem that confronts man is that of getting along in the world of which he finds himself a part; and to Social Realism it seems reasonable to assume that man will find it easier to get along in the world as he gets to know it better. Knowing the world becomes essential to living in it; the problem of knowledge is related to the problem of existence.

We can learn about the world only as we experience it, through the contacts that we have with it. The bedrock of experience are the sense-data, and our progression toward knowledge begins with the impressions registered upon our senses. The world, as we perceive it, is a tremendously complex affair; it is futile to attempt to know it in its wholeness. Man isolates the elements of physical reality as they impinge themselves upon his consciousness, and studies them; in terms of their physical make-up and relations and their operational qualities he gets to know them. By adding up single items of knowledge, single *facts,* man comes to know the world as it is. Through successive accretions of such items of knowledge and their empirically-evident relations, by making small beginnings simultaneously in different places, by fitting facts together in the fashion of a jig-saw puzzle, we construct a mind-picture of a growing fragment of world. Mastery of the relatively unchangeable world of matter is the first step. Science has been extremely successful in supplying us with precise and trustworthy information regarding the world of matter, and the method of science needs to be and is being extended to all living nature, to provide equivalently sound information there. In essence, the scientific method is the empirical method, sharpened and objectified to the point where it is maximally effective in analyzing, in isolating, in observing under various conditions, and in discovering the constituent elements and the operational qualities and effects of data of sense-experience. If anything can, the unlimited extension of the scientific method may ultimately provide a comprehensive basis of fact concerning the world of sense-experience, to serve us in marking out sounder directions for our living. So far, science and the scientific method have gone only part of the way.

Man's concern with knowing reality is related to the problem of living. Knowledge is sought, not primarily for its value as knowledge, but as being instrumental in the conduct of life. It is true that reality is independent of man, but man does not seek to know reality for its own sake. The object of knowledge is to obtain information serviceable in living. Man must know in what way he is affected by everything in nature, and those things that affect him most he must know best. "Of what consequence is it to me?" becomes a question of extreme importance. Knowing the consequences, actual or possible, of particular realities, man is able to achieve certain effects and to avoid others, and even to re-create nature so as to secure either a consistent recurrence or a consistent avoidance of certain effects.

Science has been admirable in reducing to precise, established, incontrovertible facts of knowledge much of the data of sense-experience; but it has not yet so reduced all of these data. Yet man must act; he cannot stand still. On the basis of what he knows or thinks he knows about the significance of things in relation to himself, he must so order his behavior as to achieve the effects necessary for the maintenance of life. Moreover, there are many things that cannot be known with the certainty with which facts of the world of physical matter, for example, can be established. Science cannot always tell man what its factual knowledge means in relation to himself; it cannot always tell him *what consequences* are best for him. Accordingly, there must be recognized different degrees within knowledge about the world, or to put it in another way, there must be recognized different types of knowledge about the world. In addition to knowledge of the factual kind, which can be reduced to certainty, there must be recognized knowledge that is substantially belief.

There is no reason to assume that science will ever be able altogether to direct human action. Regardless of the extension of science, there will always be a large place for human belief. Belief arises from the inability of man always to obtain verified knowledge pointing inevitably in one direction. Belief is necessary to bridge the gap in human experience between knowing a thing in its impersonal relationships and knowing how it may serve to secure the most desired consequences in human living. (Consequences are not only events that happen to man but events that he brings to bear upon himself.) Beliefs are the flexible elements in human cognitive experience; whenever there is room for the exercise of option belief steps in.

Like factual knowledge, belief arises out of experience; [29] there is nothing supernatural in its origin. It supplements and extends factual knowledge to the point where action is possible. There is no doubt that the extension of factual knowledge will cut into the area of belief, though it will never altogether eliminate it. Belief is verified pragmatically, in terms of its consequences, though never with the finality possible with factual knowledge; ultimately belief is at the mercy of the human will. Wherever possible belief should be based upon factual knowledge that has itself been thoroughly verified; it ought never to go contrary to any factual knowledge the verification of which it cannot question or the relevance of which it cannot deny. In the absence of completely factual knowledge, beliefs that have been applied in living and pragmatically tested offer an indispensable basis for making value-judgments; such beliefs may be credited with having been productive of consequences that, to the best of human judgment, bettered human living. Belief is dangerous only when it seeks to go contrary to established factual knowledge or when it becomes identified with such knowledge; or, its empirical nature temporarily obscured, it comes to be regarded as supernatural or infallible or unchangeable.

Nature of Values.—Human values derive from the basis of factual knowledge and belief that man possesses. Accordingly, values change with experience, as new facts are uncovered and as man forms new beliefs. It is futile to define with finality *the* goal, the *summum bonum,* of human living. The goal of living is whatever, consistent with his established knowledge and beliefs, the human being conceives it to be, and it changes in the course of continuous human living. Generally speaking, man seeks to make his life more secure, his living better, more satisfying, more worthy of what he considers himself to be. But security and the good, satisfying, worthy life are outcomes of the way in which

---

[29] Belief is not used in a religious sense (i.e., in the sense of "faith"). Science and belief are used here pretty much as Socrates used the terms "knowledge" and "opinion."

man experiences the world. Materialism and idealism are both conceptions that have in the course of time undergone considerable change and exchange, and many a high idealism has come in later years to be taken pretty much for granted.[80]

Human existence, however, has a cumulative continuity that is different from the chain continuity of biological existence. Human values remake reality; man makes changes in the world in accordance with the values that he sets up, each individual adding something to the world as he finds it. The impressions linger, and each successive individual is thus brought into contact with the one before him. The experiences of individuals in successive generations tend to draw them together in common world-outlook. Values overlap. A generation of individuals may ultimately repudiate the values of the preceding generation but (1) it must, in any event, begin with them, and (2) it is never likely to repudiate all of them. When to this are added the important facts that scientific knowledge is of a growing, cumulative nature, and that beliefs are tenacious in their hold upon people, it is easier to see that there is an overlapping, an enduringness, a cumulativeness in values. No generation creates all of its own values. Human beings build on what has gone before. They do not need to accept the past in its entirety; neither can they ignore it completely. There is a core of value that is common to all human beings, and this core is growing all the time. As science extends the areas of knowledge, the core of common values is extended.

A human being, born into the world, is born into values. His experiences are not "naïve" experiences; they are charged or loaded with value. Whether he likes it or not, the values that he receives are the only values he has, and at least the core of them has received sufficient verification in experience to merit thorough trial. The society into which the individual is born has the choice of helping him, through systematic guidance, to develop an understanding of these values and the reasons for them, and to influence him in the direction of at least tentative acceptance of them; or it can permit him, without much direction, to attempt to discover for himself, through "natural experience," what these values are, on what they are based, and, out of his

[80] The simple wearing of clothes, for example, must have been at one time the expression of a high ideal.

limited knowledge, to decide whether they are worth adopting. Because the values which society induces the individual to accept are admittedly imperfect and will not, under ordinary circumstances, be adequate to serve him throughout his lifetime, is no reason why society should not actively sponsor them. It is possible to compel an individual by force to adopt certain values, but it is not possible to deceive him for any length of time regarding their validity. Subsequent events in his experience will establish or disprove the validity of his values; in terms of these results, values will be retained, rejected, or altered and improved. New experiences will yield new values, and these will be continuously synthesized with the old. Where values are founded on tested belief, the utmost effort should be made to persuade the individual to accept this belief, at least up to the point where he can fairly test it in his own experience. Until we can get something better, what we have is the very best. The manner of living of the individual, regardless of what it may ultimately become, should begin by "following suit." Society must undertake the responsibility for "showing the suit to be followed." The proper induction of the individual into society as it is, is a first condition for his own and society's further improvement.

Value of Society.—Viewing empirically the manner of human living in the world, what is most striking is that this living goes on in societal relationship, and that the necessity of society is a fact no longer even questioned. Whatever the circumstances under which society originated, it is a reasonable inference that society, in continuous human experience, has proved itself such a value in human living that man has consistently and consciously taken care to maintain it (i.e., that human beings together have done so). The societal way of life, though it is probably only a means to the end of individual living, has become one of the guarantees of that living, a good *for* the individual to be balanced against goods *of* the individual. The fallibility of individual knowledge and belief has made society a necessity. The collective experience of individuals has reinforced, and, where the common welfare is affected, replaced the experience of the individual as a source of and a test of values. The factual-knowledge-basis and the belief-basis of value, small and uncertain in the experience of the individual, have become more substantial and more trustworthy when growing out of the common experience of the group. As a validating medium, collective experience has been judged more reliable than individual experience.

In the course of its history, society has developed modes of procedure that operate to ensure its integrity and continued existence while it performs its function of substituting common for individual experience as a basis for living. Society has worked out ways of arbitrating among conflicting individual beliefs, of determining what should be common as against individual ends, of working changes in itself in a common and orderly manner. Social procedures have been developed even for social change, all to the end of preserving the vital value of society. Social procedure as a general value is greater even than the values it serves to secure at any particular time; the latter will most certainly change with time, but the fact of social procedure is necessary for the continuance of society itself. What the precise nature of the relationships among the individuals in society shall be, where the dividing line shall be drawn between what is common and what is individual, no one can state with finality. These are values that change with experience. There is no rivalry between the individual and society, it is to be understood. Society is a coming-together of individuals, to realize in a cooperative way what is ultimately a good life for each individual; societal arrangements are merely means toward the realization of this end—they ought to change in a manner required to maintain their consistency with this end (and with the one other of maintaining society itself). If a more positive generalization may be ventured, it is the very commonplace-sounding one that the degree of mutual dependence within the group ought to vary directly with the difficulty that individuals have in realizing desired ends through their own effort. But that even this is no "law of nature" but a much more uncertain outcome of human experience may be noticed in our present social situation.

Human living is in a world dominated by the fact of society. Ways of living are not individually created, but are taken over from a social group; the values motivating these ways are resultants of long social effort; the experiences themselves are impressions of a world that is continuously being remade by the joined efforts of human beings. To state this as fact is not at the same time to confer on social action any special sanctity, nor to overestimate the degree of unity and cohesiveness in society and to underestimate its particularism, nor necessarily to conceive it statically. Society is made up of individuals acting upon each other. As such, society is ever in process: the individuals comprising it are constantly at work altering its values and its processes, this way and that, in accordance with changing experience. Not even in totalitarian countries is society altogether a unity. In any society whatever, the total living of an individual is in some way characteristically his own. But it is an inescapable fact that individual living is dominated by common social values. Individual experience is within the larger setting of social experience. Human development is in terms of a social milieu. Continuous movement toward a better life is possible because man takes over ways of living existent in society, and, cognizant of both ends and means, pushes on toward new ends and better means. Human development begins with the comprehension and acceptance of the values approved by society, continues as the individual, in the course of his living, tests, refines, alters, discards, adds to values—within the freedom that society allows, and in socially approved ways—and cooperates with others in using the results of his own experience in the building of new and better common values.

The Meaning of "Mind."—In its view of the nature of mind and the manner of its operation in experience, Social Realism tends to be agnostic and empirical. Its agnosticism is in the nature of a reaction to a previous unfounded dogmatism. The tendency of human beings to theorize from a small basis of fact has led to disastrous consequences. Working from the premise that reason is primary in human action, theorists constructed an elaborate picture of mind and mental organization and a theory of educational method to go with it. The faculty psychology and its concomitant theory of mental discipline were contrary to common sense. It remained for scientific psychology to discredit them completely. Until science itself ascertains with some degree of certainty the nature of mind and the manner of its operation, it is necessary to take an empirical and a pragmatic view.

To be "real" by pragmatic definition, mind must be operative in assisting the individual in achieving life-extending and life-bettering consequences; mind must be apparent in the outcomes of living and in all the processes by which these outcomes are attained. Mind must be an observable quality of the human being in action, and must be developed in and through its overt manifestations. We do not know what mind is but we do know how it is supposed to work. By assisting the individual to carry on better the processes of his life experience, we are incidentally instrumental in the training of mind. To realize this goal, it is necessary not so much to theorize about the nature of mind as to study the individual, to find out everything we can about him, and then, *taking him as he is* and not some idealized version of him, to help that individual to become more effective in formulating and achieving his ends cooperatively in society.

To act thus is not to deny the existence of mind; it is rather to postpone categoric formulations of it until science has "bagged all the facts." It is hardly necessary to state that judgment based on observation of the human being in operation, fortified by the facts that science has already succeeded in establishing, would serve to refute many of the notions long accepted. Man, then, would be pictured not primarily as an analytic, calculating, detached intellectual being, but as an *acting, behaving,* flesh-and-blood person; a creature impelled by emotion fully as much as by "reason," given to forming habits because habits are time-and-energy economies that leave room for other types of activity; not an "all-or-none" being but rather a creature of parts, with specific interests, biases, talents, and "intelligences." Knowledge can best be gained through the slow uncompromising analytic-and-synthetic method of science; and in the study of man as a perceiving, conceiving, judgment-forming, and acting being, the method of science may ultimately succeed in placing on a sound, verified, precise knowledge-footing that for which we must at present rely on observation and common-sense judgment.

Summary.—Social Realism finds its chief values in the twin facts of science and society. Insofar as definite incontrovertible knowledge of the world we live in is obtainable, it will be gained through science. The scientific method must be extended into every area of experience, and the knowledge thus gained must be used to the greatest possible extent in the formulation of values. Science, however, cannot in itself fully establish an adequate basis for value-judgments. Scientific knowledge must be supplemented by belief, which may be regarded as a kind of interpolated knowledge necessary to relate fact and its possible consequence in human living. Belief grows out of human experience as a legitimate cognitive outcome, and is validated pragmatically in human living. Belief occupies a crucial place in human living; it is closer to action than is factual knowledge itself, and is therefore more decisive in achieving the consequences which make or break human life.

On the basis of his knowledge of fact and his beliefs man must choose his values. Since values thus arise out of experience, and experience is a changing thing, it is impossible to set up the final goals of human living. As man obtains more knowledge of the world or as he alters his beliefs, his goals change. Values are validated in experience. Human experience, however, has a continuous cumulative quality (to which the continuity of knowledge and belief considerably contribute), and man individually is not faced with the tremendous task of creating a whole new set of values for his living. Man is born into society, and that means into a set of operating values.

The fact of society itself is incontrovertible evidence of the continuous faith of human beings in the greater reliability of collective over individual experience as a means of obtaining factual knowledge, beliefs, value-judgments based upon them, and the arrangements for realizing these values, all of these adding up to more secure and better individual living. The fact of society guarantees to the individual a better kind of life than he could achieve for himself. Social experience as a collective source of human values must be maintained. Society is, however, a means to an end—the end of better individual living. It is impossible, therefore, to prescribe with authority what shall be the optimum organization and arrangements of society; these depend on the needs of the individuals constituting that society. Society is a fluid rather than a set arrangement; its principal activity is to provide for its individuals better goals of living and better means of attaining them. In the course of its history, society has developed certain procedures whereby it could perform this function, with a minimum of risk to its own integrity and existence. As a value for human living, the maintenance of such procedures (if they are procedures truly based on the concept that the individual is the end of living) is greater even than the particular values that these procedures produce. Translated into our own terms, this means that adherence to democratic processes, democratic ways of doing things, is more important than any single issue that may be settled by these processes.

An individual is born into a society; his development is within a social milieu. The adjustment of the individual must be in terms of the values that are dominant in his society. This is not to assert either that the values are perfect or even adequate or that the society which enforces these values is very much worth adjusting to. (No society is good that does not recognize the simple facts that it exists for its individuals; that all its values grow out of experience, should be validated by experience, and change with experience; that belief that goes contrary to factual knowledge is either mistaken or vicious; that no man or group of men can claim infallible authority; and so forth.) But the individual can't help himself; only in terms of the dominant social values can he understand his environment; only as he begins by adjustment can he go on to participate in the task of *making society better* without threatening the existence of society itself. The development of the individual does not cease with initial adjustment; it goes right on throughout life. In the process of his development, the individual will discover new values and improve the old ones, and in harmonious social cooperation with others will work to make his society a better place to live in.

We can assist the individual in this development only as we know the kind of being he is. For a long time we were misled by ill-founded theories which, on the basis of a premise that man is primarily a reasoning and not an acting being, evolved an elaborate but fallacious view of mind, its organization and operation. Common sense and science have combined to discredit these theories. Unfortunately it is easier to discredit a false theory than to build a sound one in its place. Knowledge of man cannot be gained through wishful thinking. It is necessary to bring to the study of man the uncompromising method of science, and until science can obtain for us the desired accurate and comprehensive knowledge, we must do the best we can with whatever empirical knowledge is available. As science comes more to our assistance, we shall be able to formulate a sounder plan of human development.

EXPERIMENTALISM

General Characteristics.—The term Experimentalism as here used denominates the theory of secondary education that develops out of the

more general philosophy of that name.[31] The ideas bearing immediately upon secondary education were drawn from the following: the
writings of L. T. Hopkins and V. T. Thayer, including collabora-
tions with which these men were prominently associated—*Integration:
Its Meaning and Application* (Hopkins), *Science in General Education* (Thayer), *Reorganizing Secondary Education* (Thayer); the more
recent writings of Cox;[32] *Democracy and the Curriculum*, a publication of the John Dewey Society; selected chapters[33] from *A Challenge
to Secondary Education*, by the Society for Curriculum Study; selected
chapters[34] from *The Changing Curriculum*, edited by H. Harap; selected chapters[35] from *The Community School*, a report of the Committee on the Community School of the Society for Curriculum Study;
and, in general, *Youth Serves the Community*, by P. R. Hanna et al.
(The selected chapters were those which, in books somewhat more
representative, seemed to project into secondary education the ideas of
the Experimentalist philosophy.) The basic general ideas, necessary
for an understanding of the principles of secondary education, were
drawn directly from the writings of Dewey,[36] Kilpatrick, Bode, Childs,
and Counts.[37]

The extension of Experimentalist principles into the area of secondary
education was not undertaken until rather recently, and, as a theory of
secondary education, Experimentalism is still in its formative stages.
This accounts for the fact that Experimentalism has not yet expressed
itself regarding every phase of a program of *secondary education* (for

[31] For an exposition of Experimentalism as general theory of education, see
J. L. Childs, *Education and the Philosophy of Experimentalism.* 1931. The
writer is indebted to this book for much of his knowledge of the basic ideas of
Experimentalism.

[32] *Supra,* p. 33, footnote 25.

[33] The chapters by Everett, Hall and Alexander, Mendelhall, Watson, and
Koopman.

[34] The chapters by Brim, Zirbes, Harap, and Rankin.

[35] The chapters by Everett, Misner, and Horton; and the Introduction by Kilpatrick.

[36] In a more general way, as one of the founders of Pragmatism, Dewey also
influenced Social Realism.

[37] It is hard to say whether Counts can properly be called an Experimentalist.
His writings in social theory have, however, been accepted as a source of reference
by some Experimentalists, and his criticism of American society is typical of Experimentalism as a whole.

example, organization), while with respect to other phases its expression has sometimes lacked precision (compared, for example, with Social Realism). This is said not in criticism, but as a fact of which note must be taken. As theory of secondary education, Experimentalism is still in process of development; many important problems have not yet been reached for detailed discussion, while others are still in the stage where various possible courses of action are being tried and tested.

For some years Experimentalism existed side by side with another Progressive theory of education, non-pragmatic in its philosophical foundations, which was identified with the thought of Rousseau and of Froebel rather than of Dewey. A basic principle of this earlier theory was a belief in the innate goodness of the child and the essential value of his natural expression. Although such thinking is no longer evident on the part of responsible theorists (at least in secondary education), there is recurrent at times, in the writings of certain Experimentalists, a lapse into the old language and ways of thinking. It is the intention of this study to regard such lapses as individual inconsistencies and not as essential breaches within the unity of the Experimentalist system. They will accordingly not be pointed out in this study. For present purposes, the theory of secondary education here presented will be regarded as resting wholly on the foundations of the Experimentalist philosophy.

The chief disagreement within Experimentalism [38] arises from a conflict between two values fundamental to Experimentalism itself—faith in the individual as a reagent who is in all things competent to direct his own experience, on the one hand, and a conviction that a democratic social environment is necessary for and even antecedent to the effective self-direction of the individual, on the other. Although both democracy and the experimental technique are accepted as essential values by all Experimentalists, there seems to be a competition among them for "prestige." It is very difficult to place one's finger

[38] To follow the course of this disagreement, refer to B. H. Bode, *Progressive Education at the Crossroads* (1938), and the series of articles in the *Social Frontier* by Childs (May, November, 1938) and by Bode (November, 1938, January, 1939). For an excellent summary statement of the two positions, see J. L. Childs, "Progressive Education and the Secondary School," *Progressive Education,* 16:411–417, October, 1939.

squarely at the root of the conflict, but the nature of the conflict may perhaps be revealed in the following alternative series of propositions.— *A:* The Experimentalist philosophy holds that individual experience is pre-eminent as a value and source of values. As a result of his experiences, the individual will reveal his own beliefs, convictions, and purposes. Democracy means chiefly a respect for the individual and his right to control his beliefs. It is a violation of both experimentalism and democracy to impose ideas upon an individual. *B:* Democracy and the experimental method are different aspects of the same condition of living. True experimental living is impossible except in a democratic society. Democracy has proved itself completely as a human value. To make possible experimental living (and that means living that holds most for the individual), it is necessary to inculcate loyalty to those social conceptions and arrangements that will make possible a true democracy.—The implications of this conflict for theory of secondary education are evident. It is interesting to note that among the Experimentalists writing in the field of secondary education both sides are represented.[39]

More so than the other systems, Experimentalism owes its rise and development to the fundamental creative thinking of one person. In the process of extension and application, however, even fundamental principles may undergo alteration. It is necessary to state that the exposition of Experimentalism as a theory of secondary education given in the following chapters is essentially from the point of view of those who have carried the doctrine and theories of Dewey into secondary education rather than primarily from the point of view of the originator.

Basic Postulates.—At the basis of the Experimentalist theory of values there is a postulate that all knowledge is empirical and that whatever man can know about the world and the method of dealing with it he can know only through experience. From the point of view of naïve empiricism (and in this, naïve empiricism is supported by the researches of modern physics) the world that we live in does not seem to be an orderly rational system, the elements of which cohere within a single framework and operate according to determined and ascertainable principle. From the point of view of our experience we are hardly

[39] *Vide* Chapter III, pp. 279 ff.

justified in calling the world a "universe," the pattern of which we can intellectually reproduce. What we experience is a succession of events, ("a rush of events"—it may be said), each of which leaves some effect upon us, and each of which is complete and unique with respect to its total configuration. The characteristics of our world seem to be movement, particularity, change. There seem to be no grounds for postulating eternal laws by which the world is governed or eternal values by which we are to be governed in it.

The problem for man is how to live in this world. Empirically there seems to be no basis for belief that the world can be divided into two elements—man and nature, and that man is outside of nature. On the contrary, the evidence of our experience compels us to assume that man is essentially within nature, a part of it, and continuous with other living things. Man is in some respects unique; so in some respects are all other things. (It seems in fact, the more we study each event in nature and each object in nature, that each event is an end in itself, and each object its own purpose for being. Nothing occurs for something else; no one exists for anyone else.) Human living is, in general, not apart from nature but within it; and it is well to start from that generality to arrive at an understanding of the respects in which human living is distinctive within nature.

It is evident that in a world of essentially unpredictable events, events that seem to recognize no law, living is precarious. Our problem is essentially a problem of securing, extending, and improving our living in this world. Our first thought must be of ourselves; we cannot either divert our energies to other things or sit back in the confident expectance that, whatever happens, we have mastered our problem of living. In whatever respect it is that we are superior to other living things (and we may assume that in some respect we are superior), we must turn that superiority to the solution of our great and pressing problem —that of living. This does not mean that we are doomed to materialistic existence, that we shall "live by bread alone"; as we progress in the solving of our problem, we can to an extent re-create the world, making it, to our way of thinking, better.

A living thing has needs; to maintain life it must satisfy them. Living seems to be dedicated to the continuous satisfaction of life-needs. An organism satisfies its needs not by drawing upon itself, but by drawing upon its environment. The environment, however, is no static, receptive affair—waiting to be acted upon: it is *world,* full of living things and much more formidable, though inanimate, events. The environment is in its turn constantly acting upon the organism. In short, living implies continuous activity—continuous satisfaction of organismic needs, continuous acting and being acted upon, continuous changing and being changed. The term that may be used to describe this is experiencing, and the unit—an experience. From the point of view of the organism, experience is related to adjustment, to the satisfaction of life-needs. Experience is an individual thing, qualitatively different with each organism. Also, in a changing world, no two experiences are alike, since each successive experience finds the organism "different" and occurs in a "different" world. An organism is whatever its experiences make it; and the unique process of experiencing accounts for the fact that no two organisms are ever identical.

All life-activity is primarily adjustive: the organism acts to obtain from the environment those consequences which are favorable to its living. Action brings reaction: every act has a consequence which in turn sets other acts into motion. Living is continuous, adjustive activity. The difference between animal and human living is that man seems to be aware to a much, very much, greater extent than the animal (though possibly not yet to as great an extent as he should be) of what is going on—what is happening to him and what he is doing. Man is capable of knowing experience—of knowing what is taking place in the course of his life-process, of defining his needs, of knowing what in nature can satisfy these needs. While the non-human organism acts to adjust itself in a blind sort of way (although it is true that the higher animals can make involved and difficult adjustments), the human being can consciously manipulate environmental factors in such a way as to achieve outcomes favorable to the continuance of his existence. Human life-activity is not only purposive; it is purposeful.

Nature of Intelligence.—Human superiority lies essentially in the capacity to behave purposefully so as to achieve needed ends. In that activity of the human organism lies the meaning of intelligence. The tremendous effect of this capacity should not be underestimated; intelligence makes "all the difference in the world." Intelligence operates in the successful control and direction of living; everything else that intelligence does is comprehended within this function. Intelligence means intelligent conduct—the satisfaction of needs, the conception and realization of life-purposes; as an abstraction, aloof from biological events and brooding far above the world of material things, intelligence does not exist.

Man behaves intelligently by using meanings. He relates actions to consequences, and on the basis of past relations is able to anticipate (and create) future events. Knowing the meaning of things, he can so conduct himself as to obtain those consequences that will satisfy his life-needs and to avoid those that will not. A meaning is a relationship that has been drawn between a thing and its consequence; to put it in another way, the meaning of a thing is its imputed operational effect. Meanings are obtained out of experience, most generally (though not always) by systematic analysis. Man mentally reconstructs his experience, and by relating things in their effect upon each other and ultimately upon himself, he draws meanings; these meanings he "puts back" into experience, using them as purposes and as means through which purposes may be realized. In that way he can "steer" his behavior, becoming increasingly adept in analysis of experience and in application of meanings.

But to behave intelligently is not so simple a matter as that. Experience is not a steady, dependable, predictable process; it is rather an ongoing, changing succession of ever-new events. No two events are exactly alike; no situation exactly duplicates another. Intelligence has all it can do to keep up with the flow of events; [40] each succeeding experience finds it somewhat unprepared. In a dynamic world of essentially separable events, man cannot in the present use with assurance meanings that he has derived from past experience. Each event, in its total potential effect, offers a new challenge. Intelligence facing a new situation must be creative—it must create an understanding of the situation and the means of dealing with it. Intelligence is conative: nothing is guaranteed. In such a world, living the Good Life cannot mean applying, composedly and with every expectation of success, to the mov-

[40] The contrast between Humanism and Experimentalism at this point is sharp. The Humanist sees human intelligence as restless in a sluggish world; the Experimentalist sees a restless world and an intelligence that needs to be alert to keep up with the movement of events.

ing continuum of present events meanings that have been accredited as true of the past. Judgments made on this basis would have disastrous consequences. Intelligent conduct is experimental conduct. This fact gives point to the statement that intelligence is not a possession, a store of meanings furnishing a supply of sound values; but that it is to be understood only in terms of human beings applying themselves creatively and experimentally to the mastery of each successive situation. Intelligence is a quality of behavior in a situation, and as such is specific to the situation and to the human being who is functioning within its scope.

Values within the Experimentalist System.—It now becomes possible to speak explicitly of the nature of human values and the manner of their operation. Values are meanings drawn from previous experience by which conduct may be so regulated as to result in the satisfaction of life-needs, whether these needs be independent of human control or those that he has himself conceived. The reference point of value is the individual human being. The source of values is experience, though not always necessarily the experience of each individual; and values are validated as they "make good" in human living. Ultimately the test of value is an empirical one: there is no sure sign that certain values "work" beyond the fact that, in the best understanding of human beings, they appear to operate favorably toward the development of the individual. Experimentalism does not hold therefore that values can ever be tested with the precision and mechanicalness possible in certain physical science, but rather that values are tested by human beings thinking conscientiously and intelligently in situations that bear upon their vital welfare. Experience is self-regulative, and there is no feeling of certainty beyond what experience itself can furnish. Values are not selfless, objective, mechanical, ready at any time to prove themselves. Values must be reinforced at any time by human faith in them, so that they may be tested fairly, so that the human intelligence may have a real opportunity to create means of realizing them, of making them "work."

The nature of experience is such, however, that values must be held as hypotheses, and when applied to the direction of events they must be tested with some of the open-mindedness and high regard for the testimony of results that is characteristic of science. Values are tested by events; they do not test events. Successive situations although they may be related in some kind of understandable sequence, have each of them in some respect a novel nature. To manipulate each situation so that it eventuates in a certain way, it is necessary to apply values creatively. Values just will not work in a pre-fabricated way. Only as values are held hypothetically, as they are applied in a creative way to each situation, and as each situation serves, to some extent, to test them, can the perpetuation of mistakes and ultimately disaster be avoided; only in that way can human intelligence be adequate to the turn of events. Human values must be in a state of continuous adjustment. Human intelligence must be continuously re-examining its workings, and must constantly be adjusting its meanings as it passes from past to present, and creatively applying its values as it passes from present to future.

But the fact that values are medial and instrumental in experience and that the nature of this experience requires that they be held hypothetically does not mean that we live in a "jittery" world, where everything is tentative and nothing is ever regarded as dependable. (The philosophy of Experimentalism itself has strong convictions, i.e., values, and it does not rule out strong convictions or values in the guidance of practical living.) The fact that each experience, when regarded as a totality, is unique in its configuration should not be taken to conflict with the fact that basic human needs are repetitive in the individual and in the race (especially is this true of biological needs), and that these basic needs are general factors constant in all human living that give rise to certain constant general values. The experimental attitude (itself, by the way, a firm value) should not be held to be at odds with the fact that we are sure of some things, that we can use them with greater conviction, and much greater assurance of getting vital results.

The experience of man has in the past accumulated many values which have been validated as far as that is possible in experience itself. These values have gone into the making of the environment, have become part of our culture (along with many other values which were never validated with reference to the vital welfare of each individual, but rather were perpetuated by force within the culture). These values, which we must take care to identify and segregate from the rest, may be accepted with the assurance that they will "work," though man needs to be intelligent in interpreting them properly in changing situations. Whether they are to be regarded as "practical absolutes" or merely as "reliable working hypotheses" [41] is a matter of difference among Experimentalists, as is also the relative weight to be given to each of the preferred values.[42] But the Experimentalist is, on the whole, not suggesting that the making of values is something that begins anew with each individual. This is impossible. The fact that an individual is born into a culture means that his experience will be influenced into accepting a great many values. What is important is how discriminating he is in his use of values, how skillful he is in adapting values, in creating new values out of the matrix of his own living, in testing values in terms of his own life-processes. Experimentalism as an educational theory does not deny the importance of its function of preserving and transmitting the cultural heritage, but it wants this heritage to be relevant and important to the individual in the conduct of his experience, and flexible enough to serve him as an instrument of creative intelligence.

Summary.—What are the principal values about which Experimentalism holds strong convictions and which it would also sponsor as basic in the direction of living? Probably the paramount value is a strong regard for each human being as an individual and a faith in his possibilities. Despite internal disagreement on the degree to which this value is to be carried, Experimentalism stands out for its belief that each individual, out of the content of his experience, can create his intelligence as he goes along. Values that have come down from the past, values that are consciously cherished or unconsciously fostered by the culture, the culture itself, are background and accessories which the individual uses in making himself continuously intelligent. The dynamic nature of experience makes it impossible for the past to legislate for the future; the present is therefore left to its own resources, having for the most part only spent values to begin with. Because each human being is himself an end of living and is equal in this respect with every other human being, and because the experience-process is in some decisive ways unique with each individual, it is impossible for any social mechanism (as, for example, government) to assign common,

---

[41] J. L. Childs, *Education and the Philosophy of Experimentalism*, p. 123. 1931.
[42] *Vide supra*, pp. 45–46.

arbitrary ends and means of living to all individuals (i.e., if it would not warp their development), nor can it permit some individuals to impose their purposes and methods upon others. It falls to each individual to make his own way, and Experimentalism has faith that he can do so. Democracy as a value is bound up with the freedom that the individual must have, and is to be interpreted as the principles of social procedure that offer to the individual opportunities for the greatest self-development. The value of the societal organism is in what it makes possible for the individual, and by this token society acquires great importance of a secondary kind. An individual is what his experience makes him, and society is the crucible of experiences. Whatever an individual becomes, he becomes within society. A society that does not make possible the experiences that are conducive to the fullest development of personality is, to the degree that it does not do so, blameworthy. To alter the offending social conditions should become the immediate concern of all individuals.

Another set of values in the Experimentalist category devolves out of a strong faith in the method of science. The method of science is to be extended into human living, and to occupy a position central in the direction of experience. The method of science has been defined in different ways at different times, and Experimentalism holds no brief for the positivistic, objectivistic, unintellectual attitude that has often characterized science in the past and is in evidence even today. The scientific method in which Experimentalism has confidence is the method by which modern science, and especially modern physics, has been enabled to learn so much about the physical world and to gain for man the large degree of control over physical nature that he possesses. The essence of this method is flexibility in thought, relativeness, awareness of alternative possibilities, a tentativeness-looking-toward-verification, an honesty of appraisal, and swiftness to act once results are verified. The world that physical science thus reveals is a world in which the scientific method is just as appropriate and as necessary of application to human experience. In a static, orderly world-system, human living might be intelligently managed through the conscientious application of deductive principles, and the experimental method would be unnecessary. But in an indeterminate world of plural possibilities, the experimental attitude is the only attitude to take, unless one can rely upon a *deus ex machina* to pull him out of difficulties. Moreover, the potentialities of the material achievements which physical science has stored up must not be overlooked; these achievements, which have made it possible for man to gain control of natural energies and ways of using them, give promise of providing a material foundation that will make actually realizable a Good Life for all.

1: The Social Dynamics of Secondary Education

I [2]

RECOGNIZING THE material and spiritual importance of the societal way of living, Humanism nevertheless assigns to the individual priority in the human scheme of things. This emphasis upon the individual varies in intensity: at its greatest,[3] it brings to mind a picture of society as a congress of individuals each of whom, conscious of his dignity and completeness as a human being, enters almost reservedly into societal relations to an extent no greater than life demands; at its least,[4] it still places the individual first, but makes unmistakably clear his reliance upon society for the realization of those values that make him a full and a free person. Whatever the degree of emphasis in particular cases, Humanism holds as common tenets that the unit of human living is the individual man; that society, though by continuous contiguity its individuals may have grown together and developed common cultural traits, must recognize the distinctiveness of each of its members; that human beings are uneven and unequal in their possibilities for development in the direction of the Good Life; that societal arrange-

[1] The contents of the following pages are based on an analysis of the writings of Butler, Foerster, Hutchins, and Kandel. The writings of Learned do not especially deal with social theory; in view of his general orientation, it can hardly be doubted that he would agree with the general principles here expressed.

[2] The Roman numerals used in this study to mark off sections have the following significance: I—General Principles, II—Evaluation of the Existent Situation in Terms of These Principles, III—Nature of Constructive Proposals.

[3] In Foerster, *The American State University, passim.* 1937. Foerster's emphasis on the individual is considerably greater than that which is typical of Humanism as a whole.

[4] In Kandel; *vide* Introduction to this study, p. 21, footnote.

ments, therefore, beyond common guarantees of the rights of "life, liberty, and the pursuit of happiness" must provide for the development of each person as far as his possibilities allow, consistent with the welfare of the whole.

The genesis of human society is to be attributed to the development in man of the rational spirit. At a stage of human development, it became apparent that to live in a harmonious, cooperative societal way was to realize one of the attributes of humanness. To share with others one's strength, one's labor, one's problems, one's thoughts, to lend and to accept assistance, seemed to the individual to be at one with living the Good Life. To realize these values, men voluntarily entered into societal organization, and in doing that, surrendered certain rights to gain certain opportunities. Human society was thus originally formed on a voluntary basis; the rights that were surrendered in no way involved the fundamental rights of living that belong to man as a human being. The motive in surrendering the lesser individual liberties was to make secure the fundamental rights of all, and thus to make secure the societal state. That every person might retain his fundamental rights and that there might be no cause for the dissolution of society, each person willingly gave up some of the less essential liberties that seemed to be unfriendly to the societal idea. Thus, "the sphere of government was carved out of the sphere of Liberty by free men who knew precisely what they were doing."[5] Wherever in fundamental matters he differed from other individuals, the individual assigned to the group the privilege of arbitration. Some rights he reserved for himself, and would not consent to have society consider at all.[6]

Succeeding ages have certified to the wisdom of the human decision to adopt societal organization, as well as of man's insistence that the fundamental rights of the individual be made inviolable by the group. The fact of human society has become one of the goods of human living. Societal living *is* a manner in which man expresses his humanness, and by which it becomes possible for him to rise higher and higher in

[5] N. M. Butler, *Annual Report of the President to the Trustees of Columbia University, 1934.* p. 25.

[6] Through force and unfounded claims of state absolutism, tyrannies have sometimes developed which deprived individuals of their fundamental rights. These governments have not prevailed. The essential human rights have always reasserted themselves.

the human scale. In and through society man realizes a better individual life, spiritually and materially. Society not only furnishes the opportunity for ethical living but, by keeping intact and transmitting the precious heritage of human wisdom, it makes ethical and effective living possible. Societal existence, once achieved through a voluntary coming-together, can no longer be conceived on such a basis. Human society must be maintained; the rights that the individual once upon a time voluntarily surrendered he can no longer withdraw. In the course of time even additional curtailments of original liberties became necessary to secure the societal structure, as society grew and the problems of maintaining it became more complicated. The individual has undoubtedly gained by each one of these concessions. To give up the few liberties that are needed to assure the continued security of the human association is a small enough price to pay for the inestimable privileges that society offers and makes possible in the way of living the Good Life.

Society has a perfect right, therefore, to *exact* of each person the obligation that he will so conduct himself as not to threaten its continued existence (to put it negatively), and the right legally to enforce this obligation. Moreover, it has a right to *expect* that each person shall so conduct himself as to actualize in his living those positive social values— of good-will and cooperation, of respect for the rights of others—that long human usage has learned to prize. For that reason, society (that is, individuals acting together for common ends) owes it as an obligation to every person to help him, as far as his natural capacity allows and at least beyond a minimal common point, to secure for himself the values that society holds in trust for humanity. But society, in extending the authority of the group over individual living, must take care to move with caution, even when it moves toward the generally creditable ends of strengthening itself or of seeking the greatest good of the largest number. Even to serve the common welfare is not sufficient reason for depriving the individual of certain fundamental rights that belong to him as a human being. Tyranny may lodge in a society as well as in an individual, and from society may be even more difficult to dislodge. Human life, human soul, belong to the individual. Society is not in itself an end of human living, but a means, and it is distortion of vision to see the means as the more elevated. In the extension of its power, society must be careful not to violate the cardinal truth that, man advances toward a realization of complete humanness as an individual, distinct and different from all other individuals. The Good Life is fundamentally a function of mind, it cannot be imposed by society. Society can teach truths, but it cannot make them real. Only the human mind can do that, and mind is a personal possession. Society not only should not, but is unable, by legislation, to confer certain rights upon individuals which by nature they are not entitled to possess. Only by guaranteeing that the essential rights of man are held inviolate can society truly help the individual to realize, to his own degree, the Good Life. Moreover, society must be mindful that the conception of this Good Life is not a finite human ideal, and that the human mind must be left unfettered and free to design and to create for itself a higher life.

The good society, therefore, while acting to maintain its security and ensure its continuance, accepts as a basic limiting principle that the individual life is the end toward which it is the means, and that this life never has and never will surrender itself to the trusteeship of society. The human spirit is a free spirit; its essence lies in its ability to guide itself. The responsibility for his life is the individual's; it rests in himself and not in society. The foundations of progress, moreover, are always a consequence of individual achievement; society may, through collective effort, elevate the living of all its individuals when these foundations have been properly laid, but it cannot itself build the foundations. The great ethical principles, the great discoveries of mankind, the artistic achievements, the mechanical inventions that have served to better the material life, were all of them achievements of the individual mind. The group has followed in the course that individuals have plotted. The good society leaves unrestricted the opportunities for intellectual inquiry; for freedom of religion that has done so much to clarify for man the meaning of his humanness. It affords opportunity for the spiritual and material advancement of each person to the limit of his capacity, provided that he does not endanger the common welfare and the individual liberties of others.

Political equality is a right to which every person living in society is entitled. This principle is an affirmation of the truth that society originated in the voluntary coming-together of its members and a recognition that the preservation of the original status of human equality is a necessary condition for human happiness. The good society guarantees and respects this equality. Whatever changes it may incur in matters that affect the living of all, it makes by common consent, in a manner by which the voice of each person is equally registered. But political equality is not complete equality. Political equality is equality of a kind, the reality of which man has been able to recognize and to ensure; it is a *fact* which man has reaffirmed as a value. But man cannot create equality when it is not there. Man cannot confer essential equality upon human beings; nature has ruled otherwise. Beyond political equality there is no other equality. Human beings are born unequal and become more unequal as they develop; and they are unequal with respect to the essential human possession—mind. The good society recognizes the basic inequality of human beings, and does not confuse the perfectly valid ideal of political equality with an untenable, sentimental doctrine of complete equality. Especially must this distinction be maintained in an interpretation of the principle of equality of opportunity. The principle itself is one of the great generalizations out of human experience seeking to realize the greatest justice to the individual consistent with the common good. The good society provides for all individuals equality of opportunity. But equality of opportunity does not mean sameness of opportunity in all things. Indeed, "to treat all human individuals equally is to treat them unequally." [7] Equality of opportunity cannot be uniformly interpreted; it must be determined in terms of individual goodness. The good society offers to its best individuals the highest opportunities, and the best individuals are those most amply endowed with mental capacity, regardless of wealth or social status. In its best sense, the meaning of democracy combines all these principles relating to human equality: recognition that each person is equally a member of society, equal guarantee of the fundamental human rights to all individuals, recognition of the undeniable fact of intellectual inequality of human beings, provision of equality of opportunity for all to advance toward the Good Life to the extent that intellectual capacity permits. The good democracy is also an intellectual aristocracy that is constantly renewing itself.

But provision of highest opportunity to the most talented does not imply a policy of unrestricted laissez faire. Equality of opportunity,

[7] N. M. Butler, *Annual Report of the President to the Trustees of Columbia University, 1929*, p. 37.

even when fairly granted, can have outcomes that are socially and individually destructive. It can lead away from as well as toward the Good Life. The realization of granted opportunity must be given ethical direction, and must at times be placed under social restraint when it operates in opposition to recognized human values. When equality of opportunity fosters selfish and unsocial individualism, societal intervention is necessary. Conversely, it is consistent with both societal stability and the highest ethical principles to intervene on behalf of those whom lack of natural talent or failure to take advantage of opportunity or even other causes place at a great disadvantage in human living. While the inevitability of inequality in human living must be respected, it is also a human ideal that security of life be afforded to all. (Humanness, after all, does lie in modifying natural conditions toward human ends.) It is the duty of society at the present time, for example, to assist individuals in gaining a measure of economic security.[8] How far society is to go in this direction cannot be decided once and for all; it is a principle that must be applied flexibly. But societal arrangements must always seek to strike a balance between the inviolable rights of the individual and the demands that society may rightfully make upon him for the assistance of others.

The good society is evaluated by the same standards as is the Good Life of the individual; it must reflect in its collective conduct—in its common motivating ideals, in its dominant methods, in its mores, in its institutions—the values upon which humanity has placed its highest approval. A society is not the independent judge of itself, answerable only to itself. Any particular society is a phase of collective human existence, the past brought down to date. Like the Good Life of the individual, the Good Life of society rests upon the total accumulated intelligence of mankind. The good society serves as a continuous bridge between the past and the present. Its processes are evolutionary and not revolutionary. It is continuously furnishing itself from the common storehouse of human wisdom with those treasures which it can use, which it can further refine, and which, if necessary, it can make over. Social progress is not always implicit in social activity, nor is the movement of mankind always in the direction of the good. Progress is an

---

[8] Though all would agree on this general statement, Humanists differ considerably in the extent to which they would carry out this principle.

achievement, an outcome of conscious application of will and intelligence. The direction of progress is, in general, toward the increasing control of life by mind, toward the substitution of ethical for natural living, toward extending mastery over material nature and using this mastery to realize approved human ends. In finding the course of progress, the only available compass and charts are the values that humanity has stored up. A society that cuts itself off from the human tradition is bound to be limited, provincial, uncivilized; reliant upon the small fund of wisdom that it has been able to accumulate in the short course of its existence and more largely upon its own unsupported intuitions, such a society is constantly running the risk of wrecking itself.

The highest criterion of goodness in society is to be found not in the externals of living but in its fundamentals—in the ethical life of each of its constituent individuals. At best the externals (productive ability, mechanical efficiency, material standard of living) are an indirect and not a very reliable criterion of goodness. Often they are altogether misleading, creating an appearance of actual goodness where there is only material "prosperity." The goodness of a society resides in the extent to which each of its members approaches in his living the humanistic ideal—a life of high ethical virtue guided by disciplined, effective intelligence. This criterion presumes a degree of success in material living— physical and economic well-being, freedom from violence, amity in human relations, the rule of law—but goes considerably beyond it. It goes beyond any mere negative restraint from perpetration of injustice. It is to be found in the positive exercise by each person of those ethical virtues that are man's chief distinction in the whole realm of living nature.

The most important factor in the attainment of the good ethical life is intelligence. A society can be good to the extent that the individuals in it are intelligent. Society originated as a voluntary association of intelligent individuals who found in societal living a satisfactory realization of a common purpose. As individuals grow in intelligence, they develop ideals according to which the societal purposes, societal processes, societal organization are improved. There can be no final statement, in terms of specific processes, of what is the good society: the good society is what individuals, as they grow in intelligence, make it. The intelligent man is also by definition the social man. To be intelligent, he must realize that the societal is a necessary and an advantageous form of living, that it aims at a finer life for the individual, that in return for benefits gained by the individual, there are reciprocal obligations. Possessing such intelligence, he not merely will take pains to keep within the restrictions that society imposes equally upon all, but he will exert his intelligence in positive ways so that it operates for the better living of others as well as for his own. If man uses the intellectual abilities that humanity has helped him to realize, and if his efforts are motivated by good-will toward others, whatever eventuates will be inevitably *intended* for the social good, and may *actually* turn out to be good. Society must have faith in the intelligence and good-will of its individuals. Beyond this, there can be no formula for social betterment. It is to the advantage of society that men be intelligent, that men be free, that their intelligence be guided, so that, in its expression, it is consistent with the highest human values. As society originally was the creation of the individual intelligence, so continuous societal betterment is an outcome of the continued growth of this intelligence. What has been said, however, must not be interpreted to mean that man's living is directed only towards social development. The good man is much more than just the social man. The Good Life is essentially the individual life. The good man strives to realize through his living *all* the highest attributes of humanness. In the process of doing that he serves society.

The ideal society has never been realized nor ever can be. Much less can it be rightfully assumed that *the* society in which a person lives, the society which *happens to be,* is *ipso facto* the good society. For a person to be devoted to the societal way of living does not mean that he is also loyally to accept the social values regnant in his particular time and place. Loyalty to society requires that there be a conscientious effort to accept prevailing social values if that can be done in a manner consistent with intellectual integrity; but societal welfare in the long run requires also that these values be criticized in the light of the more permanent values of mankind, and, failing by this test, that they be replaced. The good man is loyal to the ideal of societal living generally, and particularly to those values prevailing in his society which have received the sanction of broader human experience; of the others he is critical, and, to the best of his intelligence and without violating the principles of ethical conduct, applies himself to their replacement. What is true of the whole of human life is true also of its social aspects: the unexamined life is not worth living. In continuously searching for a better life himself, the individual cannot keep from searching out the defects existing in the societal situation. The good man is not, therefore, one who accepts without question societal things-as-they-are: but in the elimination of defects he is guided by a regard for the necessity for rational procedure, by a respect for human rights, by a proper sense of proportion toward the values involved. However necessary it may be to alter the societal *status quo,* it is necessary to begin with it. And the ability that is required both for understanding and appraising society and for conceiving and executing improvement is a function of the degree to which the individual has acquired the highest wisdom that the human past has been able to offer.

A good society rests upon a broad base of individual goodness. If that is true, it follows that society can become better to the degree that more of its individuals attain a high degree of ethical living and intellectual effectiveness.[9] This the good society must seek to have its individuals do. Human beings are not alike and society cannot make them alike; their differences are indeed, in a manner of speaking, to be cherished. But an attempt must be made to raise all individuals to high minimal levels of ethical and moral living, of knowledge and the effective exercise of judgment and the reasoning processes, of appreciation of beauty, of performance of the important activities and processes of daily living. Beyond the common level, the attainment of individuals in ethical insight and intellectual power will be as varied as are their potentialities; and the good society will indeed give most assistance to the intellectually most deserving. But societal progress does come in two ways: by

[9] What follows is not acceptable to Foerster. It is his view that so considerable a number in the population is ineducable, that it is futile for society to try to raise itself on a basis of *mass intelligence.* Society can, with better results, concentrate upon improving the opportunities of its more capable individuals. When society does operate on a high level of common intelligence, that fact must be attributed to chance or heredity rather than to what society itself has been able to accomplish through educational processes.

In taking this position, Foerster is alone among the Humanists *here* represented. The position, however, is not an uncommon one among Humanists generally. *Vide,* for example, A. J. Nock, *The Theory of Education in the United States.* 1932.

elevating the common level of living of all individuals, and through the highest development of its best individuals. Toward both of these objectives the good society must direct itself.

II

Evaluating the contemporary American society in terms of these general principles, Humanism finds something that is laudable but considerably more that must be criticized. It is an undeniable fact that American society is at present undergoing deep and far-reaching change. The basis of the change is the success of science in understanding and mastering the physical world—in inventing machines to do the work of man, in evolving a technology that has made it possible to increase many times man's capacity to satisfy his material wants. There is no denying that the speed with which the change has come has created large problems: of an industrial-economic nature, as, for example, the problem of restoring a balance between production and employment, between production and distribution to the consumer; of more than only an industrial-economic nature, reaching into the social, cultural, religious, emotional, intellectual phases of human life. Nevertheless, our age has managed to exaggerate even the admittedly tremendous effects of the change it is undergoing. For one thing, our age has appeared to see in this change a transformation in the character of human life itself. It tends to see itself as something new under the sun, as unique in human history. Conscious of its differentness, it has broken from its moorings in the past. The past is old, old-fashioned; we are young and new. For another thing, change has become idealized and rationalized into a "philosophy" of change, and this "philosophy" has proceeded to operate on the assumption that everlasting change, uncertainty, precariousness,[10] rather than constancy, certainty, assurance, are the natural and desirable conditions in human living. Change has become identified with progress; what is new and different is also hailed as good. We have thus been further encouraged to turn our backs upon

[10] In section II, under each theory and in every chapter, the evaluation is strictly in terms of the particular theory of secondary education considered. The characterization is, therefore, not necessarily such as this writer would himself make.

the horse-and-buggy past and to deal only in immediate presents and futures.

The foundations of culture are not in material things but in the nature of human beings. And although the nature of things can change with considerable rapidity, human nature cannot. Human nature is accustomed to material changes: it, in fact, begets them. (It is easy to forget that industrial revolutions are products of the human mind.) Human nature changes slowly, and when it does, the change is not merely a resultant of the pull of inanimate forces, but the result of a conscious, deliberate effort by mind itself. Changes in material externals do not necessarily signify equivalent changes in the fundamental problems that have always concerned man and will always concern him. The higher reality is in human mind, and it is to this we must feel bound. It does not follow that because human nature produces changes, it is in turn changed by them.

Changes there have been, and of the utmost importance, and with increasing rapidity changes continue to develop. But that is not sufficient reason for our present self-consciousness of being different and unique, for cutting ourselves off from the continuity of human experience, for breaking with the rightfully trusted values of the past. That is what we have done, and more: in our awe of change and its material effects we have lost sight of the supreme human value—mind. We have become unidealistic and anti-rational. Instead of relying upon mind to achieve for human beings freedom from the control of nature, we have invented a "pragmatic" way of life: we set adjustment as our goal, we blame nature or economics for our troubles, we pattern "laws" of human conduct upon the behavior of rats in mazes, and when "the world is too much with us" we go to psychoanalysts to tell them all about it.

The American people have, to their great credit, attempted to fashion their living in accordance with the great values of democracy and personal liberty. But we are in serious danger of debasing our democracy and of losing our liberty. The equality that democracy guarantees has become distorted into equalitarianism. Equalitarianism cannot be defended as a fact of nature or as a human ideal. Democracy means individual freedom, political equality, and equality of opportunity, but it does not mean equalitarianism. It is impossible for human beings to be all alike, and uniformity would be undesirable even if it were possible. Like the guarantee of political equality, the guarantee of liberty is inherent in the concept of democracy. But our liberty is being threatened today from two sources: first, by those who have interpreted liberty as license, as justification for lack of restraint and exclusive concern with self; second, by those who, reacting against the evils brought by excessive individualism and driven by fear of a dark future foreshadowed by the great "changes," are urging collectivism and the domination of the individual by the group.[11]

Individual liberty is one of the highest values that it has been given man to possess. But liberty is not a gift into possession of which man automatically comes at birth. Liberty is a possession that is achieved, that comes with the flowering of the intelligence, with ethical character, with self-discipline, with recognition and assumption of social responsibility. Liberty without trained intelligence is no liberty at all but the most dismal kind of slavery—slavery to ignorance, to superstition, to prejudice, to fear; liberty that is interpreted as license is intolerable in society. Yet, for a long time, American democracy has been inclining in the direction of the kind of liberty that means social irresponsibility. Business ethics have tolerated a conception of liberty that expressed itself in ruthless competitive struggle for gain, for self-aggrandizement, for material power. The same concept operating in social relations has resulted in widespread disregard of the law, in a high degree of criminality, in a lowering of standards of morality, in a neglect of human life. On the other hand, with emphasis upon "machine," upon "technological change," and so forth, there has developed among many a lack of faith and confidence in the possibilities of man as an individual. There is noticeable a tendency to seek spiritual comfort and material safety in numbers, to try to achieve en masse what each person does not have the fortitude to attempt separately. Following the example of some countries, where the individual human spirit never did achieve the freedom that learns to face with resolution and confidence the problems of living, there have developed in our society collectivistic theories and programs which, in the name of economic betterment for all, would

[11] This concern is not equally shared by all the Humanists. It is strongly felt by Foerster and Butler. Hutchins and Kandel seem to be of the opinion that an extension of social control, if wisely done, would be at the present time desirable.

destroy individual rights to be cherished even above material security. Already social action has gone a considerable distance in this direction.[12] "From the point of view of humanism . . . this absorption of the individual into the mass and this development of the mass into a means of attaining the maximum of economic and material power is a return to primitivism. . . . To substitute the social animal for the social man is to renounce the dignity of man which rests upon the freedom of individuals." [13]

Changing economic events have undoubtedly made more difficult the problem of establishing the material basis for secure living. An economy of scarcity has given way to an economy of potential plenty, and the change has caught us unprepared. Technological development has greatly reduced the need for human labor, and created a problem of technological unemployment. Extreme economic individualism has added to the disjointedness of our economic situation. But these problems are not to be solved merely by casting away old values and operating with no values at all. The mind of man will have to invent new social means of coping with these problems; but it cannot do so except on a humanistic basis—on a basis that recognizes the superiority of man over nature, that has faith in his possibilities, and that guarantees to him his inalienable rights.

The misinterpretation and the misuse of the right of liberty are symptomatic of a general loss of a true sense of values that has resulted. We have magnified certain values far beyond their proper importance, and we have unwarrantedly minimized others. Spiritual values, religion, retain little of their old significance; they have been overshadowed by naturalism and materialism. Reason is directed toward material achievement, and not toward the ends of ethical, humanistic living. With materialistic preoccupations have come strife and disunions of every kind. Reason directed toward ethical ends is productive of individual development and societal betterment; directed primarily toward material ends, it breeds competition and strife, degrading the individual and weakening society.

We are paying the penalty for an irrational and unwarranted faith in science. Over-impressed by the success of science in mastering the

---

[12] This represents the viewpoint of Foerster and Butler only.
[13] N. Foerster, *The American State University*, p. 229. 1937.

world of matter, and induced by those who would carry the legitimate pursuit of science into illegitimate scientism, we have allowed ourselves to become reliant upon science for the guidance of our living. Science does not possess the power to provide such guidance. "Science has been compared to a time-table which tells us how we may proceed in any direction but which is silent as to our destination." [14] We have abandoned philosophy and looked toward science, and we are confused and in despair because science has failed us.

This, in sum, is the criticism which must be made of American society. Its weaknesses are intellectual and moral self-isolation; idealization of change and identification of change with progress; surrender of old and tried values, and failure to replace them with others of equal worth; consequently, moral and intellectual decline; a false notion of democracy substituting equalitarianism for equality and license and absence of restraint for self-disciplined freedom; the threat to the rights of the individual arising out of a feeling of spiritual and material insecurity; economic unbalance and resultant social-economic difficulties; frustration that comes from reliance upon science as a way of life. Perhaps the most serious single weakness is the general temper behind which we have taken refuge—the temper of pragmatism. The spiritual sterility of this outlook, its pessimistic attitude toward the possibilities of man in the world of things, its idealization of opportunism, all operate to make it difficult for us to face courageously and to attack with intelligence and determination each of the social problems that confront us.

As against this, and to the credit of American society, it must be said that many of its weaknesses are imperfections and blemishes arising out of its considerable achievements. American society has chosen the way of democracy and individual freedom. In the face of difficulties it has maintained in large degree the liberties of the individual. Its errors have been errors of exaggeration and sentimentalization. Though lately it is veering toward anti-intellectualism, it has up to now admirably shown its faith in the possibilities of man by its generous support of education. Its material achievements have raised the standard of physical living and offer possibilities for a better human life, if only they could be properly directed. The achievement of science has been an achievement

[14] *Ibid.*, p. 236.

of which the human spirit may well be proud, although its pretensions to pansophism have been disastrous in their common consequences.

III

The troubles with which American society is afflicted are as much spiritual and intellectual in their origin and nature as they are industrial and economic. Periodically in the course of his history, man has been subjected to changes in the material foundations of his living. In such times, troublesome problems are bound to arise. The only way to deal with them is with clear-headedness, with resolution, and with faith in the human possibilities. This period of change that we are at present undergoing is possibly more critical than the others have been, and its problems are more severe. Especially, then, in grappling with them we must keep our intellectual balance and retain our faith in tried values. Above all, we must retain our faith in the idea that the only way of life for man is the one that sets man above nature. Physical comforts and the satisfaction of physical needs make possible the Good Life, but the Good Life is not *within them*. Of what value would it be to solve our economic problems if in the process man had to surrender his liberties, if ethical living became impossible and man had to return to crude primitivism, if man had to surrender faith in his own possibilities as an individual human being and return to the ways of the herd?

The problems of society cannot be solved by social formula or by social fiat but by the patient self-application of intelligent, disciplined human beings. Problems are not solved by society, but by individuals, by the pooling of the products of their individual intelligence and effort. It is the responsibility of education to help to produce individuals who are sufficiently intelligent, sufficiently concerned, and sufficiently per-severing in the right way, to solve these problems. Especially must education emphasize in the development of each individual those virtues which are at this time not commonly present in the human character and intellect, and which help to account for the fact that our efforts are not being very successful.

Through the development of right individuals, there must be a restoration to their proper place in human living of these values— spiritual, ethical, moral, intellectual—which have proved their worth and their goodness in the long course of human history, and which are not in our time sufficiently prominent. A high valuation must again be placed upon responsible, socially-conscious liberty, upon honor, justice, personal responsibility, moral uprightness, upon rationality, emotional refinement and restraint, upon the essential dignity of the human being. There must be a rejection of opportunism and subjectivism: notions of relativistic truth must be given up as senseless and unworthy; absolute standards of truth and knowledge must be restored, and by them all proposals must be evaluated. The quest for material goods and increased power must be subordinated to the search for the good ethical life.

In the political arrangements of society there must be a return to a true conception of democracy, the conception of Jefferson, which harmonizes the need for individual liberty and the rights of man with the fact of the essential inequality of men. There must be achieved a better balance between the rights of the individual and the requirements for societal stability. In this balance, a true conception of human freedom will be discovered. Education must help to secure individuals who freely and knowingly enter into all their human responsibilities, exercising their rights as free men, but also carrying out the obligations to which their membership in a human organization commits them. At the same time, there must be a return to a conception of individual worth that is based upon the possession of mind. This, too, is implicit in the concept of democracy. Without withholding the respect that is due the human being as human being, it is nevertheless necessary to recognize differences in achievement, and to estimate worth on the basis of achievement and possibilities of achievement. Especially must the leadership that a democracy develops be a leadership provided by its intellectual aristocracy.

The ideals of American society, assuming a return to these values, must be more clearly defined in the future than they have been in the past. Validated against and in accord with the best that the past has achieved, they must be set up as objects of allegiance to which all men must subscribe. American society must achieve a sense of unity, stronger than any it has ever had, to overcome the various unfriendly ideologies that now threaten it; all along the line there must be a re-integration to overcome the looseness, the negativism that has crept into American life. But the unity of American society must be part of a larger whole, part of a sense of an active belonging to the whole of the human race. No true cultural feeling is possible without the feeling of humanism. There must be, fundamentally, a return to the humanistic temper. A world of complex material problems demands the use of reason to the extent that no simpler world does. But even rationalism, unless it merge the world of material things with the world of spirit, is barren. There must be a return to religion and its elevating and refining influence, a return to idealism, with its human ends pitched high above those of nature. Of necessity, the agnosticism, the obscurantism, the anti-intellectualism, and all the other arid negativisms now riding high must be overthrown. These tasks constitute in essence the social function of education.

SOCIAL EVOLUTIONISM

I

To the Social Evolutionist society is pre-eminent both as the means by which a continuously better life is made possible for the individual and the race and as an end of human living. Society makes available to every individual the learnings, essential for survival and human advancement, that have come out of the total experience of the race. It offers to the individual an environment in which most of these learnings are already operative; he needs but to become assimilated into that environment to share in a manner of living that it has taken mankind long ages to achieve. It offers the individual a means for securing the cooperation of others in the solution of life-problems; living thereby becomes easier. Apart from this, societal living is one of the goals toward which human living aspires, one of the true ends of living. The Good Life must be lived within the societal medium; no other kind of life would conceivably be satisfactory.

It is true, in the final analysis, that the ultimate end of nature is the individual life; but this life is so dependent for its well-being upon others, and in turn influences so many others, that it has come to be impossible to think of the individual as an independent entity, with goals of living that can be dissociated from the goals of the rest of society.

There need be no conflict between the individual and society and there should be none; but if a choice must be made between promoting individual ends (short of life itself) and those of society, the priority of the latter must be recognized. It is to be understood, of course, that there is nothing supra-human about society. Society is made up of living men and women; beyond that there is no society. But it must be understood also that society is more than merely an aggregation of individuals, living together. It is an organism—an organism, as it were, created by man—and with its welfare is tied up the welfare of every individual.

Like every other living thing, man seeks adjustment in nature. But human adjustment, unlike that of any other living thing, is not dependent for success upon the slow transmission by heredity of proper adaptive traits; nor is human adjustment the adjustment of a single being facing alone the immensity of nature; nor in human living must the learnings of bitter experience be renewed in the life-history of every member of the species. The human organism is endowed with a capacity for mind. Mind, or the ability to make the right adaptations to environment, developed in the course of living. At a certain stage of its development, mind brought into being society. Since then mind and society have cooperated in making possible and in facilitating human adjustment, or rather, mind has carried on its adjusting activity within, and through, and with the help of society. Society is a concrete and permanent tribute to human adaptive capacity as well as at least a limited insurance of success in future adjustment.

The origin of society is thus to be explained in terms of the growing adaptive ability of man. Whether the first forms of group life emerged as a result of man's conscious intending or of his unconscious yielding to some strong but undefined instinct, man soon came to recognize that in societal living lay a better way of satisfying life-needs. The value of society, once tried, proved itself. As man grew in adaptive ability, he experimented with different forms of societal organization through which he might better achieve his ends. He developed techniques to secure and to foster human cooperation in society: methods of communication, principles of common procedure, common ways of doing things. Society became the field of human operations and the means of human progress. Since the emergence of society, the method of human progress has been by social rather than by organic evolution. Unquestionably society is one of the great achievements of man seeking adjustment; in the natural history of mind it stands as a great event.

Basically what makes the human organism superior to every other living organism is its capacity for tremendous self-development. The physiological basis of this is a highly developed, complex, sensitive nervous system. The self-development of which man is capable makes realizable for him a new kind of adjustment—an adjustment that consists in steady changes in self and in environment in accordance with consciously conceived ends. An important factor in human self-development is man's ability to profit not alone from his own experience but from the experiences of others. And it is this fact that society utilizes to greatest advantage, to the inestimable benefit of mankind. It cannot be said that man has yet fully taken advantage of all the possibilities for better living that society offers. Indeed man has often abused society and spurned its benefits. Despite this, the influence of society remains paramount in the life of civilized man.

Society enables every human being to utilize in his own adjustment the values that have come out of the experience of other men, in the past and in the present. We are all of us seeking better adjustment all the time. Out of our experience come discoveries, inventions, insights that throw new light on the meaning of life and serve better to attain its ends. A learning gained in the course of one man's experience society can make available to all other men. Thus made available, the learning can remain forever the property of the whole race; society preserves and transmits it. Many learnings of a vital nature, acquired in the long course of human experience with much toil and pain, thus do not have to be relearned. Man can build upon the experience of his predecessors. In the course of centuries, society has become a vast reservoir into which have been poured all the learnings that mankind has accumulated. Every generation, every individual adds to the number. Equipped with these learnings, man does not have to rely upon his own meager experience to serve him in his adjustment. Without himself having stumbled, he can avoid certain pitfalls of nature. Though he may himself be incapable of great creative achievements and inventions, he can enjoy the results of the achievements and inventions of others. Society makes available for him a vast number of learnings crystallized, assembled, and ready for use. He and his generation, having at their disposal the benefits of the entire racial experience, can make a steady climb toward higher goals.

Not only does society make available to all the great learnings out of human experience, but it represents an attempt to gain the ends of adjustment cooperatively, through a pooling of human effort, ingenuity, and strength. Man does not face his problem of adjustment alone; together men have harnessed nature to serve their common purposes. Methods have been evolved for furthering human cooperation—methods of formulating goals, methods of procedure for achieving them, methods of communication, methods of organization. To a great extent society has achieved a revision of the cruel law of nature that only "the fittest" survive, and has placed within reach the possibility of the assured survival and progress of all. The learnings that society makes available and the methods of cooperation that have been devised help the individual to overcome personal handicaps that nature may have bestowed. Society exerts an equalizing influence on human beings: it helps every individual to rise to the general level of living which it exemplifies. In the process of societal adjustment the essential differences in adjustive capacity with which men are by nature endowed are greatly (though not altogether) reduced. Other and more desirable *consciously acquired* differences take their place—differences in intellectual interests, in technical skills. The latter differences are harmonious with the ends of common living.

The value of society must not, however, be judged merely in terms of that conception of adjustment which is common in all nature. The end of human living is not merely survival or comfortable physical existence. Man is continuously defining the ends of his living. In the final analysis, human adjustment is what man thinks it is (provided that nature does not prove him wrong). The ends of human living, subject to the broad condition of survival, are for man to establish. Man has chosen to regard living in close interrelatedness with others as one of the aims of his living. Society has become the framework within which all other ends of living are to be realized. Companionship makes for human happiness, and loneliness makes for human distress. Man finds comfort in living and working with others, in sharing their experiences, in participating in common in life-activities. This comfort of the spirit is, too, an end of living, and society makes it possible.

The emergence of society brought into human life a whole new set of values which have demanded integration with the other values of living. The maintenance and progressive improvement of society has become a condition attendant upon satisfactory human life. It has become part of the total purpose of the individual life to contribute toward societal welfare. A person can no longer think of himself alone, but of himself in relation to others. Every event in the life of the individual has some corresponding social effect; in the evaluation of human action, the social effect must also be considered. Nothing in human life can be considered good if it is in some way detrimental in its effect upon society. Whatever is good must also be social.

It has been said that the ends of human living are not set. Human life is in evolution and man is constantly conceiving and establishing new goals; yet, in moving from lower to higher levels, man must take care not to contravene any of the fundamental principles of adjustment. Societal evolution is an integral part of human evolution. It is impossible to speak of the perfect society or to prescribe any society for the future. As man moves progressively toward higher levels of living, he evolves progressively different societal conceptions and forms. The history of the human race is also the history of the evolution of societal organization, procedures, and institutions. From inferior societal adaptations we have gone to superior; from the rule of the blood feud as a personal means of redressing grievances we have come to the rule of impersonal law and justice; from government by the strong and government of one man by "divine right" we have come to government by all the people; from the principle of excluding or exterminating offenders against society we are working our way toward the practice of assisting in their rehabilitation; from a conception of societal prestige as resting on martial glory we are very slowly moving to a conception of societal prestige resting more on peace and the welfare and security of all citizens. Society is thus in evolution, and it is impossible to predict what forms or actions of society will be good for the future. Mind is an emergent and society itself evolves in emergent, unpredictable fashion. On the other hand, racial experience indicates with unmistakable clarity those learnings which a society is to heed if it would thrive, grow strong, move upward. Like the human individual, society must in its own experience take advantage of these learnings if it would make progress. The learnings are both positive and negative in character: there are certain general principles of adjustment that society must not contravene if it is to survive as society; there are certain principles of societal procedure that will assist it in maintaining itself on any existent level and to go higher. These learnings are available to us through an analysis of the experience of the past; up to the present time our knowledge of them has been empirical, unsystematic, imperfect; with the development of a science of society it is hoped that we will be able to identify these learnings more systematically and precisely.[15]

Generally speaking, a society can perform its functions in human living to the extent that it is strong and united and operating harmoniously. A society is an organism, the various elements of which must be integrated toward a common purpose. Influences that draw people together—a common law, common ideals and interests, concern with common problems, common institutions—are for that reason good; influences that tend to pull men apart—excessive competition among individuals, self-concern, unconventionality, disrespect for the authority of law—are bad. Excessive individualism, emphasis upon the rights of the individual as against those of the group, tend to weaken the societal organism. This is not to be taken to mean that individuals have no rights; indeed, "both common sense and the history of mankind . . . coincide in the conclusion that the interests and welfare of society are best served by recognizing a wide range of individual rights and liberties. . . ."[16] But the determination of individual rights must be made with a view to their effect upon the common whole.

The good society is democratic. The concept of democracy is inherent in the concept of society itself; to realize best its purposes in human living, a society must organize and conduct itself democratically. Society is good to the degree that all its individuals are achieving satisfactorily their common goals of living. It is in the implications of this that the meaning of democracy lies. Society is a great equalizer; democracy is the means of making equalization systematic and effective to a

---

[15] In general, Judd is more insistent upon the use of scientific techniques in the analysis of social experience (for the purpose of obtaining guiding values) than are Bagley and Morrison.

[16] W. C. Bagley, *Education and Emergent Man*, p. 126. 1934.

high degree. The concept of democracy is itself an evolving concept, but at least that much may be said about its essential meaning. The emphasis in democracy is on equality, but also on cooperation, on the spirit of "togetherness," on the principle of mutual assistance so as to enable all to rise to as high a level of common living as possible. Democracy is much more than a political concept—with emphasis upon liberty of person and identity of political and civil rights.[17] Democracy has implications that are cultural and economic, that affect man in every aspect of his living. The good society is not paternalistic: successful adjustment requires that every individual be able "to stand upon his own two feet" in every one of the important life-activities. But at the present stage of social evolution, it is necessary to reconsider the concept of democracy from the point of view of its implications for greater economic equalization.[18]

It follows from this that the concern of society is to be for all its members equally rather than for any special group. It is the duty of society to assist all individuals to rise to a point where they can make successful adjustment in their common environment. This means that society must exert even greater effort on behalf of those who are handicapped in inherited native endowment than on behalf of those more favored. It is not true that the equality to which human beings in society are entitled can be reduced to equity of opportunity.[19] Disregarding as much the accident of meager original endowment as it disregards the accident of social or financial status, the good society will bring even the most backward individual up to the point where he can operate with efficiency on the common cultural level. Being a unitary thing, society cannot afford not to do so. It is not true that a society needs to pay most attention to the proper development of its brightest individuals. "It would be easy to show that an intellectual aristocracy is just as reprehensible as an aristocracy based upon family or upon wealth."[20] And society need not worry excessively about the problem of securing a proper leadership. "The safest guarantee of sincere and responsible

[17] Contrast with Humanism, *supra* pp. 58 ff.
[18] Within Social Evolutionism there is disagreement as to the lengths to which it would be proper to go in equalizing economic status. Bagley and Judd would go farther in this respect than Morrison.
[19] W. C. Bagley, *Determinism in Education*, pp. 24 ff. 1925.
[20] *Ibid.*, p. 26.

leadership lies in a level of informed intelligence among the rank and file that will enable the common man to choose his leaders wisely and scrutinize their programs with sagacity, and encourage them to relinquish the duties of leadership gracefully and speedily when they go wrong." [21] Human progress is in and through society. All human beings must move together if higher levels of living are to be reached. This does not mean that they are to move in perfect unison. Individual differences cannot be wholly obliterated, nor should they be. The initiative of the few is the indispensable condition of progress: some daring and original spirits must always be in the vanguard; the great learnings of mankind originate with them. But not even these gifted people can draw very far away from the rest of society; societal living does not allow it. Fortunately the human organism is so constituted that it can assimilate and adopt for its own use learnings that it is not itself capable of originating; the ordinary person can use to very great advantage in his own living the invention of the genius. And in education society has one instrument (there are others) that enables it to communicate to all the learnings that originate with a few.

The good society is notable for the large degree of personal self-discipline and positive social-mindedness that characterizes all of its members. The qualities that have enabled man to reach high levels of living are pre-eminently those that are summed up in the term "self-discipline"—self-restraint, ability to persevere in the face of difficulties, ability to abide "by the rules," ability to hold to a steady course determined by remote ends rather than to yield to immediate impulses, all under the self-guidance of the individual rather than under the compulsion of enforced authority. The good society shows in its collective demeanor that a high degree of self-discipline is operative in the conduct of all its individuals—there is respect for properly constituted authority, obedience to law, regard for established human rights, order, coolness and level-headedness in the face of emergency, general regard for effort and respect for accomplishment, superior regard for cultural than for material achievement. History shows that no society has remained on a high level of civilization that failed to reveal these qualities in high degree. And these qualities must be present individually in large proportions not only in some or in many or in most but in all its members.

[21] *Ibid.,* pp. 26–27.

The good society keeps open the channels by which men may move toward a better kind of life. It is not a closed society, operating by principles that are regarded as absolute. A large degree of conformity is necessary, or society cannot operate as an organic whole. But society must remain cognizant of the fact that "final" ends have not yet been formulated and, indeed, never will be. Without extending to individuals that degree of license that would make true societal existence precarious, societal authority must take care not to interfere with essential individual liberties that are indispensable if civilization is to exist. Society must, indeed, take positive measures to assure individuals the freedom to experiment, to try new things, to express new ideas, to deviate from common social patterns, to as high a degree as is compatible with its welfare. Society must anticipate the need for changes by providing the orderly processes through which suggested changes may be translated into accepted practice. Though there must be respect for proper authority, the good society is not authoritarian. Questions on which popular judgment differs must, pending scientific confirmation or the decisive verdict of experience, be decided by consensus. Consensus, once taken, does not preclude further trial and experimentation. The good society takes note of results, and, when results so direct, does not hesitate to change its decision.

It is evident, of course, that the good society presumes a high degree of intelligence on the part of all its members. A society contributes to its own goodness to the extent to which it makes systematic provision for communicating to every individual those racial learnings that can serve to make him a highly adaptable, social person. Education—universal education, indeed—is more than a luxury: it is a necessity without which no society can be fully adequate. In universal education there lies the hope for the kind of progress that man has never before made even in society—a progress that is continuous rather than, as human progress has characteristically been, saltatory. "The development of the universal school is the latest scene in this great drama of social evolution." [22]

These are the general attributes that the good society must possess. It follows very easily that no particular society is ipso facto good: like the good individual, the good society must embody in its living, in cor-

---

[22] Bagley, *Determinism in Education*, p. 31. 1925.

rect proportion, the great positive learnings of our racial experience. These learnings do not identify themselves; they must be very carefully sought out and then identified. It rarely happens that all the necessary learnings are empirically identified and naturally adopted. Particular societies are all imperfect to a degree; and the decline and fall of many societies in the course of history shows that essential learnings have often gone unheeded. The fate of a society is like the fate of a living organism: it must satisfy the conditions required for adjustment or perish. In the identification of essential racial learnings, the rigorous methods of science applied to an analysis of social experience of the past and present are of great value. Once properly identified, these learnings may, through the instrumentality of the universal school, become assimilated into the whole of the societal organisms. Barring the emergence of some unforeseen evolutionary force that may interfere, it is within the realm of possibility for every society to become a "good" society.

Though society has organic structure, it has no separate existence apart from the individuals who make it up. A good society presupposes good men. What is the good man? The good man is, first of all, the social man. *Social*ness is not necessarily a trait with which man is endowed by nature. It is a trait that is communicated through learnings and toward the ends of which personality is shaped. Man is born neither social nor unsocial; he becomes social to a degree in the course of natural development, and can become much more so through education. Long ago man learned that living in society is an indispensable condition for good human living; socialness is therefore a necessary ingredient of the good human character. To be social means (1) to be a self-disciplining person; (2) to possess positive social attitudes, ideals, interests and to act in accordance with them. The social man is not merely the natural man: the social man acts from motives higher than those merely natural. He determines his actions not only by reference to himself but by reference to others who may be affected. When required, he sacrifices personal want to ethical principle, selfish desire to social need. At all times he subordinates impulse to conceived purpose.

The good man is also the intelligent man. Socialness itself involves not only volitional control but intellectual power. But goodness presumes more than socialness. The conception of human ends is not a finite conception that may at any time be closed. Man is always moving toward a higher kind of life. The direction of movement is not determinate; it is continuously being decided by man himself. Man maps out his own directions, and whatever fate awaits him, to that he must adapt himself. It is not sufficient, therefore, merely to reach a level that has already been realized—to become adjusted to conditions as they are. Man must be made competent to participate in conceiving new and better ends of living and in adapting himself to new conditions that are constantly developing. Social progress depends upon it. When, in addition, society has already reached so high a stage in evolution that its normal life-processes are complex, changing, of a high intellectual order, then adaptability becomes not only an added asset to the human being but a necessity without which he cannot properly exist. Ours is such a society, and adaptability of a high order has become a second requisite characteristic of the good man.

II

From time to time in the course of its evolution, society has had to pass through critical periods of transition. In a process of emergent evolution, this is inevitable. In both the organic and the social process, a new emergent creates a crisis; a period of readjustment follows, and a consolidation; when all is over, an important advance has been made. There is very strong evidence that American society is at present passing through such a critical period. "Human life, in our day, has reached a crucial stage in its evolution. Old adjustments have become obsolete and new adjustments have not reached sufficient maturity to be effective." [23] In the nature of things (since we have been operating on a higher level of adjustment than did previous societies), the crisis is more severe than others have been. If we do not lose control of ourselves, if we do not throw over all the values that we have inherited from long human experience, if we remain level-headed, if we persevere, when it is all over there will probably emerge a new social order that will be better than the last.

As is normal in periods of transition, there is a momentary loss of

[23] C. H. Judd, "This Era of Uncertainty in Education," *School and Society*, 44:359, September 19, 1936.

balance, an upset, a disjointedness in the social scheme. Different types of developments do not keep abreast of each other; more than normally there are social lags. Owing to the fundamental character [24] of the present crisis, the loss of balance and the confusion may perhaps be expected to be greater than in other transitional periods. But the seriousness of our situation is greatly aggravated by complications arising in part from certain inherent weaknesses in American society, and in part from fallacious social and educational theories that are current. In a period of social change it is more than ever necessary to hold tight to those values that make for steadiness, for order, for strength, for social unity, and to get rid of those defects in the societal organism that make for unsteadiness, for weakness, for disunity. We have not done so, and, to make things worse, there are theories that justify and rationalize our neglect. As a result there is a much greater threat to the security of society and to the chances for uninterrupted societal progress than is fully warranted by the nature of the transition.

The basis of the crisis is economic. The invention and the application of machines to industrial processes have changed the economic foundations of our living. We have become potentially able to produce enough to satisfy our material wants, and to do this through the use of automatic, human-labor-saving machinery. Our economy is highly industrialized, highly mechanized, potentially highly productive; these economic facts are basic in determining our personal welfare. But to these developments we have not made corresponding adaptations in other economic and in social and political areas. This is at the root of our difficulty, and the circumstances are such that even a solution of this problem would bring other trying problems in its wake.

Though our economy has changed from an economy of scarcity to one of potential plenty, and we can produce material goods sufficient for the needs of all, we have not learned how to utilize this potential abundance for the benefit of all the people. "Even today the industrial system is open to the charge that it is not organized in such a way as to promote the highest degree of welfare either of workers or of society. It has required the chastisement of a deep depression to induce employers in general to share liberally their incomes with their employees and to re-

[24] Morrison would be less inclined to regard these changes as inherently fundamental than Judd and Bagley. *Vide* Introduction, p. 22, footnote.

duce the hours of labor to the point where individuals may be released from the demands of profit-making far enough so that they may have much leisure for activities which yield personal enjoyment. Industry has advanced on the side of mechanics more rapidly than it has in its treatment of human beings." [25] We have it in our power substantially to raise the standard of living of all, but for the most part we are still operating as if hardship in the obtaining of needed things were a law inscribed in nature. Though it has tremendously increased our productive capacity, the mechanization of industrial processes has created a problem of technological unemployment. To a large extent, our failure to solve this problem—to spread employment—has nullified the value that inheres potentially in our productive capacity. Our difficulties pursue each other in a vicious circle: unemployment makes for low purchasing power; this in turn results in restrictions upon production, even when the need for the products is great; restrictions upon production do not tend to alleviate the unemployment situation. We have never fully unleashed our productive machinery. Our abundance has remained potential abundance.

The next years should witness a comprehensive attempt at adjustment. It will be necessary in some way to afford to all greater economic advantages. Ultimately the problem of unemployment will have to be solved by redistribution of labor—by reducing working hours per man, by spreading employment much more widely. But these achievements, should they be realized, will in turn raise other problems. Material abundance has in itself certain hazards. Successful adjustment, under any conditions, still calls for the exercise of great qualities of strength, endurance, self-discipline. There is danger in growing soft when material security is guaranteed. It is not well to eliminate from human life the need for hard work, for great and sustained effort aimed at overcoming certain obstacles. "Our highly industrialized civilization rests upon mechanical slavery. A civilization resting upon slavery has within it the seeds of its ultimate disintegration. Effort and struggle and a certain amount of competition are fundamentally essential to progress." [26] If and when our civilization succeeds in providing for all a larger measure of material security, there will still be the problem of

[25] C. H. Judd, *Education and Social Progress*, p. 109. 1934.
[26] W. C. Bagley, *Education, Crime and Social Progress*, pp. 5–6 (Quotation

channeling the energies of the people toward higher levels of work and toward great social and cultural achievement.

As a result of rapid industrial expansion we have changed rather quickly into a closely interdependent society. But we have not discarded some of the mores that have come down from a much simpler kind of existence. Foremost among them is an excessive individualism, which, if ever it was appropriate in any society, is certainly not appropriate in ours. Individualism of another, less rugged but equally self-centered, kind has been further spread by some of the childish and enervating educational theories that constantly emphasize "personality," "child-interests," and so forth. (It is possibly as a result of this latter weak, undisciplined individualism that we have at times gravitated toward "an extremely awkward kind of communism."[27]) Other things we have outgrown and with respect to which needed reforms have not yet been made are antiquated governmental units (creating artificial areas of demarcation among people who are essentially interdependent), and a taxing system that is based upon an agrarian concept of wealth and not upon a money economy. Our society then is in a condition of discord. Industrial development has run far ahead of corresponding social adjustments, and even when organic unity is regained there will lurk in the emerging civilization potential dangers.

Intensifying these problems, moreover, are disintegrative influences that spring in part from weaknesses in our culture, in part from current social and educational theories already mentioned. These influences are as much a danger to the American social structure as the problems inherent in the economic crisis. American society has to some degree always been lacking in the unity and harmony that society requires to function as an efficient organism. We have been a melting pot into which have been introduced peoples of diverse racial and cultural origins. This has had results of immeasurable benefit in the building of the American culture, but it also has been responsible for some social stresses and disturbances. (Perhaps the native-born element has been more responsible for these disturbances than the immigrant.) The

abridged). 1931. Quoted with permission of The Macmillan Company, publishers.
[27] H. C. Morrison, *School and Commonwealth*, p. 167. 1937.

physical conquest of a large part of a continent, the problems of main-taining existence under difficult conditions, life on a wide and continu-ously moving frontier, have combined to make of Americans a people of great energy and vigor and initiative, but also a people who are in-clined to be reckless and lawless. "To our shame be it said that we are, as a nation, the most lawless in Christendom." [28] This fact has added a great element of uncertainty and danger at a time when we must marshal all our moral resources.

The last century has seen in the United States a great development of democracy. The principle of equality has been extended, and the common man has gained greater rights for himself. This development must be rightfully regarded with great pride. The increase in the general standard of living for most of the population (in spite of the economic troubles previously related) must also stand as a great achieve-ment. But accompanying these gains there has been a general lowering of moral standards, a general let-down in the emotional tone of the entire population.[29] This had been noticeable a long time prior to the depression. Along with the moral and emotional let-down, there was an intellectual weakening—a relaxation of intellectual vigor, of stand-ards of intellectual achievement. When the depression came we were discovered to be lacking in both moral stamina and intellectual ingenu-ity and enterprise. In a period of transition, it is especially necessary to retain a strong sense of discipline, of proper perspective, high moral standards, keen-wittedness, intellectual enterprise, and courage. Of these things we are not sufficiently possessed. Confused by change, we are going too far toward surrendering values that history has proved of inestimable worth: perseverance, the ability to work, respect for society and its institutions, self-reliance, regard for the lessons of experience. And there have developed strange doctrines to mislead us further. There have come into existence social philosophies and educational theories that justify when they do not actually glorify individualism, opportunism, lack of discipline, and conduct that is motivated by "wants" and not by principle.

[28] Morrison, *op. cit.*, p. 120.
[29] This strong indictment of present-day society on moral grounds is not char-acteristic of Judd. In this respect, Judd is inclined to view present American culture more tolerantly.

III

Society in evolution must expect periodically to be confronted with crises. Evolution is not mechanical; progress is not movement in directions precisely laid out. Mind is inventive, creative. Achievements of mind influence human living in new ways. Progress requires trial and experimentation, and constant vigilance. But man must master crises and not be mastered by them. He must not be tricked, in the confusion of the moment, into giving up those values which society after long effort has finally realized. Above all, in a period of crisis, man must preserve his moral stamina and his intellectual keenness and vigor, and must not permit those influences that are equally injurious to individual and social adjustment to make inroads.

In the present transitional period we have not behaved up to specifications. We have not shown sufficient moral courage and intellectual enterprise in attacking its problems. We are in many cases letting go of those values to which all humanity must hold fast. We have permitted the integrity and strength of American society to become greatly impaired. The cause has not been entirely or even mainly the intrinsic severity of the crisis itself. It is true that the crisis has been severe enough. But even prior to the advent of the present emergency there had developed debilitating influences in American life. Intensifying the natural difficulties arising in the course of a serious transition, they place us under even greater handicaps in our efforts to secure successful adjustment.

The problems confronting American society must be solved. Our society must go on to attain a better balance between the economic foundations and the other social adjustments. The principle of equality must be extended to make a more perfect economic as well as cultural democracy. It is necessary to improve the economic situation of all the people. Material resources must be better distributed. We must solve the problem of unemployment, and, after that, the manifold problems that will come when the need for productive effort has apparently been reduced by the machine. Our responsibility will by no means be over when the economic problems are solved. We must devote our energies to the building of a civilization that will be distinguished for its social and cultural accomplishments. Far more than we have been able to do, we must contribute to the culture of the world. It goes without saying that we must eliminate from our own society crime, ignorance, immorality, narrow-mindedness, inefficiency and corruption in government, and raise to high levels the moral, emotional, and intellectual tone of all the people.

How all this is to be done, no one yet knows. We must go about achieving these things through a process of broad social experimentation. The application of the methods of science to the study of our problems—the study, for example, of the recent trends of our civilization [30]—will give us clues as to how to proceed. Eternal intellectual effort is the price of progress. Without surrendering any of the values to which we should cling, we must also contrive new values. Successful adjustment is the criterion against which we must check all our accomplishment. Failing, we must try again. Only time can tell what is right. All our problems will not end with our safe emergence from our present dilemma: other problems are sure to follow. We may as well throw away the "blueprints" for a "new social order." A social order is not blueprinted: it evolves. We cannot prescribe a new and better social order any more than we can prescribe a new and better human physiology.* The improvement of the social order is a continuous thing, requiring invention and adaptation. Mind invents and adapts. Each new invention brings forth in turn adaptations to it. How this has operated in the case of recent inventions—the motion picture, the radio, the airplane—is too clear to require explanation. By a process of continuous invention and adaptation we will emerge from our present difficulties.

The two great traits that serve man in successful adjustment are *social*ness and *adaptability*. Possessing these traits, a person can in the course of normal living effectively cope with whatever situations happen to arise, and, operating through society, can help to raise his living to higher levels. Possessing them in even greater degree, he is as prepared as any one can be to deal with the troublesome problems of

---

[30] This point is made in particular by Judd. ("The Curriculum in View of the Demands on the Schools," *School Review*, 42:17–25, January, 1934; and elsewhere, *vide* Bibliography.)

* *Vide* H. C. Morrison, *School and Commonwealth*, pp. 191–192. 1937.

even a transitional period. Man cannot be guaranteed success in his operations; he can, however, be equipped so that his chances of success are good. Properly equipping a person for his tasks in the present situation consists of transmitting to him all the social learnings through the help of which one may acquire social, adaptable personality.

SOCIAL REALISM

I

In the philosophy of Social Realism society is conceived as the living-together of individuals in order that there may be realized the values that inhere in the collectivization and common interpretation and management of experience. The fact of society stands to human beings as a guarantee of a much larger measure of personal welfare and happiness in living than they could obtain as individuals. The value of society in the scale of human values is thus very high. The welfare of individuals depends upon the effectiveness with which society gathers and cumulates its experiences as a basis for making judgments, upon the intrinsic wisdom of these judgments, upon the effectiveness with which they are enforced and with which they assist individuals in the solution of their problems. Society is not ipso facto good; whether it is good depends upon whether it is geared in its operation to assist in the living of the individuals who compose it—in other words, upon the pragmatic effectiveness of its social processes. But the value of society as society is unquestionable; besides its collective possibilities, the possibilities of individuals are insignificant. Of course, society is not an end in itself: it is at its best when it serves well the needs of its individuals. The goodness of society redounds, therefore, to the good of its members. There need be no conflict between the societal and the individual good, but no allowance for individual "rights" or "privileges" or "wants" is justifiable when the granting of these would interfere with the well-being of society.

The fact of society stands squarely in the center of the problem of human living. Of crucial importance to man is the problem of knowing the world; knowing the world is closely tied up with living in it.[31]

[31] *Vide* Introduction, pp. 33 ff.

Man comes into the world equipped with an apparatus for knowing it; that is the only respect in which he is superior to other forms of life in nature. The world exists and is real irrespective of man and his knowledge, but to live successfully within the world man must know what is going on about him, what things in the world affect or can be made to affect his living, and in what manner. The basis of knowledge is experience, that is, the contact that man makes with the external world about him. The avenues of knowledge are the senses. On the basis of sense-impressions of things man forms judgments that bear upon his own life-conduct; he forms these judgments not because of any choice of his own, but because he is forced to do so; to maintain life, he must act. Out of experience thus come judgments operative in the guidance of living, judgments that go back into experience. Judgments are based first on hypothetical belief, later on increasingly verified belief that itself rests upon a growing core of scientific knowledge. Man's success in living depends upon the manner in which his judgments result in consequences favorable to himself. The use of experience as a source of knowledge and belief is central in human living.

Life is precious, and individual judgment based upon individual experience is an uncertain, fallible thing. Sense impressions are elusive, and the senses themselves are often deceiving. Individual experience is limited. Unfortunately also individual judgment is sometimes seriously unbalanced by a number of factors that ought properly to be regarded as irrelevant and unnecessary.[32] Yet to maintain life, much less to improve it, man must be constantly "reading" his experiences aright, and acting upon them properly. Society represents a much more reliable way of getting *vital* knowledge out of experience and applying it in the conduct of living. In society individuals pool their experiences, and thereby extend them immeasurably. They collect and compare and analyze sense-impressions—and out of their investigations of the phenomena of experience comes definite, factual knowledge. The judgments on which life-activity is to be based are made in common: the voices of many individuals are heard, the merits of different proposals are considered, ultimately the best judgment of which human beings are at the time capable is obtained. Society affords a better means not only of obtaining judgments out of experience but of testing them in

[32] *Vide* Chapter II, p. 175.

subsequent experience. As long as experience serves in human living (and there is nothing else that does), societal experience can be of greater service to man than individual experience. The unity of society must not be overestimated. It must not be thought that societal living has utterly abolished individual aspects of living and has made of all men complete conformists to convention; but the principle of collectivizing experience is the principle in terms of which the meaning of society must be explained.

What is of primary importance in society is *the method of living* that it makes possible for man. But of very great importance also is the content that it gives to human life. Man not only lives in a real world but he remakes the real world. A judgment is *acted upon*. It results in some change (as far as man is concerned). If subsequent experience proves the judgment to have been sound, then the judgment itself is passed on, and the condition in which the change is embodied is made permanent. Society is thus extending experience and the benefits that come from experience not only horizontally but vertically. Knowledge that has been acquired, beliefs that have been verified, judgments that have proved wise, conditions through which certain desirable effects have become permanent, are all passed down from individual to individual. The proximity and the interlocking nature of human living in society make this possible. There is no question that society makes human living easier, the farther it goes. Not all the beliefs that society transmits may be "true," not all the knowledge may be real knowledge, not all judgments may be valid, but there are *some* things (indeed, a great many things) that the individuals of a new generation do not have to puzzle out for themselves, and, as time goes on, the number of these things mounts. Man is born into an environment in which many of his experiences are anticipated for him and many of the proper ways of dealing with these experiences are given to him. The mores that he encounters and falls in with, the social institutions which he gets to know and to which he becomes adjusted, the things he learns to do, are all of them ways of dealing (with more or less success) with the world.[33] As the individual grows towards maturity he himself contributes increasingly out of his own experience to the total stock of knowledge, beliefs, values, and actions based upon

[33] *Vide* T. H. Briggs, "Mores," *Secondary Education,* pp. 440–477. 1933.

them. Thus society offers a content derived out of experience by which man learns successively more and more about *the world in relation to himself*. And this is the knowledge that serves him in his living.

Society emerges thus as an outstanding value. Human life is not only impossible but inconceivable without it. Continuous human experience has of course so confirmed societal existence that there is no question of doing without it. The questions that do arise, that are constantly arising, are questions relating to the manner in which society can best carry out its functions. But indisputably social experience has displaced individual experience as a basis for human living; societal judgment is considered, in general and in the long run, much more reliable than individual judgment. In the individual's own life, society is the dominant factor: the experiences that he thinks are his own are experiences that society has put in his way, the values that he cherishes are values that society has given him (whether or not he knows it), his very occasional revolt against established convention is itself proof of the otherwise constant influence of society. That is as it should be; for society, other things being equal, guarantees the individual a life that he could never attain for himself. Of course the good society (as will be explained later) fosters certain important individual liberties and even extends protection to a certain amount of non-conformity. That is the way in which societal advance is made. New experiences are all the time being added to the common total. The established values of society are under scrutiny all the time; it is literally true that revisions and modifications are constantly being made. Occasionally the dominance of the social may result in a certain amount of injustice to the individual: it is true that sometimes the individual genius finds himself persecuted for non-conformist convictions that ultimately turn out to be truths (for society tends to exercise a jealous guardianship of its rights). But in the long run, in spite of mistakes that society occasionally makes, the societal course of life is the safest for human beings.

It must be stated categorically that society (or the state, as it may be called) is not a supernatural creation with a "destiny" or purpose apart from the lives of the human beings who make it up. The purpose of society is to serve individuals in their living. But it must be asserted just as emphatically that society does possess a corporate existence, apart from the individual existences of its members. Society is "individuals-in-their-relations," [84] and these "relations" are just as real as the "individuals." Society has an existence of its own, equivalent in its way to the existence of individuals. The reality of society is the reality of human beings in their collective aspect. Thus the experiences of society, the judgments of society, the well-being of society, the needs of society are just as real as those of individuals. It is true that individuals have a private existence apart from society as a whole: this private existence is of course within society and is permeated by social experience, but in a sense it does not concern society in its collective aspect. Such a private life must be reserved for the individual; it is a part of the totality of existence. (Individuals entering into society are not absorbed completely as are the elements entering into a chemical compound.) But when societal values and private individual values are in conflict in matters where collective existence is affected, then individual values (when they cannot be reconciled) must be subordinated.

No one can decide once and for all what ought to be the optimum relationship between the individual and society, what demands society should or should not make upon the individual. Social experience may have displaced individual experience as the principal basis for the direction of human conduct, but as long as there is experience, human judgments will keep being formed and being changed. The relations that shall prevail between individuals and society are determined by human beings; they are no more infallible than are human judgments about anything else. People change their minds as they interpret experience differently or as experience changes. They have often changed their minds as to what shall constitute the best individual-societal relationships. As in everything else, facts and beliefs that have received verification in experience ought not to be lightly discarded: relationships that in the past have shown themselves to be instrumental in preserving society, in making it work, should be greatly cherished. At the same time, however, people are continuously trying to improve the manner of their living: it may be to the societal interest to make certain adjustments in the interrelationship of individuals.

[84] Quotation from Dewey, in *Issues of Secondary Education*, Department of Secondary School Principals, *Bulletin* No. 59, p. 130. 1936.

If any general principles can be formulated, they are the following: Human beings live in society primarily to obtain greater security and better living for themselves. It was not altruism but necessity that prompted them to surrender certain liberties upon entering into the communal life. They surrendered these liberties not to any other individuals but to society as a whole. The criterion by which to determine whether a change is needed in the societal relationships is the criterion of practical necessity; when the welfare of enough individuals in society demands it, a change must be made. When individuals find it relatively easy to meet the demands that the socially-accepted standards of existence make upon them, with relatively little assistance from and therefore dependence upon others, the amount of freedom and the extent of the "rights" that they enjoy can naturally be relatively great; when it is more difficult to satisfy the needs of life in relative independence of others, when the exigencies of life-experience make greater cooperation necessary for the attainment of common ends, then the "rights" of the individual compared with the group must be more greatly restricted. But, whatever the circumstances, when changes are made they must be made by society as a whole by regularly constituted societal procedure, and great care must be taken against the tyranny of any group or against over-haste in action. The longer a type of relationship has proved itself in experience, the more carefully and deliberately should changes affecting it be made.

The principles governing the internal relationship of individuals in society apply also to the consideration of the formal organization of society. No one can establish with finality *the* form of societal organization that is "good." Determination of the formal arrangement of society is according to values growing out of experience; in the course of time man has made use of different kinds of organizations, and changed them when they no longer served his purpose. Societal arrangements are not governed by independent criteria, they are not ends in themselves; they must be judged with reference to the ultimate purpose of the society which sustains them. Political, social, economic institutions existing at any given time are good if they contribute to the advancement of the living of all the members of society, and are good to the extent that they do so. Man is never quite satisfied with the societal organization and arrangements that he has achieved, nor should he be. In an effort toward improvement, societal institutions are constantly undergoing some alteration. The good society never hesitates to make a change when circumstances operating in the lives of a sufficient number of people make them think such a change is necessary. Whether society is right in making that change only subsequent experience can tell.

The introduction of the word "good" calls for some explanation of its meaning. In human living there are no absolute "goods" and there are no perfect "goods." It is hard for man to become reconciled to the fact that his ideals are not perfect. The course of human history is strewn with ideals at one time highly regarded, later discarded as not good enough. All human values arise out of experience, are set up by man himself, and are verified or disproved by later experience. Generally it may be said that ideals are constantly in process of being perfected, that human "goods" are constantly being made "better." A human judgment of what constitutes the "good" is, like all other judgments, fallible; never is it so perfect that it cannot be improved. This is true of the judgments of society as well as the judgments of individuals. Societal judgments should be made with the understanding that they are not perfect or complete. In time individuals, on the basis of their experience, will note that certain societal values have become outmoded, that certain ideals need adaptation or revision or new definition. When these individuals have persuaded a sufficient number of their fellows to take a similar view, the societal ideals will be "repaired."

The "good" human life, therefore, is always in process of becoming better—both with respect to the individual and with respect to society. This is as true of the good life in contemplation as it is of the good life in actuality. Man is the final arbiter of values, and man is forever reconstituting them. There is no such thing as *the* good society in the absolute sense; there is *a* good society in the sense in which its contemporaries understand it. And since human beings can entertain different conceptions of what is good without necessarily being *proved* wrong by events, it is conceivable that at one and the same time there may be in existence a number of different "good" societies. Such a view may seem shocking to the idealist who is accustomed to thinking about the universe in a monistic way, but it is the only proper view for man unaffected by delusions of grandeur regarding his place in the universe. Experience is the ultimate basis of all purposeful living; and experience is not everywhere and at all times the same, nor does the same experience lead different individuals inevitably to the same conclusions.

That does not mean that society is to be subject to no evaluation at all. Human conduct is evaluated ultimately in terms of practical consequences; so must be societal conduct. The ultimate purpose of society is the improvement and advancement of the lives of its individuals. Society is good to the extent that it carries out this purpose —to the extent that its ideals are such as to produce in the end consequences favorable to individual human living, to the extent that its practices are effective in realizing these ideals. This is no shadowy criterion. It is true that what constitutes a "favorable consequence" is often subject to human interpretation, and human interpretations can differ. That is the human limitation, and mankind cannot but respect it. It accounts for the fact that different societies, presumably composed of intelligent individuals, are differently constituted and head in different directions. But it must not be overlooked that experience is a great teacher, that human beings have agreed in the past and agree in the present that a great many consequences are desirable, that a great many others are not, that certain ideals lead inevitably to disastrous consequences, that certain ideals are in themselves reflective of degenerative tendencies that have already set in. No society that recognizes such ideals as the latter can be accounted good.

In a sense it is much easier to evaluate a society negatively. No society is good: the ideals of which contravene the lessons of experience and are reasonably sure to lead to consequences which are patently disastrous or which men have united in calling undesirable; that is not organized for the benefit of the individual, that is organized as an end in itself; that favors a special group as against the whole, that neglects the welfare of the majority while conferring special privileges upon a minority; that is not organized in such a way as to promote the attainment of its constituted ideals; the individuals of which do not cooperate effectively as a society.

Far more important than the exact nature (content) of the societal values at any one time is the maintenance of the societal method of procedure. Societal ideals come and go, but *the ideal of society itself* must always remain. Man must continue to live within and through society. It is essential, for example, that when differences of opinion relative to important values arise, society be not broken up or seriously weakened. It is essential that, when changes need to be made in the societal framework, these changes be made without upsetting society. A good society anticipates all this by developing in advance procedures to arbitrate differences among individuals and to regulate social change, procedures to keep society operating smoothly at the same time that many of its values are being subjected to critical scrutiny and continuous modification, that it is absorbing many changes. These procedures have been developed out of previous experience, are validated by experience, and are being improved all the time. In the course of time we have developed methods of legislation, law-enforcement, and adjudication, methods of settling political disputes, disputes between individuals, disputes between capital and labor, methods of obtaining social judgments on questions of social policy. The value of adhering to societal procedure can hardly be overestimated.[35] It is sometimes overlooked that *the fact of law* is more important than is any law at any given time, *the fact of judicial procedure* more important than any verdict rendered at any time, *the fact of law enforcement* more important than the apprehending of any single law-breaker. Whatever its ideals at any particular time may be, a good society regulates itself by procedures that assure its continued functioning as society.

One of the procedures that society has in the course of time worked out is the method of consensus. Whenever a choice is involved resting upon judgment, a good society has recourse to the method whereby each individual registers his opinion. The opinion of a specified number, usually agreed upon in advance, prevails. The method of consensus is justifiable in theory and enforceable in practice; experience has proved it to be the soundest way of guaranteeing societal existence. Of course the method of society may be overdone; no question that can be answered scientifically, no doubt that can be resolved empirically in such a way · that it can be completely dispelled, ought to be

[35] For application of this principle to education, see T. H. Briggs, "Propaganda and the Curriculum," *Teachers College Record*, 34:468–480, March, 1933.

subjected to such a decision. Belief can never prevail over scientifically verified knowledge when the two are opposed, and a wise society will agree (as one of its procedures) not to submit questions to the arbitration of beliefs when they can be settled with much greater certainty of correctness. Moreover, the method of consensus must not be allowed to displace the use of expert judgment. A wise society does not rely upon the direction of well-meaning laymen when the practiced skill of an expert is called for. Finally (it must be remembered that) a verdict thus rendered is not infrequently wrong; there never has been a judgment, in fact, that at some time was not improved, or corrected, or altogether replaced. Societal living is characterized by a continuous succession of judgments arrived at by consensus, and society has found that to be a wise method for governing itself.

Very closely related to the principle of consensus and, in fact, prompting it is the principle of democracy. Democracy implies simply a recognition of the fact that each individual is equally a member of society, that he must be treated equally with every other individual, that he has a right to participate in the direction and management of society, that he has a right to register an equal voice in all matters coming under societal jurisdiction. Democracy is not a privilege to which people must aspire, as some social theorists are fond of saying; it is a principle inherent in the fact of society itself. Society was formed for the benefit of its individuals—no other explanation of its existence is equally plausible. If this be true, then all individuals should share equally in the direction and management of society and in such benefits as it agrees to extend. The principle of democracy is as sound in practice as it is in theory: practically no other way has been conceived that is even nearly as effective in promoting individual happiness in society and in promising the continued existence of society by reliance upon the good will of its members, without resort to compulsion.

Democracy involves the acceptance of the principle that all members of society have equal rights and an equal voice in the determination of societal policies. This is the heart of the democratic concept. Arising from it but incidental to it are such rights as the right of personal freedom, freedom of speech, religious freedom, equality under the law, etc. Beyond this general statement of democratic principle *as method of procedure* it is impossible to go. They are wrong who maintain that democracy implies a guarantee in advance to the individual of certain specific inflexible rights. Democracy can make no guarantees in advance beyond affirming the sovereign right of every individual to share in the control of society and assuring him of equality of treatment. Strictly speaking, democracy makes no guarantee at all. Society does: were there no society, there would be no need for democracy. Society can make no guarantee in advance that would ultimately hamper the continuance of its function as society. Society seeks to realize its purpose, which is the advancement of the living of all individuals. To that end it recognizes all individuals as equal (in the dual role of directors of society and recipients of its benefits) and extends to them all the privileges of equality. At all times these should involve a large measure of individual liberty, as large as is consistent with the ultimate aim of society. This means that the exact amount of freedom that individuals possess must vary with the condition of society: a society operating under certain conditions of living can afford to extend a larger measure of freedom than a society operating under others. In the period of colonization and settlement and early agricultural and industrial development of the United States a large measure of individualism was perfectly proper; at the present time "the historic American tradition of individualism (is) no longer a sufficient philosophy to guide men through the social and economic transformations of the century." [36] When it becomes more difficult for members of society to maintain themselves as individuals, when conditions bring people together in closer proximity, when the need for harmonious cooperation is greater, then the measure of personal freedom that society extends to individuals must be restricted. This is not at all inconsistent with the principle of democracy; it is in fact implied by that principle. But the rule of social necessity must never be carried to the point where it is forgotten that society is maintained for the benefit of its individuals, that personal restrictions unduly imposed defeat the ends for which society exists.

By the same token it is wrong to maintain that the principle of democracy implies the need of providing special opportunities for those who are intellectually gifted. [37] Democracy implies that there be equality of opportunity. Equality of opportunity cannot be interpreted as

[36] *Issues of Secondary Education*, p. 129.
[37] Cf. Humanism, *supra*, pp. 59 ff.

identity; neither can it mean that brighter individuals be singled out for preferential treatment. Every person must be helped to develop as far as he can, *in ways that he can*. Society has need of a great many different talents. Individuals possess a great many different talents; every individual possesses some talent in terms of which he can contribute to the common good of all other individuals in society. Equality of opportunity demands that every person be given a chance to develop his common and his special talents in a way that will best fit him to serve himself and to serve society. The I. Q. is not the only index of a person's potential value to society. Moreover, it is not necessary to worry unduly about the training of potential leaders. (The I. Q. is again not an indication of natural capacity for leadership.) The first concern of a democracy is for the training of its citizens. "The success of democracy demands more than enlightened leaders. Leaders find it difficult to serve only the interests of the entire group when opportunities present themselves so frequently to exploit their position of leadership to their own profit." [38]

The conception of goodness in the individual is strongly influenced by the fact of society. Individual goodness involves, of course more than socialness: not all traits in the individual are relevant to society (for example, religious faith, esthetic sensitiveness); not all individual actions should be perfectly conforming; not all the individual's thoughts should be such as are the common possession of all other human beings. But goodness does presume a high degree of socialness. The good man is necessarily social: no individual who does not contribute to the common societal welfare and to its ultimate progress can be accounted good. Socialness, moreover, presumes active contribution: the social worth of a person is not appraised by reference to certain abstract qualities (of intellect, for example) which he may possess but does not (or not yet) exercise in a social way, but by the manner in which he uses his qualities, whatever they are, to achieve social ends. It has been said that society, in the pursuit of its function of helping individuals in their understanding and management of experience, has need of many different kinds of contributions: it has need of talents of a mechanical

---

[38] H. R. Douglass, "Adapting the Curriculum of the Junior High School to the Needs of the Pupils," Department of Secondary School Principals, National Education Association, *Bulletin*, 45:135, March, 1933.

kind as well as of talents of an abstract intellectual kind; it has need of traits of quickness and alertness as well as of the trait of plodding persistency. No individual possesses aptitude for all these things; individuals differ greatly with respect to the special aptitudes that they possess. It does not follow, therefore, that superiority in any one thing entitles a person to special eminence or distinction in point of social worth. The person of high abstract intelligence who contributes to the wellbeing of society is worthy of no greater praise than is the person of high mechanical proficiency who does the same. The scholar is intrinsically no better than the artist or the statesman or the civil engineer. In terms of their special capacities, aptitudes, and interests, all individuals must be given equally the help that society can extend.

A pragmatic conception of society must recognize the fact of the existence of *particular societies* as well as of *general society*. If society is defined as a community of individuals sharing experience, cooperating in the making of common judgments on the basis of this experience, directing their living in accordance with common ends, then it is a patent fact that there are at the present time, within the common framework of human society in general, many distinct particular societies. An individual lives in not one but in many societies surrounding him in a concentric way. Some experiences, some ideals, some ends and means of living he shares with all humanity; others he shares with a more limited portion of mankind in general, let us say, with the Western civilization; still others he shares with successively more limited groups, ultimately coming down to more intimate experiences that he shares with his family and personal friends. For practical purposes the particular society to which an individual belongs must be defined or delimited, and the definition must be made in operational terms. Generally speaking (though exceptions are numerous and at the present time particularly prominent) the political state represents a group, the individuals of which have agreed, by virtue of their common ethnic origin or their geographic proximity or their common interests, to come together and to live together, to abide by common rules, to pursue common purposes by generally common methods. Not only have they agreed to do so, but they have done so. By a pragmatic criterion, the political state is at the present time the most important societal unit.

For practical purposes this societal unit must be regarded as *the* particular society in which the individual lives. That is not to say that the influence of the smaller groups within this society—the local community, the cultural group, the circle of friends, the family, can be neglected; nor does it mean that the relationship of this particular society to other particular societies, to the world of human beings at large, can be overlooked. The mistake must not be made of exaggerating either the unity or the distinctiveness of the particular society as here defined. No state is at any time a perfect unit in the sense that it is perfectly integrated, that its dominant ideals are understood and accepted by all, that it is homogeneous with respect to its culture. There are always smaller groups within it competing for the allegiance of the individual. The larger the society, the more numerous the original groups comprising it, the generally less cohesive it is. There will be many interests operating at cross-purposes, there will be different and perhaps contradictory ideals reflecting religion, cultural background, and economic status, there will be different sets of mores. Nevertheless there will be binding common ideals, common experiences and judgments about experience, common ways of doing things, common mores, and common institutions. These the particular society must have, if it is to be, by definition, a society. On the other hand, to recognize the political state as a definite societal unit is to not overemphasize its distinctiveness. To recognize membership in a political state is not necessarily to be nationalistic or provincial or narrow or limited. Every particular society to some extent shares in the experiences, the purposes, the methods of mankind as a whole; every human being possesses to some extent traits which are universal. Human knowledge, human interests, human sympathy must extend far beyond the particular society. Perhaps the purposes of individual living will ultimately be best served when particular societies grow toward each other, when they unite, when they cooperate in their common endeavors. But as long as particular societies exist, it must be recognized that with respect to some experiences, ideals, and ways of behaving, they are distinct from all others.

The good man must be well-integrated with his particular society, must be loyal to the political ideals which motivate it, must partake in its culture, must contribute to its common welfare, and must work for its gradual improvement. Considering the nature of the particular society, this is no easy thing; the political state is always trying to strike a balance with the smaller social units comprising it; the individual must always maintain a nice balance between the different groups claiming his loyalties—his family, his community, his state. But devotion to the larger ideals of the operating society, participation in its large undertakings and furtherance of its endeavors are necessary. Integration does not mean complete conformity in all things. Without surrendering those traits that make him a person different from all others, that stamp him as an individual, the good man is loyal to the common and accepted ideals of his particular society and subscribes to its institutions. Without integration a democratic society cannot maintain itself at all. "Democracy needs social integration; it needs citizens who believe in its ideals and are so loyal to them that they consistently seek the democratic way of life." [39] Integration does not presume a blanket endorsement of all societal ideals and practices; it does not presume a blindness to the patent fact that societal ideals are imperfect and in need of improvement; nor does it assume a withholding of criticism. Criticism, re-evaluation, effort at improvement are part of the life-experience, and societal experience is incomplete without them. But social integration does imply an absorption of self into the group life, a harmonizing of personal outlook and personal activities with the group outlook and group activities, an acceptance of societal purposes and methods and criticism of them, not in the spirit of the dissident but in the spirit of the co-worker. Integration implies a moving together with others, not ahead of them or away from them.

Social integration, in turn, requires that the individual begin with a sympathetic understanding and acceptance of the ideals that dominate society. However he may ultimately criticize them and work to change them, he must begin by understanding them and by trying to become adjusted to them. This much society has a right to exact of its individuals; both theory and practice justify such enforcement. Theoretically, societal ideals, other things being equal, have greater validity than do individual ideals. Human ideals develop slowly and are tempered in the fire of experience. The wisdom of society, as it is expressed in ideals guiding human conduct, is likely to be much greater than the

[39] T. H. Briggs, "Should Education Indoctrinate?" *Educational Administration and Supervision*, 22:583, November, 1936.

wisdom of the average adult individual, not to say the immature individual. The average individual does not invent his own language, his own mathematics, his own way of building houses, his own way of using tools; he takes them all from society. When he has understood them, learned how to use them, become thoroughly familiar with them, he becomes competent to contribute to their improvement. The same is true of ideals. The brightest minds of each generation show us new ways of interpreting experience, and formulate new ideals for our criticism and acceptance; but even they must begin by trying to understand, by trying to become adjusted to the ideals that prevail. Practically speaking, no other course is possible. To allow each individual to make up his own mind about what values he will recognize and what he will not, what laws he will accept and what laws he will flout, etc. is to invite disintegration of society. Society must enforce the social integration of every individual in order to preserve itself. On the other hand, true integration requires that the imperfection of society be not concealed or glossed over, that along with sympathetic understanding and at least provisional acceptance, there be wholesome resolve to effect improvement.

II

American society is today undergoing basic changes. So far-reaching are these changes that the habits of thinking about society and social practices that have served us in the past are no longer adequate for the present and for the future. Changing experience brings with it the need for revaluation and re-formation of previous judgments, and for reconstruction of ends and means. That is our problem at present. There is no use in longing for "the good old times," in seeking to recall what cannot be recalled. The promise of American society lies in the present and the future and not in recapturing the past.

Generally speaking, American society has always been somewhat deficient in the degree of social integration that it could achieve. Perhaps that is the nature of a democracy. In a democracy integration is more the result of voluntary effort by its individuals and less a result of compulsion by the state than in any other society; and that is as it should be. It must be remembered, however, that lack of social integration weakens society and renders it less effective in dealing with vital common problems. The social problems emerging from the basic changes in society portend for the future the need of a far greater degree of integration than American society has yet achieved. It has become exceedingly difficult "to live and to make a living" in society without the most careful kind of social planning and the closest kind of social cooperation. The changes that have brought people within one society closer together have also brought together the people of the world. While that is undubitably a good thing, in the practical world it has also made for competition among societies, competition not only in trade but with respect to political and cultural doctrines. If American society is both to serve the interests of its own individuals and to withstand the great competition presented by highly-integrated, totalitarian, anti-democratic societies, it must, in its way, organize for democracy. The planless, drifting society may have served in the past; it will not serve in the future.

The ideals that should guide American society today are not clearly known. "The ideals of our society have not been formulated with sufficient definiteness to be understood, approved, and sought by potentially cooperative citizens." [40] For the most part our ideals survive as slogans of an earlier era, and many of them are out-of-date. There is need, as a result of the changes that have been wrought, for a redefinition of democracy and a redefinition, or perhaps it would be truer to say a completely new formulation, of the aims of our society. These must serve as the Magna Carta of American democracy, to guide our way in the future. All our energies must then be coordinated and directed toward a realization of these aims.

A new formulation of the goals of American society is made necessary by the great societal changes that have occurred. At bottom these changes arise out of the very great advances in science and out of the very large-scale application of science to industry, to communication, to recreation, to every aspect of social and personal living. The changes that technology has produced embrace the economic, the political, the cultural, the spiritual. Every aspect of experience has been penetrated. Industrialization and the accompanying development of mechanized

---

[40] T. H. Briggs, *Secondary Education*, p. 114. 1933. Quoted with permission of The Macmillan Company, publishers.

means of communication and transportation have brought people together in physical proximity and greater material and psychological interdependence. We have come to live together in great cities, to work together, to be dependent upon each other economically. The nature of work has changed radically, and at the same time opportunities for work have become scarcer. The application of mechanical devices to the performance of the routine activities of everyday life has changed a great many of our fundamental habits. The nature of our leisure-time activity has been fundamentally affected; the changed character of the home and the introduction of mechanized and commercialized amusements have helped to bring this about. In the hurry and pressure of events, the family and the church have lost a good deal of their influence for ethical living. With the growing complexity of society, special interests and pressures have multiplied. It is difficult to keep one's balance among the many things that compete for one's attention and influence. Intelligent citizenship among other things, has become much more difficult of achievement. "Within more than thirty years, but markedly within the last generation, changes have taken place in government which make it increasingly difficult for the citizen to play his part wisely in either local or national political life. The rapid growth in the complexity of social, economic, and industrial activities has been accompanied by a corresponding growth in the complexity of the governmental machinery designed to regulate these activities. Merely to vote wisely at the present time—to say nothing of taking a more active part in political affairs—demands of each individual a knowledge of events and issues, of persons and forces, far beyond the knowledge which was once deemed adequate for reasonably competent citizenship." [41]

It is necessary to examine the significance of these changes on each phase of American life more closely, and it may be well to begin with the economic. "During the past generation we have had a development in technology that is revolutionizing our economic and consequently our political world. It is unnecessary here to repeat the uncertain figures of how few men can now perform in less time and with more efficiency the work formerly done by many. The undisputed fact is that there has been a spectacular increase in productivity in all fields of work, and

[41] *Issues of Secondary Education,* p. 43.

that the increase has not yet reached its limits. The results are an over-abundance of every commodity with a constantly decreased demand for human labor to provide it. The consequent disruption of our economic world has brought a horde of problems that are not yet solved by economists and statesmen."[42] At the same time that there is overabundance of every necessity there is hunger. There is unemployment, and for many people there are no prospects of employment to come. There are great extremes of wealth and poverty, for among other things, technological development has been accompanied by concentration of productive and distributive power, and therefore of wealth, in relatively few hands. There is waste, duplication, cut-throat competition. While some of these may be acute maladjustments of a but temporary nature, technological development has resulted in problems that promise to be continuing: the decreased need in the future for human labor is sure to make work-opportunities scarcer; the increased mechanization and routinization of work activities threatens to deprive people of greatly needed intellectual exertion and stimulation; the shorter working day is sure to result in increased time for leisure.

The period of unrestricted, opportunistic individualism is undoubtedly over. "The present world-wide economic depression . . . has emphasized the fact that no generation of mankind has yet thought through the problem of providing for the wants of all. Each man has been trained to provide for himself and for his family, hoping that out of such individualistic uncoordinated efforts an effective economic system would emerge. It is now apparent that this way of approaching the work of the world is no longer adequate to maintain society at its present level of technological progress. Society is faced with imminent and catastrophic breakdown unless great masses of people, not merely a few inspired leaders, learn to evaluate intelligently and to cooperate responsibly in a great variety of new plans for providing and sharing more good things than we have ever known how to provide or distribute."[43] The present economic situation makes inevitable for the future a method of procedure by social planning, a greater coordination of

[42] T. H. Briggs, *Secondary Education,* pp. 119–120. 1933. Quoted with permission of The Macmillan Company, publishers.
[43] *Issues of Secondary Education,* p. 43.

energy, and a consequent greater centralization of power in government. A planning society produces what it can consume or utilize and no more, and this it makes available to all its members. Necessarily there will have to be some restriction placed upon private individual enterprise, although care must be taken not to destroy individual initiative, the will to work, and not to take away essential personal liberties. Necessarily there will be a more equitable distribution of wealth and of those things that make for material well-being, and national resources will be used for the common good and not exploited for private gain. How this is to be done, no one can at present tell; we shall have to find out by a process of invention and social experimentation. The meaning of democracy and the purposes of our American society must be redefined so that this invention and experimentation may get under way.

As for the permanent problems with which we are faced with respect to employment and the use of leisure time, it is easy to see that in these both society and education have new responsibilities. The present acute problem of unemployment may be solved by a redistribution of working hours among a much larger working population, but a problem of employment will still remain. Technology has changed radically the task of preparing for a job and of finding a job, and the conditions of working at it. One can no longer become vocationally competent incidentally through a general education; on the other hand, one cannot adequately prepare for a vocation by learning merely the routine skills involved. Work-opportunities are fewer, and fear of not finding a job has become general among youth, as fear of not keeping it is becoming general among older adults. The vocational adjustment has become the critical adjustment in human living: lack of a job has become a focal point of personal disintegration just as the possession of a job is a strong potential means of continued integration. Even with those who have jobs the proper use of increased leisure time has become a problem. It will require the exercise of the greatest ingenuity on the part of both society and education to deal with such problems as these.

However, the effects of the changes on societal living have not been only economic. There are implications for political citizenship, implications for personal, cultural and spiritual growth. The problem of maintaining a democratic way of life has become difficult. The natural complexity of the societal situation is aggravated by the fact that there are at large many agencies attempting to influence public opinion to their own (often anti-democratic) ends. Propaganda devices and techniques have been developed to a high point of efficiency. Organized pressure groups have learned to exercise a control far greater than their numbers warrant. Under these conditions the task of maintaining a society operating democratically and operating intelligently offers a great challenge. The very conditions that make social integration more than ever necessary make it also more difficult to attain.

The changes wrought by technology affect also the cultural development of the individual: while technology restricts, mechanizes, and hopelessly routinizes human labor and leaves the individual much free time, the physical restrictions of the urban home and the availability and attraction of equally routine, mechanical, and commercialized amusements deprive him of much of the need and opportunity for self-application for intellectual, artistic, and spiritual improvement. Education is faced with a large responsibility in individual development, the responsibility for instilling intellectual and artistic interests so potent that they will propel the individual into such activities long after the supervision of the school over his development has ceased.

These are some of the things with which society must deal in the reconsideration of its aims. There are, however, no short-cuts to a good societal life. There are at present many people who see the weaknesses in the present social order and who can suggest the steps that society needs to take to straighten itself out. These people need to make their influence felt among the adult population, they need to campaign to bring about the societal reform. But in not a few cases the good intentions of these people are marred by their indifference to the need of following the accredited societal procedure. They wish to impose their (genuine) blessings upon society. But at least as important as the blessings themselves is the fact that society must consent to receive them. The societal way of doing things must be adhered to, even if the slowness of its movement provokes impatience. "Those who advocate significant changes in our social or economic order have a primary responsibility to present their arguments to their fellow-citizens who as partners in the great corporation of democracy must accept or reject their proposal." [44] That is the true way to the social reconstruction at present greatly needed.

III

In spite of the gloomy prophets there is nothing wrong with American society that clear-thinking and good and energetic teamwork cannot correct. A return to the past is unthinkable: the significant changes that have occurred make that impossible. On the other hand, it cannot be expected that the situation will right itself. The present miscegenation of the old and the new distinctly represents a menace to democracy. New conditions spell also the end of planless social drift. It is necessary to redefine the values of American society and to harness all energies for their realization.

For that purpose there is needed a planning agency. Whether or not this agency is to be under governmental control is not of primary importance. The best minds of the country must be drafted for the purpose of studying the situations and translating needs into purposes and concrete proposals for action.[45] Transmitted to society as a whole, clarified, discussed, modified, accepted, these proposals should serve as a chart to guide American society through the problems of the immediate future.

In formulating these social purposes, the planning commission would have to take note of the following social facts that stand out in a review of the current situation: that economic conditions at the present time call for a restriction of unlimited individual prerogative, that there must be economic planning, that there must be greater governmental regulation of economic life; that all this must be done without excessive infringement upon certain liberties—civil, economic, religious—lacking which societal living would be irksome; that there must be reinterpretation of the concept of equality of opportunity, assuring individuals some measure of security and ultimate success without removing or

---

[44] T. H. Briggs, "Propaganda and the Curriculum," *Teachers College Record,* 34:475, March, 1933.

[45] An attempt to do this has already been made by the Committee on the Social Economic Goals of America of the National Education Association; *vide Journal of the National Education Association,* 23:5–12, January, 1934.

greatly lessening the incentive for the expenditure of individual effort; that democracy in general must be redefined in terms that would include a degree of economic as well as political security; that it follows inevitably that there must be some redistribution of wealth and material resources; that readjustments must be made in the matter of employment; that society will probably be called upon to take care of adolescents to a still later age than at present; that some steps will have to be taken to relieve the economic situation of older people; that the whole problem of employment has important implications for the future cultural development of the people; that intelligent practical living has become a difficult thing; that the intelligent exercise of democratic political citizenship has become still more difficult; and that the maintenance, in general, of democracy under these conditions has become a challenge to American society.

Once the ideals have been formulated and accepted it will be necessary to organize and coordinate all efforts to the attainment of these ends. Planning will have to be continuous and permanent. It will be necessary systematically to foster the conditions that serve these ends and just as systematically to eliminate those that hinder them. Devotion to democracy will have to be instilled to a greater extent than ever before. Social integration will have to be carried to greater lengths. And every societal agency will have to do its part.

EXPERIMENTALISM

I

To the Experimentalist the individual human life is the supreme end in nature. Each human being is, as a totality, different from every other; but, as a human being, each commands equal regard. The Good Life cannot be conceived in terms of a mass or group pattern; it must be conceived in terms of an individual operating in his own circumstances toward his own ends. "If a general principle be demanded, the experimentalist says that is good which promotes the happiness and growth of individuals and does not interfere with the happiness and growth of other individuals." [46] The fact of society looms very large in

[46] J. L. Childs, *Education and the Philosophy of Experimentalism*, p. 227. 1931.

human life: man is nurtured in society, his experience is social experience, his personality is a social product. But society is distinctly a means to an end: everything about it is influenced by the fact that it serves the end of individual living. Though living in society man does not surrender his essential individuality; above all he does not permit society to think for him. Society does not exist as an entity separate from and independent of its individuals; it *is* individuals dynamically interacting with each other. Its character is formed as the purposes of individuals cross each other, establish alliances with each other, compromise with each other. A societal good is whatever assists in the realization of the legitimate purposes of the individual.

The end of human living is adjustment in nature. To an extent, adjustment is self-definable: whatever contributes to health, to extension of life, to physical well-being, contributes to adjustment. But beyond this point, the ends of human living are defined by man himself, on the basis of his own experience. Human happiness consists in the realization of those ends which man finds to be favorable for his living. Through the instrumentality of meanings drawn from his experience, man envisions consequences for himself which he regards as desirable, and so directs the course of his living as to obtain them. Man succeeds to the extent that the consequences that he achieves through the management of his own experience are favorable; he fails to the extent that he does not achieve desired consequences or to the extent that such consequences as he achieves turn out to be unfavorable. Life is a continuity of ever-changing experience. Succeeding events constantly offer new problems: each oncoming situation presents the individual with a challenge of (1) what it means, (2) how it can be translated into consequences ultimately favorable rather than unfavorable to living, (3) how these consequences can be realized. The large element of uncertainty must be provided for. Man, therefore, embarks upon his course of action experimentally: he is constantly alert, studying the effects of his actions and making modifications in his own planned procedure as he goes along. Intelligent living is guided by hypotheses rather than by inflexible laws. It distinguishes between ends and means, constantly adapting means to gain favorable ends. It never becomes attached to means per se, cherishing them because they have the blessings of tradition or the sanction of authority.

In essence, human conduct is adjustive or integrative. In order to live, the human organism, as any other, must maintain a "life-sustaining equilibrium" with the surrounding forces of the environment. Everything that man does is pointed toward that end. Every action in which the organism is involved has some effect upon it, good or bad, or possessing a degree of both. An effect is good if it operates to maintain the "life-sustaining equilibrium" or to restore it; an effect is bad if it operates to disturb the equilibrium or to fail to bring it about. The equilibrating process is a continuous process; man is acting all the time to maintain that essential balance which is living. Not always is he successful; each human life is marked by successes, partial successes, and failures. Judged in terms of their effects, failures are of two kinds: there are failures to obtain the consequences essential to the carrying on of the life-process—if the consequences are sufficiently essential or if the failures occur often enough, these may be destructive of the life-process; there are failures to obtain consequences desired by the organism but non-essential (as it is afterwards proved) to the maintenance of the life-process—if common enough, these failures, though not necessarily fatal, will have a disturbing effect on personality. In the nature of things, frustration in attempted satisfaction of legitimate needs has a deleterious effect on the human organism.

In the course of adjustive activity having as its purpose the maintenance of the life-giving balance between organism and environment, human beings resorted to societal living. They developed relationships among themselves, (undoubtedly) first cooperating for the attainment of their several *individual purposes*. To facilitate such cooperation they invented a method of communication, a method of organization, principles of procedure. While societal living may have been in its early stages an experimental undertaking, the value of society as a permanent *general* arrangement soon proved itself. It was patent that society possessed important values in facilitating the adjustment of individuals. Two things occurred: (1) individuals came to see themselves as possessing more and more purposes in common, so that society became a method of attainment, through collective activities, of to-some-extent common ends, (2) societal values came to be secondary values in human living—to maintain a good society became a purpose incidental to the realization of perfectly individual ends. No one any longer questions the value of society. It has become one of the great human values.

This, however, does not alter the fact that society is a means to the end of individual living. Societal living must make it possible for each person better to realize the ends essential to his living. To the extent that society does not do this, to that extent it is bad; a special arrangement in society that interferes with the satisfaction of vital individual needs is a bad arrangement, regardless of how hallowed it is by tradition. The formal organization of society, its institutions, its ideals, its practices are all of them intended to serve the purpose of individual happiness.[47] Now it happens that, while the *fact* of society is a permanent fact of human existence, never to be discarded, the particular formal organization prevailing at any time, the institutions, the instrumental ideals, the social practices, are not. Ideally they must be adjusted to changing experience. These things are not "goods" in themselves. A social institution, for example, is a means of realizing consequences considered at a particular time to be favorable to the individuals making up society. With changing experience new consequences may be visualized or the old means of achieving the same consequences may cease to be valid. In that event, the social institution needs to be modified to suit the changed situation, radically altered, or perhaps altogether discarded. The fact is; however, that social institutions have a tendency to linger long after they have outlived their usefulness. To be of greatest service they must be viewed in the same way as is every other means to an end—experimentally. That does not mean that social institutions are here-today-gone-tomorrow affairs. It does mean, however, that social institutions must be modified in the light of changing events, and that a process of continuous modifica-

---

[47] In this connection there is to be noted the strong tendency of some Experimentalists to distinguish between "society" and "the state." "In a democracy . . . government is something less than the state, and the state something less than society, society being the most inclusive term applied to the facts of human association, the state the fundamental legal conceptions through which the will of society is expressed, and government the state in action at any given time." (G. S. Counts in "The School and the State in American Democracy," a paper presented before a meeting of the National Council of Education, Cleveland, Ohio, February 27, 1939.) Where the state does not express the will of society, these Experimentalists would appeal over the head of the state to the people themselves. For the tremendous educational implications of this, *vide* pp. 281 ff.

tion of them needs to be regarded as the ordinary rather than the exceptional state of affairs.

The fact of societal living (as will be seen later) exercises a tremendously important influence on individual development; among other things it extends very greatly the meaning and possibilities of human intelligence. But there is one thing that societal living does not do: it does not change the essential character of the life-experience or the essential meaning of intelligent living. Experience is still a particular affair, specific to every individual. There is no such thing as a collective or common experience: there is a common situation which will yield as many different kinds of experiences as there are individuals involved. Sharing an experience with others does not mean deriving from it meanings and consequences identical with those of others. Individuals interacting in a common social situation do not sign over their intelligence to anyone else or to the group as a whole. Intelligent human conduct is conduct that is guided by the individual in accordance with meanings drawn from his experiences. Individuals living in society retain the obligation to live intelligently. In disagreements affecting a number of persons, the will of the majority may prevail; but individuals do not yield the right to think for themselves, and the obligation to act in accordance with their own ideas, when such action does not interfere with others. The principle here is not to be interpreted to imply that every person must have his own way: society must be maintained; to maintain society it is often necessary to go contrary to the wishes and even the genuine needs of many individuals; there is a quite legitimate place for social method that, in case of dispute, recognizes the precedence of the whole over any of its parts. But the principle is to be interpreted to imply that a social action does not, by virtue of the fact that it is a *social* action, acquire intellectual merit, and that it cannot be assumed as axiomatic that it operates for the welfare of all the individuals affected by it.[48]

An organism, at any point in its life-process, is a uniquely individual thing. Man, though living in society and exhibiting social character, does not surrender his inherent individuality. In fact, it is through his

[48] In this respect Experimentalism differs fundamentally from Social Realism. *Vide* pp. 95 ff.

interactions in society that he fully acquires individuality as well as social character.[49] The experiences that he has are his own experiences; the meanings that he obtains from them are necessarily his own meanings; the consequences of his interaction with the environment are, generally speaking, consequences for *him;* the impressions that consequences make upon his character are different from those made upon others. "To be a person means to be biased." [50] Individuality implies freedom to differ. A person living in society does not surrender his freedom to differ: he does not become a conformist. But individuality, freedom to differ, imply a selection. Individuality is not differentness in all respects; neither is freedom the right to do anything one pleases. "It is a superficial understanding of the nature of a person, and of the nature of freedom, that leads one to assume that to be a free person means to be equally open to all sorts of possibilities. Were all things equally desirable and possible, a person would have no important preferences." [51] Societal relations are to a great extent the interactions of the preferences of individuals. No rule-of-thumb procedure can be suggested for regulating the preferences of individuals so that they do not constantly jostle each other, but intelligent living in society assumes the maintenance of a nice balance between the individual, operating for the realization of his own purposes, and other individuals, operating for the realizations of theirs. If what has been said suggests a picture of society as no complacent, settled, orderly state of affairs, but as a state of continuous interplay of individual purposes, of continuous give-and-take compromise, then that is as it should be. "Adaptation is thus a continuous process of reciprocal modification." [52]

The fact of societal living does not serve to alter the nature of intelligence in human living. Intelligence is instrumental in effecting better adjustment; that is the end with respect to which it must be evaluated. An action taken by society is intelligent to the extent that it actually operates to improve the adjustment of its individuals. It is

[49] "In its broad sense, the experimentalist conceives education to be that total process by which we become individuals. Individuality is not something given at birth; it is an achievement." J. L. Childs, *Education and the Philosophy of Experimentalism,* p. 135. 1931.

[50] *Ibid.,* p. 149.

[51] *Ibid.*

[52] *Ibid.,* p. 243.

not intelligent per se—because it is a social action or because it follows precedent or because it obeys the dictum of authority. If a social action operates in a manner to interfere with the adjustment of the individual, directly or indirectly, positively or negatively—to impair his health, to keep him from satisfying his physical needs, to restrict his liberty, to deprive him of his individuality, then that action is, with respect to the individual, unintelligent, and, though he may accept it momentarily, it should provoke from him a response in the direction of correcting the situation or at least effecting an acceptable compromise. Intelligence, moreover, is experimental; it cannot be sure of success. An intelligent act is, in a sense, a tentative act; it leaves the way open for amendment or modification in the event that it is not altogether successful. Now social action may be attended by greater pomp and circumstance than is individual action. It may not only be more impressive, but it may actually be wiser with respect to the needs of the individuals whom it serves. But to be intelligent, it must still be hypothetical. That fact that it is social does not also render it certain-to-be effective. Society does possess a greater fund of valid meanings than are available to any individual. It does "know most of the answers" better than does the individual. But it does not know all the answers; and those that it knows are constantly rendered less valid by changing experience. Individuals, therefore, cannot place their trust unquestioningly in the wisdom of social action; they must be ever on the alert to note the consequences for individual living of the action that society takes, and, when necessary, must press for social changes.

The need for social change is not self-evident. It is not sensed first by "society" itself, nor by the individuals whose purposes the conditions of the societal status quo are serving well. It is sensed first by the individuals in whose living societal means no longer operate to produce needed ends. These individuals analyze their experiences and discover the causes of their maladjustment. (The judgment of individuals is, of course, not fallible either. Its validity has to be borne out by subsequent experience.) The existence in society of conditions inimical to individual needs is *altogether independent of the formal recognition of that fact.* For any one of a number of reasons, society may not recognize, through a collective verdict officially rendered, these conditions as existing. But whether they are recognized or not, the conditions *may* still exist; not to have their existence confirmed by even a single intelligence does not alter the fact that they may be there. Denying a fact or repudiating it does not serve to make it non-existent; its non-existence can be assumed only if it has no effect upon living.

Human progress is contingent upon many things. It presumes first of all an acceptance of the fact that society exists to serve the aims and purposes of all its individuals, that all its arrangements and practices are with a view toward this end, that the signal for needed social change is the failure of social conditions, as they are, to satisfy human needs. It presumes further an acceptance of the experimental way of living, with the attitude that means are to be regarded as tentative until they are successful in securing needed ends, and that ends themselves are constantly modified by new insights growing out of experience. Social action must be firmly founded on all the meanings collected out of the past experience that are relevant to the particular situation, and must be carried out with thoroughness; nevertheless it must be regarded as hypothetical, and re-examined at the first sign of a felt irritation in the experience of individuals affected by it. Finally, human progress is contingent upon the presence in society of active, individual intelligences which are both critical and creative, which are quick to note disturbances in the equilibrial condition essential to life, are capable of discovering the locus of maladjustment and of suggesting constructive measures for improvement, and are persistent enough to have them considered and tried out by society.

Considerable has been said in maintenance of the thesis that the individual is the end of living, that societal living does not imply the surrender of individuality, that intelligence is a prerogative of individuals and not of society, that human progress depends upon the persistent exercise of critical and creative individual intelligence. It is necessary, however, not to underestimate the tremendous positive effect of society upon individual development, or the importance of socialness as a human trait. Society is an inherent and inextricable and inseparable part of the environment into which an individual is born and in which he operates. The natural environment for civilized human beings is also a social environment. Man has remade nature in accordance with his own ends, and is remaking it all the time. The environment into which a person is born is suffused with human meanings. Interacting with this environment a person takes over its meanings, and with these as tools, learns how to direct intelligently his own living. Society has assembled a great many meanings out of past experience: some it has embodied in concrete and established things— in changes it has made in nature, in relations it has established among human beings; others it holds as a reserve to draw upon when necessary. In language it has invented an effective and economical way of communicating meanings as well as a way of effectively and economically deriving meanings from experience (that is, language is not only a means of communication, it is a means of thinking). In the course of the life-process an individual interacting with his environment is constantly obtaining meanings from society, using them in his own experiencing, and incorporating them into his own personality structure. The personality that he has is a personality developed in course of the experiencing process, and it is a personality socially-built; the intelligence with which he behaves is an outcome of the experiencing process and its instruments are the meanings obtained in large part from society. "The individual self is literally built out of the interactions of the human organism with its natural-social environment." [53]

Human experience is social experience. The conditions that operate to foster or to disturb the life-sustaining balance in individual living are social conditions. Society is to a large extent thus involved in determining the all-important fact of success or failure in individual living. To the extent that the individual is able to manipulate the elements of his social experience to achieve necessary ends, to that extent is society good; societal conditions that set back the efforts of the individual to realize needed ends are to that extent bad. It follows inevitably that society, if it is to have an integrative effect upon personality, must itself be integrated, must itself operate with a consistency of purpose and an effectiveness of means to ends. "Any adequate culture will be a balanced whole, each part of which should articulate with all the other parts so that all aspects of community living may go on well together." [54] A conflict in social ideals or in social institutions and practices cannot act to the advantage of individual living. Lack

[53] J. L. Childs, *Education and the Philosophy of Experimentalism*, p. 242. 1931.
[54] W. H. Kilpatrick, in *The Community School*, p. 8. 1938.

of balance in the environment serves to thwart the effort of the individual organism to integrate itself; it is bound to have an injurious effect upon personality development.

A human being born into society is born into values most of which he adopts in the course of his own living. Many of these values the individual accepts almost automatically as he learns to cope with experience. But no societal values can be ultimately acceptable that in the course of the individual experience-process are not validated. Social ends and means must justify themselves in individual existence; if they consistently and definitely do not, the individual is justified in taking steps (along with other individuals similarly affected) to induce social changes that will establish values more compatible with the greatest good to the largest number. Like all other meanings, the meanings that society accepts and sets up as values are hypothetical in nature and valid as long as they work. They are constantly being put to the test in individual experience; under ideal conditions they would be continuously modified or reconstructed in accordance with new insights derived from experience.

For the most part, however, societal values do possess a large measure of validity: they represent meanings which in the past have been more or less successful in effecting certain outcomes. How much validity they possess at any one time probably depends most on how intrinsically relevant they are to the prevailing social situation in which they serve as regulative principles. Some values are always much more valid than others. Some, by repeated verification in experience, have acquired a very great prestige: they are values which the individual may accept almost with the certainty that they are valid if properly used (that is, if they are used flexibly, if they are continuously adapted to situations). Other values require much more cautious and circumspect attention: they are to be accepted tentatively and to be given careful trial. The effects which they achieve in individual experience serve to establish their validity.

The principle that societal values must validate themselves in individual experience should not be interpreted to mean that the individual, developing in society, must take an agnostic or disbelieving attitude toward the values which social experience is seeking to foster within him. The values that have completely proved themselves in human experience should be accepted by the individual with the full assurance that they will work: such values are, for example, democracy, justice, law, experimentalism itself. They must be accepted by the individual almost on faith, whether or not in his immediate experience he recognizes their validity. His personality development must be guided in such a way that these values become a part of his working equipment. Other values cannot be accepted with nearly as much assurance; while still others must be regarded with suspicion even if they have the support of social convention behind them. In any event, a human being does not begin by creating out of his own experience the meanings that serve him in the guidance of his living: he receives and accepts most of them from society and uses them in interpreting his own experiences and in achieving his purposes. Personality is, in any case, a social product; the intelligent personality is the one that discriminates, in the management and control of its own living, between societal values that are utterly trustworthy and those that must be watchfully regarded.

Through society the individual becomes capable of the effective management and control of his own experience; by undergoing an experiencing process within society he acquires the meanings through which he can effect more securely his life-adjustment. An individual would be much poorer in meanings were his experiencing not within a social realm. Social experience is thus a builder of intelligence. A person is not born with intelligence; he is born merely an organism with certain immediate organic powers and a capacity for learning how to deal effectively with experience. In the course of living in society, this capacity can be very greatly developed: the individual can acquire a sufficiency of meanings, an effective method of using meanings in experience, and a corresponding personal equipment of effective behavior patterns. Regardless of individual differences, with proper guidance each person can become, through a process of social experiencing, an intelligent person.

In the light of these general principles, it becomes possible in summary form to characterize the good society. The good society is, in the first place, so organized as to promote the ends of individual living; and, for that purpose, each individual is recognized as the equal of every other—this in spite of the patent fact of individual differences.

Human beings cannot be compared. Each man is in his own way an individual, and must be accorded the dignity of recognition of his individuality. What makes democracy pre-eminent as a social principle is its inherent recognition of both these truths: of the principle that society is a means to the end of individual living, and of the principle that each individual is essentially the equal of every other. "High regard for the individual is probably the most distinctive and pervasive characteristic of democratic living. In democracies, personalities are held to be precious, unique, and not capable of duplication. The optimum development of each individual, irrespective of birth, economic status, race, creed or color, is to be encouraged and nurtured both because of the enhanced enjoyment of individual living which comes through full development of distinctive qualities and because of contributions which such distinctive qualities make to the common life." [55] Beyond this democracy cannot be defined: it cannot be defined in terms of the particular arrangements which express this principle, because arrangements must be relative to situations. At different times, the principle of democracy calls for different kinds of political and economic action. But all of the time democracy implies a recognition of the essential equality of each person and of his right to maximum self-development.

The good society is of necessity the experimentally-minded society. "The experimentalist believes that the distinguishing characteristic of a democratic society is that it is precisely the kind of society that does cherish individual variations, desires, and aspirations, instead of seeking to crush them out in the interest of some static social arrangement. Consequently a democratic society must ever be a changing society. Its traditions and institutions are to be subjected to continuous reconstruction in order that they may better serve the needs and promote the growth of those individuals whose lives are conditioned by them. The concern of such a democratic society is not to absorb the individual into its already developed social tradition. While such a society seeks to afford fair opportunity for all to nourish their lives on its tradition, it is equally concerned to provide for its own continued growth

[55] The Commission on Secondary School Curriculum (V. T. Thayer, chairman), Progressive Education Association, *Science in General Education*, p. 36. 1938.

through the perpetual reconstruction of the social fabric. Concrete individuals with their unfulfilled desires and purposes afford the focal points around which such social reconstruction can take place." [56] The ultimate reference is always the well-being of every individual, and with respect to that end all social means are evaluated.

The good society is the well-integrated society; the conditions within society must be such as to assist rather than to hinder the individual in his efforts to achieve satisfactory integration. Social arrangements, social practices must be consistent with one another; to the extent that these are inharmonious or in conflict with one another, satisfactory individual integrating activity and adjustment are more difficult.

Corresponding to these characteristics of society, there are characteristics of the good man. The good man is first of all an individual. True individuality does not conflict with socialization; rather it is inclusive of socialization. Individuality is a product of social experiencing. It is itself not a fixed thing but is continuously developing, taking its character from the social conditions that foster it. The complete person is the individual who operates in terms of his own purposes and is propelled by his own intelligence. Implicit in individuality is creativeness and criticalness; the man who is not constantly evaluating, who is not constantly analyzing experience, who is not constantly comparing ends and means, who is not continuously creating new ends out of the insights of his own experience is the incomplete man. The good man is necessarily the democratic man, recognizing the essential equality of all human beings and the right of each to maximum self-development. Society is always, in a sense, seething; individuals are working not only together but also against one another, that is, crossing purposes with one another. Only when the equal right of each individual is recognized and becomes a guiding ideal of conduct is the good society possible. Such a society is made possible by democratic individuals. Implicit in a democracy, as it is in individuality and socialization and creativeness, is the trait of experimentalism. The good man recognizes that meanings are hypothetical guides to action, and comports himself in such a way as to make that principle a reality. Finally the good man is the continuously integrating person—integrating his own activities

[56] J. L. Childs, *Education and the Philosophy of Experimentalism*, pp. 228–229. 1931.

around his life-needs as a center, and acquiring in that way a wholesome well-rounded personality as well as a genuine rapport with his environment.

II

The development of science and technology has radically transformed our modern culture. With amazing rapidity an agrarian culture has been changed into a highly industrialized one. Fundamental economic changes have brought equally fundamental social changes, and the present American society in which we live is new and radically different from any previous one that ever existed. But that is not all. Science has brought into existence a method: we have invented a method of invention. The fundamental changes that have occurred came with remarkable speed, and the speed with which change is taking place is constantly being accelerated. This rate of change is something new in history; it is probably the most momentous phenomenon of our time. Human living, inherently dynamic, has become a much more dynamic process.

Although the marvelous development of science and technology has ushered in a new era of living, and has actually created a new culture, we have not yet adjusted ourselves to it and to the changes it has wrought. In fact, out of the fundamental changes that have taken place have come tremendous conflicts in American life. We are today an "unbalanced culture." [57] Adjustment, already made difficult by the rapid rate of change, has become much more difficult because we are in conflict with ourselves. "The major difficulty resides in the fact that the march of events has proceeded very unevenly in the several parts of the social structure. Thus science, technology, and invention, with their devastating implications for traditional practice and thought, have moved much more rapidly than government or even economic arrangements. Within the field of economy, moreover, methods of production have changed far more radically than methods of distribution. And the prejudices, the ideas, the thought of the people with respect to many basic social relationships and institutions have remained relatively static for generations. An intellectual equipment

[57] W. H. Kilpatrick, in Introduction to *The Community School*, p. 8. 1938.

suited to the age of the ox-cart, human energy and handicrafts lingers on in an age of motor cars, mechanical power, and automatic factories." [58]

"The strategic essence of the current social situation is economic"; [59] that is where the central maladjustments lie and that is where fundamental social reconstruction will have to reach. The richness of the natural resources of the country coupled with great technological development have made possible the attainment of a productive power sufficient to supply the material wants of all. No longer need man make his living by the "sweat of his face"; no longer need want and poverty be a usual condition in society. The productive power that we command makes it possible for us to achieve for all any reasonable standard of physical well-being to which we might subscribe, and to turn our attention then "to the tasks involved in the rational, humane, and esthetic ordering of life." [60] But that has not been done. To some, indeed, this abundance has already come, in far greater measure than they require. On the whole the physical standard of living has been raised. But for a large portion of the American people there is still poverty and want, while for the large majority of the people there is little more than what is essential for the most fundamental needs. Far from being largely concerned with cultural and spiritual things, we are more than ever concerned with material things. We are materially and spiritually a "depressed" society. The making of a living is in most cases attended by toil and worry. We suffer from a huge problem of unemployment. Our youth are faced with lack of opportunity. Even those employed are affected by a chronic feeling of insecurity. The potential rich life that we can make contrasts in a ghastly way with the realities of experience.

We are producing much more than has ever been produced before, though we still hold our productive power in restraint; but without question we are not yet producing enough of all things to satisfy the legitimate material needs of all the people. The anomaly is, therefore, that considerable of what is produced never reaches the people who are

[58] G. S. Counts, *The Social Foundations of Education*, p. 507. 1934.
[59] W. H. Kilpatrick, "The Social Philosophy of Progressive Education," *Progressive Education*, 12:289, May, 1935.
[60] Counts, *op. cit.*, p. 511.

in need of it. While crops are being destroyed and cattle slaughtered, while goods rot in warehouses, and merchants, unable to sell the wares that others want for, are driven into bankruptcy, and while machines are idle, a great many people are not able to satisfy the most fundamental human needs. We have not been able to coordinate production with distribution. We are still governed by the idea of value fixed on the scarcity principle: to hasten "recovery," for example, we artificially restrict production and raise prices. We have misused technology rather than used it intelligently; we have wasted rather than enjoyed our natural resources. The machine is a priceless boon to mankind, but we have not yet learned to use and direct it in the common interest. "And so today men starve in the presence of plenty. Here is the most terrifying of the many contradictions found in contemporary society."[61]

The development of technology has acted to bring people together in mutual economic and social interdependence. The making of a living has in fact become a cooperative enterprise. The elements of the culture have become thoroughly interrelated. Every aspect of the life-experience has been affected. The invention and perfection of new forms of transportation and communication have brought together in closer community not only members of society but the peoples of the world. "Through these agencies, the isolation and self-sufficiency of family and neighborhood have been destroyed and modern man has been ushered into a world of wholly unprecedented extent and complexity."[62] The tendency of technological development is inevitably in the direction of fostering group thinking, group cooperation, group life—whether in the community or in the nation or in the world. Collectivization of human enterprise, even in our unbalanced social order, has become a fact.

But we fight against the recognition of the full implications of this fact. Very largely responsible for the disjointedness of the present situation is the fact that our social thinking and our social action are governed by concepts evolved within an earlier culture and no longer valid in the present. Our thinking in terms of man and society has not kept pace with the development of technology. We stubbornly refuse to concede that many of our social institutions, social practices, even

---

[61] *Ibid.*, p. 516.
[62] *Ibid.*

social ideals are, in the face of the changes that have occurred, out-moded. Many of these we have mistakenly identified with democracy, and this has increased our reluctance to revise them. We are in fact ruled by tradition rather than by an intelligent regard for and under-standing of the meaning and needs of democratic living in the present social situation.

Standing as a kind of symbol of all the outworn concepts that con-tribute to the mismanagement of our social living is the doctrine of individualism. The harmful effect of this doctrine penetrates beyond economics into politics, into culture and education. In economics we see it operating as the so-called laissez-faire principle (in actuality not altogether a laissez-faire policy) and causing untold harm. To that principle may be laid the present evils of production for private profit rather than for human need, the strangle-hold of a financial oligarchy on the economic life of the nation, the general emphasis on materialistic success, the waste and private spoilation of the country's natural re-sources, the waste and senseless competition in industry and business, the periodic interruption of productive processes, and much of the temporary, seasonal, and chronic unemployment. In an undeveloped society, individualism may serve as a spur to human initiative; a meas-ure of individualism may be compatible with the needs of intelligent living. In a complex, highly-integrated technological society, extreme individualism is not only an anomaly, but one that threatens to destroy society itself.

The doctrine of individualism [63] has perverted men's thinking about the meaning of societal living, about the meaning of democracy, about the function of government. At best individualism is a divisive force, and contrary to the needs and implications of societal living. Living in society demands a large degree of harmonization of purpose and effort, while individualism pits man against man and group against group. Individualism makes dominant the element of competition. Under it government is accorded the role of a policeman keeping order; more often than not government fails to play even this role with fairness, and, falling under the influence of the powerful social group, is "converted into a dispenser of special favors and privileges

---

[63] Experimentalism makes a strong contrast between this sort of individualism and *individuality* as social product. *Vide* p. 122 and pp. 129 ff.

to those who have." [64] Social agencies and institutions intended to advance the spiritual and cultural life of all members of society tend to align themselves with the powerful economic groups and to support their selfish purposes. And, in our day, individualism has succeeded in identifying itself with democracy, and marches under its banner.

Under the governing conditions of our present civilization, the ideal of individualism is altogether incompatible with democracy. While present social-economic conditions persist and individualism remains as a guiding social ideal, liberty and equality of opportunity must remain empty slogans. There is no liberty possible without a measure of economic security, and equality of opportunity must appear a bitter fiction to many who feel themselves doomed to poverty and despair. In the present situation democracy cannot be conceived in purely political and legal terms—the right of suffrage, equality under the law, etc.; the concept of democracy must embrace the ideal of greater economic equality, greater economic opportunity, and a large measure of economic security to all. Democracy must be restored to its true meaning as a recognition of the right of every individual to maximal self-development in society. Social and economic practices must be brought into line with this principle. Only on this condition can political liberty survive in the modern world.

The whole human ideal of democracy, to recognize and to gain which has taken humanity many centuries of struggle, is threatened. There is developing a growing pessimism concerning the value of democracy. Not only is democracy vigorously under attack by rival authoritarian doctrines, and fighting for its very life, but many of its friends have begun to have misgivings about it. "In their theoretical advocacy the friends of democracy adopt a defensive and even an apologetic tone. The best they can say is that while democracy is not as good as it should be, it is not as bad as it might be. Cataloguing and commending its merits, conceding and lamenting its defects, and consciously balancing argument against argument, they arrive at the tentative conclusion that democracy is a trifle superior to any rival order of society and life, as if diverse social systems were readily commensurable. Moreover, in an age when great choices have to be made, when positive and determined social action has to be taken, democracy is denominated the middle way.

[64] Counts, *op. cit.*, pp. 514-515.

Obviously if such a conception of democracy should prevail, its worst enemies could ask for nothing better." [65] There is noticeable everywhere a growing tendency to compromise with democracy. There is an admission that democracy has to some extent failed, when the fact is that the failure of our society is not due to the failure of democracy but to the unfortunate identification of democracy with outworn social practices. Democracy must regain its true meaning, namely, as a way of life that promises the greatest good to all the people under the direction of the people themselves.

Ours is a "depressed" society, and though everyone is affected, the youth of the land are affected most of all. They are indeed in the way of becoming a lost generation. The inconsistencies existing within society, the discrepancies between ideals and actualities—between what youth are taught to believe and what they themselves experience—have had a distressing influence on their personality development. An unbalanced society cannot produce wholesome, balanced individuals. The economic difficulties of society and the dark prospects that face youth arriving at maturity serve further to deepen their depression. For many there is no employment immediately available, and hardly a promise of any in the future. There seems to be no chance for economic security and the general stabilization of personality that comes with it. Study after study of the attitudes of youth give evidence of the frustration that they at present feel, unable to take up their duties as members of society, unable to marry, unable to look forward to the realization of their hopes and ambitions. In a real way the future of American democracy is tied up with the future of the country's youth, and, unless changes are made in the social-economic structure of society to brighten the prospects for youth, the future of democracy is not secure.

III

As stated previously, we possess in technology a potential means of supplying the material wants of all on a level not previously known. Technological development "has at last made it possible for man to create a society in which an entire population would be sufficiently emancipated from the grinding struggle for the bare physical necessities

[65] G. S. Counts, *The Prospects of American Democracy*, pp. 6–7. 1938.

to permit all to share in the realization of the finer possibilities of existence." [66] Granted that we need to go much farther than we have in developing a spiritual and intellectual culture, the first step is to extend to all a large measure of material security and to release their creative energies for other and finer things.

This is not possible as long as the traditional individualism prevails and with it the "erroneous ideas of personal liberty and property rights which now tragically prevent the management of our new corporate processes for public rather than for private ends." [67] Individualism is not compatible with the corporate existence that we at present lead. "Inherited ideas of individual competition, of private profit, and of the right of each man to do as he pleases with his own, need reconstruction if they are to fit the facts of our interdependent, corporate age. Thus new behavior patterns consonant with the facts of this new social interdependence must be woven into the economic, legal, and political conditions of our country. Such patterns must also be permitted to penetrate into the mental and moral dispositions of individuals. A new social philosophy is demanded." [68]

Individuality must not be confused with individualism. Individuality is a quality of the total behavior of personality without which that behavior is not genuinely complete; individualism is merely a hollow doctrine of an age that is past. "Individuality is not a static term. When conditions change, individuals conditioned by those social changes must also change. We need today a new individual, an individual not fashioned after the pattern of the individualism of the agrarian, pioneer life, but an individual integral with the deeper social tendencies of our present industrial corporate civilization." [69] To obtain such individuality (and this should not seem paradoxical) we must first secure greater socialization, greater socialization as a means to individual happiness. There is need for a greater sharing—of values, of thought, and of action and the fruits of action. Our means of living must be socialized but the end toward which we aim must be democracy, not authoritarianism. Democracy in essence means a recognition of the individuality of every

[66] J. L. Childs, *Education and the Philosophy of Experimentalism*, p. 237. 1931.
[67] *Ibid.*, pp. 237–238.
[68] *Ibid.*, p. 238.
[69] *Ibid.*, p. 239.

person, of his right to exist as an individual. Our social system must be so reorganized as to make this possible.

There is needed a fundamental reconstruction of the social order. We must face the full implications of the fact that we have entered an era of collective living: our social concepts and arrangements must be consistent with the needs of this era. Inevitably there must be an approach to a collective economic order.[70] But collectivism is a broad category: it can lead society in many directions. The American people must make their choice of a collective economy that recognizes the historic American commitment to the principles of democracy. Whatever social order ultimately emerges must recognize the worth of every individual man and woman.

Precisely what the arrangements of the new social order shall be cannot be immediately stated. Planning, continuous planning, will be necessary to keep the new social organization geared to the demands of an industrial economy. But a few of the general principles have already shown themselves to be incontrovertible for a democratic society. Enterprise established on the principle of unlimited private profit must go. For it there must be substituted a system that makes possible a true equality of opportunity, a modicum of economic security for all, a real and not a feigned democracy. Natural resources must be utilized not for the benefit of the few but for the welfare of all. Control of the economic order must be in the hands of the people. Science and technology must be administered for the benefit of all. Government must apply itself to serve all, and not to protect the privileges of a few.

Change has come to stay. We cannot set back time; we cannot go back to an era when the problems of existence were relatively simple. We possess in the scientific method a method that can be as successful in giving us mastery of our own affairs as it has been successful in giving us mastery of nature. We possess in experimentalism an attitude that can help us not only out of the current crisis but out of difficulties that are bound to present themselves in the future. We must adopt this attitude so that we may guide ourselves in our social undertakings by scientifically weighing our decisions, by relating means to ends, with the ultimate end of advancing the living of every individual.

[70] For the general attitude of Experimentalists toward economic collectivism, *vide* p. 443, footnote.

2: The Psychological Foundations of Secondary Education

*I ***

To HUMANISM the concept of human development connotes not merely growth of the human being naturally toward maturity but growth that is steadily inclined in the direction of a certain well-defined way of life. To develop is to move in the direction of a Good Life as it has been conceived by the universal mind of man and verified countless times in human experience. This Good Life consists primarily in living in accordance with certain ethical and intellectual values which, in the judgment of mankind, emphasize man's humanness, his distinctness from all other living things. Although ethical considerations are primary, living the Good Life presumes a high degree of effectiveness in dealing with material things and employing them toward human ends. The Good Life of man is universal in conception, but living it is an individual matter. Each man enters into it in his own way, realizing it to an extent of which he is capable; to the extent that he does realize it, to that extent does he become a good, worth-while person. Development implies a high degree of individual intelligence of a critical and creative kind. The conception of the Good Life is neither finite nor static; its limits are continuously receding as are the limits of the horizon; individuals are, by virtue of ethical or intellectual qualities, constantly extending it. Speaking generally, however, the development of

* The Roman numerals used in this study to mark off sections have the following significance: I—General Principles, II—Evaluation of the Existent Situation in Terms of These Principles, III—Nature of Constructive Proposals.

131

the individual is a process of approaching, in his own living, this universal.[1]

Thus, development is movement toward a manner of living that, in the crucible of the whole of human experience, has been proved to be finest. The process that undertakes to assist each individual in development must be a process that guides him in this direction. Human development is not necessarily "natural" development; whether it is "natural" or not in specific cases depends upon whether man is content to accept nature as his ideal. In the process of its development, the human race has altered a good many of what apparently were "ends of nature"; it has tried to substitute restraint for impulsiveness, mercy for vindictiveness, temperance for immoderateness, the rule of justice for "the law of the jungle." To what degree human development is to be "natural" and to what degree it shall be "forced" depends upon the extent to which each individual is by nature endowed with desirable attributes. For example, to the person who shows himself to possess traits of loyalty, honesty, courage, tolerance, and human sympathy, further guidance in this direction is not "forced" but "natural." But in every case, proper human development requires some modification of the original characteristics that man, as a living thing in nature, would normally show, in favor of those characteristics that man has learned especially to style as human. Stated rather strongly and from the special viewpoint of the New Humanism: "As Aristotle suggested, we become human largely by resisting our own natural tendencies, pulling ourselves back to the mean just as people straighten pieces of wood that are warped."[2]

The secret of humanness lies in possession of mind. Although Humanist theories differ as to the essential meaning of mind, the manner of acquirement of its original content,[3] and its general method of development,[4] there is no disagreement that the effect of mind is revealed in

[1] Kandel is also inclined to maintain that a universal conception of the Good Life is further modified in terms of the characteristics of a particular culture.

[2] N. Foerster, *The American State University*, p. 254. 1937. The New Humanism is a special type of Humanism with certain additional and distinguishing principles. It has in this study been absorbed and generalized within the larger framework of Humanism.

[3] *Vide* Introduction, pp. 14–18.

[4] *Vide infra*, pp. 139 ff.

the Good Life in terms of ethical and humane conduct and effective intellect. Right character and effective intelligence are the twin requisites of the good man, and, though they are not to be artificially separated, they are *both* to be emphasized. Human development is toward the end of acquiring such character and such intelligence. Though there is further difference of opinion as to what degree the two are conjoined and how far development of effective intelligence can be relied upon automatically to bring with it desirable character,[5] there is also agreement that, of the two, intelligence is the basic factor in human development. Without a substantial basis of intellectual capacity, the realization of the Good Life is impossible, and, conversely, development toward the Good Life is possible and likely to a degree governed by the possession of the intellectual capacity. It is conceivable, of course, that moral virtues and emotional refinement may be achieved in a blind, unknowing sort of way, but they cannot be used in that way. Moreover, the higher the moral virtue, the greater the intellectual capacity that is necessary even for its acquirement. The development of effective intelligence may not of its own accord secure completely desirable character, but intelligence is undoubtedly joined with character. Human development is fundamentally the development of effective intelligence, though moral and emotional training are concomitant with it. Native intelligence is the prime factor in human development and is indispensable to it. It limits and circumscribes the degree of humanness that can be attained, an index of intelligence is an index of potential humanness, though no guarantee of it. The process that aims at assisting in human development must address itself primarily toward the realization of the power latent in the intellectual capacity, and its absolute success is conditioned by the extent to which that capacity is present.

Intelligence may be defined as capacity for dealing with (that is, obtaining, arranging, using) the meanings of things. Humanness connotes the power of awareness of the *nature* of things. Man's distinctiveness in nature is founded in his capacity to "know" things, to translate the concrete but meaningless objects of his sensed experience into specific meanings and cohering patterns of meaning in such a way as to obtain conceptually a vision of the world that exists. Meanings not only give order, place, and purpose to the objects of experience, but they

, [5] *Vide infra*, pp. 138 ff.

offer clues to the further existence of things. They are not only the means and the stuff of knowing the world but the means and the stuff of dealing with it. Intellectual power comes with the possession of meanings and with knowing how to deal with them. Intelligence is the capacity that determines to what extent intellectual power may be achieved. It is the capacity for dealing with concepts, with abstractions from the concrete; for reducing the world of sense-objects to a system of abstractions, and for dealing with the world through the means of abstractions. The higher the capacity of the individual for dealing with abstractions and for dealing with the world through abstractions, the greater his intelligence. It is unfortunately impossible to measure the capacity of anything except in terms of some appropriate content. The intelligence of a human being can be estimated in terms of the actual success that he has had in dealing with ideas drawn from the store of the human heritage.

Appraisals of human intelligence made both empirically and scientifically have proved beyond question that human beings differ greatly with respect to original capacity. Human beings, of course, vary among themselves with respect to many distinguishing features, traits, and tendencies; variety is a common quality in nature. But variation with respect to capacity is the most fundamental of all variants among human beings. It is a variant which decides to what extent it is possible for a human being to develop toward absolute "goodness." As far as we can ascertain, the gift of intelligence is a gift of nature, and nature has been most lavish in presenting it to some and niggardly in withholding it from others. Human beings are born greatly unequal with regard to this most important factor of humanness, as they are born unequal with respect to the other great factor in living—physical health. Regardless of the quarrels that are now going on about undefined and perhaps undefinable terms, the fact remains that man is powerless to create intelligence or to extend it beyond its natural limits. Man can assist in the flowering of intellectual promise, in its realization, in conversion of capacity into power; or man can by neglect doom intelligence to barrenness. But man cannot create or extend capacity. It is present to a degree and to that degree it can be realized. Whether this capacity is present in some individuals in such small measure as to render them for practical purposes ineducable, is a matter upon which Humanism does not fully agree.[6] (The preponderance of belief is in favor of the principle, in general, that all normal people are educable.)

Intelligence is a unitary capacity, just as character and intellectual power are unitary traits. Every person is intelligent to a degree, and that degree is a general index of his capacity to carry on effective thinking in all situations. It is possible, of course, for intellectual capacity to be realized more fully in some types of activity than in others, but that is an effect of natural inclination, special interest, or training. Intelligence is susceptible of development as a whole, and it can be made generally effective. Effective operation within a specific situation is dependent upon ability to understand that situation, to gather its meanings, to relate them to others, and to give them concrete expression. The more meanings a person possesses, the bigger, the more comprehensive, the more searching they are, the more thoroughly they are related to each other and organized in broad coherent patterns, the more skill a person has in dealing with meanings (in obtaining them, relating them, giving them concrete form)—the more likely is that person to operate successfully in the specific situations that confront him, even when he has had no prior specific training in them. "The man who has learned to think and to reason and to compare and to discriminate and to analyze, who has refined his taste and formed his judgment, and sharpened his mental vision, will not indeed at once be a lawyer, or a pleader, or an orator, or a man of business . . . but he will be placed in that state of intellect in which he can take up any one of the sciences or callings I have referred to, or any other for which he has a taste or special talent, with an ease, a grace, a versatility, and a success to which another is a stranger."[7]

The higher the intelligence, therefore, the more general is its potential effectiveness. The person of superior mental capacity, equipped within reasonable limit of his capacity with important meanings and with knowledge of their relations, and trained in precise and effective intellectual techniques, can be relied upon independently to apply himself to the mastery of specific situations with maximum assurance of

---

[6] The one not in otherwise common agreement is Foerster. *Vide supra*, p. 63, footnote. Note in later chapters the effect of Foerster's thesis upon his theory of secondary education.

[7] N. Foerster, *The American State University*, p. 203. 1937.

ultimate success. The process of assisting such a person in the development of ethical character and operational effectiveness may well concentrate on the development of general intellectual power. On the other
hand, the lower the intelligence, the more limited is its general effectiveness. The person of limited mental capacity is not capable of acquiring
a sufficient number of important and well-ordered meanings, or intellectual power sufficient to serve him adequately in mastering the specific situations to which he applies himself. The process that undertakes to assist such a person toward moral and effective living must
supplement general intellectual training with specific training in moral
habits and the particular knowledges and skills that the specific life-
situations require. Between the two extremes of highly superior intelligence and markedly inferior intelligence, there is, of course, infinite
gradation, and to that gradation the (educational) process must accommodate itself.

The higher the intelligence, the better does it lend itself to development through abstract means. Intelligence is the capacity to deal with
the world through the instrumentality of meanings. The higher the
intelligence, the easier does it find it to deal with meanings—to begin
with them, to assimilate them, to linger over them, and to end with
them; the lower the intelligence, the greater is its need to begin with
concrete data, to linger over them, to revert to them, never in fact to
remain very far from them. The process of assisting the more intelligent
person to develop *general* intellectual effectiveness may well be carried
on through a subject-matter of meanings; the process of assisting the
less intelligent person, as far as his capacity allows, to develop general
intellectual effectiveness must be carried on through a subject-matter
that embodies meanings within a more concrete context. This general
psychological principle, of course, harmonizes with the principle that
potential general effectiveness is proportionate with intellectual capacity.
Translated in terms of educational method, the result may be stated as
follows: The educational process seeks to help each individual to acquire, to the limit of his capacity, important general meanings and the
ability to use them. The method (situations, techniques, materials)
through which these meanings and this ability are imparted will in
various degrees be characterized by abstractness or concreteness, according to the intelligence of the person who is being educated. With indi-

viduals of more limited intelligence, the educational process must further fortify general intellectual training with training in specific knowledges, habits, and skills, referent to specific situations. This also requires the use of method emphasizing a large degree of concreteness. The result is that individuals of inferior intelligence are throughout to be trained through more concrete educative instruments, individuals of superior intelligence, with more abstract instruments. Differentiation of educational method is thus a necessity for the realization, in varying degrees, of the common ends of right conduct and material effectiveness.[8]

The twin objectives of the developmental process are the attainment of ethical and refined character and effective intellect. The two factors, however, are not independent—effective intellect underlies right character and is basic to the Good Life. The question is whether, in the process of human development, effective intellect may be of itself relied upon to assure right character, or whether additional training of the emotions and inculcation through habituation of right conduct are required. The answer to this question finds Humanists in disagreement, though the area of disagreement is restricted. In general, the higher the intelligence of a person, the greater are the possibilities of his achieving truly ethical conduct in living; potentiality for right character is therefore a function of intelligence. Moreover, to the degree that a person possesses intelligence, to a corresponding degree can the moral virtues and refinement of the emotions follow naturally from intellectual training.

It is agreed by all, therefore, with respect to those individuals of ordinary and of limited intelligence, that intellectual training alone will not suffice to produce that emotional restraint and discipline and positive practice of good moral habits that characterize the Good Life. Just as, with intellectually inferior individuals, general intellectual training must be supplemented by specific training of a practical sort in order to obtain the desired effectiveness in material things, so must general

---

[8] The term educational method is here used deliberately in preference to possible more specific and definite terms. Humanism is in disagreement in interpreting to what extent differentiation of method requires the use of different *types* of educative materials or whether adequate differentiation may be achieved with the use of at least a common core of materials, suitably adapted to the varying intelligences of individuals.·

intellectual training be supplemented by specific moral training in order to obtain the desired conduct in social living. The latter is even more important than the former; for, while people of limited talent can occupy themselves, with personal benefit to themselves and without complaint from society, in humble practical callings not requiring a great deal of intellectual power, it is a social necessity that these same people, irrespective of intellect, reveal in their common living a high degree of honesty, tolerance, patience, emotional restraint, self-discipline, and so forth. With individuals of ordinary intelligence, therefore, the developmental process must aim at good character both through intellectual training and through additional moral training of a habit-forming kind, given both prior to and alongside of the intellectual training. With the most backward individuals, indeed, the process of moral disciplining must often continue beyond the limits where intellect can follow. The ideal, generally, is to have habit ultimately merge with reason, to have character possess both a rational and an emotional foundation. Wherever possible, discipline should lead to self-discipline.

With respect to the mentally superior individual, however, there is disagreement. Can, in the case of such an individual, intellectual training alone with a minimum of special emotional and moral training, be trusted to produce in every respect—ethically, morally, emotionally as well as intellectually—the good man, or must the developmental process deal specially with emotional and moral as well as with intellectual training? For an obvious reason, the issue can be even further narrowed. Even the superior individual, up to a certain stage in his development, must have training in good moral habits, both through the medium of and in addition to his intellectual training. Good conduct, emotional refinement cannot wait until intelligence has developed. Good habits, once ingrained, themselves later reveal the reason for their being. Self-discipline comes so much more easily if it is preceded by discipline. Children, irrespective of intelligence, must receive moral and emotional training with their intellectual training. The disagreement then is with respect to the later stages in the process of development of the superior individual (that is, with respect to higher education), and here it remains unresolved. The issue is whether higher education shall emphasize moral and esthetic training or whether such training is a by-product of the intellectual process. It is the contention of Kandel that education is more than intellectual training; physical, moral, and esthetic training is equally important for the whole man.[9] On the other hand, Learned states:[10] "Give a youth ideas that are big enough and important enough, and you can with proper guidance marshal behind them all the emotional resources and moral qualities of his nature."

Important both as an instrument of character development and also as the means of making man generally effective is the training of the intellect. The transformation of intellectual capacity into intellectual power is the prime condition of human development. Intellectual power is an outcome of the acquisition of intellectual content and intellectual method—of the acquirement, in other words, of many and important meanings, of methods of organizing them and applying them. Determination of the method of assisting the individual toward the maximum intellectual development possible for him is the crucial problem of the educational process. And with respect to this problem, there exists within Humanism a serious breach, the origin of which is discernible in the different mind-concepts.[11]

It is the conviction of one group that intellectual development comes most effectively and most economically through a process of formal discipline.[12] The essence of formal discipline is the subordination of means to end. The end of intellectual training is the independent acquirement by the individual of important ideas and of methods of using them. The process of intellectual training is important only as it contributes to this end. The materials and methods of the developmental process must be selected from the point of view of their contribution to the method of thinking—of formal handling of meanings, of their technical arrangement and disposition. Given a method of thinking, the individual can go on to get the important meanings for himself. (In the background, there is to be seen a conception of the human mind as not so much a creative as a receptive instrument, and a theory of ideas as things-complete-in-themselves, capable of undiminished existence with a form separable from substance. Training the

[9] I. L. Kandel, *Conflicting Theories of Education*, pp. 39, 125. 1938. Butler and, to a lesser extent, Foerster side with Kandel.

[10] W. S. Learned, *Realism in American Education*, p. 29. 1932.

[11] *Vide* Introduction, pp. 14 ff.

[12] Hutchins and Foerster; *vide* Bibliography.

mind is thus in the nature of sharpening it to the point where it can apprehend, or raising it to the point where it can reach, ideas.) The first stage of development is formal training; up to this point it does not matter what meanings the materials used in training themselves convey —they are being used for their technical and not for their content value. They are to equip the mind with intellectual tools, techniques, and general habits and ideals. Some materials are of course better equipped to perform this function than are others. Beyond this stage a second set of materials will furnish the ideas when the intellect is ready to receive them. These ideas will then, through proper use of the tools, be assimilated in a highly concentrated and expeditious manner. Those individuals who do not possess the mental capacity to deal with ideas as such, will, as soon as they have to the best of their ability obtained the use of intellectual tools, apply them in working with radically different—with concrete—materials. Through these materials they will obtain whatever ideas are implicit in these materials and in addition specific practical knowledges and skills.

The contrary view [13] is that the human mind is not an inert thing that will be passively acquiescent while it is being trained in the formal techniques of thinking; nor are ideas of such a nature that they can be satisfactorily communicated without some form of suitable context. The mind is an active, sensitive instrument that is continuously registering impressions drawn from the experienced world, and, for better or worse, creating its own meanings. The technique of good thinking is developed in terms of some content, not independently of any. Ideas are inherent in things and can be derived from them. The prime requisite of developmental materials is that they be meaningful; the more meanings there are and the more important they are, the better do the materials serve developmental purposes. Other than that, one material is as good as another for the development of the technical intellectual habits and skills. Although some material of a formal nature must appear, it is better on the whole to select materials for their ideational content. This content ought, wherever possible, to derive from a context to which the individual himself is no stranger; for example, from the context of his culture. The function of materials is still largely disciplinary—they are not so much ends in themselves as means of

[13] That of Butler, Kandel, and Learned; *vide* Bibliography.

intellectual training. But the fact that they are psychologically close to the individual will (1) ensure a greater motive for learning, (2) facilitate the transfer and ultimately the successful application of methods of thinking. Since all meaningful materials are equally good for training purposes, the training process becomes more flexible, and it is easier to adapt method to individual capacity in most minute gradations.

Both views, however, unite in emphasizing that the developmental materials must be carefully organized, must possess internal coherence and gradation. In proportion as they possess these qualities are they likely to possess developmental value for the learner. Both agree, too, that sustained and continuous application is essential.

II

The basic general weakness of the psychology [14] that is effective in contemporary American education is traceable to the general philosophic attitude or bias that it reflects. This attitude or bias is pragmatic and positivistic, or, to put it negatively, unidealistic and anti-intellectual. Modern psychology, in its practice, does not seem to recognize that man *is* essentially different from other living things, and that the essence of humanness, the quality that makes him different, is mind. Psychology has, in fact, lost almost entirely the conception of mind. It has reduced human conduct to behavior, and behavior is interpreted in terms of chains of S—R connections. Through acceptance of its tenets, the educational process has almost ceased to be regarded as the general training of the character and intellect and has come to be regarded as inoculation in specific knowledges, habits, skills, and attitudes. Not only the conception of man as intellectual being, but the conception of man as ethical being has been lost sight of. Man is regarded as merely a superior and more complex kind of animal, different in degree of structural development and therefore only in material effectiveness from other animals. Human conduct is appraised from the same level of motivation as is the behavior of animals. Satisfaction and annoyance are the prime movers. Whatever is natural is to be respected. Observe animal behavior or study the naïve conduct of young children, and you are competent to generalize as to how mature and cultivated human be-

[14] That is, of the various tendencies in psychology.

ings are to be expected to think, to feel, and to act. On such bases, are "laws of learning" evolved for human beings. Modern psychology is indeed a pedestrian, workaday affair. It is content with little, provided that it can go out and get its "objective" facts, and reduce them to figures and formulae.

The prevalent spirit of scientism has greatly contributed to this condition. Psychology has comparatively recently become "the science of psychology" or "experimental psychology." Insofar as the scientific spirit and the scientific method have been extended into psychology, that development is good. But "science" has not stopped there. Science has entered the realm where only values of the mind belong. Psychology has ceased to take its cue from true philosophy; it no longer troubles to study the part with some (even tentative) understanding of the whole. Man is not studied from the point of view of what he *should* be and what he *can* be, but from the point of view of what he is, at his simplest and most naïve; and even that, in the name of "objectivity," is simplified and atomized. Psychology has busied itself with fact-gathering, and is so involved in this task that it has not stopped to ask for what purpose it is gathering facts and what they really mean. "Statistics are in the saddle and ride education. We are experimenting and measuring. But statistics are incapable of discovering educational values. We have been experimenting since the beginning of the century, but without any sense of direction or goal." [15] Reflecting the spirit of the age, the science of psychology has become anti-rational. Not being able to prove "objectively" that mind exists, it has banished mind from the scheme of things, and accustomed itself to proceed in its calculations without benefit of mind; not being able to reach an agreement in defining intelligence, it has proceeded to measure it; not being able to prove (in minuscule experimental operations where confirmation of the fact of transfer would have been not an event but a miracle) that sufficient transfer of training occurred, psychology concluded that only under certain conditions can a limited amount of transfer take place.

The general attitude of prevailing psychology reflects some of the crudities of the present age—its materialism, its demand for "facts" rather than theory, its worship of "results." Possibly this attitude repre-

[15] I. L. Kandel, "Our Adolescent Education," *Educational Administration and Supervision*, 18:569, November, 1932.

sents to some extent a reaction against the very crude and pretentious faculty psychology of earlier times; when this was discredited, it became something of a fashion to jibe at armchair philosophies and at theories that could not be demonstrated in a laboratory. At any rate, educational psychology finds itself in the hands of a pragmatic, positivistic behaviorism. Behaviorism is in accord with the equalitarian spirit of the age which holds that all men are equal, "equal to anything, apparently," [16] that all men can be taught all things. It also holds that the training of men is not unlike the training of animals. The consequences of this outlook have been to lower the morale and weaken the moral stamina and intellectual power of the American people in a critical time that calls for these qualities.

Specifically, the general criticisms here made may be illustrated and confirmed by the following instances. Modern psychology neglects or distorts the obvious truth toward which the fact of individual differences points. The most important difference among human beings is the difference in intellectual capacity, and with respect to this all men *are* different. Yet modern psychology refuses to recognize the obvious implications of this fact. Equality of opportunity is in effect, and with the apparent support of psychology, interpreted as the right to learn the same things and to try to achieve the same outcomes. At the same time, however, psychology is inclined to attribute exaggerated importance to differences in "interests," as if interests were endowed with a mystic quality that made them inherently good. Interests tend to become the determiners of learning whether or not they lead away from those common goals toward which all mankind should aspire, whether or not they lead to any significant goals at all. The result of neglecting truly significant differences of capacity has been an effort to find a standard of intellectual attainment that could be appropriate for all; this standard has become the standard of the average. Mediocrity of attainment has become established as an objective, and the superior students have found it easy to attain this objective without extending themselves. The result of glorifying interests has been to coddle the individual, to make him self-centered, often to reduce the educational function to mere satisfaction of whim. Psychology has contributed its share to the

[16] N. M. Butler, *The Meaning of Education,* p. 159. Revised edition. 1915. Charles Scribner's Sons, publishers.

making of undesirable individualism, to the distortion of the meaning of liberty, to the weakening of democracy.

There is no generalized intellectual power to be developed; there are only specific knowledges, habits, skills, and attitudes to be acquired. Preparation for vocation becomes one concern, preparation for home-making another concern, preparation for the proper casting of the political ballot still another. Since abstractions are not gripping in their interest to the average mind, principles are neglected for facts, ideas for "experiences," and generalized ability for concrete skills. Knowledge is no longer formative in function; it is instrumental and utilitarian. Since there are many kinds of utility, the materials of education are multiplied to meet the popular "need." When the criterion is utility, one subject is as good as another. When it becomes impossible for one person to study all the subjects which have been brought into the cur-riculum by reason of their being useful and interesting, specialization follows. A scoring system has been introduced, and credits are tallied until the score shows that "education" has taken place. Even practical subjects have potential educative value, but this value has been greatly reduced by a breaking-down of logical organization, by releasing the learner from the necessity of continuous application, of follow-through, so vital to intellectual development. What we have descended to may be sadly called a "rabbit theory of education." [17]

III

Educational psychology cannot be properly reconstituted until there is recovered an idealistic, rational world outlook, and until science is re-established in its proper relationship to philosophy. The science of psychology must be harnessed to the service of human values. As a science it cannot have the objectivity and independence that is possible in the realm of physical matter; its findings are subject to the superior assessment of philosophy. Moreover, the truths that have been con-firmed by reason and experience must not be held to be impeached simply because proper methods have not yet been devised by which they can be given scientific validation. In its present stage of develop-

[17] N. M. Butler, *Annual Report of the President to the Trustees of Columbia University, 1936*, p. 27.

ment, psychology is but an infant science: the time has not yet come when the empirical wisdom of centuries can be dismissed because it is unsupported by the "findings" of scientific theories operating as free agents.

The naturalistic conception of man as a somewhat superior order of animal must be abandoned in favor of a humanistic conception. In mere physical constitution, man may be a continuation of the animal organism, but the possession of mind endows man with possibilities that elevate him far above the rest of nature. The undeniable fact of mind must be recognized, and not dismissed, as by the behaviorists, as something that cannot be studied and therefore does not exist. The motivations of conduct that are present in man as a gift of nature are not the motivations toward which human development must aim. Human conduct must be identified as a conscious, self-conceived, and self-created thing. That such conduct is in some respects similar to animal behavior must be recognized, but it must be recognized that man has gone far beyond mere animal living in most respects, and can go much further. No one can deny that men often act contrary to self-interest, natural impulses, and physical satisfactions. In the possibility of moral discipline lies the possibility of humanness. The validity of ethical motivations as mainsprings to human conduct must be confirmed. The laws of human learning need to be redefined on an idealistic basis. The catering to desires, euphemistically regarded as "needs," must cease. In the place of these, there should be an endeavor to satisfy genuine moral and intellectual needs. The pleasures that human beings derive do not all spring from the same source as animal pleasures; men do find satisfaction in contemplating a job well done, in effort usefully expended. Even recognition of only partial success in an undertaking admittedly difficult is rewarding. Psychology must cease also to idealize the individualistic tendencies in man. Human development is in the direction of a common Good Life. Human beings are individuals, but their individualities possess a large common measure of ideals and ideas. This is inherent in the conception of the Good Life of mankind.

In restoring "mind" to its rightful place in the guidance of human living, psychology must recognize intelligence as the basic factor in human development. Psychology will have to cease viewing the educational process as a process of conditioning the individual in the successful performance of specific tasks. Intelligence is a general capacity; trained in a general way, it can serve man in the successful performance of a multiplicity of specific tasks. The training of the intellect and the right training of character (both through intellectual means and in other supplementary ways) must be established as the twin objectives of the educational process. The outcome to be sought in training the intellect is the large general and versatile effectiveness that comes with the possession of broad knowledge, sound methods of thinking, judgment, intellectual balance and discrimination, taste and sensitivity. The mechanistic outlook that typifies modern psychology must be surrendered, and with it the whole of the S—R paraphernalia. It is necessary to face the fact that on the actuality of transfer of training depends the possibility of human development. Everything in human experience substantiates the reality of this fact. It is equally necessary, however, to avoid the mistake of explaining transfer as simply (and as crudely) as did the advocates of the faculty psychology.[18] The materials assisting in human development are to be chosen for their developmental rather than utilitarian value. These materials shall be possessed of important meanings, and the meanings organized in coherent, systematic form. Application to them is to be continuous and sustained, so as to allow for the gradual maturing of ideas. Such materials are needed to replace the scrappy units of "practical" subject-matter at present in use. Thoroughness of learning must replace superficiality. Emphasis upon the formation of right character and the development of total intellectual effectiveness needs to replace the piecemeal accumulation of facts of knowledge and of skills up to the point where the learner "has enough." A sensible attitude that measures learning in terms of real development will have to replace the present mechanical and artificial credit system.

The fact must be admitted, however distasteful it may seem, that capacity for intellectual development is an inherited capacity that education can realize but not extend, and that in this capacity, as in other inherited traits, men strikingly differ. Acknowledging this fact,

---

[18] Butler, Kandel, and Learned unqualifiedly reject the faculty psychology. Hutchins and Foerster hold to a theory of formal discipline that is much like that formerly held by the faculty psychologists, but there is no evidence that they themselves accept the faculty psychology. It is possible, of course, to be a formal disciplinarian without being a faculty psychologist, viz., Plato.

educational agencies will face the problem of planning education in terms of the individual. It will then be realized that an attitude of equalitarianism in education is a futile attitude, and that it can result only in injustice to all. Justice to the individual as well as to the larger society demands that each individual be assisted to develop to the limit of his ability. Opportunity shall then be provided for the ablest to go farthest, though each person must in some degree learn to live the Good Life. Psychology can then turn to the problem of inventing suitable ways and means of facilitating the development of all. It is to be recognized that, in its essence, intelligence involves abstraction and the use of abstraction. On this basis, there must be devised suitable differentiation—not differentiation that leads away from common goals into specialism, but differentiation that enables each in his own way to attain the common Good Life.

SOCIAL EVOLUTIONISM

I

The continuous, progressive evolution of the human race toward higher levels of living is consistent with the process of nature itself. All life is in process of organic evolution. The human race, however, evolves also in another way. In the human race, transmission of those traits that are instrumental in achieving a higher type of adjustment is effected not only organically, through a process of biological heredity, but also through social heredity.[19] The learnings that the race has acquired in the course of its experience are transmitted by social processes. Human progress toward high civilization, indeed, owes more to the continuous accumulation and refinement of learnings transmitted by social heredity than to the refinement and development of traits and powers by the natural biological process. Man uses the learnings out of experience thus acquired, basing upon them his subsequent adjustive behavior. To them he owes his present actual high status in nature and his comparative success in making adjustment.

A racial learning may be defined as either a discovery that has in the

[19] "Social heredity" is a term in common use by Social Evolutionists. *Vide* W. C. Bagley, *The Educative Process*, p. 18. 1905.

past given some new insight into the meaning of human adjustment, or an invented technique through which a certain established end is more easily attained. Racial learnings take the form of ideals, attitudes, knowledges, intellectual and mechanical tools and techniques, individual and social practices. Progress implies, of course, that there is a continuity of such learnings. Human ends are not all of them set; man is constantly moving toward new ends that he himself conceives. Such new ends emerge as new learnings. In the process of realizing new ends, either old techniques are worked over, refined, perfected, or new techniques are invented. These are also new learnings. Thus human life may be seen as a continuum of learning during which learnings previously acquired are used, or are modified and used, or new learnings altogether are attained. As man moves from lower to higher levels of living there is a constant sifting of learnings in search of those that are needed and pertinent. It is obvious that the particular learnings that serve a human being in his adjustment are relative to the level of living on which he tries to make that adjustment. Highly refined learnings of an esthetic-appreciational character would be of no service to the savage in a primitive environment; an eye-for-an-eye kind of morality would not serve as an appropriate learning in civilized society. The Good Life is not absolute; it must be defined in terms of a particular environment at a particular stage in human evolution.

The concept of human development implies a progress from the condition in which a human being is at birth to the point where he can make successful adjustment in his environment. The goal of development is to enable the individual to lead the Good Life as that can be conceived in his environment in the light of the progress that the race has already made. This means that, except in a perfectly primitive environment, development is not synonymous with natural growth. A child born into a complex, highly advanced environment will never, by means of his natural growth alone, learn successfully to adjust in that environment; there is nothing in the blood stream or anywhere else in the human organism that will by itself raise the child to the level of living that his culture has achieved after generations of building on learnings slowly extracted out of experience. Civilization is not transmitted biologically. With regard to natural potentialities, a child born into the world at the present time is not very different from the child born to primitive man of long ago—in fact, in terms of physical potentialities, he is probably not as good. Were he capable of surviving at all under the rigors of a primitive environment, the level of living that he would naturally reach would not be very much higher than that of the primitive child. The modern child, however, is not born into a primitive environment but into a highly advanced culture. He has a long way to go before he can begin to adjust successfully within that culture upon its existing level, even farther to go if he would raise the existing level to a higher one. Development, in this case, obviously cannot be fully served merely by natural growth.

Fortunately the human being is an organism endowed with marvelous adaptive capacity. The behavior of man is not determined for him by heredity; experience (that is, the learnings out of experience) fashions human behavior. Man is possessed of a nervous system that gives him high adaptive capacity. By heredity, it must be said, he is also endowed with certain general proclivities. But it is the learnings that he gains out of experience that truly decide the character of his adjustive behavior. Left to himself, he probably would soon learn the adaptations that would enable him to live on a low level of adjustment. But placed under guidance and given concentrated, systematic *instruction* in the racial learnings, he can in a relatively short time become the kind of person who can successfully make adjustment within his own advanced environment, and in time remake that environment in accordance with ends that he himself conceives. His remarkably flexible and impressionable organism enables him to receive learnings, assimilate them, and return them in the form of adaptations that are appropriate to his own environment. What learnings he must assimilate, how long a period the instructional process requires, depend of course upon the nature of the environment or the culture in which the adjustment is to be made. What must be emphasized is that, almost literally, a person can learn how to live; he can become something that at birth he showed no signs of being. Accurately it may be said, "Within the human cerebrum a new world is created."[20] The manner and qualities that his behavior assumes are those that are judged best to fit him to live within his environment. Since the environment in

[20] C. H. Judd, *Psychology of Social Institutions*, p. 12. 1926. Quoted with permission of The Macmillan Company, publishers.

which man has now for a long time lived is a social environment, and since human adjustment is within and through society, the manner and qualities that individual behavior assumes are such as have been judged to be entirely compatible with societal ends and societal methods. "The individual becomes an embodiment of social tendencies. The individual nervous system is in this way taken over by society, and the modes of behavior exhibited by the individual become those which are determined by society's needs and modes of operations quite as much as by natural personal traits. . . . There are no phrases too strong for a description of the transformation that society makes in the human individual." [21]

Sufficient has been said to convey that satisfactory human development is not possible merely by "natural growth." A human being does not develop in the same way that a vegetable grows. Proper development involves the most fundamental kind of transformation in what might be called original tendencies of human beings. It involves much more: in a positive way, it involves the production of a finished article out of raw material. In the process of development something is created—a personality, a mind. During this development, an individual takes on a set of conduct dynamics: impulse, passion, desire for physical satisfaction, fear of pain—the dynamics of conduct that characterize man "in the state of nature" or man acting in accordance with original tendencies—make way for action that is controlled by reasoned ends and ethically desirable motives. He also acquires a new set of responses to situations, new methods of doing things, new tools with which to achieve desired ends. He becomes the kind of person who can successfully adapt himself in his social environment. With respect to method, the concept of development implies controlled, purposeful, effortful assimilation of learnings, rather than the easy, un-selfconscious, and uncontrolled process inherent in natural growth.

The ability that serves man in his adjustment and that basically accounts for his supremacy in the animal world is the ability to make the changes that are required for the continuance of life, and progressively to make more of the changes that produce for him the kind of life that he wants. In this respect man is immeasurably the superior of all other living things; it is this that puts man into a class of his own.

[21] *Ibid.*, p. 328.

The ability to make adaptations (it is necessary to bear in mind that ends of living are adaptations also) is essentially what is implied by the term "mind." Of all living things man is by nature endowed with the most highly organized and complex nervous structure. This nervous structure makes *possible* a high degree of adaptability—makes it possible but not necessarily inevitable, nor does it determine the degree of adaptability that a person can ultimately attain. Some degree of adaptability is of course inherent in the nervous organism of the human being, in the makeup that he inherits; only some experience is required for that adaptability to reveal itself. A greater degree of adaptability is achieved as a result of the learnings accumulated in the course of natural living; even among savages, the adult or the older man is normally more adaptable than the immature individual. Most of all, adaptability can be achieved through the *systematic* acquisition of racial learnings; one becomes most adaptable by assimilating and utilizing as his own the adaptations that have previously been made, in corresponding circumstances, by other human beings. Such adaptations are the use of language, the use of tools, the use of number, living in societal organization and using social processes and institutions, the ability to interpret phenomena of nature in their relation to human life, and the like. Equipped with these learnings, the civilized person is infinitely more adaptable than the mature and most experienced savage. It is not, however, that the civilized person in his nervous system possesses potentially a significantly greater adaptive capacity, or that he is more adaptable to begin with; he achieves very much greater adaptability through the learnings that he acquires.

What generally seems difficult to comprehend is that adaptability is a function of learning. Adaptability is in the first place made possible by the highly developed human nervous organization; animals lower in the scale cannot achieve anything like a comparable degree of adaptability regardless of the training that they get. The human nervous organization enables man to assimilate learnings out of experience, and to change as the learnings seem to direct. Some degree of adaptability, therefore, is immediately obtainable out of natural living. But the fullest degree of adaptability is obtainable only as the joint product of heredity and environment, with environment as much the greater factor of the two. Mind, defined in terms of making adapta-

tions to environment, is an extensible product.[22] It goes without saying that mind cannot be treated as a luxury possession that can be
given to some and withheld from others.

It becomes pertinent now to apply the concept of adaptability to a
statement of the objectives of human development. It is common to
hear intelligence defined as native or inherited capacity for adaptive
behavior, and personality as the sum total of the traits that reflect a person's innate potentialities. Both definitions are ill-advised. Of what
relative importance is it to know the capacity for adaptive behavior
that a person inherits and inherently possesses? In the course of his
life-process he never relies upon this alone. It is of the greatest importance to know the capacity for adaptive behavior (the adaptability)
that he attains. Mind is achieved in the course of the adjustment
process; it should be defined with reference to that process. It may be
a matter of satisfying a laudable curiosity to know what degree of
potential adaptability is inherent in the nervous system that one inherits; but it is a vital necessity for an individual to be assured at least
the minimum of adaptability that is adequate for successful adjustment
in a particular environment. Such adaptability can never casually result from heredity alone, or even from heredity plus a natural experience process; such adaptability must be purposefully, effortfully
achieved through the systematic assimilation of racial learnings. A
child born into the world possesses no language, he cannot use tools,
he does not comprehend society and its function, he does not know
the meaning of things. These are factors in adaptability. Without
them, the child's capacity for adaptation is limited; unless he acquires
these learnings, it remains limited. It is therefore much more to the
point to define intelligence functionally in terms of inheritance *and*
learnings. "The term general intelligence should provisionally be
accepted as connoting the most important function of mind, namely,
the ability to control behavior in the light of experience. . . . General
intelligence is determined in part by physical heredity and in part by
environment. Probably the most important environmental pressures
are those represented by systematic schooling. The contribution of
systematic schooling to general intelligence is probably equal to the
combined contributions of native endowment and the informal pres-

[22] Contrast with Humanism; *vide* p. 134.

sures of the average social environment."[23] And again: "This capacity for adapting means to ends is obviously what we mean by the term intelligence; hence effective intelligence may be regarded as the product of a disciplinary process, as I have defined such a process."[24]

It cannot be denied that individuals differ with respect to the immediate adaptive capacity that their biological inheritance makes possible. Were this gift of biological inheritance the more important factor in the ultimate development of adaptability, individuals would naturally go on to achieve widely varying degrees of success in adjustment. Ultimately there would be a regression to the rule that is characteristic of sub-human life—the survival of the fittest (that is, those who are rendered most fit by the accident of biological heredity). Human organization, however, is in part for the purpose of revising and improving this law of nature so that survival is possible for all. Systematic learning can operate greatly to overcome the handicap of inferior biological heredity. If adaptability is a joint product of heredity and learning, a compensatingly greater emphasis upon learning can overcome the drawback of inferior heredity. Irrespective of individual differences at birth, all can be helped to acquire the high degree of adaptability necessary for successful adjustment. In the course of development, therefore, people do move closer together toward a common high degree of adaptability. "While the slow learner may never catch up with the bright learner, he does in many cases tend to approach him."[25] The effect of initial difference can never be completely overcome, and perhaps should not be; there is need for the genius who towers above the others and shows the way toward higher orders of living. But a high degree of effective intelligence can and should be developed in every individual, regardless of heredity.

The same general attitude must prevail in thinking concerning the nature of personality. An individual inherits tendencies to behavior, and were he not subject to training, these tendencies might color and

---

[23] W. C. Bagley, *Determinism in Education*, pp. 157–158 (Quotation abridged). 1925.

[24] W. C. Bagley, *Education, Crime and Social Progress*, pp. 107–108. 1931 (Quoted with permission of The Macmillan Company, publishers). Both Morrison and Judd support this thesis. (Morrison, *Basic Principles of Education*, p. 106. 1934; Judd, *Psychology of Secondary Education*, pp. 484–485. 1927.)

[25] W. C. Bagley, *Education and Emergent Man*, p. 114. 1934.

ultimately dominate personality. But tendencies may be either intensified or modified or completely overcome by learning. In the process of development, certain tendencies of the individual are deliberately weakened, some of them are deliberately intensified, new tendencies are deliberately fostered. It is unnecessary and undesirable to think deterministically of human personality as being dictated by inherited tendencies. It is much better to think of it as "the sum total of what an individual has come to be by learning the cultural products of social evolution." [26] Regardless of the inherited tendencies of an individual, he can by assimilation of social learnings develop those traits of personality that would establish him as a desirable and effective person within the medium of the social environment. As in the case of adaptability, the development of personality tends to bring people closer together rather than to carry them farther apart. The traits that are most desirable and most effective in adjustment within a common social medium are common traits.

The objectives at which the process of human development aims are adaptability and social personality. Actually socialness and adaptability are closely related; in a social environment, no one is truly adaptable unless he is also at the same time social in every important respect. The objectives complement each other in cooperating toward successful adjustment. They are both developed in the course of the same learning process. Possessing a high degree of adaptability and strong social personality, an individual is fitted as well as he can be to make increasingly successful adjustment in his environment. Both objectives are in their specific meaning a function of the environment in which they are to operate and of the conception of human adjustment in which they are to serve; the more highly advanced the ends of human living, the more complex the environment, the greater the degree of adaptability and of social personality required.

Adaptability consists of the capacity accurately to visualize life-needs in a continuous, progressive manner and to make the responses necessary in every case to satisfy the life-needs. Inherent in the concept of adaptabilty is the ability to modify and control behavior in the light of past experience, to conceive and to realize ends remote in time, to devise means effective in the accomplishment of desired purposes, to

[26] H. C. Morrison, *Basic Principles of Education*, p. 39. 1934.

make needed changes in self and in the environment, to see things in their right relationship and according to their true value. Adaptability is the greatest value operative in adjustment. Human history has been one of the continuous growth of adaptability, and one, therefore, of progressively greater success in living. It is the function of the developmental process guided by social agencies (that is, education) to make of every individual as highly adaptable a person as the particular environment requires. Adaptability, of course, cannot be guaranteed; it operates in a future that cannot be prescribed by formula. Strictly speaking, a person cannot be rendered adaptable in advance. Adaptability, however, can be and must be induced by learnings; those adaptive techniques must be communicated to the individual through which it *becomes possible* for him to adjust himself to the situations that may arise. It is conceivable that even with these adaptive techniques in his possession, the individual may not successfully adjust himself to every situation in the future; but without them, successful adjustment is altogether impossible. The adaptive techniques or learnings that make for adaptability are language (or the means of human inter-communication as well as of symbolic thinking); number (or the method of viewing and knowing the world in its quantitative aspects); understandings of the nature of society, the role that it plays in human adjustment, and the manner in which it carries on its social processes; conduct controls or motivations that make easier the realization of the ends of living within a social environment; understandings of the meaning of things in nature, including the meaning of human life; the use of tools and machines; the use of methods of thought by which man has attained his present level of living and by which he may go farther. Possessing these learnings the individual is equipped to adjust himself successfully to his environment; giving him these learnings is the closest that society can come toward rendering him adaptable.

Social personality is exhibited in the ideals, attitudes, traits, habits of behavior that set off an individual as a desirable, cooperative member of society. Implicit in social personality are a high degree of self-control, unselfishness and concern for others, willingness, when occasion requires, to subordinate personal to social needs, personal response to ethical rather than "natural" conduct motivations, the habit of acting from reasoned judgment rather than on impulse. In a social environment, proper social conduct (interpreted in a positive as well as in a negative way) is an indispensable condition of successful adaptive behavior. The same developmental process that aims at adaptability must aim also at social personality. In the nature of things, social personality can be more strictly controlled than can adaptability. It is possible by training to help a person acquire the learnings that make him a social person. The discipline process must, however, give way to continuous self-discipline if the end of social personality is to be attained. There is no need to fear that the disciplining process will interfere with the attainment of that resourcefulness which marks the adaptable person. In the cooperative adjustment that characterizes human living, individual resourcefulness is most truly effective when it is paired with social consciousness and social concern.

Adaptability and social personality can be achieved most effectively and in the shortest time through systematic training. Systematic training implies selection, concentration, and organization of learnings; it implies instruction. In training for adaptability and social personality, formal instruction plays a more important role than natural learning through experience. For several reasons the method of natural experience alone is not adequate for the purpose of bringing about human development. In the first place the learnings most needed (for adaptable and social personality) may not be available in the environment in such form as to be properly assimilated through a process of natural experience. It often happens that needed learnings are not operative in a particular environment; or needed learnings may be present and operative but they may not be easily recognizable by the immature individual. The method of natural experience, therefore, exposes one to the hazard of missing learnings necessary for successful adjustment. Secondly, the process of natural learning through experience is a slow and uneconomical process. The individual has far to go in order to come abreast of the progress of the race. However long the developmental period, it would not be long enough under this method to enable him to encounter and take possession of all the learnings. Concentration of learnings is required, and organization for effective assimilation. Systematic instruction therefore carries the brunt of responsibility for development. The period most appropriate for such instruction is the period of human infancy (that is, the period prior to the attainment of physical adulthood). For this period, special agencies and processes must be devised that will, in the most effective manner possible, instill those learnings so that adaptable and social personality may be realized.

From what sources are the necessary learnings obtainable, and in what forms are they available? In the first place, the supreme agency that makes possible the preservation and transmission of learnings is society. In the processes of society, taken in its entirety, the learnings are embodied; in its records, they are preserved. The only means of access to the great racial learnings is through society, and that a full complement of learnings may be obtained, society must be considered in its total, aggregate form, in the past as well as in the present. It is true that most of the essential learnings are inevitably transmitted from particular society to particular society and, at any one time, are to be found embodied in the daily life-sustaining activities of any civilized culture—in its mores, in its institutions, in its economic processes, in its religious beliefs and practices, in its intellectual and artistic expression.

But never should it be taken for granted that the learnings embodied in a particular society are (1) all proper learnings, (2) all the learnings that there need to be. Particular societies of past and present have been much too casual, much too thoughtless, at best much too empirical, in the manner in which they themselves have accepted, used, and, in turn, transmitted what in reality are the precious and life-ensuring learnings. History shows that some civilizations in the past thoroughly disregarded important racial learnings until eventually they (the civilizations) disappeared, and a glance at the present shows that particular societies are still being reckless in their disregard of the lessons of past experience. Many factors are involved in the application of all the proper learnings of past experience to the events of present living, and something may easily go wrong. Human beings are naturally reluctant to surrender what seem to them to be easier and pleasanter modes of living for what may seem to be more arduous ones; or certain individuals with sufficient authority may find it to their interest to perpetuate wrong or pseudo-learnings and to bar the transmission of true learnings; or a society may be misled as to the identification of the proper learnings; or the means of transmission may be faulty, and proper and sufficient learnings may not have been communicated to a sufficient number of individuals of the rising generation. In any event, no particular society at any time exemplifies in its collective conduct all the important learnings out of the past experience. It is true, of course, that the very existence of a society on a high level of culture is testimony of the fact that it *does* to some extent carry on its adjustment processes in accordance with most of the essential lessons of experience (else it could not survive or at least maintain itself on its high level). It is necessary therefore to make careful analysis of society and, by reference to the past, determine which of its processes may and which may not serve as examples and instruments in the systematic training of its young people.

A much more reliable medium of racial learnings are the school studies which in their present form have gradually evolved out of the past. Into these has gone much more considered and disinterested thought. Societies perished not so much because they did not possess within their school studies the proper learnings but more because the learnings were not made available to every individual, or, for one reason or another, were not heeded. The school studies represent an attempt to assemble in an empirical but systematic way the adaptations that are considered to have been effective in adjustment, and to integrate them in a manner that will make easier their assimilation. The learnings present in the school studies are often stripped of their bodily contexts and offered as highly condensed, generalized ideas. Their organization is coherent and logical and graded. On the whole, they represent a highly concentrated, economical, and valuable medium of learnings. Their use is essential in the systematic training of individuals. On the other hand, it must be admitted that while human living, the environment, and the adjustment process change, the school studies have a tendency to change much more slowly, and they often retain learnings after the need for them has gone;[27] that, since school studies—once launched—tend to evolve in an empirical way, they do not contain all the learnings they should contain and would contain, were they scientifically analyzed and reconstructed; and that school studies are more often organized from the point of view of those who have discovered the learnings than from the point of view of those who have to assimilate them. The last is possibly the most serious charge

[27] Judd is more emphatic in making this point than Morrison and Bagley.

that can be brought against the present school studies. Science—the science of society and the science of psychology—affords, however, a means of (1) analyzing society with a view to discovering systematically the important learnings and incorporating them into the school studies, (2) reorganizing the school subjects from the point of view of the psychological needs of the learner.

It remains to consider the precise nature of the developmental process in the individual human being, and, with respect to this, Social Evolutionism contains two somewhat different views. According to Morrison,[28] development is through a process of continuous assimilation of unitary learnings, arranged in serial fashion. The acquisition of a learning is always expressed as some accretion or some change in personality—a new attitude is formed or a new ability is acquired. Through a succession of such specific accretions or changes, a social, adaptable personality is built up. A learning, though it is a single characteristic, is general in its effect. "They (the learnings) are not acquired adaptive responses, but every true learning makes possible innumerable adaptive responses, as experience of life varies." [29] Having acquired a learning, a human being is to that extent more adaptable, to that extent more social. All true learnings contribute to the formation of character (to the volitional and moral and esthetic aspects of personality) as well as to the attainment of intellectual adaptability. The developmental process consists in thus acquiring bit by bit an adaptable social personality. The learnings are not merely acquisitions which the individual accumulates and stores away; they enter into the fabric of personality, become integrated, become part of the living structure of the individual. As a result of proper training, the individual becomes a kind of person "who will sense or feel what is the right thing to do and possess the specific ability required for its execution." [30]

A learning is a product, an effect on personality. Learnings are obtainable through appropriate subject-matter and learning activities. The subject-matter and the learning activities are not in themselves the

[28] H. C. Morrison, *Basic Principles of Education,* Chaps. VI–VIII. 1934.
[29] *Ibid.,* p. 240.
[30] H. C. Morrison, *The Practice of Teaching in the Secondary School,* p. 20. Revised edition. 1931.

learnings; they are the means through which the learnings are conveyed and assimilated. Corresponding to each learning or group of learnings, there is an appropriate unit of subject-matter, assimilation of which will produce the desired learning or learnings.

The theory of Judd and Bagley [31] adheres a little more closely to the "emergent" interpretation of the nature of mind. Mind develops in the course of training, through acquisition of learnings. The higher mental processes are, however, qualitatively different from the lower. While mental activity on the lower levels may be characterized by automatic, single responses to fixed situations, mental activity on higher levels is characterized by continuous conceptualization, by the organization and retention of complex patterns of ideas, and by the use of these patterns in a way that makes possible a wide transferability of learnings. On higher mental levels transfer of training is the rule, not the exception. The higher mental activity is realizable only in man, and the capacity for it ultimately resides in the complex nervous structure that man possesses. "In this cerebrum there are possibilities of organizing neural processes in ways utterly impossible in the meager cerebrums of all animals below man. The human cerebrum is quite different in structure and function from the lower parts of the nervous system. To think of the organized processes in the cerebrum as though they were like the processes which take place in the lower parts of the nervous system where reflex arcs explain all that occurs, is to ignore all the teachings of modern neurological research." [32] Adaptability is a general function of the cultivation of the higher mental processes; it results from the acquisition of large systems of ideas, from the ability to generalize, from the ability to relate ideas properly, to analyze situations in terms of the ideas inherent within them, to make successful transfer. The learnings, of course, do enter into and make over human personality, but they are available also as a kind of large reserve content, ever at the beck and call of the individual to serve him when the occasion requires. The higher learnings do not function automatically or semi-automatically; their release involves a great deal

---

[31] C. H. Judd, *Education as Cultivation of the Higher Mental Processes*, 1936; W. C. Bagley, *Education and Emergent Man*, 1934.

[32] Judd, *op. cit.*, pp. 157–158. Quoted with permission of The Macmillan Company, publishers.

of conscious selection and discrimination. The matter of motivating the individual to make effective release may be left to the natural compulsions of the adjustment process, or may be facilitated through the inculcation of strong ideals [33] that will impel a person to try to do the right thing.

It follows, therefore, that adaptability (and socialness which is implicit within it) is not obtainable merely through the acquisition of a large number of unit learnings. "The psychology of the higher mental processes teaches that the end and goal of all education is the development of systems of ideas which can be carried over from the situation in which they are acquired to other situations. Systems of general ideas illuminate and clarify human experiences by raising them to the level of abstract, generalized, conceptual understanding." [34] On higher developmental levels there must be emphasis on the organization of ideas, and on methods of dealing with broad systems of ideas so as to obtain desired results in specific situations. The training process must be carefully graded; on higher levels both content and learning activity must be qualitatively different from those on lower levels. Systematization does not take place automatically; it must be taught. Progressively in the training process it must obtain greater emphasis.

II

In general, the psychology that is at present exercising the dominant influence in American education is based upon a faulty conception of the nature of man, of the nature of mind, of the meaning therefore of human development. Man is viewed not as an emergent but as a being who, in conduct dynamics and mode of operation, is continuous with the animal world, though superior to it. Mind is viewed not as an emergent function, itself developing in course of the adjustment process, but in a deterministic and mechanistic manner, as a kind of inborn capacity to establish fixed connections between stimuli and responses. Nature and natural tendencies play roles of exaggerated

---

[33] W. C. Bagley, *The Educative Process*, pp. 207 ff. 1905. Judd believes that transfer of training can take place irrespective of the formation of ideals.

[34] Judd, *op. cit.*, p. 201. Quoted with permission of The Macmillan Company, publishers.

importance; development itself is not regarded as the *building* of personality as much as the *liberation* of personality. Psychology is in general overnaturalistic, oversimplified, mechanistic. Allied with this psychology there is a soft pedagogy that defends and rationalizes, in educational value-terms, the weaknesses that the psychology presents. The most serious trouble confronting American education today is the weakness of its underlying psychology.

One of the important achievements of American education and of American culture in general has been the development of an educational science, embracing both the social and the psychological aspects of education. Nothing could be more laudable than the attempt to introduce into the study of man the precise and systematic methods of science.[35] Already the introduction of the scientific spirit and method into education has produced important results.[36] But on the whole the science of education (especially in its psychological aspect) has been guilty of the same kind of thinking that has overtaken psychology as a whole. It has tended to be deterministic, and to promote injurious deterministic doctrines. It has been guilty of overnaturalizing the conception of man: on the basis of studies of animals and young children, it has proceeded to make generalizations purporting to explain adult conduct. It has invented an apparatus of stimulus-and-response, and proceeded to explain complicated human behavior in exceedingly simplified terms. It has been instrumental in spreading unsound notions of the nature of mind, and on the basis of questionable data and dubious conclusions it has tended to break down popular belief in the validity of transfer. Altogether it must be said that science has actually not given the great service of which it is capable, although it has made some contribution.

As a consequence of the basic mistakes that psychology has made, there are current conceptions of worthy human conduct that are more appropriate for man in a primitive state of nature or for an immature and untutored child than for civilized men and women. Human conduct is explained and rationalized in terms of pleasure-pain motivations: we act in one way or another because we are impelled to do so by fear of pain, by desire for pleasure, by expectancy of reward, by dislike

[35] *Vide* p. 76, footnote.
[36] For example, in the teaching of reading.

of annoyance. Discipline in human conduct is decried as unnatural. It is forgotten that the capacity for self-discipline is the capacity that has served man most outstandingly in his long climb to the top. There is little use in studying animal behavior or child behavior in order to find the controls that should actuate highly developed adult human behavior. They are not there. The truly ideal qualities of human behavior must be acquired. And their identity is discoverable through a study of the race's history and a comparison of those civilizations that attained high eminence with those that never did.

It is but a step from a psychology that thus overnaturalizes man to a "progressive" psychology that glorifies the "interests," the "felt needs," the "self-expression" of children. In recent years such a psychology did develop. It has served to carry to an extreme some of the weaknesses present in the principal prevailing psychology. It has further confused the concept of human development, setting up the "interests" of children as guides to be followed. It has intensified the already existent individualism, the distaste for anything that requires discipline and sustained effort, and the lack of respect for propriety and law and order. It has fostered an interpretation of freedom not as a necessary *end* of education, not as an achievement that comes with self-disciplined, socialized, adaptable personality, but as a kind of "divine right" with which every child is endowed. In a time of fundamental transition it is particularly important to retain the qualities that make for social cooperation, for individual strength and endurance, for self-discipline. The psychologies influential in education have not been such as to encourage the emergence of these traits in young people whose training they have affected.

Basic in any educational plan is the conception of mind which it holds. As has been stated, the conception of mind by which current psychology is guided is oversimplified and in many respects unsound. With the (unjustified) rejection of the transfer theory there apparently has also been a rejection of the idea that there are *higher* and *complex* mental processes, not only quantitatively but qualitatively different from the lower. We have reduced our thinking about thinking to the lowest terms—to reflexes, instincts, S—R bonds, and the like. We have forgotten one very important thing—that mind develops in an emergent manner. It progresses not in a regular, continuous, mechanical way, but by a series of uneven, discontinuous steps, each step characterized by activity of a qualitatively different kind. "The view that all mental activities can be explained in terms of elements which are of the simplest and most primitive type overlooks altogether the principle that organic compounds always exhibit qualities different from the qualities of elements that are synthesized in these compounds. Protoplasm as living tissue has qualities which the elements comprising it do not possess. It is the fact of organization which accounts for life. . . ." [37] Using nature as the ideal and operating thus in mechanistic terms, we have constructed laws of learning that professedly describe human action. The laws of learning "are rather hypotheses based very largely upon neurological speculation—hypotheses which are fairly, though not entirely, satisfactory explanations of the conditions under which learning takes place on a very primitive plane— namely, the plane of specific habits and specific meanings. They are entirely inadequate as explanations of or guides to the higher type of learnings, including the mental functions that we recognize under such terms as deliberation, judgment, choice." [38] Yet their validity has been widely accepted.

The net result is that we are without much knowledge of the workings of mind on its higher levels, and since our values are pitched on low levels, we do not seem to be aware of what we are missing. It need hardly be said that our education is not often successful in instilling in its individuals the highest racial learnings either of a volitional or of an intellectual kind. On a high level of living, human beings are motivated in their conduct by high ideals and carry on their thinking in terms of large, well-organized ideas. That every human being may reach a high level of living systematic training is necessary; but it is hardly possible for training successfully to realize this purpose if it refuses to recognize either high ideals or important organizations of ideas.

Along with a simplified conception of mind have developed unsound and dangerous notions concerning the significance of individual dif-

[37] Judd, *op. cit.*, p. 154. This particular criticism is more reflective of Judd and Bagley than it is of Morrison.

[38] W. C. Bagley, *Education, Crime and Social Progress*, p. 110. 1931. Quoted with permission of The Macmillan Company, publishers.

ferences. Educational science has very creditably attempted to measure general intelligence. The instrument that it has developed has not been equally creditable. The intelligence test is a crude instrument: [39] there is confusion as to what it really does measure, whether innate capacity (which is hardly measurable) or some kind of achievement. At any rate, the intelligence-testing movement tended to give currency to the notion that intelligence ought to be regarded as innate adaptive capacity, realizable but not extensible by training. Out of this has come the pernicious deterministic influence in education. Since individuals possess at birth varying capacities, it seems to follow that throughout life they must maintain their respective differences in the degree of adaptive power that they can attain. Heredity (and, according to some individuals, race) seems to be the chief determinant of ultimate human adaptability. On the basis of inherited capacity, individuals are labeled superior or inferior. The importance of individual differences is exaggerated. Individuals are separated from one another and then are given specialized training, either superior or inferior, according to their capacity. It is forgotten that human beings develop adaptive power as a product of both assimilation of learnings and initial adaptive capacity; that handicaps of heredity can be very largely overcome by greater stress on acquired learnings; that in the course of development, individuals actually do overcome inferior heredity. It is forgotten that the great undertaking of society is to bring all individuals up to a high point of common adjustment, irrespective of their initial endowment; that individual differences, for the most part, affect method and not ends.

All these facts combine to explain why the process of training that is supposed to lead toward social personality and high adaptability has become training in a large assortment of differentiated and petty activities. The great racial learnings that especially at this time should be at a premium no longer figure most prominently in education. And the results are evident in the manner in which we are weakened morally and intellectually in the face of the crisis in which we are currently involved.

[39] Bagley goes much further than this in criticizing the intelligence test. *Vide Determinism in Education*, pp. 11–32. 1925. Judd, on the other hand, is inclined to be more lenient.

III

The psychology that is to underlie the educational process must rid itself of its naïve "naturalistic" [40] bias, and must regain a true understanding of the nature of man and mind and the meaning of human development. It must rid itself of the static conception of man and nature that it now has, and see them as part of an evolutionary world-process. They are both in process of development—nature through organic evolution, man through social evolution much more than through organic. The learnings gained by the race in the course of its development do enter into and change subsequent individual human behavior, and man is continuously and progressively becoming a different being. If at one time, to act out of fear of pain or desire for physical pleasure was "natural" in man, at the present stage of human evolution, to subordinate fear and pleasure as conduct dynamics, to act out of ethical and altruistic motives may be considered equally "natural." Once that fact is recognized, psychology will be able to re-evaluate the entire process of human development—its meaning, its objectives, and its method.

It will be necessary to identify the learnings or adaptations that are of greatest value to man, and to inculcate these as traits in the personality of every individual. Psychology will learn to regard both personality and intelligence as *outcomes* of learning. Those personality traits will be especially cultivated that tend to make a person self-disciplined and social, and they will be cultivated in all individuals regardless of original or "natural" tendencies. Intelligence will be conceived in terms of adaptability, a finished product, and not as a capacity that is as yet innocent of all knowledge and ability. Adaptability will be regarded as capacity emerging out of the mastery of the important knowledges, the techniques, the use of the tools that the racial experience has made available. Intelligence will be seen as something that is indispensable to the survival of every individual, and not something that can be present in some and absent from others. By

---

[40] The term naturalism is here used not in the same sense in which it is used by Humanism (pp. 141 ff.). Social Evolutionists are themselves naturalists. The reference is here to a "naturalism" reminiscent of Rousseau.

every means available, every individual will be assisted in obtaining a high degree of effective intelligence.

When that is done, it will be the task of educational science to analyze out of racial history the important racial learnings, to discover the precise method of human development and the manner in which the mental processes operate on higher levels, and to prepare the learnings for economical and easy assimilation by man. The knowledge of the method of human development and of the operation of intelligence on higher levels will undoubtedly be the most difficult to obtain. But science will be able to obtain this with less difficulty if it does not lose sight of the fact that mind operates as a truly emergent function. Psychology will recognize that the higher mental processes are qualitatively different from the lower; it will not try to study the higher mental processes as if they were nothing but longer and more complex reflex chains, but as processes involving conceptualization, organization, analysis, choice, judgment. After that, psychology will be able to reconstruct some of its notions regarding the transfer of training. It will be recognized that, however transfer of training does take place, it is central in the developmental process. Some of the conceptions that now serve as unsatisfactory substitutes for developmental training will be automatically eliminated.

A sound psychological basis is indispensable to the intelligent guidance of instruction. Laws of learning serve a most important purpose. The present so-called laws of learning must be identified for what they are—only partial descriptions of the conditions under which learning takes place on the lower levels of behavior. Once the true manner of human development is known, laws of learning will be formulated which will be applicable to those intellectual levels where ideals operate as conduct controls and keen judgment rather than mere automatic response is required. Even on the lower levels, a theory of the nervous system more acceptable than the present will have to be evolved.

The method of science introduced into the study of human life promises to be of inestimable service. But the scientific method must cease to be used in deterministic, mechanistic, oversimplified ways. It is of great importance to measure intelligence, but we have not yet created an instrument that can do this except in a very crude way. It is of great importance to ascertain the precise emphasis in content and technique of learning that a particular individual requires, but science has been rather more effective in segregating students and in placing on some of them an unwholesome, undemocratic, and untrue stigma than in helping them through content and method. Science must come to regard individual differences as problems of method rather than of aim: while the effects of initial differences in capacity cannot be entirely obliterated and should not be, education must through diverse methods help to raise all individuals toward a high general level. Such differences in outcome as will prevail among individuals will be differences in special intellectual interests, in aptitudes, in tastes, in total qualitative personality, rather than differences that set off people as inferior or superior, as being much less or much more social and adaptable. The science of education has indeed been of some service already: in the development of achievement tests, in the systematic improvement of instruction (for example, the teaching of reading), the preparation of individual study materials (workbooks, etc.), the systematic study of educational administration, in the development of some sound laboratory techniques. If it can overcome some of the handicaps that modern thinking in psychology has placed upon it, science will be able to cooperate in showing the way to a real understanding of human behavior.

SOCIAL REALISM

I

Competent human living consists in the ability to interpret and to use the objects of experience in a manner to make them serve desired, life-sustaining ends. Ends and means in human living are both outcomes of what man knows or thinks he knows about the world. The problem of living is inextricably tied up with the problem of knowledge. Mankind does not move in a predetermined course, nor is it guided by absolute ends. With growing experience comes greater, more certain, more exact knowledge and more sound and secure belief; on the basis of these man conceives new ends for his living and contrives new means to realize these ends. Generally speaking, the object of human life is to secure and to better itself in nature. To a certain degree nature itself defines these terms: the man who is hungry or ill or cold is not successfully "securing and bettering" his living. But beyond such obvious instances, what constitute security and goodness are themselves definitions growing out of human experience. At different times man has recognized different ends. Most frequently ends are not completely discarded; they are revised or altered and perfected to make them consistent with new knowledge that has been added or new beliefs that have been acquired. Human life thus has continuity, by virtue of the fact that human experience is cumulative and yields a constantly growing core of trustworthy knowledge and belief.

The cruciality of the problem of knowledge is undoubtedly at the basis of human society. The need for society grows out of the need for maintaining life. Society offers a broader basis of experience on which to act than does the individual life, a method of making sounder and more reliable judgment on the basis of experience, and a method of more effectively acting in accordance with judgment to obtain desired ends. Individual experience has become integrated within social experience. The ends and means of human living are not for the most part those of the individual, but those worked out *in community* by human beings. In return for the "security and betterment" of living that society offers, man has consecrated himself to a societal existence. But what has been said before about the general nature of human ends and means holds for society as well as for the individual: societal ends, like individual ends, cannot be evaluated according to any absolute criterion. The greater society's fund of human experience, the greater the wisdom that it has acquired out of experience, the greater its knowledge about the consequences for human living of the events of experience—the generally better are the ends of societal living. When "all the facts have been bagged," it is quite certain that our living will be established on a much sounder basis than it is at present; even then, however, large questions will exist about the rightness and wrongness of things.

No more than an individual, can society "prove" or "guarantee" that it is "right"; unless practical consequences forcefully show otherwise, society assumes that it is "right." Practically it is necessary, therefore, to recognize the existence, along with the general human society, of *particular* societies in which human beings live. A particular society is a (generally large) group of individuals who feel keenly their kinship in experience, who are bound together by more or less common ideals, who cooperate among themselves more than they do with outsiders for the realization of their common ends. Particular societies often differ from each other with respect to the values that they recognize, and it is hard to prove that one society is more "right" than the next; nevertheless, the individual, to live effectively within his society, must become integrated within it, must accept its ideals, and cooperate in its way of living.

Individual development is not in any direction marked out by "fate," nor is it according to any common and fixed and permanent set of values established by man. It is in the direction of acquiring a certain set of ends and means that characterize the particular society into which an individual is born. Possessing these ends and means, the individual is integrated within his society and enabled to carry on, competently and successfully, his life-activities. To a great extent, a person grows in this direction naturally. To maintain life adequately, he must get to know the world in which he finds himself and must understand the experiences that he has; the society around him, in large measure, provides the world "in which he finds himself" and the experiences that he has. The knowledge that he obtains is, in large part, the knowledge that society makes available. The individual, therefore, can hardly keep from taking on "the protective coloration" of his society—from reproducing its particular ways of living. Many of these ways he acquires almost unwittingly, without any conscious expenditure of effort. But this method of growth is not sufficient. The individual must become consciously adjusted to his social environment: he must not only take over the ideals of his society, but he must understand them, personally accept them, become consciously devoted to them; he must not only learn to use the common processes, but learn to use them with maximum effectiveness; he must cultivate the social virtues not incidentally but systematically; and he must discover those ways by which he as an individual is most apt to contribute to the betterment of the common life. True human development is in the direction of becoming a desirable and effective member of one's society—a person who can operate in it as it is, and cooperate with others to improve it. It is for that reason that society has assumed the responsibility of guiding individual development, and has created agencies and prepared activities through which a person may, in a relatively short time, become a desirable and effective citizen.

It follows that the general social process by which an individual is assisted to become a socially-competent person (that is, the process of education) is not necessarily a respecter of "natural tendencies." Its object is to render the individual competent to live in a manner that society regards as good; to realize this it must help the individual to learn to perform effectively those life-activities which together comprise the social conception of the Good Life. Effective performance of these life-activities implies the acquisition of specified ideals, attitudes, knowledges, modes of behavior, and operational techniques. Regardless of personal inclination, each individual must learn all those ways of doing things that society considers desirable and necessary in a good citizen. Regardless of the precise kinds and degree of native ability that he possesses (provided he be a normal[41] person), each individual must be made in his own way competent in the performance of all the life-activities which society deems important.

A definition of human development given thus (1) in pragmatic terms, (2) in terms of adjustment to a particular society, is open to the danger of misinterpretation. For one thing (to consider the latter point first), it may be interpreted to imply that the motivating ideals and the resulting life-activities of any particular society are perfect or, at any rate, beyond criticism, and that adjustment implies complete and unreserved acceptance of them without the possibility of criticism. Such an interpretation would be incorrect. A particular society, it must be evident, is a portion of the whole of humanity. Some experiences, ideals, knowledge, operational techniques, it shares with all mankind. In some respects it is different. A person making adjustment to a particular society is adjusting not merely to a limited group, but to a cross-section of mankind. He acquires ideals, attitudes, and modes of living which are universal as well as those which are special to his society. He learns in what respects his society is like others, in what respects it differs from others, and why. In the process, the

---

[41] For a definition of normal, *vide* p. 181.

characteristic ends and means of his society are evaluated and subjected to criticism. It must be easily evident that no society is ever perfect, that no society ever "stands pat," that each society is constantly revising its aims and improving its methods. Along with its ideals and methods, the individual learns something of the needs and limitations of his particular society. Adjustment does not imply blindness or insensitiveness to existing defects; on the contrary, it implies noting the imperfections, trying to learn their causes, and planning suitable remedies. On the other hand, inherent in the meaning of adjustment is that there be a sympathetic understanding of what society has been trying to do and loyalty to its purposes, a falling-into-step with others, a resolve to cooperate with all other individuals in maintaining society and in improving it, a resolve to abstain from reforms through unsocial shortcuts [42] and until such a time as one has acquired all the facts and skills that make him a competent member of society.

The "goodness" of an individual is measured in terms of his ability to achieve the consequences which, in the judgment of mankind as exemplified by his particular society, have a favorable effect upon his living. Pragmatically that can be the only interpretation of the meaning of mind, namely, the ability to bring about desirable and desired effects in living. Man comes into the world possessing an operating equipment that makes this possible: he can see and take note of the world about him; he can take note of the effect upon him of the impact of things, and can register these effects in his memory; he can compare effects and note resemblances and differences. In terms of their constituent elements and qualities and in terms of their consequences for himself, he can discover meanings. He can thus identify and catalogue the objects of the world insofar as they impress him. Beginning with mass perceptual data, he can emerge with a good deal of tried and systematized conceptual knowledge, and with a good many sound beliefs as to desirable courses of action. His knowledge and his beliefs strongly influence his course of action: in order to achieve consequences known or believed to be desirable, he takes this course of action, devises these techniques, forms these habits. Knowing the world is the starting point for intelligent living in it. But knowing the world is not in itself intelligent living. In the final analysis, the

[42] *Vide* Chapter I, pp. 95 ff.

efficacy of mind lies in the *achievement of desirable and desired consequences*. It does not lie only in perception, it does not lie only in conceptualization, it does not lie only in making judgments. All these are part of the whole—very necessary preliminaries, it is true, but preliminaries. They are the means of which pragmatically effective life-behavior is the end. Perceptions and conceptions and judgments that have no influence on human action may have some value of their own for academic purposes, but their vital significance is nothing.

In human experience it is not unusual to confuse the means with the ends, the part with the whole. The object of the help that society gives the individual in development is to enable him to become pragmatically effective in doing all those things that in the common judgment of society contribute to desirable living. Of course, the developmental process is not a simple one: it requires long natural maturation; it involves physical, emotional, moral, intellectual training; it involves the acquisition of knowledge; etc. But all these are means contributing toward an end. The object of development is not complete with physical training or with emotional training or with the acquirement of methods of reasoning. All these must culminate in the right kind of behavior, in the effective performance of desirable and desired life-activities, if the developmental process is to be adjudged a success. In the past, we have often appraised adjustment in terms of adequacy of preparation for it, and mind not in terms of pragmatically effective behavior but in terms of accessory equipment. Just as success in crossing a street safely cannot be judged in terms of the keenness of sight of the pedestrian, his acuteness of hearing, and nimbleness of movement, so effective living cannot be judged in terms of a fund of ideas and methods of thinking that a person may possess. The educational process must culminate in the manifestation of the actual behaviors that society regards as constituting effective living.

Effective living in a complex environment calls for a by-no-means simple or brief training process. It would be very desirable to avail one's self of shortcuts, of indirect means that would insure satisfactory human development, of general methods by which the specific life-activities comprising human existence could be competently performed. A very long time ago people began to speculate about this problem and to fashion theories of human development. One of the results, until lately very influential, was the theory of formal discipline, usually allied with a special picturization of human behavior based upon a concept of mental faculties. By indirect training with certain formal (or formative) materials, each of the faculties could be developed in a general way. The effects of general training would be carried over into the very many different situations that go to make up the life-experience, and would render a person equally capable in the performance of all of them. In the same way, by a kind of general character-hardening process—by a process of overcoming obstacles to the point where character was "formed"—one could become equipped with the specific conduct-attitudes and habits necessary for proper living. The theory was attractive because of its neatness and the simplicity to which it reduced the training process. It did, however, place somewhat of a strain upon human credulity, and when carried to extremes it offended common sense. Science ultimately sided with common sense and succeeded in discrediting the faculty psychology as well as the general notion of moral training by the hurdle method. Transfer of training was shown to take place only under certain conditions and in limited degree.

"Although psychologists are not yet entirely agreed on what the mind is or on how it learns, retains, and applies its knowledge, they are unanimous in rejecting the simple and attractive notion that the mind as a whole can be so trained that it will be effective in all later challenges of whatever kind. They wholly reject the notion of an automatic and inevitable transfer of training in one field to any and all others." [48] Deprived of this attractive and fallacious theory, we are forced to restrict ourselves to what science and experience have made available to us in the way of a method of helping each individual to become a socially-effective person. Science and experience have both furnished us with a great deal of information about the nature of man as a behaving organism, but neither has as yet furnished us with reliable shortcuts in the way of general methods that would insure proper human action in a wide variety of situations. Eventually science may, but pending this it is necessary more than ever to concentrate on desired *ends* of development. Each person must learn to do com-

[48] T. H. Briggs, *Secondary Education*, p. 134. 1933. Quoted with permission of The Macmillan Company, publishers.

petently certain things which his society considers of major importance in living. In the absence of reliable general methods it is necessary
to focus on these actual activities, and to give individuals practice
in properly performing them. "It is sound psychology to assume
that one best learns to do something by doing it under skilled direction."[44] The process of training for social competence must go by
no devious routes but must aim straight at its objectives.

In the course of this process, however, the positive contributions that
both science and experience have made toward an understanding of human nature and development must not be slighted. Although the facts
that have been gathered so far do not add up to any such complete
and easy psychological system as that which science recently helped
to discredit, they do reveal a great deal about the nature of man and
the conditions under which (therefore the methods by which) human
development takes place. With competence in the performance of
the societal life-activities as the aim, it is possible to formulate certain
psychological principles with the help of which adequate educational
methods may be worked out.

In the first place, experience makes abundantly clear (and the facts
of science do tend to confirm) that man is essentially a behaving
rather than a thinking being. The impulse to action is inherent in
the impulse of life itself. Man is propelled by inner dynamics to
adjustment-seeking behavior. Reflection, thinking, is a medial process:
it is not so much the motor that drives the machine as the searchlight
that illuminates the way. Instinct, desire, emotion are the primary
factors in human conduct. Emotion is far more potent in influencing
behavior than reason: it not only exerts a stronger pull but it influences
reason itself. Emotionalized attitudes "condition the reception, the
interpretation, and the retention of ideas, thus being to a large extent
determiners of thinking; they integrate an individual with others; and
more than anything else they stimulate to action."[45] The effect of
emotional stimulation is stronger and retained far longer than the
effect of the intellectual. These statements may not harmonize with

[44] T. H. Briggs, "Indoctrination in Education," *Educational Forum*, 1:139,
January, 1937.

[45] T. H. Briggs, *Secondary Education*, p. 380. 1933. Quoted with permission
of The Macmillan Company, publishers.

the idealized picture of man sometimes painted by the philosophers, but they are borne out by the facts of experience. Thought is instrumental in purpose and medial in position; it is not normally an end in itself. The social process aiming to help the individual become competent in the performance of his life-activities in society cannot afford to ignore the training of the emotions. "Unable to explain them, pedants may close their eyes and continue their denial, and scholars satisfied with a reactionary educational program may regret their potency. But those who realize their responsibility for pragmatic education that will affect the whole individual for effective social living must accept the challenge to train the feeling attitudes as well as the intellect." [46] In the developmental process every effort must be made to instill in the individual as *emotionalized attitudes* those attitudes which society regards as desirable and necessary.

Experience also makes it clear that habit plays a large part in human behavior. A habit may be defined as a "more or less pattern form of response to the same or similar stimuli." [47] Truly man is "a creature of habit": human conduct consists in large part in making responses that have been habituated. Habits perform a great service in human living: they are economizers, conservers of intellectual and physical energy, shortcuts in purposive action; habituation and routinization of common and unchanging responses make possible a greater concentration of human attention and effort on the less familiar and more difficult responses necessitating conscious thought. "Relatively a small proportion of specific activities grow out of immediate rational thought; the great majority are controlled by habits of individuals and customs of groups of which the individuals are members." [48] Habits are thus unavoidable; they are caught from individuals and groups operating in the social situation in which development takes place. Not only does the habituation of a great many responses become one of the aims of the developmental process, but habits, and especially the characteristic habits of a group, or the mores, become an important means of social integration.

Psychological science teaches that if learning is to take place and

[46] *Ibid.*, p. 374.
[47] *Ibid.*, p. 372.
[48] *Ibid.*, p. 440.

be long retained, the learning experience must be attended by satisfaction and must be confirmed by repetitions. Both these laws must
be operative in the training process that aims at the inculcation in the
individual of proper emotionalized attitudes and necessary habits.
Lacking complete data about the nature of the learning process we
must all the more heed the facts that we possess. The laws of learning
describe the conditions under which the learning of desired responses
most effectively takes place; in the process that is to culminate in
the effective performance by the individual of the desired life-activities,
the laws of learning must provide large direction.

It has long been evident that an individual shows greater competence
in some activities, that fall within the common categories of his life-
experience, than he does in others. The person who displays great
competence in situations requiring mechanical skill may not display
equal or similar aptness in situations requiring language facility or
in situations requiring social sense or in situations requiring abstract
thinking or in situations requiring artistic skill or artistic sensitiveness.
On the other hand, many an intellectually gifted person has seemed
to be almost "constitutionally inept in every department of manual
skill." [49] The tremendously important implications of this would long
ago have struck us had we not been befuddled by a theory of mind,
growing out of nothing but speculation, that represented human
capacity as a unitary thing that could expend itself with equal effectiveness in any number of particular situations. It must be said in truth
that there appears to be some common integrating or unifying factor
that relates all human abilities. The rule seems to be "correlation" and
not "compensation": a person who shows great skill in the performance
of one activity is likely to be superior also in the performance of other
activities, though not in the same or even approximate degree. Some
individuals can be characterized as generally exceptional, others as
generally average, others as generally below average. But for purposes
of training for effective social living, the fact of differentness is *more
striking* than the fact of resemblance. In the first place, it cannot be
assumed that an individual will, through training received in one;
automatically perform with the necessary effectiveness the other life-

---

[49] The *New York Times,* January 21, 1940, Section 6, p. 1. The quotation has
been borrowed for its aptness of expression. The context is not relevant.

activities. Yet competent human living demands just that, namely, that the human being perform with the needed degree of success every one of the important activities that make up the totality of the life-experience. For purposes of training, therefore, each of the important life-activities must be regarded as a separate objective, and each must be specifically sought and cultivated. The fact that human competence varies in the performance of the various life-activities shows that, although they may all be related by some common unifying factor, from the pragmatic point of view each of them possesses a specific total quality, and offers therefore a specific challenge. In the second place, if individuals seem naturally to do some things better than they do others, the things that they can do best ought to provide the particular respects in which they make their special contribution to society. A complex society has need for many different talents: if not every individual can contribute all the needed talents, then each individual should contribute that for which he seems to have greatest aptitude.

The implications for training clearly suggest themselves. It has been proved by experience that in the cases of some individuals an almost generalized training is instrumental in promoting competence in a large number of particular things. The chances are that to some degree there is a carry-over in training from one activity to another. (The precise amount of carry-over depends upon the degree of similarity between the two situations—that is, the number of identical elements existing—and upon the degree to which conscious search for similarity has been fostered.) The method of training ought to base itself upon the principle of transfer as far as it safely can. But the responsibility of the training process is to see to it that in every learner competence in the large activities that together make up human life in society is developed; and in the absence of any scientific data that would sanction the contrary, the safest thing to do is to treat each life-activity as a separate objective of learning.

The general fact of individual differences has, of course, been so completely verified by experience and by science as not to need any reaffirmation here. But what experience (and now science) has also verified, though it is not so generally recognized, is that, given the same amount of training, individuals differ from one another in competence in *specific* things. Differences between individuals are not broad general differences; they are a multiplicity of specific differences. No two individuals are alike in the specific traits, habits, skills, knowledge that they possess, just as no one individual possesses all specific skills to the same degree. Training not only does not reduce or level many differences but actually serves to bring them out. This fact is extremely important, for regardless of the mechanism through which heredity operates, the only conclusion that can be reached is that capacity for doing certain things, in fact, *capacities* for doing certain things, exist prior to training. And the conclusion is inescapable that these capacities are endowments of inheritance.

From the pragmatic point of view, therefore, regardless of the fact that a common factor is present, the total intelligence of the individual must be regarded as a complex of specific capacities implanted by heredity. Another way of saying this is that, for practical purposes, a person may be regarded as possessing *intelligences* or different *types* of intelligence. How specific these capacities or intelligences are we do not as yet know; we can, however, easily recognize such different capacities as the capacity for abstract thinking, the capacity for carrying on social relationships, and the capacity for motor activity. Intelligence cannot for practical purposes be regarded as a unitary generalized capacity (unless we mean by it only intelligence of the verbal, abstract kind). A person may possess one kind of intelligence to such a degree that it expresses itself in certain marked special aptitudes, and at the same time be singularly lacking in another type of intelligence. Merely to know a person's general intelligence (by arithmetically averaging all his capacities) serves no very great purpose. The specific capacities are inherited: no other explanation could account for the fact that (1) people seem naturally to shy away from certain types of activity and to be naturally attracted by others, all this without previous special training, (2) the extent of training being constant, people still differ very greatly with respect to the competences that they achieve in different activities. On the basis of present evidence it cannot be said that the various capacities, although they can be realized in the course of training, can themselves be extended by training.

Acceptance of the empirical fact that individuals differ inherently with respect to capacities exposes one to the charge of being a determinist. Insofar as determinism implies pre-judgment and discrimination among individuals, the charge is without warrant. The whole matter of human capacity must be regarded pragmatically. The criterion is always the socially desirable life-activities; from this point of reference human capacities are defined. A child born into the world possesses a number of different capacities in different degree. But (1) we have no way of prognosticating the extent to which each capacity is possessed, and the capacities can be actualized only through experience, (2) a capacity can express itself through a great many different activities—it does not necessarily predispose an individual to a particular activity. The activities in terms of which we *conceive* capacity are the activities of our social culture; we present these activities and through them the individual reveals his capacity. In another culture the life-activities might be qualitatively different and therefore the capacities would be different. (For example, in a very primitive culture, the capacity for tree-climbing would be a very important capacity; in our culture we do not ordinarily think of this as a capacity. To offer an example in the negative, in a society in which no vocal language was used the capacity for speech would never be recognized as a capacity.) Capacities must not be conceived as empty vessels brought into the world ready to be filled with a certain substance. Capacities are revealed in the course of learning activity. All individuals must learn how to perform with competence the most important life-activities. In the course of learning them (and perhaps through certain devices that short-circuit the learning process) individuals may show that they possess a high degree of mechanical intelligence and a relatively low degree of abstract intelligence. This fact must be noted, and, wherever possible, provision must be made for learning how to perform the needed life-activities through means that do not place so much reliance upon abstract intelligence. We have the choice of recognizing this fact and making provision for it, or just ignoring it and pretending that it is not there.

There is no validity in the contention that any considerable number of the population is ineducable.[50] In the first place, normality or subnormality cannot be defined in terms of one characteristic; and the people who declare for the principle of inherent ineducability generally have in mind only abstract intellectual capacity. Normality must be defined in terms of all the characteristics that contribute to effective

---

[50] Cf. Humanism, p. 135, footnote.

social living: the normal individual is "one who takes, or who as a result of his development may be expected to take, an acceptable part in those out-of-school groups to which he naturally belongs under the conditions of American society."[51] The individual possesses a number of different capacities: it is most unlikely that he would possess no capacity by virtue of which he could contribute to the common Good Life. No one person can or should develop all capacities equally; the capacity that should be most developed is the capacity which is naturally the greatest. The world has need of a great many talents; no one can do all things equally well. Each person should do those things especially for which he shows greater natural aptitude. One capacity is well worth developing; it can become the center through which a person acquires competence in all life-activities. In the past the emphasis has been so largely on the training of the capacity for abstract thinking that other types of capacities have been overlooked or discounted. In the modern world, a capacity for mechanical work can be just as valuable to the individual and to society as the capacity for abstract thinking. Low academic intelligence alone cannot possibly be interpreted to mean that a student is ineducable.

In the second place, it must be restated that no one knows what a person's capacities are except as they are revealed in the course of activity. There is no index of capacity except in terms of something that has been done. The intelligence test has had in some cases almost uncanny success in revealing abstract thinking power, but it by no means tests with equal success other types of capacity; and even that device presumes a period of learning. The aptitude tests that presume to indicate special abilities in advance of learning have more negative than positive value. The best way to earmark capacities and discover special aptitudes is through revealing and exploratory activities, designed for that purpose. No one can tell in advance of actual learning experience, by any device that has been invented, that a physically normal person is ineducable.

It is a sound maxim that a person ought to develop furthest in those socially desirable and desired respects in which he shows most aptitude. Satisfactory living in the modern world demands, in addition to general effectiveness in all the life-activities, a large degree of specialization.

[51] *Issues of Secondary Education*, p. 28.

The basis for specialization ought to be in the aptitudes that a person possesses. Aptitudes (and interests, with which they are closely allied) serve also as means of all-round development. Interests radiating from the special aptitudes may be led into every important human activity, and may be effective in evoking the effort and energy needed to master these activities. Development, then, that is based upon special aptitudes need not only lead into specialization but, with proper guidance, should culminate in the acquirement of all the needed ideals, attitudes, habits, knowledges, and skills.

The pattern for training the individual for pragmatically effective living in society is as follows: it is necessary to establish with all possible definiteness the nature of the important life-activities prevailing in society, and the specific ideals, attitudes, knowledges, and skills that performance of them demands. The individual must be helped to acquire competence in each of the important life-activities. It will at once suggest itself that the number of life-activities is very great and that it is impossible to train people for the thousands of little things that they will have to do in the course of their living. But it should be noted that the human life-experience can be marked off into complexes of activities under certain general categories: citizenship, health, family life, vocation, use of leisure, etc. The activities within each complex are sufficiently related so that a considerable degree of transfer of ideals, attitudes, knowledges, and skills might be expected to take place, if that were specifically taught for. Within each of these complexes of activities, the individual must be trained for social-competence; in addition he must develop certain special skills of a socially useful character that will distinguish him as an individual and as a worker in the society of which he is a part.

Method must be adapted to individual differences. It is not true that ultimate competence in common life-activities presumes common means of training. The same goals of education can be reached from different directions: each person's special aptitudes and special abilities can become the means of approaching all the other objectives. But this is not said in approval of the idea of automatic transfer. The development of a person's particular aptitudes does not automatically result in competence in the other life-activities; the other life-activities must actually be learned. The aptitude is the avenue of approach.

We live in a dynamic world, and life-activities do not always remain the same. While we train for competence in prevailing life-activities, we must also provide for the future. The best way to assure that the individual will throughout life be continuously learning things and adjusting himself to new situations is through interests. Interests are the dynamics of human learning. Equipped with strong and varied interests as a result of previous learning-experience, an individual will continue to learn and *to render himself* competent in the performance of the various life-activities that changing experience brings. Training cannot provide for the future except through interests, but if it establishes strong and varied worth-while interests, it does enough. Liberal education has been defined in many ways, but it is probably most properly defined in terms of variety and depth of interests; the truly liberally educated person is characterized by the number, the variety, and the depth of his interests, and by the manner in which they serve his continued development.[52]

One more thing needs to be made explicit. Training for future competence can be effective only as the immediate needs of the learner are also satisfied in the process. The satisfaction of immediate needs is therefore an important aspect of the training process. In the course of maturation, in the course of natural experiencing in the social environment, the growing individual develops certain needs. The needs of the adolescent are different from those of the younger child; the training process must satisfy both. The training process must also throughout take cognizance of the psychological characteristics and abilities of learners, of what they can and what they cannot do. Human behavior, for example, is purposeful, and the socially competent individual must be able to operate in terms of long-range purposes. But for the immature individual the immediate purpose is a far more potent conduct dynamic than the long-range purpose. The training process therefore must begin by helping children to realize first their immediate purposes, and gradually guide their behavior "in the light of increasingly remote but always clearly understood and appreciated, social and personal values."[53]

[52] T. H. Briggs, *Secondary Education,* Chapters XXIV–XXVII. 1933.
[53] *Ibid.,* p. 257. Quoted with permission of The Macmillan Company, publishers.

II

On the whole, the tendencies of the psychology of American education are in the right direction. It is true that considerable of the influence of the older and discredited psychologies still remains, and that there are a great many facts concerning the nature of human development still to be discovered. But, if psychology could obtain the needed guidance of social philosophy, and if the psychological data that we have garnered were systematized and actually applied (verbally we accept many things to which we have actually not yet become reconciled), American education would be quite well off. At any rate, there have been in recent years very gratifying developments in the psychology of education.

Chief among these developments has been the discrediting of the faculty psychology and of its allied educational theories. The concept of intellectual training by formal discipline, the principle of automatic transfer which it avowed, were attractive because of their simplicity and neatness. They were, however, untrue. Since the overthrow of the faculty psychology we have been operating on an empirical psychology buttressed by an ever-growing body of scientific knowledge. We do not yet know precisely what mind is, nor precisely how it operates; many principles of procedure, therefore, remain unclear. But the empirical knowledge that we can rely upon and the scientific psychology that has been developed under the leadership of Thorndike offer a basis for mapping out at least the outlines of a sound educational method.

With the discrediting of the theory of mental discipline, there has come a shift toward a pragmatic conception of the training process. The view that training is primarily for competent social living and that method ought to be subordinate to this aim and consistent with it has taken hold. There has been some effort to meet practical needs and to develop competence in the important life-activities. Considerable pioneer work has been done in analyzing the life-functions, in cataloguing the life-activities with which education must deal, and in breaking them down into ideals, attitudes, knowledges, and skills. Subject-matter has been installed in the curriculum on that basis. On the whole, the shift away from the faculty psychology and the theory of formal discipline has caused us to rethink the entire problem of human development from the pragmatic point of view.

Another creditable development has been (at least a partial) acceptance of the fact of individual differences and a recognition of its implications for education. To a degree we are today differentiating the learning activity of students. We are attempting to discover their capacities, aptitudes, and interests, and to use these as bases of educational guidance. The junior high school has been established, and among its major functions is the exploration of student aptitudes and interests; the influence of the junior high school has extended to all of education. It cannot of course be said that the training which we provide at present to our very many students is appropriate to their individual needs. The fact is that it is not. The school at the present time still favors the generally bright student over the average and lower-than-average, still favors the academic-minded over any other type of student. But the fact is that some headway has been made in providing for individual differences.

The utter rejection of the preposterous idea that what is difficult and unpleasant is by the same token educative has resulted, for the most part, in making the training process more effective, as well as more pleasurable to the student. More attention is being paid to student needs and to student interests. Learning activities have been introduced which have greater intrinsic interest and the immediate values of which are more evident. Attempts have been made to discover the needs of the student at different stages of growth and development, and to satisfy these needs. The school has become a generally happier place to work in as well as a more effective educational institution.

On the other hand, it must be said that these developments represent only a beginning. In every case theory has gone far ahead of practice. Many things that we know need to be done, yet remain to be done. In some respects our attempts have been half-hearted (for example, in training for vocational competence, in training for leisure); in some respects we have not yet broken with tradition (for example, a good deal of the subject-matter in the curriculum today was originally disciplinary in intent); some things that we have attempted to do we have done very inefficiently (for example, curriculum reconstruction).

Our advance derives chiefly from the fact that we have thrown over speculation and unlikely theories for verified facts of either experience or science. We have developed and are further developing a science of psychology, and it has served us well. But our attitude toward this science and our use of it have not been as intelligent as they should be. We have not worked cooperatively, we have not coordinated our resources, we have not systematized our knowledge, we have not always checked our facts, we have tolerated some rather inexcusably imperfect techniques; worst of all we have not applied the verified knowledge that science has actually obtained for us. Our knowledge of the facts of human behavior is altogether greater than our use of it.

Although psychology has rid itself of the notion of discipline and automatic transfer, it has still not rid itself of some of the practices that stemmed from that. There remain many learning activities the justification of which can be attempted only in disciplinary terms. The learning-activities are still on the whole too academic, catering to those who are superior in abstract thinking power. We neglect the training of the emotions. We have laws of learning but do not apply them, so that often the students are alienated rather than educated by our efforts. The popular mind which is so influential in shaping the character of education is still secretly impressed with the disciplinary idea, and tends to regard learning-activities that have as their purpose the training of the emotions, the training in proper social attitudes, in the nature of fads and frills.

Some of the principal adjustments which the individual must make successfully have been neglected. We have not yet faced the reality of the demands of training conceived as preparation for pragmatically effective living. Good citizenship we still tend to regard as a kind of general outcome of an intellectual training process; accordingly our efforts in the making of citizens have been ineffective. The vocational adjustment, the most crucial adjustment in our present living, has received only half-hearted attention; one of the two most important objectives of education is thus almost completely unrealized. Preparation for some of the other life-activities has been similarly defective—education for leisure, education for family life, even health education.

Probably the sorest spot in our entire educational process is the incomplete provision made for individual differences. Some provision is better than none, and, as has been said, some provision has been made.

But on the whole the training process is still inappropriate for the larger number of students affected by it. Those faring best are those who probably least need our help—the brighter students. The academic studies are, for the most part, least unsuited to them. At the same time it cannot be said that the brighter students are compelled to work up to capacity; many of them develop a "get-by" attitude. The less bright students are really badly provided for; for the most part they struggle along with work for which they have no capacity, in which they are most unlikely to discover aptitudes, and in which they have no interest. Such education cannot possibly result in the attainment of social-competence. On the whole we provide better for the satisfaction of the immediate needs of younger than of older students, partly because we do not as yet know very much about the psychology of adolescence, partly because the academic studies are inherently incapable of satisfying the real-life adult needs of the older students.

A few words must also be said in criticism of a rather widespread tendency that has appeared during recent years on the part of many people toward sentimental and obscurantist thinking concerning certain aspects of child-development. Much of this thinking centers around such terms as "experience," "integration," "interests," "child-centeredness," etc. Development is regarded as unfolding from within, as a result of expression of "natural tendencies." Interests are interpreted as if they were inherent in children, as if they existed prior to experience. "Self-expression" is fostered, regardless of its nature. Objectivity, definiteness, system, aiming at predetermined goals, are decried. Psychology must free itself from the influence of this sort of thinking, and proceed on the basis of sensible empiricism and science.

III

We must face squarely the implications of the overthrow of the theory of mental discipline, and build solidly on the psychological facts that science has provided for us. In the psychology of Thorndike we have a sound, though not yet complete, basis for developing an educational procedure. The laws of learning offer reliable guidance for the formation of the desirable and needed emotionalized attitudes and habits. In the law of effect we have a verified principle the implications of which go far beyond mere educational method. We need additional dependable data, but in the meantime we must collate, examine, systematize, and use, wherever we can, the data that science has already uncovered. In the future we must proceed more systematically, coordinating our efforts and our results in the interests of greater efficiency and economy. The hope of education lies in a fruitful empirical and scientific psychology properly geared to a guiding social philosophy.

More completely than at present the problem of individual development must be seen from a social and a pragmatic point of view; very much more than at present the implications for method of this conception must be carried out. We can be satisfied with no half measures. Having abandoned belief in large and automatic transfer, we must take steps to provide for direct, specific, and systematic training in the effective performance of the important life-activities. Every important area of experience must be represented. We must know exactly what we are teaching for, and for that purpose the broad categories of experience must be broken down into their constituent ideals, attitudes, knowledges, and skills. We must use the principle of transfer to the greatest advantage: as much transfer as is possible we must seek to obtain. For the rest we must rely upon specific training. Subject-matter, throughout, should be considered instrumental in purpose.

We must utilize to the full our empirical knowledge of the fact that there are capacities rather than that there is a capacity. We must explore the capacities of students, and discover those things which they are best qualified by nature to do. The special capacities that an individual possesses to the highest degree must become his special means of development as an individual and as a citizen. He must become especially competent in those things for which he shows the greatest aptitude, and through them make his special contribution to society. It is self-evident that a subject-matter much more appropriate than the present to capacities of a non-intellectual kind must be found or devised.

An appropriate subject-matter will make it possible truly to provide for individual differences, not half-heartedly as at present. In terms of his particular capacities, aptitudes, and interests, each individual will be helped to develop social-competence. With an appropriate subject-matter it will be possible to help the student develop deep and varied interests to a much greater extent. The difference between providing for individual differences and not providing for them spells the difference between success and failure in education.

In its attitude toward differences in capacities, the school will not be deterministic. It will not in advance mark off an individual as ineducable. It will provide opportunities to explore capacities and to discover aptitudes in various types of socially useful work. However humble the talents that are thus uncovered, they will become the special centers of the individual's development toward social-competence. Effective training in terms of individual needs implies unremitting and alert guidance, and such guidance the school will have to furnish.

Much more attention than is customary at present must be paid to the satisfaction of important immediate as well as assured future needs. More data will have to be obtained both empirically and scientifically about the needs of adolescents resulting from the natural physical and psychological changes that accompany growth to maturity, as well as from the exigencies of the present social situation. With regard to older adolescents now in school, especially, is such information badly needed.

EXPERIMENTALISM

I

Man is an organism interacting with its environment. The human being is part of nature and continuous with the other living things in it. Human aspiration and human achievement are to be understood primarily in terms of the biologic process, and not in terms remote from it. The conception of the Good Life of man must rest upon an understanding of the nature of experience. As is every other species in its own way, the human species is unique in nature; the uniqueness of man lies in the fact that, by virtue of understanding the life-process, he is able to guide it. Man is capable of intelligent living; in essence the Good Life is the intelligently-lived life. Not only is man as a species unique, but each person is, as a total being, different from every other person. What makes him different is not chance or primarily heredity, but the nature of the biologic process that he experiences. The forces that he and the environment bring to bear upon each other, the consequences that unceasingly follow, serve to make of each person an individual. For an understanding of the meaning of individuality as well as for an understanding of human behavior in general, it is necessary to turn to an explanation of the life-experience process.

Living means interacting. While the impulse for life itself resides within the organism, the maintenance of life depends upon a continuous interaction with the environment, the consequences of which are favorable to the continued growth of the organism. (Organism and environment are not actually separable. The organism is part of its environment; their separation in discourse is for the purpose of focusing attention upon one of the elements of environment, the organism, in its interrelations with all the others.) Organism and environment are in constant interaction, changing and being changed; every action in which the organism is involved has some consequence for its living. The organism may be regarded as an energy system that keeps renewing itself through continuous contact with the surrounding environment. The environment must be regarded not as a static, passive recipient of activity but as a continuous flow of active forces.

Organismic behavior is purposive. Every organism has the urge to maintain life, and that impulse propels its activity. An organism maintains life as it succeeds in maintaining "a life-sustaining equilibrium," [54] with the surrounding forces of the environment; the optimum state toward which it heads may be termed "complacency." But the equilibrium is constantly being disturbed by organismic and environmental activity. "Characteristically in life strain arises between organism and environment. The organism is therein stirred to act, perhaps to seek, perhaps to shun or avoid. Looked at within, this strain is called urge or want or wish. Looked at without, efforts result, i.e., physical movements which tend to satisfy the want and so reduce the strain." [55] Such activity is going on all the time, and as long as the organism can achieve the balance favorable to its own living, just so long can it maintain life. The higher the organism, the more actively does it participate in the carrying on of its life-process, the more actively does it foster the conditions that are favorable to it. The higher animal organisms can "learn" from experience to make those responses that will produce the favorable effects. Ultimately these responses are incorporated into

[54] J. L. Childs, *Education and the Philosophy of Experimentalism*, p. 72. 1931.
[55] W. H. Kilpatrick, *Remaking the Curriculum*, pp. 22–23. 1936.

behavior, and the organism develops a certain pattern of behavior, that is, it becomes changed in order to meet better the "stipulations" of its environment.

Human behavior is distinctive in that it is not only purposive but can become increasingly purposeful. The human being is capable of acting in a way consciously to conceive, seek out, and attain those consequences that are favorable to his living. Man can not only "learn" from experience in the way that animals can, that is, learn to expect certain consequences to follow from certain acts and establish suitable reciprocal or compensatory habits, but he can enter *understandingly* into experience, analyze it, reconstruct and redirect it to suit his own ends. These ends always relate to his own personal integration, to the maintenance of the life-giving balance between himself and his environment. "Since personal integration is not self-contained, and involves a satisfactory internal adjusting to the ever-changing demands from the external situation, it requires no further words to show that the fact of integration is never completed but always in moving process. It is, however, true that a certain relative degree of integration is both desirable and possible. A satisfactory sense of security depends upon it." [56]

All rational human conduct is always in some way related to the adjustment process; that is not to say, however, that man is constantly preoccupied with meeting the needs of physical existence. What man conceives as a condition necessary for existence is sometimes largely up to man himself; increasingly man has established as necessary for his existence conditions not found elsewhere in nature. Nor is man content to take nature as he finds it; progressively he has reconstructed nature in accordance with his own conception of how things should be. A large element of idealism has resulted from the human understanding of the essential nature of experience.

Alone in all living nature, man has the capacity to "know" experience —to develop meanings out of situations and to use these meanings in directing himself in new situations. Through analysis of the experience process in relation to himself—through a knowledge of how the environment is acting upon him, in what way it is affecting his living, in what way he must respond—man can so direct his behavior that the "life-sustaining equilibrium" is maintained. What is called intelligent

[56] *Ibid.*, p. 74.

living is therefore purposeful: it is so directed as to produce *intended* consequences. The ultimate thing with respect to which a person is intelligent is the life-process; the immediate instrument is meaning; the manner in which intelligence is expressed is in adjustive action. Intelligence is not an abstract quality existing in isolation from the experience process; it is expressed in adjustive behavior. The intelligent man is the man who, through intentional action, is achieving effects favorable to his living.

The dynamic, changing nature of experience complicates very greatly the problem of behaving intelligently. The environment is not a unity acting in single fashion upon the organism; it is rather a succession of events or happenings, each with a somewhat different background and direction, and with a different potential consequence for the life of the organism. Each event, for the intelligently behaving person who seeks to understand its meaning and control its consequences, presents a new challenge. Each event is different also because the organism, which is part of the event, is a little different. Moreover, not one but a number of different events operate simultaneously in the life of the organism, and many of them are interrelated. Intelligent living does not consist therefore in the application of old meanings to the immediate management of new situations; it is rather the use of old meanings in order to create or achieve the meanings inherent in a new situation. Management follows upon understanding. Intelligent behavior is constantly in the making. Thinking is continuously inventive, continuously creative. It goes almost without saying that meanings thus *created* cannot be confidently applied with the assurance that they will "work"; they must be "tried out," they must be regarded as working hypotheses, until they are corroborated and thoroughly substantiated by subsequent experience.

Intelligent behavior, therefore, is not only purposeful and creative, but it is behavior that is characterized by an experimental attitude. The intelligent person does not rest assured in the correctness of his diagnosis of experience until after the desired consequences have been achieved. And since new situations are constantly presenting themselves that supplant the old, and since each situation has some impending consequences for living, intelligence is an ever-active thing. The intelligent person is one who is continuously directing his behavior in new situations so as to achieve consequences that will turn out to be desirable for him.

Every human being inherently possesses the capacity to "know" and to "understand" experience and the capacity, therefore, for intelligent behavior. This is what makes him, rather than any other kind of being, a *human* being. Individuals differ among themselves in the extent to which they can direct and control their experience, but all possess an initial capacity. The extent to which they ultimately obtain this power is not determined by heredity, but is a function of the experiencing process—of the experiences they have, of the manner in which they deal with these experiences, of the meanings that they obtain, and of the manner in which they use these meanings subsequently. (In spite of the fact that certain ultimate limitations are imposed by heredity, it is impossible to tell to what extent an individual can develop the power of intelligent self-direction. Suffice it to say that with the proper experiences and with the proper guidance, any individual organically normal can become intelligently self-directing.) Intelligent behavior is an outcome of an experiencing process; not only intelligent behavior, but personality, character—the individual human being at any stage of the interactive process—as well. Every action upon the human organism results in some modification of it. By a continuous series of modifications human structure is built. Personality is thus the formed organism at any given stage of its formative process.

Intelligence and personality are developed in the course of an experiencing process. They cannot be developed by passive assimilation of abstracted, condensed, cut-and-dried meanings, and by the inculcation of ideals, attitudes, and habits extracted from their context of experience. Intelligence is a quality of behaving: it is revealed in behaving and it is acquired through behaving. Personality is the organism at any stage of its behaving process; the only way to develop personality is in the course of behavior. It is possible to give a person a store of knowledge, a stock of meanings, but this is not most important; what is of principal importance is the *experience of dealing with experience.* Knowledge at best consists of imperfect interpretations of experiences-that-were: face a new situation and you create new knowledge. What is more important for the attainment of intelligent living than the acquisition of a stock of meanings out of past experience is an understanding of the changing nature of experience, an ability (using meanings as tools) to analyze experience and to "see" the new meanings that are involved in it, an experimental attitude toward meanings thus obtained, the proper manipulation of succeeding events to obtain desired consequences.

Human development is through experience; what a person becomes depends upon the experiences that he has. Theories that conceive of development as a process of unfolding from within are unfounded. In themselves, moreover, experiences do not guarantee any particular direction; unless properly managed, experiences are as likely to have a hurtful as a beneficial effect upon personality (i.e., are as likely to be miseducative as educative); experiences not properly analyzed or not inherently possessing significance for the control and guidance of future living do not necessarily lead to the development of effective intelligence. Of tremendous importance in their relation to the ultimate development of effective intelligence are the nature of meaningfulness of the experiences involving a person and the method that he develops of dealing with them.

An experience is an individual thing, specific to an organism at a particular time. The experiencing process in its wholeness, or the summation of specific experiences, is different with each organism. The human personality that results from this experiencing process, is seen in its entirety, a unique personality, identical with no other. The specific situations in which it operates and the terms on which it operates in them are as those of no other personality. The same must, of course, be said of intelligence: the settings from which meanings are taken, the meanings that are taken, and the purposes for which they are used, are unique with each person. Intelligences, like personalities, are incommensurable. Each human being is a true individual, a self, with his own make-up, needs, and purposes. Since each life is as good as every other, each individual personality with its complement of needs and purposes must be respected. Human intelligence becomes evaluable only in terms of the individual, and the Good Life is, in a true sense, an individual thing.

Man is born into a social environment. This fact is as significant as any pertaining to human existence. The environment within which man interacts is not a "naïve" environment, but one that has been largely re-created by man, and in which man himself prominently figures. The effects of the interaction upon the human organism are not likely to be as simple as would be those in a "naïve" environment; to cope with them, to "take them in hand," the individual must quickly learn their many meanings. Experiencing in a social situation is a much more complicated process than experiencing in a simple, "natural," environmental setting; and the more involved the social situation, the more complicated the experiencing-process. In a social situation man cannot guide his experiencing except through the instrumentality of a great many meanings. These he obtains from other men, from his contacts with them, most often through the medium of language. Social experience is itself a great purveyor of meanings: by interacting with others, one is constantly obtaining meanings which he uses in the conception and realization of his own purposes.

By the same token, experiencing within a social environment tremendously extends one's capacity for intelligent living. Mankind is continuously extending its knowledge of nature and its ability to cope with experience. Human intelligence is cumulative in the sense that it piles up meanings serviceable in the control of living—not only meanings in the abstract, but as they are embodied in patterns of behavior, in institutions, in tools, etc. Social contact offers an opportunity of communication of meanings from man to man; language has been developed to make that communication more perfect. An individual develops as in the course of his experience process he acquires societal meanings which he uses in the direction of his own living; were he entirely dependent upon meanings created by himself, he would be greatly limited. The mind and personality of man are thus social products as they are products of experience. But there is no contradiction between this fact and the fact that, in the course of an experiencing-process, there emerges a person who is an individual in the true sense of the word. Individuality, "self" is truly a product of social experiencing.

Society is an inherent part of the environment in which man operates; the conditions existent within society are an inherent part of the total environmental conditions to which he reacts. The "needs" which the individual seeks to satisfy are needs occasioned by the action of the social environment upon him; whether he can by his action satisfy his needs depends very often upon the prevailing societal situation. It is easy to see that society exerts a very important influence for or against personal integration. Social conditions that make it difficult to achieve "a life-sustaining equilibrium" impede the development of the individual; social conditions that facilitate the achievement of such balance promote individual development. Since the social situation, much more than the natural environment, is very greatly subject to human control, it can be evaluated as good or bad. To the extent that the social situation takes cognizance of the need for individual integration, to the extent that it helps the individual to realize his life-sustaining purposes, to the extent that all its means are in accord with each other and consistent with this end, society is good.[57]

The fact that man carries on his life-experiencing in a social situation does not alter the essential nature of the experience-process. Experience is still a dynamic, changing thing. It is still an individual affair. Intelligent living remains creative. A hypothetical, experimental attitude toward the utilization of meanings is still essential. The meanings that a person obtains from society he must interpret in terms of his own situation; in the course of living they are certain to be modified. At best such meanings are instruments that he will find very useful in the conscious direction of his own living; but not infrequently he will find that they are imperfect, in need of revision, or even altogether invalid.

The fact that meanings are sponsored by society is no sure proof of their validity. Their validity is always to be proved in individual experience, and that is where it stands or falls. Rarely can it be said that meanings have been validated in social experience beyond any peradventure of doubt. When one stops to think about it, there is no such thing as literally "social experience": social experience consists of experiences of many individuals operating to realize their individual purposes. The life of each person affords a continuous test of the meanings that society conveys. The importance of the latter is that they can be of great service in the conduct of the individual life; failing in this, they cease to be important. This does not mean, however, that the meanings conveyed by society are all in equal degree hypothetical, that they all should carry the same relative weight in their influence on indi-

[57] *Vide*, p. 122.

vidual conduct. The meanings offered by the social environment are "weighted" meanings: side by side with those which the individual must accept tentatively and must test in his own experience, there are meanings which, by their repeated and thorough validation, he may accept and trust implicitly. Some of the latter are so important that he must accept them almost on faith, use them, and build his own personality around them, or he will not be able eventually to realize his full intelligence. In this respect, societal meanings are no different from those which the individual extracts from his own experiences: some of them have much more assured validity than others.

Human development is within and through an experience-process taking place in a social environment. Development takes place throughout life; its constant objective is the successful integration of environmental forces around the individual as a center, and one of its outcomes is the integration of the individual organism itself. It cannot be said that intelligence is ever attained—intelligence means behaving intelligently, and each new situation presents a fresh challenge to intelligence. Nor is integration of the organism anything that can be achieved once and for all. The organism is continuously integrating—each event acting upon the organism creates some disturbance in the equilibrium which the organism must act to eliminate. The problem in human living, however, is how to bring the immature individual, freshly projected into the social environment and not yet familiar with its meanings, up to the point from which he can himself carry on intelligently the experiencing process and continue independently his personal integration. The problem is not one of giving young people an intelligence and a personality, as it is one of helping them, in terms of their own experiences, to learn how to control and direct their immediate and future living.

The process of "natural" experiencing within a social environment would, to a certain extent, serve to give an individual significant meanings, provide him with a method of dealing with experience, and give his personality proper direction. But that is not enough. In the early years of his life the individual must have the advantage of guided or systematically directed development. The indiscriminate experiences of natural living must be supplemented by experiences that leave with the individual the most significant meanings that he needs for his own present and future use. The individual must not only learn to deal with experience but he must learn to do so with maximum effectiveness. He must accordingly be guided and assisted in analyzing experiences, deriving meanings, applying them creatively in the reconstruction of his own experiences. The direction that his developing personality takes must not be merely a resultant of the uncontrolled forces of the environment interacting with him, but must be controlled so that he becomes, much more surely and quickly than he otherwise would, a socialized, creative, consciously and effectively self-directing individual.[58]

A process of "intentional" learning is therefore a necessity in human development: its object is to help each person to become an intelligently behaving and self-integrating individual. In the course of this "intentional" learning the young person takes on meanings necessary in the intelligent conduct of his own experiences, acquires under guidance the power of dealing with these experiences, and the personality that is conducive to intelligent social living. But while the process of "intentional" learning is much more concentrated than the learning that results from a process of "natural" experiencing, the nature of this learning and the conditions under which it thrives are very much the same.

Learning is a natural outcome of living: to experience is inevitably to learn. A human being is continuously learning, that is, adapting his behavior in the light of meanings arising out of experience. Learning is not to be considered as something imposed upon or added to experience; nor does learning necessarily involve repetition. Learning has two aspects—a creative and an incorporative. An individual learns when he creates a response to a new situation. This response he also incorporates into his own organismic structure, and it becomes part of his operating equipment—his personality—to remain until it is modified by a succeeding learned response. This must be precisely the nature of the guided or "intentional" learning-process. Such a process cannot consist of filling the individual with disembodied meanings but must consist of presenting him with meaningful, significant experiences. To be significant, experiences must be an integral part of the social situation

[58] With respect to the degree of control that would be proper, there is difference of opinion among Experimentalists. (*Vide* Introduction, pp. 45–46.).

in which the individual finds himself and must be related to his intrinsic needs. "The simplest definition of a good learning situation, then, represents an individual facing realistically his own situation." [59] The more such experiences an individual has, the more significant they are (assuming that skilled guidance is present), the more fully and more quickly does development take place. In some cases learning occurring within experiential context may have to be supplemented by some systematic repetition of meanings as such, but in every case it should be remembered that such repetition is supplementary to experience and not a substitute for it.

All learning is purposive. Human activity is in response to human need. The organism acts to resolve some tension, to relieve some disturbance in the "life-sustaining equilibrium" with the environmental forces. It "learns" as it modifies its behavior in response to a challenge to its life-interests. The learning that characterizes the process of guided development must be purposeful; the experiences presented must establish some vital contact with the learner himself. If that is done, the consummation of learning becomes a matter of concern to the individual; unless that is done, in spite of repetition and even temporary "retention," no learning takes place. If purpose is present, the intrinsic difficulty of what-is-to-be-learned is a secondary matter: purpose itself is compulsive of effort.

Whether or not learning is consummated and its underlying purpose realized is of very great importance in personality growth. Activity, once gotten under way, must culminate in the realization of its end, or personality suffers. Frustration in effort to satisfy wants or needs is inimical to wholesome living. Proper personality development implies continuous integrating, a continual return to a state approximating equilibrium. It is necessary, therefore, to present to the learner experiences which strike a sympathetic chord within him (which promise satisfaction of felt needs) and with which at the same time he is capable of satisfactorily dealing. Conversely, it is disastrous either to neglect to provide experiences through which actually-felt needs can be satisfied or to provide, for such needs, experiences that are too difficult for the individual to comprehend, to learn from, and to deal with.

[59] L. T. Hopkins, "Emerging Emphases as to Learning," *Teachers College Record*, 40:120, November, 1938.

Needs do not originate spontaneously within the individual;[60] they are created in the course of the life-experience process. Needs are determined not only by a maturing human organism acting upon a social environment but by the conditions of that environment acting upon the individual. Needs will vary at different times in the life of the organism; they, in fact, keep changing continuously. The "intentional" learning process must be organized so that its experiences are adapted to the individual at the particular stage of his development, but that does not mean that the learning process takes its cue entirely from the individual. Not only do imperceptibly felt needs become strong and articulate through experiences properly presented, but sometimes new needs are created. One of the marks of human development is the number and variety of needs which a man is at once trying to satisfy; the relationship between needs and experiences is a mutual relationship.

An organism is by definition a whole. An organism responding to a situation, learning within it, is responding as a whole. Learning does not take place partitively. "Not only does the individual respond to a situation as a whole; within himself, he operates as a whole. As he deals with a situation, he learns physically (acquires a certain deftness, changes certain glandular responses, etc.); he responds emotionally; he builds attitudes; he finds out what will work and what won't work in analogous situations; and he organizes, on his level, the meanings which the situation has for him—all of these responses being in progress at the same time. This means that it is impossible to separate the individual, except for purposes of study, into physical, intellectual, or emotional parts. Any response which he makes is always a resultant of physical, intellectual, emotional, and environmental factors; each phase of personality is influenced by and dependent upon the others, all acting simultaneously. This interaction is so marked, and the inter-

---

[60] This is an important point of difference between the Experimentalists and the non-Pragmatic Progressives. The thinking of the latter seems to be governed by a tacit assumption that needs "originate from within." The guidance of learning thereupon becomes a process of (1) discovering children's needs (2) providing experiences that match or are appropriate to these needs. This principle seems to be implicit in the term "the child-centered school." For a criticism of such thinking *vide* B. H. Bode, *Progressive Education at the Crossroads*, pp. 62–72. 1938.

connections among the parts so extensive and intimate, that a change in any one field may manifest itself, not at the point of origin, but in other parts of the organism which constitute the whole. And what he learns at a given time enters into the peculiar combination of longings, desires, attitudes, skills, understandings, that will motivate his response to the next situation." [61]

The "intentional" learning process is a guided process. Guidance is the direction of learning in experiencing so that individual capacity for continuous self-direction in living may result. The guidance process must be careful to shape itself in accordance with the principles of learning enumerated above.

II

A psychology, no less than a social philosophy, is an expression of a larger world-view, both the strengths and the weaknesses of which it reflects. The psychology which until recently dominated American education and which is still the most prominent, though in recent years headway has been made in another direction, is to be criticized basically for its alliance with an atomistic and mechanistic world-view, the principles of which it seeks to transfer into the study and guidance of human behavior. This world-view is that of the Newtonian physics, which has itself recently been disproved and discarded by modern science, postulating a fixed universe held together and operative according to discoverable laws. Movement is at a regular rate: change, though occurrent, is predictable. "The recently discarded Newtonian science outlook analyzed the world ultimately into small material particles. These and their motion constituted all phenomena. Opposed to matter, mind was spectator only, no actual factor. From these scientific method followed: (*a*) Banish the subjective and personal, it can only disturb; (*b*) Analyze every complex thing into its 'elements,' study these. Whatever is found true of them in separation holds still true in any complex whole." [62]

Educational psychology patterned itself upon this science. It too

[61] The Commission on Secondary School Curriculum (V. T. Thayer, chairman), Progressive Education Association, *Science in General Education*, pp. 20–21. 1938.

[62] W. H. Kilpatrick, *Remaking the Curriculum*, p. 16. 1936.

became "scientific": mechanistic in its view of personality and of the environment in which personality operates, analytic and atomistic in its approach to the study of the human "mechanism," "objective" in its methods. The concept of mind, being an inclusive and "abstract" concept that could not easily be handled as a whole in objective fashion, was reduced to elemental terms: intelligence became an aggregate of specific capacities. Human conduct could not be studied in its wholeness: it therefore was analyzed out into its "constituent" specific attitudes, habits, and skills. Ultimately these were reduced to their lowest terms, and there emerged the concept of the S—R bond as the representative unit of human behavior. Psychology became more and more physiologic: complicated human actions were explained in terms of neural connections. A static view of human experience sanctioned the interpretation of development as becoming conditioned to fixed responses; "laws of learning" were evolved upon which a more effective conditioning process could be based. Generally, whatever did not lend itself to easy definition, objectification, and measurement was denied consideration; whatever did, in due time became measured and catalogued. Testing became a favorite device for getting "facts." Scientific psychology "seized avidly upon 'standardized tests' as permitting an education founded on atomistic objectives as interchangeable as Ford parts, and as allowing, besides, a non-thinking type of evaluation. It tried to make education mechanical, partly to have it more easily controlled from without and above." [63]

For "scientific psychology," in spite of its pretensions to objectivity, is not impartial. Its bias is directed toward the maintenance of the *status quo*. It refuses to intervene in the prevailing social conflicts, and thereby allies itself with those who at the present time have the dominant hand and who are interested in preserving the inequalities of the present situation. Its dualistic view of world and organism gives aid and comfort to those who see nothing wrong in the present disharmonious and unbalanced social environment. Its conception of individual differences is not calculated to emphasize the dignity and importance of human individuality. Its method of "education" is not calculated to develop individuals who can undertake an intelligent reconstruction of the present situation.

[63] *Ibid.,* p. 18.

The "education" based upon this psychology regards the world as a static world of separable elements, and human behavior as the making of fixed responses to these "stimuli." Intelligent behavior consists in making the responses, previously learned, that are appropriate to certain situations. Training for intelligent living consists in identifying the important life-activities, and in arranging that each person shall gain competence in the exercise of every one of them. Correspondent to each of the life-activities there are set up objectives: the goal of education becomes the acquisition of the specific attitudes, knowledges, habits, and skills involved in the exercise of the catalogued activities. The development of child-personality is neglected for preparation for adult living; immediate needs are for the most part ignored, and the crucial problem of achieving an integrating personality is not recognized.

The changing modern world demands a creative, flexible intelligence. What the scientific psychology offers is a complement of fixed habits and skills, and knowledge that is regarded not as something created in the course of passing experience but as something, handed down from the past, that is final and unchallengeable. The medium through which these are sought is not the living experience itself, but subject-matter that is "set-out-to-be-learned"; so that the student does not even get the practice of dealing with experience under guidance. Training is given in the spirit of "once-and-for-all"-ness: at the end of the road there is "character," or "good citizenship," or "vocational competence." It hardly seems to matter that many of the things for which the individual is being trained are in conflict with each other, for wholesome personality integration is not a factor. The unity of the organism is not recognized, and training is now for this and now for that.

The "scientific psychology" probably errs most grievously in its interpretation of the meaning and implications of individual differences. The treatment is typically atomistic: individuals differ from each other with respect to many traits; therefore each trait becomes a unit category according to which individuals are to be classified. It is overlooked that the unit is the individual himself, the complete person, and that the fact of total individuality is much more important than is the fact of difference in specific traits. It is overlooked that individualities as a whole are incommensurable, and that each individual must therefore be accorded a respect equal to that given to any other. Rather, on the basis of a single trait serving as common denominator, individuals are compared, and quantitatively rated. The most important of these common denominators is the "intelligence quotient." This is an aggregate rating of more or less specific intelligences, which, furthermore, are regarded deterministically: the I.Q. becomes a basis for predicting the future development of the learner, as if intelligence were an inborn capacity that needed only to be unfolded. Students are labeled bright, average, and dull, and segregated from each other. Grouping becomes "homogeneous" with respect to intelligence, and on that basis training is differentiated. It is overlooked altogether that no true homogeneity is possible; that if students must be grouped, the best basis for grouping is purpose or interest; that a common learning situation need not interfere with truly individual learning, and that there are many values in having students, who differ as individuals, learn within a common situation. True to its general tendency, the prevailing "scientific psychology" oversimplifies and mechanizes the whole principle of individual differences.

The psychology under criticism followed a psychology that had become intolerably formal. But this psychology too, caught in the vise of a sterile scientific outlook, has become formal. In attempting to govern itself "scientifically" it has overlooked or repudiated concepts of the utmost importance to an understanding of human behavior—the concepts of experience, mind, personality, integration. There are ample signs that a new psychology is coming to the fore, a psychology not unscientific but more truly scientific than its predecessor, that yet places great value upon human mind and personality.

III

What is needed is not primarily a revision of specific principles as much as a change in the whole outlook of the dominant American psychology. Educational psychology must abandon its alliance with the atomistic and mechanistic Newtonian science and must reorient itself in accordance with the world-view of modern science, namely, that world is a moving, changing flow of forces operating according to no completed plan and held together by no internal oneness. The dynamic nature of world and its indeterminateness must be recognized. Following this, psychology must base itself squarely on the fact that man is a biological organism interacting with the environment, and not a being either above the environment and superior to it, or one which passively absorbs environmental learnings. In the study and understanding of human behavior, central place must be accorded to the concept of experience. Mind or intelligence must be seen as inherent in the experiencing process—as the capacity of the human being to guide and control his own experiencing. It must be recognized that intelligence is an outcome of an experiencing process, and that the development of intelligence is the central problem of human development.

The meaning of intelligence must be illuminated by the nature of the experience-process as well as the nature of the world in which it takes place. An experience is a particular affair specific to every organism, and it changes with every situation; yet every experience finds the human organism reacting as a whole to a situation that affects it as a whole. It must be seen therefore that intelligent living cannot be carried on through the instrumentality of responses operating as fixed habits; that intelligence is continuous behavior that is creative and experimental, that involves continuous reintegration of old conduct-patterns and formation of new ones in a manner that is to some degree unique with every individual. At the same time it must be seen that intelligent conduct is a unified whole, and not something that can be analyzed in terms of discrete elements. Provision must be made for the development of an intelligence that is personal, flexible, and creative. Psychology must address itself to the problem of helping each person to become a continuously intelligently-behaving being. Each individual must be helped "continuously to learn from experience" in his own life-situations.

Recognition must be afforded to the fundamental function of integration in the life-process. It is necessary to realize that human activity is motivated by the need to maintain a balance between the organism and the circumstances of the surrounding environment, that all human behavior is therefore purposive. Purpose must be given a central role in human development: it must be viewed as the starting point for human activity, and the end toward which it is directed. Growth toward intelligent living must be seen as the continuous formulation and realization of purposes. A purpose must be seen as engaging at one time the whole of personality, and not elements of it. And the very close relationship between the satisfaction of purposes and wholesome personality development must not be overlooked, as well as the negative implications for personality integration of failure to realize essential purposes.

The true nature of learning must become evident. It must be made clear that learning is not anything added to the experience-process but that it is an essential step in that process. It must follow, therefore, that learning takes place, not through the assimilation of inert subject-matter, but through participation in significant experiences; that the starting point of learning cannot be the artificial stimulation of interest in essentially uninteresting subject-matter that is called "motivation," but that it is the perception of genuine purposes and the desire to satisfy real needs. It is necessary to admit as a fact that learning is inherent in all living, that it goes on all the time; that the objective, therefore, of an "intentional" learning process is to help the individual to develop a better *method* of learning from experience.

The true meaning and implications of the doctrine of individual differences must be made clear. A proper understanding of the experiencing process will serve to show that each person is a unique being, and that an admission of the fact of individual differences is first of all an admission of the fact of human individuality. Differences in specific traits are subordinate to this essential difference. Each learner will therefore be regarded as a separate problem for education; providing for individual differences will mean first of all guiding the learner through an educative process that is essentially his own. Individual personality will be respected; accomplishment will be evaluated in terms of individual purposes. The needs of the individual will be the prime factor in guiding his learning process. Whether the learning-situations in which he participates are common or not will depend upon these needs. Devices that segregate students on the basis of particular traits, and make for a semblance of homogeneity where there really is none, will not be used.

Finally, a psychology that is properly oriented to the dynamic nature of the universe and of human experience within it, and that is properly understanding of the nature of human needs, will not conceive of the "intentional" learning-experience apart from the social environment in which the learning takes place. The essential interrelatedness of individual needs and the factors and forces governing the environmental situation will become a cornerstone upon which a method for guiding individual development will be built.

3: The Meaning of Secondary Education

HUMANISM

I*

T HAT EACH individual may realize to the full his capacity for living the Good Life, education is necessary. To Humanism, education is not a process that merely assists the human being in his natural development; such development alone would not require very much active assistance. Rather, education is a process of guiding, controlling, and sometimes redirecting natural development so that the human being develops in the direction of a certain accepted and valued manner of living. Natural development is implicit in mere living; an organism that lives, develops. In itself, development is neither good nor bad; goodness or badness in human beings is a characteristic of the particular direction which development takes. Long ago, man decided that what was merely "natural" was not, by virtue of that fact alone, good enough for him. Man develops in ways that *he evaluates* as good. To insure that such development would become a permanent fact of human existence and that human-life-to-come would never again revert to the "natural," man invented educational processes and agencies.

Human society is itself testimony to the degree to which man has developed beyond the "natural," at the same time that it is a guarantee that human life can never again be merely that. The free development of man in society, unassisted by special processes or agencies, would not, of course, in any real sense be "natural"; it would be turned by human values in man-made directions. But not even such free development

---

* The Roman numerals used in this study to mark off sections have the following significance: I—General Principles, II—Evaluation of the Existent Situation in Terms of These Principles, III—Nature of Constructive Proposals.

within society is identical with or even proximate to what is meant by education. The purpose of education is to guide the human being to the highest type of life that is realizable by man. Such a life is governed not by natural impulses but by ethical motives; it is characterized not by instinct but by intelligence. It is a life not of nature but of the mind working upon nature. It is free with a freedom that comes with discipline, it is good with a goodness that comes not with naïveté but with understanding. The goal of education is a long way beyond what is typical in nature. It is considerably beyond, too, the *actualities* of human life. Human actualities compromise with ideals. Man has never attained perfection. The ideal is still to be realized. Educational values are not merely tied to the existent, and cannot be obtained merely by a disclosure of *what is*. Education aims at perfection, at a Good Life that as yet may be existent only as an ideal. It seeks to make human beings not only as others have been or as they are, but much better. Education fully expects to fall short of its ideal goal (in fact, it must, since new conceptions of the ideal are constantly developing), but in the attempt education may carry man farther than he has ever gone before.

Education, then, aims beyond nature and beyond society—at the highest conception of the Good Life. The educational process cannot therefore be identified merely with the experience of living in society and receiving from it casual and unsystematized, if potent, direction. In the process of being educated, a person of course grows into society —he learns its makeup, its ways, its purposes, its efficient forces, and he learns what society demands of him as an individual. But for a person to stop there would be to stop short of the educational ideal: he must know what is "beyond the horizon," he must be able as an individual and as a cooperating member of society to fill up the gap between the actual and the ideal, he must help to attain for himself and for society a higher life. That is the general meaning of education.

The term "education" is variously used, of course, popularly and in a technical sense. It is not uncommon to hear that "education is life," that "the city educates," and so forth. Such uses are generally quite justifiable in their special contexts. And it is undeniable that living is educative (there can be no disagreement on this!) and that "the city" (not only among the Athenian Greeks, who gave the expression currency) is an extremely important means of education. But for the sake of later avoiding inconsistency in the use of terms, it is necessary to adopt a more restrictive definition of education. Education is the process or complex of processes by means of which each human being, in the course of his growth toward physical maturity, is helped to develop the character and intellect that render him desirous and capable of living the Good Life as the best of mankind have conceived it. As such, the period of education is a stage within a much longer process of growth, learning, and development; it is the stage extending through the long period of human infancy,[1] the stage when human nature is most responsive to direction. Of necessity, the period of education is a period of concentrated learning, of preparation looking toward application in the future, of "deferred" values. Not that these features are necessarily absent from human development in any later period, but they are *par excellence* distinguishing features of the educational period. The period of education is one in which much learning must be concentrated into a relatively short time. It is the period in which the individual must come abreast of mankind in its development, and must be inspired to carry that development farther. Ideally education should be followed by self-education, with the individual, throughout the rest of his life, continuing intelligently to direct his own development. It is in terms of this definition that the Humanist insistence that education does not aim at merely "natural development" must be interpreted.

Education deals with individuals, operates through them and in terms of them. It aims at a common Good Life for all humanity by trying to produce individuals so highly developed—physically, intellectually, emotionally, morally—that they will invariably achieve it. The responsibility of education for social reconstruction is indirect; education deals with individuals, and individuals apply their character and intelligence to the betterment of the common life. Social problems, of course, furnish education with cues as to where its emphasis must fall in the guidance of individuals; education, therefore, must be sensitive to societal needs. But education is not in itself an agency of societal reform—whether economic or political; nor can those who discharge educational functions indoctrinate the young in what they privately believe are desirable modes of social action. The function of

---

[1] Humanism, of course, also recognizes the need for organized adult education as a special and supplementary kind of education.

education is to transmit to the individual the highest human values, moral and intellectual. In these values is implicit the manner in which social problems are to be solved. The values which education is charged to transmit originate not in scholastic establishments, but in the judgment of mankind. In dealing with immature individuals, education is honor-bound to respect that judgment. Education is the carrier of civilization, not the creator of it; its content is the message of mankind to man the individual, and its duty ends when it has delivered its message. Education begins with the child, unaware of the possibilities of mind and of its achievements, and ends with the adult, possessing a measure of the world's knowledge and capable of using it independently in ways to which humanity has given its approval.

On the other hand, the devotion of education to the realization of human ideals renders it to a degree independent of society. In a broad sense, education is the servant of society; it operates within a framework of social experience, it is supported and maintained by society, and it must repay for this support by the large social benefits that it brings. But education is a servant who is free to criticize his master, who, in fact, is obliged to do so. Society maintains education not that it may re-create human beings in its own image, but that it may make them the best human beings possible. In possessing such men and women, society is amply rewarded. Education is thus in a sense above society. It draws wisdom and inspiration from the whole of human heritage, and not exclusively from the values that happen to be dominant in its particular setting. While cultivating in the individual devotion to the societal ideal, it must cultivate also devotion to certain great human truths that may go contrary to special societal tendencies or preferences. The allegiance of education is first to man, second to society. A society, in the particular sense, is not per se good; whether it is good or not depends on whether it is in accord with certain values. When a society tends to operate in ignorance of or to disregard these values, it is the duty of education nevertheless to cultivate these values in the individual, and through the individual to revive them in society. Education has thus a critical and a therapeutic function in relation to society. How else could a society right itself, how else could it correct its weaknesses, how else could some small degree of continuous social progress be assured? Education does not sink or swim with society;

through its broader view of direction it helps society to keep to a true course. It is degrading for education to become the political instrument of a state, or the mere means of propagating one or another economic or racial ideology; and in the long run it is ruinous to society. Wise societies have realized the truth of this principle by granting education, especially on the higher level, a measure of freedom to criticize. This is the meaning of "academic freedom." And a good education shows itself worthy of this freedom by exercising wise restraint in the use of its critical prerogative, except when, in a period of conflicting values, society goes counter to that which the moral authority of mankind sanctions.

Education achieves its aim of helping the individual to progress toward the Good Life by helping him to acquire the twin possessions of right character and effective intellect. Given these, the individual will do the rest; giving these, education fulfills its task. It is obvious that the Good Life is not a general abstraction but a concrete affair of thousands of small incidents; that the Good Life presupposes the happy solution of varied and important problems—of vocation, of marriage and family, of political citizenship, of leisure. But possessing right character and good intellect, a person can attain for himself the satisfactory solution of all these problems. "If the schools can prepare individuals for their common vocation as citizens with intellectual interests, with a certain body of enduring knowledge, equipped with an open mind, trained in the methods of thinking, and inspired with a full appreciation of their social obligation, the future may be left to take care of itself." [2] Mind and character are not specific, temporary acquisitions. Properly trained, they can operate effectively as general functions. When educational agencies have done their work well, self-education follows upon education, and continues throughout life the development of character and intellect already brought to a satisfactory level by education. There is no need to be concerned as to whether right character and intellect in the individual are sufficient to produce the good society; a society is good if enough individuals in it are good. Given individuals of good character and intellect, the good society will take care of itself.

[2] I. L. Kandel, "Secondary Education and Social Change," *Kadelpian Review*, 15:354–355, May, 1936.

It has been stated[3] that the basic factor in human development is intellectual capacity or intelligence; that the degree of excellence of character and intellect which is potentially realizable is a function of the amount of native intelligence with which an individual is endowed; that intellectual training, therefore, is basic in the educational process. It was said, moreover, that generality of intellectual effectiveness is itself a function of capacity: the higher the native intelligence of a person, the more can that intelligence be trusted to operate generally in terms of both ethical conduct and material effectiveness; the lower the intelligence, the greater is the need for additional training in specific moral habits and attitudes and in specific knowledges and skills of a practical kind. Furthermore, it is well known that wide differences in capacity exist among individuals, that this capacity is inborn and cannot be extended by education, and that the capacity of which a person is possessed determines the extent to which he can realize humanness. On the other hand, it is true, also,[4] that the Good Life of man presumes societal living, that a society is as good or as bad as its individuals, that the continuance of societal existence and its improvement demand respectively (1) that all individuals possess a high minimal common measure of goodness, (2) that, with time, this common measure be enlarged.[5] Combining the implications of the psychological and the sociological facts—the fact of natural human inequality and the fact that society demands a measure of ethical and intellectual commonness—one is enabled to see emerging the great educational problem that confronts man in society.

Mankind has an obligation to assist each individual to develop morally, emotionally, intellectually, as far as his capacity allows. This is his right by reason of being a human being. For mankind-living-in-society it is a necessity (that is, greater even than an ethical obligation)

[3] Chapter II, pp. 133 ff.

[4] *Vide* pp. 56–57.

[5] This principle is not acceptable to Foerster. With respect to what follows in this section, it is necessary to keep in mind that Foerster makes the following important reservations: Since a considerable number within the population is ineducable, it is not feasible to try by education to raise the common intellectual denominator of the population as a whole. It is better to concentrate on the education of the able. Secondary education continues to be selective, although not as exclusive as in the past. The good society rests not on a high common denominator of living but on the life and accomplishments of its best individuals.

to raise all individuals, almost irrespective of capacity, up to a high minimal common level of moral and material living—the higher the better. When society does this, it acts not alone from idealistic considerations; it acts to preserve itself. Societal living means interdependence, it means sharing, it means having-in-common, it means, to a certain extent, *living*-in-common. In no other way, exclusive of this, could man realize his humanness; in no other way could society survive. Were there no society, to assist an intellectually poor person to realize such possibilities as he does possess would be an act of philanthropy; in a society, such an act is a necessity. Individuals must be brought up to as high as possible a common level of living. That may even require artificially reducing disparities among individuals, so to speak; or, to state it in another way, it may require the raising of the unpromising individual to the very utmost of his realizable level. Of course, above the high common level, there will be individual levels as infinitely varied as are the capacities of individuals themselves. The Good Life is an individual affair, realizable and realized in different ways and to different degrees by different people. But the common denominator of good character and effective intelligence must be sought for all. How high the common educational level shall be, cannot be absolutely determined. It is a function of the moral and intellectual status that society, on the whole, has already achieved. That is one of the things that educational agencies within a society must define. And one of the crucial problems of education is, once the extent of the desired and possible common level of living has been defined, how to help every individual to rise to that level, often in spite of the handicaps of a poor native intelligence.

To emphasize this as one of the "musts" of education is not, however, to sanction the neglect of the other great function of education. To strive to raise all to a high common minimal level of good living is not the highest educational ideal. The Good Life, as has been said, is an individual affair. New visions, new ideals that constantly operate to elevate and refine human life are the products of individual mind and effort. The progress of mankind is made possible by the achievements and example of individuals. It is the life of each person and not the life of society as a whole which is the "end"; and it is toward this "end" that education must direct itself. Education has an obligation to each individual, regardless of the common level, to help him reach a level of living as far as possible above that. The greater the individual's equipment of native intelligence, the farther must he go in his general development. If the other function of education is essential for preserving societal existence, this one is essential for realizing man's potentialities as a human being, and, among other things, for preventing society itself from stagnating. Without neglecting the first, education must carry out its second responsibility. And it must not be imagined that in a democracy it is much more important to secure an enlightened common citizenry than it is to develop an intellectual elite. Especially in a democracy is it necessary to possess, in the forefront of a generally enlightened and trained people, a highly cultivated leadership.

In translating, now, these general principles into specific statements of purpose of education in American society, it is necessary to review the prevailing societal situation. The fact that we are a democracy means that more than under any other type of societal organization we are a society governed by the intelligence of all the people. The existence of every person in our society depends to a large extent, not upon the good-will and intelligence of a single individual, but upon the good-will and intelligence of all the people. A despotism may possibly maintain itself upon a low level of popular intelligence if its rulers are consistently enlightened (though history shows that even this is doubtful). But a society of free men makes imperative an unusually high base of popular intelligence, precisely as such a society also requires assurance of equality of opportunity for each individual to advance as far as he can. Popular education in this society cannot be limited to mere indoctrination of social ideals and procedures, nor to the mere acquirement of literacy. The second determining social factor is the degree of our material development and complexity. To live adequately in our society requires considerably more knowledge, more intellectual discernment, more judgment, more versatility and adaptive power than was ever required in any previous society. To live the full measure of the Good Life is an even more difficult achievement. And the closeness of living within society, the interdependence of individuals, requires that the high intellectual attainments be the property of every person and not merely of a few. Today the acquisition of only a mechanical routine for living is no longer adequate, save for the intellectually most backward. Of all others, a large degree of independent, general intellectual power is required. A third social condition, deriving from the second but one which must be taken into account separately, is that the rapid and continuing mechanization of productive and distributive processes has steadily pushed upward the age at which the young person can usually find employment. This age is now near the close of the adolescent period. It would be unwise, therefore, even if it were otherwise possible, to limit common education to education in childhood and early adolescence. Education must accept responsibility for the continued development of adolescents until society is ready to receive them.

These conditions combine to point irresistibly to the conclusion that life in American society requires a new high common level of education. The common school must realize ends in terms of intellectual effectiveness far beyond those realized by any common school previously. For this reason, and for the reason that society is obligated to care for adolescents until they can make their way independently, the period of common education must be greatly extended. As matters stand at present, this period must be conceived as reaching up to the age of eighteen and even to twenty. Whereas in former times education during later adolescence properly was selective, such education must today be the common right of every individual. Beyond this stage, however, education must continue to be strictly selective, offering the highest opportunities of a collegiate and university training (at public expense) only to the ablest individuals.

Common education does not, however, mean the same education. It does not mean that the outcomes of education are the same for every individual, or that the processes are the same. The first is impossible; the second is undesirable. Common education means, in the first place, a common period of education in which each individual will be given opportunity to become the best possible person—physically, morally, intellectually, emotionally—that he is capable of becoming. Within this period, each individual will be expected to develop that high degree of good character and effective intelligence that the Good Life in American society requires of all persons. Beyond this, each individual will develop in both general and special characteristics and abilities to the extent to which and in the manner in which his intellectual capacity, his interests, his special aptitudes, and his special opportunities allow. The superior person will go much farther than the average, the average farther than the inferior. The period of common education is a period of common educational opportunity; each person will go as far as he can, in the process of attaining or mounting above that common level which society sets up as the minimal ethical and material qualification of all its individuals.

The term "secondary education" denotes the education which comes between the end of the primary school, the purpose of which is to help the child to gain the most common attitudes, habits, knowledges, and tools that he needs for present living and for continued development, and the time, near the end of adolescence, when the youth emerges with the varying measure of character and intelligence required in living the Good Life. In terms of age, secondary education may be defined as extending from the age of twelve to the age of eighteen or twenty. As such, secondary education is included within the confines of common education; it builds upon the foundations of the primary school to realize the ends of common education. Secondary education is not selective, though it serves as a basis upon which selection of promising individuals for higher education must be made. Secondary education and primary education form a unitary process. The break occurs at the end of the process, between secondary and higher education, and at this point the break should be sharper than it is. Secondary studies must be eliminated from the educational work of the liberal-arts college, and that college be either reconstituted on a truly higher liberal basis or dismantled altogether and replaced by [6] new educational forms.

[6] Humanists disagree on the value of the four-year liberal arts college. Hutchins urges the dismantling of the present four-year unit, integrating the lower (or junior college) division with the secondary education, and expanding the upper division into a three-year graduate school of arts. (R. M. Hutchins, "Education and the Public Mind," *Proceedings* of the National Education Association, 71:163–167, 1933); Foerster strongly pleads for the retention of the liberal-arts colleges, on a more definitely liberal and advanced basis. (N. Foerster, *The Future of the Liberal College,* 1938); while Butler sees the need for both junior colleges and four-year liberal-arts colleges. (N. M. Butler, "The American College and the American University," in *The Meaning of Education,* pp. 261–280. Rev. edition 1915, and "Problems of Higher Education in America," *School and Society,* 39:15–17, January 6, 1934).

Insofar as secondary education, within the general function of common education which it shares with the primary school, may be said to have a specific function, it may be stated as follows: to build upon the foundation of the primary school, to operate in the light of the character traits and the intellectual attainments that the learner already possesses, to advance, intellectualize, and systematize its procedures in the light of the developing powers and maturity of the adolescent.[7] In addition, secondary education must be, even more than primary education has been, sensitive to the developing differences in the abilities of individuals. As differing capacities become realized, individuals tend to draw further apart in intellectual power and in intellectual interests. In these respects, learners of secondary-school age are more different from each other than they were in the primary school. However adequately common processes may serve (if they do) to inculcate the common fundamental knowledges, habits, and skills of the primary school, common processes do *not* serve for the realization of the ends of the secondary school. Secondary education, apart from being more advanced in its subject-matter and method than primary education, must also be more differentiated. Differentiation may mean variation in kind of subject-matter, in degree of adapting a generally common subject-matter, or in a combination of the two.[8] Secondary education has surrendered its selective privilege, but for that reason all the more must it hold to the principle of differentiation. From the time that the secondary school receives the learner until the end of the road of systematic, formal education does educational method have to be planned with a view to its appropriateness to the capacity of the educand.

The last principle is not, however, to be interpreted to mean that a separate education is to be invented to suit the taste of each individual. Taste and capacity are not to be confused. The mind of man labors collectively in one grand effort to discover what for human beings is the Good Life. The meaning of the Good Life, once its outlines are distinguished, becomes the common end to which all individual living

[7] For an interesting statement of the psychological meaning of secondary education, *vide* N. M. Butler, "The Scope and Function of Secondary Education" in *The Meaning of Education,* pp. 210 ff. Revised edition. 1915.

[8] Humanists differ in interpretation of the principle of differentiation. *Vide* Chapter IV of this study, pp. 306 ff.

is directed. The personal tastes of the individual need to be respected, both out of regard for him as a person and as a way of facilitating the attainment of educational ends. But personal tastes need not be consulted with regard to what shall be the general end of education. Capacity, on the other hand, must be considered both with respect to means and to the extent to which educational ends can be attained. The capacity of the individual determines how far he can go in the direction of realizing educational values, and by what route he can best attain them. Education is affected by capacity; education, in turn, affects tastes. The school is mistaken when it offers to take its principal direction from the interests of its students.

If secondary education is to be differentiated in terms of individual capacity, it is necessary to describe more specifically the meaning of secondary education in its differentiated aspect. It has already been said [9] that character and intellect are single generalized traits in man. Morally, the good man is not good in some things and bad in others. He is good or bad "all over"; moral goodness is a general characteristic. Intellectually, the good man is resourceful, inventive, discriminating, sound, and thorough in all things, and not only in some. Intellectual goodness is equally a general characteristic. Were this not true, the Good Life would be the difference in a bookkeeping balance between credits and debits, and preparation for the Good Life through the learning of principles would be impossible. The greater the intelligence of the individual the greater is the reliance that can be placed upon "transfer" power into all situations demanding ethical conduct and material effectiveness. The intelligent person, generally trained, can be trusted to make happy and suitable adjustment to the various situations that arise in the course of living, to learn easily and effectively the various specific things he needs to know. With such a person, the object of secondary education should be to develop to the utmost, in the time that is allowed, general rectitude of character, wholesomeness of outlook, emotional refinement, sensitiveness, balance, and intellectual power drawing upon a large fund of important ideas. On these rather than on preparation for vocation, for political citizenship, for worthy home membership, for intelligent consumership, and so forth, should emphasis be placed. Given the large attainments of character and

[9] *Vide* p. 135.

intellect, a person can make these "adjustments" for himself. Such a person will very likely continue his education beyond the secondary period—either exploring more widely and more deeply the fields of the higher learning in the college, and perhaps himself contributing, in the university, to the advancement of learning, or following his special talents or interests into some area of professional preparation. For him, the secondary school does not need to try to anticipate specific life-problems either of vocation or of home or of society.

For the person at the lower end of the scale of intelligence, on the other hand, training culminating in the emergence of general traits, however desirable they are, of character and intellect is insufficient to prepare him to meet adequately the demands of life. Where understanding is at best dim, general traits do not carry far enough. For such a person, general moral and intellectual development must (1) come through training in specific concrete situations, and (2) be reinforced by habituation in important types of conduct, knowledges, and operational skills. Far less than in the case of the very intelligent person can reliance be placed upon broad ideals, ideas, principles, methods of procedure; far more must reliance be placed upon indoctrination in specific attitudes, upon inculcation by repetition of facts of knowledge, upon habituation in specific skills. With such a person, secondary education must aim at a considerable degree of specific preparation for vocational activities, domestic responsibilities, civic duties; secondary education will, in fact, be given *through* materials drawn from these activities. In his case, education must approach its practical ends in a more straightforward way. Such a person is not likely to continue education beyond the common terminus, and the secondary school is doubly bound to equip him, before he leaves, with the knowledges and skills that living in society makes necessary for all individuals.

It need hardly be said that between these two extremes there is almost infinite progression in capacity. Individuals do not fall into two types, or three types. Secondary education must be adjusted to the capacity of the student; for every student, the right education. But whether individualization calls for a sharp qualitative differentiation in types of subject-matter, or for a much more gradual adaptation of a common core of subject-matter with the qualitative differences previously described present only at the two extremes, is a point of issue.[10]

Especially with regard to vocational training, it must be admitted that a problem confronts secondary education. When the secondary school was selective, no problem existed; in a simpler society, the task of finding or creating a suitable occupation was, for a well-trained individual, not very difficult. At the present time, for all except the very best individuals, it is. Secondary education, extended to the point where it is part of common education, requires that the school assume, for all but the top group, some responsibility for training of a commercial, industrial, semi-technical, or semi-professional kind. The emphasis on vocational training should be made to vary inversely with the intellectual ability of the student. The method must also vary with capacity. Only with the least bright can vocational training be interpreted as specific training in the skills needed for a particular job. Throughout it must be remembered that progress in intellectual development is from a specific concrete to a general abstract. Even in vocational training (except with the least bright) facts should point toward principles, skills toward general method, and all of them together should combine to present a clear, understandable, coherent picture of the Good Life in action.

II

The conception of secondary education that is today prevalent in the United States is of course expressive of the values that dominate contemporary American life. Secondary education reflects the strengths and the weaknesses of American society. In a society that has demonstrated its ability to maintain the democratic way of life, that in large degree does afford a chance to those with ability, regardless of humble beginnings, to rise to the top, that has confidence in the educational process and supports it with generosity, secondary education would be expected to reflect these admirable characteristics. In a society, however, that carries the concept of democracy to the extreme of equalitarianism, that permits equality of opportunity often to breed selfish opportunism, that is materialistic, undisciplined, contemptuous of the past and of

[10] *Vide* p. 137, footnote.

tradition and prideful of itself—in such a society, education is bound
to possess certain serious defects. When these defects, moreover, become incorporated in educational philosophy and in educational
psychology, and become rationalized and idealized indiscriminately
with the other more desirable traits, they become doubly difficult to
dislodge both from society and from education.

In response to the educational demands made by life in a democratic,
highly industrialized, complex society, education has been extended
horizontally and vertically. Common education has been extended
upward, and it has taken in the secondary period. Secondary education
is on the road toward becoming universal. We have set as our aim
the raising of the general level of living of every man and woman
in the United States, and we have taken steps to realize this aim. We
have given to every normal boy and girl access to the secondary school.
To this extent, what we have done is highly commendable.[11] Beyond
this point, our efforts have not been so wisely expended.

Perhaps the most serious charge that can be made against American
secondary education is that it has identified equality of educational
opportunity with sameness of opportunity. Equality of educational
opportunity is a virtue in any state; in a democracy, it is an indispensable condition. But equality of educational opportunity must be
interpreted in the light of individual differences, not in disregard of
them. The secondary school has been thrown open to all students,
but secondary education has not been differentiated according to the
types and degrees of ability that the students represent. All have been
treated as equals. A common measure of education has been applied.
Bright and dull, both are offered opportunity for the same education,
and are judged by equal standards. Since this is not easily done, the
common standard has been depressed so that it.is actually realizable
by most students. There has been differentiation of many sorts—
differentiation according to "interests," according to "practical needs,"
and so on, but no real differentiation according to the intellectual capacity of students. American secondary education suffers from mediocrity—it is pitched on the level of the average student, its expectancy of
attainment is average. The chief sufferers have been, of course, the
bright students, but through them American society as a whole has

[11] Foerster is excepted. *The American State University*, pp. 172 ff. 1937.

suffered. Even before a theory of education came along to justify and rationalize willfulness and the withholding of effort unless "motivated," the American people had suffered from a general lowering of standards which, if secondary education did not actively beget, it certainly did nothing to correct. A high order of common living requires that the best minds show the way; this guidance has for a long time not been sufficiently available.

It was inevitable that a school which treated all its students alike should in time reduce education to the level of practical training. As long as the secondary school was a selective institution, it was relatively easy to maintain a true perspective of its educational function. With a heterogeneous student body representing more than half the available population, it became impossible to retain a high type of training and have common standards too. The high type of training went. Out of the naturalistic and materialistic tendencies already present in American society, there emerged a new psychology the central idea of which was that it was possible to know and to guide human conduct without a knowledge of mind and without worrying too much about mind. A psychology of education arose around the behavioristic principle that education was conditioning. Secondary education, for almost all students, has become a matter of practical training—training in fundamental processes, home membership, vocation, worthy use of leisure time, and the like. Secondary education has lost its idealistic *purpose* —its purpose of assisting individuals in the recognition and realization of the Good Life—and become a humdrum preparation for the routine of social living. It is apparently the belief of pragmatic behaviorism that mere intellect is not sufficient to ensure worthy home membership, that a man has to be "trained" for it. Secondary education has become training for this "adjustment" and that, and since the vocational problem admittedly looms large among the modern problems of living, secondary education has become job-minded even in the case of superior students who do not require vocational training in the secondary school. The use of vocational materials and activities is not necessarily inconsistent with liberal education, but even this use must aim at something more than vocational skills—it must aim at the "sound mind in the sound body." Secondary education has no faith in the general competence of moral and intelligent human beings to solve successfully their life-problems; it has attempted to show them how the myriad of life problems are to be solved. Since all individuals are not equally concerned with all these problems, secondary education has been divided and subdivided according to "interest" and "practical needs." Thus we witness the anomaly of essentially the same type of education that leads off into different directions. Specialization exists, but it is not the specialization of means to attain common general ends or specialization of individual ends upon a base of common ends already attained. The same kind of thinking has further been productive of parochialism in secondary education. The common Good Life has been reduced to a community affair.

The present crisis in national and in world affairs demands of the American people strenuous self-discipline, devotion to ideals long sought and partially gained, self-possession, rationality, clear thinking, trust in mankind. In all of these important things, secondary education has failed the American people. Like the rest of American education, it is falling under the spell of a theory that encourages "experimentation" with human values, that counsels against definite loyalty to anything except the "experimental attitude," that sets up the individual as the arbiter of morality. When respect for law and justice, morality and religion, orderly processes, the rights of others, when steadfastness and uprightness of character, and devotion to ideals are more than ever needed, secondary education turns to the cultivation of the "personality" of the individual. Self-interest, "felt" needs, desires become the accredited mainsprings of conduct. In the same way, secondary education has not lived up to its responsibility for the high cultivation of the human intelligence. No school that is obedient to a pragmatic psychology and that conceives as its duty the practical training for routine functions can produce in human beings a high order of intellectual power.

Secondary education has fallen victim to the panic that has spread from the overemphasis on the "change" that has occurred in our living. By a strange twist of logic, material changes seem to require as a necessary corollary a change in human nature, and a change in human nature calls for a new conception of education. It is forgotten that human beings make changes, and that it was a race of men "traditionally" educated that instituted the present changes. There is also heard frequently the suggestion that not only must education be radically changed but it must take over the leadership of society and guide it in the specific direction that the "changes" indicate. The principle that free human beings are capable of directing themselves and that the primary responsibility of education is to help produce such individuals is repudiated. Some educational leaders have already made a design of the new social order, and all that society has to do is to follow instructions. Fortunately this threat to democracy is only an academic one; actually society will never permit the school to lead it in directions that are not acceptable to it and are not sanctioned by the wisdom of human experience.

Finally, secondary education has suffered from those who, disdaining philosophy, have turned to science for spiritual guidance in educational problems. Lacking faith and direction, these men have resorted to fact-finding and experimentation. Secondary education has accumulated a great many facts about itself, and, not knowing what to do with them, it has gone on accumulating more. Amid pseudo-philosophies with mistaken ideas and a pseudo-science with facts but with hardly any ideas at all, amid societal weaknesses that require correction but strongly resist it, secondary education, with the great task that it has undertaken of raising the educational level of a whole people, is indeed confused and misled.

III

A theory of education is an expression of a theory of life. An idealistic theory of education can truly spring only from such a theory of life. It is useless to expect an age that has turned its back upon humanistic values in living to recapture humanistic values in education. Revival in education will come with a general revival of faith in mind, the power of mind, and the values of mind. A new theory of society and a new psychology will have to be integrated to form a new theory of education. The essence of the new theory of society will be a recognition of the meaning of freedom, of the meaning of equality, of the meaning of democracy, of the meaning of the Good Life for the individual and for society. The essence of the new psychology will be a recognition of the meaning of *human* development as against both natural growth and animal-like conditioning. Out of the integration of the two will come a theory of education that is idealistic and intellectual. It will aim at the realization of the Good Life, and it will achieve its ends through the physical, intellectual, moral, emotional development of the individual. Under such a theory, secondary education will be restored to its true function. It will not "integrate personalities," nor will it endeavor to dictate to society, nor will it train individuals merely in utilitarian skills. Working within the setting of the American culture and in conformity with its democratic ideals, it will help to raise each person in ethical character and in material effectiveness to a high common level, and, beyond that, as far as the individual's capacity will carry him and in the particular directions in which his intellectual interests and aptitudes incline him. It will recognize the societal need for a high common level of living, but it will also recognize and respect the basic fact of differentness among human beings. In extent, the secondary school will be common to all persons to the end of the adolescent period,[12] but in its specific objectives and its processes it will vary with the capacity of each learner. It will aim toward a common Good Life for all, but it will realize it to different extents and in different ways with different individuals. It will recognize that the Good Life is expressed in certain ethical virtues as well as in material power, and it will endeavor to inculcate in all individuals the virtues of kindness, of sympathy, of humility, of self-restraint and self-possession, of tolerance, of courage, of personal responsibility, of concern for others, of love of justice and of truth, of order and decorum, of patriotism, of love of God, and the power that comes with knowledge, with good methods of acquiring and of using knowledge, and with the intellectual virtues of open-mindedness, honesty of judgment, thoroughness. Secondary education will recognize that human intelligence is basic in its whole process, that, above all else, education is the training that converts intellectual capacity into intellectual power. It will once more concede that intellectual power can be generally effective and can be generally gained, and the process of secondary education will become a process of training the mind so that it produces a maximum of such effectiveness. The materials of education will be chosen by what they contribute to these ends in terms of the capacity of the learner. The essence of

[12] Foerster is excepted. *Vide* p. 213, footnote 5.

intelligence will be recognized as the capacity, through the instrumentality of meanings, to know the world and to live in it. According as this capacity is greater or less, the specific purposes of secondary education will be decided. To each person, his proper education. There will be neither a single standard common to all, nor the kind of flexible adjusting of standards that soon ceases to challenge human effort. Secondary education will be truly differentiated. The most gifted people will be trained in the most important ways, and they will be selected to continue their studies in higher institutions. The others, each to his appropriate degree, will be trained so that they become independent, responsible citizens of society, and, more important, in the eyes of the world, good men.

SOCIAL EVOLUTIONISM

I

That civilization may renew itself in every generation of man, that each individual may attain to the level of living that his society has reached and progress beyond it, that the entire race may thus continually move in an upward course in its living, education is necessary. An education that serves the individual serves the race; it is at the same time an agency of individual development and of racial evolution. Born into the present advanced and highly complex environment, the individual could never "naturally" adjust himself to it on its own level; adjustment within such an environment presumes the power to make successfully certain adaptations which the individual does not inherently possess and which he could not "naturally" obtain. The purpose of education is, in the course of his own maturation, to equip the individual with those learned adaptations that render him capable of living on the general level of his environment and of helping to raise that level. The great human capacity for self-adaptation enables man to acquire, by learning, needed traits that function as effectively in adjustment as do traits transmitted by physical heredity. While man has evolved very little in organic structure during the whole of the historical period,[18] human life has changed very greatly for the better. By the

[18] W. C. Bagley, *The Educative Process*, p. 17. 1905.

same process that it enables man, the individual, to rise to a higher level of living, education enables the race to make progress through social rather than through organic evolution. In either case there is assumed a continuous, unfailing transmission of those adaptations that the race has learned to make, and a process of assisting the individual, in the course of his own growth, to acquire these adaptations and to make them operate in personal behavior. That is in essence what education tries to do.

From this, two principles relating to the value and meaning of education can by inference be derived. It can be inferred at once that education cannot in any sense be regarded as a luxury, for the individual or for society. Education is among the most essential necessities. It is not merely for "culture," or for intellectual, emotional, or spiritual "refinement." It is not a privilege to be fully enjoyed by some (whether by a social or by an intellectual "elite") and only partly by others, depending upon whether they are lacking in one thing or another. And to deprive a person of any part of the necessary education on grounds of insufficient "native intelligence" is just as reprehensible as to do it on grounds of insufficient wealth. Equally pointless is any controversy as to whether education inherently deals only with intellect or with intellect and emotions both. Education has as its purpose to assist every individual to become the kind of person who can make adjustment to his environment, who progressively can do it better. Education performs a life-giving service; through transmission and inculcation of necessary learnings it helps every individual to become a person who can put to vital uses, for himself and for others, the energies with which nature has endowed him. Withhold these learnings, and you make it impossible for him to achieve the full life of which he is capable. The problem of individual differences does not by any means create a dilemma. Individual differences there always have been and always will be; regardless of individual differences, however, every person must be rendered capable of making successful adjustment to his environment. Individual differences may constitute a large problem of method, but they do not affect the meaning of education. With respect to the problem of living, all men are alike, and education must succeed in equal or similar degree with all of them.

The same valuation must be placed upon education when that is regarded from the point of view of society. From this point of view as well education is not a luxury. In order that society may not degenerate, it must take care to instill in all its members the ideals, the attitudes, the knowledges, and the skills that are needed for effective common living, and to make of these individuals independently social and adaptable men and women. Society without education cannot maintain itself; society that extends education to only a portion of its population cannot flourish or improve. Education cannot, of course, in itself assure societal goodness—it is incumbent upon the society of adult individuals to maintain the values that education transmits. Nor, when a societal breakdown comes, can education always be held responsible; it is the society as a whole that must assume responsibility. But education—the effective transmission of the right learnings and the process of assisting in the proper development, through them, of every individual—is the first bulwark against societal breakdown and the first indispensable condition of societal progress. It is thus rather childish to inquire whether society can afford to maintain effective educational agencies and activities; it is a good deal like inquiring whether an organism can afford to remain healthy. " . . . It is as unreasonable to question the ability of the United States, or of any of the states, to maintain an adequate and proper school system as it would be to find fault with the organs of digestion on the ground that the body cannot afford the blood supply essential to their tissues." [14] Impressed with the truth of this, society has recently created an instrument—the universal school—that assures to all the dissemination of at least the essential learnings and some degree of training in the qualities necessary for successful living.

The second principle that can be inferred relates to the meaning of education as distinct from growth and natural maturation and the degree of self-development that is implicit in these. While both growth and maturation take place in the course of the educational process, education implies much more than that. By a process of natural growth and maturation in a perfectly simple environment a person may develop certain satisfactory adaptive responses that would enable him to make moderately successful adjustment on a fairly low life-level. He could not, of course, achieve for himself anything approximating that order of living which we can call civilization. In a complex societal en-

[14] H. C. Morrison, *School and Commonwealth*, pp. 165–166. 1937.

vironment, where development in the course of ordinary growth and maturation would not be "natural" but would be the resultant of many social forces exerting pressure in various directions, a person by a process of "self-development" or "self-education" might acquire, on his own, sufficient of the needed learnings to become a very satisfactorily adjusting person. Indeed, many such self-educated individuals have risen to positions of high eminence among their fellows. But it is unlikely that a sufficient number of individuals would, by such a process of development, be enabled to rise to a point where they could make successful adjustment. At any rate the risk is too great and the issue is too vital. Long ago society instituted the practice of providing systematic training, during the period of infancy and youth, looking toward successful adjustment. The family in the home, the church, the school, and from time to time other social agencies and processes, supplement with direct instruction the learnings informally acquired from the social environment.

"The school is essentially an instrument which society has used for transmitting to each generation in the body politic the discipline, the enlightenment, the culture which represent the education of the period."[15] But the school does more than that; it helps to translate into the experience of the individual learner the racial learnings that it makes available. Schooling and education are of course not synonymous; throughout all of life man may be said to assimilate learnings —from the racial as well as from his own experience—that serve him in adjustment. But insofar as education may be used in a specific sense to mean that systematic training in racial learnings which is given to every person, especially during youth, to enable him to achieve a degree of personal development adequate for successful adjustment, schooling may be said to be an indispensable adjunct of education. In fact, in recent years the school has been assuming a more comprehensive and responsible role in the educational process.

It may perhaps be necessary explicitly to repudiate a notion that has, by implication, already been made untenable. Education, it has been stated, is in very large part a process of systematic training of the individual in those learnings that, when acquired and used as adaptations,

[15] H. C. Morrison, "A Definition of Secondary Education and Its Implications," *High School Quarterly,* 17:115, April, 1929.

enable him to carry on adjustment on a high level. It is necessary to repudiate any suggestion that proper education comes about through unfoldment of one's inherited or inner potentialities. In the first place, though one does possess certain innate general tendencies, it cannot be said that one inherits potentialities for one thing or another.[16] There really is not very much that can be unfolded. In the second place, and speaking positively, education seeks to establish in every individual certain tendencies that successful living requires and that he does not, to begin with, possess. Education, for example, seeks to make of every individual a self-disciplining person. Now self-discipline is not a quality that is inherent in human nature; in fact it may be shown that behavior that may be called instinctive is totally lacking in qualities of self-discipline. Yet, the self-disciplining personality is a desired outcome of education. The same may be shown to be true of other traits that successful living makes essential; they are not inherent in human behavior to begin with, and to establish them it is sometimes necessary to counteract other more natural tendencies. Education in the broadest sense means the acquirement of experiences that serve to modify inherited adjustments toward social ends. It must be emphasized that education is not the liberation of personality, as that is popularly understood. There is nothing to liberate. Education is rather a process of building or creating personality. That is in a sense liberation, too. In fact the personality that through the medium of learnings has acquired the power to operate independently with effectiveness in its environment is the truly liberated personality.

Used in its technical sense, education implies preparation; it implies preparation for independent, successful living in the environmental culture surrounding the individual. The educational process, to be sure, cannot offer guarantees of complete and continuous consequent success. Life is an evolving, developing thing. Adjustment is continuously taking on new and added meaning, and producing new problems. The function of education is to make of everyone the kind of person who can contribute to the achievement of new ends of living and who can solve successfully the new problems. This implies the power of continuous self-adaptation to whatever conditions arise. Adaptability is the essence of mind; the growth in human adaptability has coincided

[16] H. C. Morrison, *Basic Principles of Education*, p. 349. 1934.

with the extension of human power in nature. Adaptability is gained through acquisition by learning of those adaptations that the race has invented in the course of its long adjusting experience. The racial learnings offer the only basis for adaptability. By making them part of his personal equipment and by using them as necessity requires, the individual can solve successfully the ordinary problems of adjustment that confront him; in the light of adaptations that he already possesses, he can go on to invent or create new adaptations that will serve him in adequate adjustment to new or especially difficult situations. The function of education is to prepare the individual for adaptability, to render him adaptable. There is nothing more and nothing else that education can really do; it cannot help the individual to solve his future problems specifically, in advance, because it does not have a very good idea of what those problems will be.

Human life at the present stage of human progress is, without any serious alternative possibility, societal life. Society has become the indispensable condition of human living on any civilized level. The Good Life at once suggests the social life; goodness must inherently carry with it the suggestion of socialness. Adaptability implies socialness. The adaptable person operates within and through a social culture; he possesses the traits that make him also a desirable member of society. Society is not a loose aggregation of individuals, but an organism that possesses the qualities of unity and relatedness. Individuals living in society must not only refrain from violating each other's rights, but must also feel themselves held together by common ideals and attitudes, and ways of living. They must be working toward the same ends and in the same general ways. They must be conscious of their interrelatedness, and that consciousness must be in control of their conduct. That a man may be complete as an individual he must be conscious of himself as a member of a group. Educating for adaptability does not mean educating each person to look out for himself. Independence does not mean aloofness. The good person needs not only to recognize strong social restraints; he must be motivated by active social sympathies and by attitudes that serve to bind society together in a strong cooperating unity.

Although it is inherently concerned with social welfare, education—it must be pointed out—does not yet deal with societal "futures." No more than organic evolution is social evolution a process that operates mechanically according to predictive laws. The nature of future human life is not predictable in advance. Mind makes its own laws as it goes along. The school is no better fitted than any other institution to tell society what lies in the future. The responsibility of education is to transmit the great racial learnings, and through them to make the individual as adept in his living as possible. That is all that education does; the individual then goes on to develop his own future. Nor, incidentally, can education proceed lightly about the business of reconstructing society. The foundations of society are more deeply imbedded in human nature than many think. "Many of us talk glibly about planning what we call a 'new social order'. We might as well talk about planning a new and better human physiology. No doubt most of us have days when we devoutly wish that just that could be done. We have come, however, to cherish only a mild enthusiasm for gland doctors; and, rough hew us as they will, our surgeons seem still to be obliged to work within the limitations imposed by metabolism and the nervous system." [17] Impatient as we may be with the shortcomings of society, it is necessary to rely upon responsible and intelligent human beings to work out their own salvation, and not to thrust one upon them.

On the other hand, it is equally bad for education to go to the other extreme and not to recognize the shortcomings of society as such. Education enjoys a certain immunity from societal restriction by virtue of the fact that it is disinterested, or rather, that it is interested in the *genuine* welfare of society. Education must not succumb to societal fashions; it must not be induced to accept as values those modes of behavior which it knows to be false and socially negative and destructive. Not everything that society accepts as good is genuinely good. Education serves best its social responsibility not by being servile to social fashions, but by being loyal to those things which stand for civilization.

The goal of education is the promotion of successful human living. This is the principal criterion that is effective in determining what, in a given societal situation, are the necessary learnings and how long a period is required for their acquisition. Ideally, this criterion should be interpreted in maximal rather than minimal terms. The question ought to be, "What learnings and how long an educational period are

[17] H. C. Morrison, *School and Commonwealth*, pp. 191–192. 1937.

necessary so that the individual can be enabled to live as good a life as
he can achieve within his social environment?" But social economics
require also that the educational problem be viewed realistically—from
the point of view of the absolutely necessary rather than the ideal. The
question must therefore be reconstructed somewhat: "What are the
learnings that, in the present social situation, are necessary for *satisfactory* adjustment, and how long a school period is required for their
transmittance and inculcation?" For the answer it is necessary to turn
to a review of those conditions that characterize "the present social
situation."

The conditions of living in our society have become exceedingly
complex and the problems difficult. We have reached a new high level
in the scale of social evolution, from the point of view of needed adaptive skill, much higher than any previously attained. The problems that
confront us are qualitatively different from those prevailing in a simple
economy. There are difficulties arising from the extreme specialization
of economic activity and from the mechanization of economic processes;
these have been accentuated by the abruptness with which we have
plunged into the period of economic transition. The vocational problem has become a difficult one: it is increasingly harder to find a job;
more and more do the non-routine occupations that are left require a
high degree of intelligence.[18] A satisfactory balance among the various
economic factors is still to be achieved, and from the economic maladjustments arise many troublesome social and political situations.[19]
Though the immediate future should see the solution of some of these
problems, many problems will still remain and new ones will undoubtedly continue to develop. The Good Life presumes a willingness and
an ability on the part of all individuals to contribute in the solving of
these problems. The general situation points indisputably to the conclusion that satisfactory living in our culture requires a degree of adaptability greater than ever before. Adaptability has always been at a
premium in human living; conditions today make it a necessity.

Adaptability, it has been said, implies socialness. But more than ever
before, special social training is a necessity. The problems before us

[18] W. C. Bagley, "The Task of Education under the New Deal," *Educational
Administration and Supervision,* 19:561–570, September, 1933.
[19] *Vide* pp. 81 ff.

have aggravated the effects of certain long existing weaknesses in our societal nature.[20] We cannot solve our economic problems or dispel the many other threats that hover over us unless we are socially strong. More than ever before, education must exert itself on behalf of socialness, and must bring to bear upon the individual the learnings that will make him a self-disciplined, socially-oriented person.

The period of human growth to maturity is the natural period of education. Our present social situation requires that education be extended almost up to the point of maturity; the multitude and difficulty of the learnings to be transmitted require that nothing less be considered adequate. Education throughout this period must be *general education* —that is, it must concern itself with the development of the general qualities of mind and character that make for successful living in our environment. General education is "concerned primarily with the production of really educated men and women, individuals who will do their life work in some special field, but who are primarily concerned with getting into intellectual or moral touch with the world, and not merely with being breadwinners and producers."[21] General education must be extended to all, and its aims must be common to all. Regardless of individual differences, all young people must, through the instrumentality of general education, be raised to the high level of adaptive efficiency that will enable them to live intelligently in their common environment. Up to the age of eighteen or twenty all young people must be trained for generally efficient living in society.

However it may have been regarded in the past, secondary education must now be regarded as part of universal general education. Whatever were its former aims (whether, as some described it, to give "liberal education" or "culture," or, as was more accurate, to offer preprofessional training to a small class of youth), its present aims must conceive it as part of the universal school for the preparation of youth for general living. Secondary education must divest itself of any aristocratic pretensions that still cling to it. It must sever its close connection with higher education, and establish a new and better articulation with the primary school. The severance of the connection between secondary and higher education will probably involve a re-examination of the

[20] *Vide* pp. 84–85.
[21] H. C. Morrison, *School and Commonwealth,* pp. 92–93. 1937.

purposes of the higher institution, and very likely its reconstruction; it is a fact that the work of the first two years of the college has not been very different from that of the secondary school. Another task that faces the secondary school is the redefinition of its aims in the light of its new purpose within general education. Primary and secondary education in point of general purpose constitute a unity. The special aims of the secondary school must be defined functionally, in terms of the developmental progress of the learner and the nature of the learnings to be administered.

The period of secondary education may be said to extend from the end of the primary period to the end of the general educational process (as defined). Experience has shown that primary education can be effectively given in about six school years, or up to about the age of twelve.[22] In terms of an age period, therefore, secondary education may be said to extend from this point up to the age of eighteen or twenty, when the student will have been able to acquire the traits—volitional, moral, intellectual—that mark him as a mature person. Beyond secondary education training of a professional character should be available to those who are most likely to profit from it. The American educational system should "draw a line between secondary schools and institutions of higher education clearly and definitely so as to exclude from admission to the higher institutions all persons not qualified for independent intellectual activity."[23]

Far more important, however, than any definition of the formal extent of secondary education is a definition of its special function within the larger process of general education. Since there is still a good deal

[22] Morrison does not accept this. Though reluctant to admit that secondary education can be defined at all in other than purely functional terms, Morrison believes that with effective teaching the primary adaptations can be acquired approximately by the age of nine. (*The Practice of Teaching in the Secondary School*, p. 13. Rev. Edit. 1931.) In his functional definition of secondary education as well, Morrison differs somewhat from Judd and Bagley. Secondary education begins at the point where the student has acquired the primary adaptations that enable him to continue learning through "study and the use of books." (*Ibid.*, p. 7.) Judd and Bagley interpret the secondary period as the period which more broadly concerns itself with advanced learnings, with the cultivation of the higher mental processes, and with progressively greater independence in study.

[23] C. H. Judd, "The Reorganization and Coordination of Secondary and College Education," *Institute for Administrative Officers of Higher Institutions Yearbook*, p. 95. 1933.

to be learned regarding the nature of human development on the higher levels, a statement of the special function of the secondary school can be given only in general terms. The goal of the educational process is adaptability, with everything in the way of volitional and social development as well as intellectual power that this implies. An individual advances toward this goal as he acquires the learnings that constitute the principal human adaptations. Some of the learnings are predominantly intellectual, as, for example, the language adaptation and the number adaptation, ideas concerning the nature of the world and of man, the meaning of society and social institutions; some of the learnings are volitional and moral, as, for example, the ideal and the habit of self-control, respect for law and justice, regard for the rights of others, cooperativeness, self-reliance, moral courage. Individual development consists in taking over these modes of behavior and these knowledges, and incorporating them into one's own living. Certain of these learnings are basic to all others, language and number among them; these must be acquired first. But systematically in the course of his development, as the individual acquires these learnings and grows and is changed by them, he becomes more capable of making the adjustments that his own living requires. When development has gone to the point from which the individual can himself carry on successfully the important adjustment activities of his environment, the process of systematic, formal education through the organized agency of the school should cease.

The multitude of learnings that the race has accumulated in its long experience, the difficulty in assimilation that they naturally present, and yet the crucial role that they play in successful adjustment in our modern environment, all argue for the need for an extended educational process. The learnings are intrinsically such that a primary and a secondary educational period are necessary. The learnings must be organized and presented in carefully graded series. Basic learnings, without which no further learning is possible, must come first. Some learnings also are needed for satisfactory immediate living; without them the child cannot adequately exist, even in an immature state. Moreover, certain needed learnings presume considerable progress toward physical, emotional, or social maturity—learnings, for example, of a biological, ethical, religious, esthetic nature; others—methods of thinking, the solution of troublesome problems—presume considerable progress in intellectual development. The point is that primary and secondary education are no mere terms of administrative convenience. Primary education is concerned with helping the child to make those primary and basic adaptations without which he cannot exist satisfactorily in his immediate life-situation and without which he cannot possibly develop further. In the nature of things, the child cannot obtain these learnings for himself; he must be given them. Such learnings are the essential habits and knowledges relating to health, habits and attitudes relating to personal behavior, essential motor and manipulative skills, the use of language in speech, in reading, and in writing, elementary number concepts, facts, and skills, knowledge concerning the physical world, concerning the world of man. Possessing these, a child can maintain himself in his immediate life-adjustments at the same time that he can take more personal charge of his continued development. In the secondary period, he continues to take on new learnings and to integrate them with the old, but in the learning process he exhibits a new and increasing independence. There is greater self-reliance in the acquisition of learnings, greater emphasis upon organization, evaluation, and application. Volitionally and morally as well as intellectually, the progression toward maturity is evident. Adaptability implies ability to carry on independently the process of adjustment, and in the achievement of such independence the process of general education must culminate.

In this, therefore, lies the functional significance of secondary education: in secondary education the emphasis is on all those things, both in content and in method, that make for volitional, moral, and intellectual independence. The approach toward such independence must be sensed. Aims, curriculum, instruction must be imbued with it. A rich content of learnings must progressively involve the use of the higher and more complex mental processes. "The minds of pupils must be exposed to a sufficient range of experiences to insure the cultivation of mental agility and adaptability." [24] There must be a development of intellectual interests to insure the continuance of "self-propelled intel-

[24] C. H. Judd, "In Defense of American Secondary Schools," National Education Association, Department of Secondary School Principals, *Bulletin,* 45:8. March, 1933.

lectual activity." [25] There must be a progressively increasing emphasis upon organization and application. The method of instruction must be based increasingly upon individual study,[26] upon the independent use of intellectual tools. Volitionally and morally there must be increased emphasis upon self-guidance and self-discipline. The end of secondary education is reached when the student is intellectually mature as well as morally and volitionally mature. General education is complete at maturity.

It is impossible at this time to describe in greater detail the special function of the secondary school. A much more precise formulation of its function, and of the specific functions of the smaller units comprising it, will be possible after application has been made of some of the general educational principles here stated and a comprehensive re-organization of the whole educational structure undertaken. In any event, trial and experimentation will be needed. Social science will have to contribute by identifying more specifically the needed racial learnings on the higher levels, and psychological science by ascertaining more accurately the manner of operation of the higher mental processes. But ultimately, the units comprising the structure of secondary education, as well as the units comprising the larger structure of general education, will be determined in terms of their special contribution to the development of the individual.[27]

It is necessary to speak briefly of the possible relationship of vocational education to the purpose of the secondary school. Secondary education is part of the total process of general education. General education has no specialistic purposes. Its aim is to produce men and women who are *generally* competent to make successful continuous adjustment to their environment. (Competence is a general capacity, and not an aggregate of a large number of petty skills. It is an outcome of adaptability.) The aim of secondary education is to build on the foundations of the primary school toward the end that the individual may achieve adaptability. The secondary school does not take on

[25] C. H. Judd, "The Reorganization and Coordination of Secondary and College Education," *Institute for Administrative Officers of Higher Institutions Yearbook*, pp. 89–101. 1933.

[26] *Vide* p. 236, footnote 22.

[27] Judd goes somewhat further in indicating the nature of a proposed reorganization of the secondary school. (*Education and Social Progress*, pp. 255 ff. 1934.)

specialized activities except as they contribute to the general end of adaptability. Vocational preparation is not therefore per se one of the objectives of secondary education. Whether, however, vocational materials can with some students be used to contribute to the ends of general development, is another question. It is a legitimate question, but it is a question of method of secondary education rather than aim, and will be so considered.[28]

II

In the United States, secondary education has developed in a manner that is unique. Nurtured by the large social and economic opportunity that is made available in a democracy and by the practical incentives for education that an industrial civilization offers, the secondary school has become an institution for almost all the people. Faced with the need for taking care of a very rapidly increasing school population, and unable to continue to apply the old aristocratic conception of a "liberal" education, the secondary school proceeded to evolve a new conception, not according to any set rules but in roughly experimental fashion, in accordance with the pressures of social forces.

The result is that the American secondary school is not like the secondary school of any other nation. It is common rather than exclusive, democratic rather than aristocratic. It stresses popular education rather than education for leadership or the production of an elite. It attempts to educate for life rather than to impart "culture." For all this the secondary school deserves great credit. On this account it ought not to pay great heed to those critics who accuse it of being not sufficiently discriminating in its admission of students, of not concentrating on the training of leaders, of departing from the traditional conception of liberal education, and so forth. The secondary school has taken the direction that an institution of general education in a highly industrialized, complex, democratic society should take.

A great experiment is not unaccompanied by mistakes, by stopgap devices and makeshift policies that remain after their usefulness is over, by repairs hurriedly made that soon call for new repairs. Moreover, a conception of education that represents no long-term planning but an

[28] *Vide* pp. 326 ff.

evolution under the pressure of different social forces must inevitably contain inconsistencies, overlappings, discontinuities. Accordingly American secondary education does have weaknesses that must be attributed to its pioneering purpose: the various school units lack articulation, there are large internal discontinuities, there is unjustified duplication and repetition and equally unjustified omission, there are incongruities such as the credit system. There is no denying that the tremendous task that secondary education has undertaken has left it with many weaknesses that will soon have to be eliminated by a thorough overhauling and reorganization of the educational structure. But this elimination of weaknesses must be accompanied not by lessening but by increasing emphasis on the democratic purpose of secondary education.

The real weaknesses of American secondary education do not lie in its excessive democratization, nor in the fact that it has discarded the old aristocratic conception of secondary education for something that it judged to be more suited to the needs of modern industrial civilization. Nor are the most serious weaknesses of American secondary education those of structural incoordination, overlapping, etc. The real weaknesses arise from the fact that secondary education has become too completely saturated with the individualistic, unsocial, opportunistic spirit pervading the modern American society, from the fact that it relies too much upon a mechanistic psychology and a soft pedagogy. These factors to a large extent have operated to neutralize the good that the extension of opportunity for secondary education might have done, and to misdirect the attempts of the secondary school to develop a program well-adjusted to our present social needs.

In a very real sense the secondary school may be charged with reflecting too faithfully the motivating attitudes of modern society. Education is of course the servant of society; it serves society, however, not by catering to its moods but by stimulating it to meet better its real problems of adjustment. Society is at present going through a critical transitional period. Some of its strains, some of its weaknesses, may be attributed to the severity of the crisis that it is going through. On the other hand, some are an expression of fundamental defects that have long been existent in the American social organism, and that present events have thrown into relief. Under the circumstances education is expected not to be ruled by prevailing fashions, not to emulate societal weaknesses, but to throw itself into the breach and work with special strength on behalf of truly needed values. In such a situation education must stress discipline, social attitudes, intellectual balance, moral courage. In a period in which mechanization threatens to reduce labor to non-intellectual routine and ultimately perhaps to rob the individual of the need for initiative and for sustained intellectual effort, education must bend its energies to make the desire and the ability to work, intellectually and in every other way, the cherished possession of every individual. But education has not done this.[29] It has chosen to go along with the times. It has accepted the leadership of a "naturalistic" philosophy that conceives of man, not as the kind of person that *he can become,* that he has it in his power to be through the help of learnings amassed in the course of social evolution, but as the kind of person that he naïvely is.

To this fact the weakness of secondary education must be traced. Secondary education has itself contributed to the general slackening of morale and intellectual stamina. It has become soft. It has neglected its socializing responsibilities. Too much attention has been paid to individual "wants" and "needs" and not enough to the duties and obligations that societal living exacts of individuals. In personal conduct the ideal of discipline has fallen into disfavor, and educational theory encourages what it calls "freedom" and "self-expression." There is too little heart for serious work. Granted that the task of providing secondary education for more than half of the available youth in the population is an enormous one, both standards and achievement have fallen much too low. The values that come with learning how to work with sustained energy, how to exert one's self to overcome obstacles, have not been realized. There has not on the whole been very much exertion; the serious endeavor that is characteristic of European secondary education is notable by its absence. As for intellectual attainment, "it is generally agreed among competent students of the problem that our average 18-year old high school graduate in scholarship is far behind the average 18-year old graduates of the secondary school of

---

[29] The criticism that follows is more suggestive in tone of Bagley and Morrison than of Judd. While agreeing with the general points made, Judd would be considerably milder in expression. *Vide* p. 85, footnote 29.

many other countries. . . . But even granting that secondary education elsewhere is in general selective, there is abundant evidence that in our laudable efforts to send everyone to and through high school, standards have been unnecessarily lowered. Both the bright and the slow pupils are handicapped by weaknesses in fundamentals that all except the hopelessly subnormal are able to master. Within the past decade the effectiveness of high school instruction has been weakened by increasing disabilities in so basic an accomplishment as reading. It is scarcely too much to say, indeed, that increasing proportions of pupils in the junior and senior high schools are essentially illiterate." [30]

The mechanistic psychology upon which secondary education is based makes it extremely unlikely that the goal of adaptability will in any case be attained. In denying the validity of the transfer theory, this psychology in fact denies the possibility of educating for adaptability; indeed the concept of adaptability does not loom large in modern educational values. Secondary education is increasingly becoming a kind of training for many fixed, specialized particulars. The subject-matter of education has been expanded tremendously, and many activities have crept in that are not educative at all. Studies which are instrumental in the narrow sense have taken the place of learnings which performed the broad service of developing social, adaptable personality. There has developed an indifference to organization, system, precision. Secondary education has indeed done its share in contributing to the bungling of many of our present problems; our general lack of adaptability is amply evidenced by our behavior in the current economic crisis.

Another effect of the mechanistic psychology operating in secondary education has been to lead people away from each other rather than to bring them together. The true object of general education is socialization, not individualization; an education, however, that has become particularized training in habits and skills cannot but lead people off in different directions. The secondary school has lost sight of its true purpose. An unhealthy determinism operating via an intelligence concept and intelligence tests has further served as a strong unsocializing influence. To some degree the old notion of an exclusive and aristocratic secondary education has given way to a new undemocratic and

[30] W. C. Bagley, "An Essentialist's Program for the Advancement of American Education," *Educational Administration and Supervision,* 24:242, April, 1938.

unsound notion that some individuals are by heredity marked as superior and others as inferior. Determinism in secondary education has led to differentiation in objectives, segregation of students, undue specialization of curricula. Secondary education has temporarily lost sight of the fact that its purpose is to raise the operating intelligence of all to a general high level.

Secondary education has suffered greatly from the influence of a "progressive" theory of education which while it tended to enfeeble the individual also tended to glorify him. To the fire of individualism, already burning too brightly in society, "progressive" education added fresh fuel. It has contributed in general to a childish preoccupation with self, to volitional immaturity, to a moral relaxation already too noticeable in society, to the lowering of intellectual standards and achievement. At the present time, curiously enough, "progressive" education is engaged in inciting American secondary education, and education in general, to take the lead in "reconstructing the social order" or in "planning a new society," as if education were gifted with a prophetic vision of the future and endowed with some special authority to take society apart and put it together again. As on education as a whole, the doctrines of "progressive" education have had a harmful effect on the secondary school.

III

American secondary education must continue to try to adapt itself to the real ideals and real needs of a democratic people and a highly industrial civilization. The fact that it has broken with European traditions with regard to selectivity and exclusiveness and so-called "liberalness" (as that is commonly interpreted in education) stands greatly to its credit. The fact that it is becoming a common school for general education is a recognition of the requirements of industrialism and democracy. The secondary school must continue in the tradition of the old American common school, raising common education to new levels. Insofar as it has neither precedents nor ready-made plans to follow, secondary education must rely for a solution of its problems upon the lessons of past experience, carefully refined through large-scale experimentation.

Secondary education must, however, regain a true perspective of the real aim of general education under present conditions of living. This involves both a realistic understanding of the nature of adjustment in a complex, technological, changing society, and an understanding of the developmental possibilities and processes of the human being. Secondary education must realize that environmental conditions of living militate against a conception of education that emphasizes mechanical responses to fixed situations and treats the higher mental processes as if they were not existent. Somehow, though its procedures are unquestionably unsuited to all the students in the secondary school today, the old secondary education had intuitively caught a better understanding of the possibilities of human development and of its general methods than does the modern school. Secondary education today must be reconstructed toward the end of training all its students, with an equal degree of success, in a modern way for modern living. It must study human behavior on the higher levels as a basis for its method, and it must canvass human history for those learnings that must furnish its content. With the help of educational science, it can do both these things. Secondary education must then satisfactorily adjust itself within the larger framework of general education, and assume that portion of the responsibility which, on a psychological basis, will be assigned to it.

Reflecting realistically on the meaning of adjustment, educational agencies will realize that adjustment takes place within society and in a cooperative way, and that society is an organic entity the welfare and strength of which are an indispensable condition for satisfactory adjustment. Training for adaptability will naturally emphasize social character, and the secondary school will do its share in developing desirable social as well as personal attributes in its individuals. Especially when there are social (and perhaps inevitable natural) forces abroad that threaten the unity of society, will secondary education energetically apply itself to this task. It will identify the desirable social traits, and will make all of its educational activities contribute somewhat to the building of them. The educational theories that cater unnecessarily to individualism will be discarded. Those elements in educational psychology that overemphasize and misinterpret the significance of individual differences among people will be removed or corrected.

Having verified scientifically what has long been empirically evident
—that the equipment of man renders him capable of tremendous development in the direction of a higher kind of living—secondary education will emancipate itself both from deterministic psychologies
which insist that human capacity is entirely subject to heredity and
that there is not much purpose, therefore, in aiming very high with
certain individuals, and from soft pedagogies which insist that "natural
tendencies," "natural interests," and "felt needs" merit great consideration and respect, and that effort and discipline are reprehensible because they are contrary to nature. Secondary education will then
cooperate within the larger framework of general education to help
build up in *all* individuals those traits that make for adaptable, intelligent living in the present situation. Regardless of individual differences all will be raised to the needed high level of intellectual ability.
Differences there will still be, but in large part differences will be in
intellectual interests, in intellectual aptitudes, in intellectual areas of
work. All individuals will attain a high degree of moral conduct, self-
control, personal integrity, social character. Discipline eventuating in
self-discipline will seem just as "natural" as behavior growing out of
pleasure-pain motivations. To the realization of such ends, the secondary school will direct itself.

It goes without saying that the flaws in the formal structure of secondary education must be removed. The inconsistencies that have
developed, the overlappings and the discontinuities that exist must be
eliminated. A comprehensive job of reorganization and consolidation
must be undertaken. But these are relatively minor flaws. They will
be corrected when it is possible for secondary education to act out of a
better understanding of its functional purpose in the broader scheme
of general education.

SOCIAL REALISM

1

The Good Life is conceived and actualized in society. Human ideals
have their origin in common social experience, are formulated by the
group, and are translated into common group practices and procedures.

Man does not live as an individual but as a member of a group; the ideals by which he is guided are those of the group with which he feels most closely identified, and that, in pragmatic terms, may be said to constitute his particular society.[31] That the individual may become effectively integrated within his society, that he may perform with competence those life-activities which in his society have been adjudged good, that he may contribute to the progressive conception and realization of higher life-activities, education is necessary. Education is without question dominated by society; it is socially inspired, directed, maintained, and supported. But it must be clearly understood that the ultimate value of education, like the ultimate value of society, is for the individual; through education he is inducted into the kind of life which his society, by common consent, accepts as good. Man does not possess innate preferences for development in special directions, but is capable of development in any one of a number of directions according to the experiences that he has. By means of education society takes the individual in its charge, and equips him with those ends and means of living of which it is itself possessed. He becomes a participating member of this group, living its life, cooperating with others in its improvement. He does not, by any means, give up entirely his individuality, but in the particular ways in which nature and his interests best fit him, lives his own life and contributes to the welfare of the group.

While there is life, there is learning. In a very real sense, social integration is going on all of the time, and man is constantly perfecting his technique of carrying on the established life-processes and developing new competences as new life-activities appear. And all of the time society exercises a broad supervision when it does not actively lend assistance to the individual. Education, with some justification, therefore, can be conceived as a lifelong process, carried on not only by special social agencies in a certain period of the life of the individual, but by the broad process of social experience during the whole of man's life. A distinction must, however, be made between this general lifelong process and that shorter, special process which has as its object to help the as-yet-immature individual to reach the point where he can take his place in society and carry on with competence its important life-activities. While in the former case the objective of learning is

---

[31] For elaboration of this point, *vide* Chapter I, pp. 100 ff.

identical with the objective of life itself, in the latter case the objective is more immediate preparation for competent societal living (and the term "preparation" must not be misunderstood and narrowly interpreted). In the period of his childhood and youth, the individual is equipped with the ideals, attitudes, knowledges, and skills through which his immediate needs of living are satisfied and he becomes capable of acquitting himself well in his role as a member of society. Helped to arrive at the point of initial social competence according to adult standards, he becomes capable of directing his own continued development and of learning effectively—directly from the whole of life-experience as well as from the special agencies of learning that society establishes.

It is in the more limited sense that the term "education" is here used. "Education" refers to the organized and systematic effort of society to guide the development of the individual from infancy to the point where he becomes capable of carrying on effectively the life-activities characterizing his society, and beyond which he can continue to develop in character and ability under his own immediate direction. The instruments which are available to the individual for this purpose are not only his own social experiences and the processes and agencies through which society as a whole operates, but special agencies maintained by society for the training of the young, agencies which provide experiences "with conscious intent of producing learning"[32] leading to social competence. The school is one, and probably the chief, of these agencies, but not the only one. The school is an agency founded and maintained by society for the purpose of guiding the development of the individual to the point where, in the estimate of society, he becomes a socially competent person. "The school is one of the agencies developed for the purpose of controlling human behavior. Its *modus operandi* consists entirely in the selection or influencing of the experiences of those who attend it. Its aim is to produce in them habits, skills, knowledges, concepts and ideals deemed to be desirable. As these types of products arise from the experience of the individual, formal education then is the provision of special experiences for special

[32] Committee on the Orientation of Secondary Education, *Issues of Secondary Education*, Department of Secondary School Principals, *Bulletin*, No. 59, p. 24. January, 1936.

purposes. This distinguishes it from informal education which is the influence upon future behavior of experience arising incidentally from the normal and natural activities of life. The school, in brief, may be thought of as providing a somewhat artificial short cut to educational objectives." [33]

Though the function of education, as here defined, is in the large sense preparatory, it must not be thought that the immediate needs and interests of the child and the youth (as well as his assured future needs as an individual) are overlooked in favor of the values and needs of the adult society. A child grows into an effective adult only as he learns progressively to deal effectively with the experiences of childhood and the experiences of youth. Education must satisfy the needs of young people at every stage of their development. As will later become apparent, the best preparation for living the Good Life in society is through the development in each individual of his interests, aptitudes, and capacities. Interests are dynamic, changing things, growing out of intimate personal experience; education that is constantly mindful of individual interests can never degenerate into preparation for "deferred" living.

In the discussion of the meaning and purpose of education, two principles are central. One relates to the responsibility of society for the individual. Out of regard for the well-being of all other individuals, society must take charge of each individual and help him to become, in accordance with its understanding, a good man. This society must do both to help the individual to achieve the kind of life that is best for him and to protect and preserve and better itself. The responsibility of society extends over the mature as well as over the immature, though in the case of the former much of the initiative is transferred to the individual. In the case of the child and the youth, the responsibility of society extends beyond what has been defined as education. "Society is responsible for the care and development of all children and youth from birth until they are able to fit successfully into social life and to discharge individually, without constant tutorial direction, their social responsibilities. The responsibilities of maturity cannot be cast upon the immature. Society should assume the responsibility of caring for

---

[33] H. R. Douglass, *Secondary Education for Youth in Modern America*, pp. 1–2. 1937.

the normal child through the home into which he is born, so ordering economic life that the parents of the child may, through honest work, provide adequate support to promote the child's physical and intellectual growth. For the irresponsible, the illegitimate, and the orphan, society must provide special institutional care or parental oversight in homes suited to the needs of individual cases. The child of normal intelligence in this group should be cared for in the public school; the entire needs of the sub-normal child may be met by the institution charged with his support."[34] The responsibility for education, therefore, does not constitute the whole of society's responsibility for the individual. The reason for this is to be found not in humanitarian considerations primarily nor in any paternalistic conception of the state; it is to be found in the pragmatic basis of society itself, in the purpose of its existence. Society is organized to promote the better living of individuals; it must undertake to do all those things that contribute to that better living. Now the continuous well-being (and therefore the care and education) of each individual is a matter vital not only to himself but to all other people living with him in society. (Society is *individuals-in-their-relations*. Individual conduct is all the time exerting some force upon the rest of society.) Society is acting properly neither toward itself nor to the individual involved unless it actively extends to him the aid that he needs in order to behave as a socially-efficient person.

The second principle is that education must be conceived in pragmatic terms. Education is effective when society becomes "a better place in which to live and a better place in which to make a living."[35] Education is appraised in terms of the social improvement that it has fostered, not in its own terms, as for example, by the number of students who are being educated, by the number of schools in existence, by the length of the school period, or by the monetary expenditure on education. The latter are all means to an end. Similarly in the education of the individual, the final criterion is the social competence that he has achieved.[36] A person is educated when he can

---

[34] *Issues of Secondary Education*, p. 25.

[35] T. H. Briggs, *The Great Investment*, p. 19. 1930.

[36] For an application of this principle, *vide* the Reports of the Regents' Inquiry into the Character and Cost of Public Education in the State of New York, 1938–1939, especially the report, *High School and Life*, by F. T. Spaulding.

take his place in society and carry on effectively all the life-activities which his society has adjudged necessary or desirable. The knowledges and skills that he acquires in the course of learning are means to this end. With reference to this end, methods of education are conceived and educational issues are adjudicated. There are no fixed or absolute laws of education as such. Whether the method of education is to be "training" or the "cultivation of the intellectual processes," whether "indoctrination" is proper or not, can be judged only by reference to their relative contribution to effectiveness in social living.

In the light of these two principles, the objectives of education in relation to society and to the individual may be more clearly understood. Education is established and maintained by society primarily for societal purposes; the primary function of education is social—to ensure the integrity of society, to ensure its continuance in accordance with its cherished ideals, its progressive improvement in the light of these ideals and of new ideals which it accepts. Education does not serve any special groups or any special interests or ideals (even when they are highly rated by absolutists) that society as a whole does not accept. The interests and the ideals that it serves are those of society, of individuals in their collective or total aspect. Since individuals are not in agreement on every important respect (in modern times even in "homogeneous" societies there exist some fundamental differences in the interests and outlook of individuals), it is conceivable that an education which is satisfactory to society as a whole may be, in some respects, considered inadequate by particular individuals. That cannot be avoided. A group within society may feel strongly that public education which does not include training in the principles of their religion cannot be regarded as adequate. The wise society will allow mature and responsible individuals to supplement the public education that is given to their children with special instruction in religion, provided that this is not carried to lengths that are subversive of the public welfare. Public education is, in a sense, a compromise. But, then, society is itself a compromise; and goodness in society lies in the extent to which it makes continuously more possible compromises among individuals.

Education can sponsor no social program that society itself does not sanction. Education is not an instrument of revolution—whether political, social, or economic—against society. Neither is education a conservative or a reactionary force that restrains or pulls back society when the latter seems to be acting contrary to its (education's) better judgment.[37] Education operates within the framework of the societal ideals, and is limited by societal limitations. Education can be no better, as it should be no worse, than society itself. It is assumed that society is continuously re-interpreting its experiences, re-examining its major and minor premises, redefining its ideals, revising its methods. (This is no idle theoretical principle. Society *is* actually doing this all the time.) In its normal course, therefore, education would be constantly revising its guiding social philosophy to make it identical with society's ideals and program. But education does not, of its own accord, step out of its assigned role in society and undertake a task of social reconstruction, however well-intentioned its aims may be, and however greatly some degree of social reconstruction may be needed. Education does not arrogate to itself what should be the responsibility of the intelligence of the whole adult community. The purpose of education is to follow and not to lead, and to follow in step and not out of step. The task of social reconstruction lies with the adult membership of society, and an intelligent society is constantly re-examining its purposes and its methods. It is true that society may be at times irritatingly slow to take needed action; it is the function of education as it is the function of every other active intelligence to prod society into action. Not infrequently social action is in the wrong direction, and keen minds are able to discern that fact. Their duty is to warn society, to try to persuade it to alter its course, to endeavor to lead society back when experience has shown it to be wrong. But society is the final arbiter. In spite of its shortcomings, human experience has shown the societal form of procedure to be the safest. Not even education has the right to depart from this procedure.

This strong statement of the social purpose of education is easily subject to misconstruction. A number of implications need perhaps to be made explicit. For one thing, education is guided by societal ideals rather than by societal practices. Societal practices never quite measure up to its ideals and sometimes fall far short; this is characteristic of human behavior. It is the task of education to socialize the individual in terms of the professed ideals of the society, and when a society is in

[37] Contrast in this respect with Humanism and with Social Evolutionism.

practice compromising with its own ideals, education must point out that fact. Education is not a pedestrian affair, an "imitation of life." Education carries a mandate from society to train individuals to live in ways that society has judged most desirable. When societal ideals are mistaken, education must necessarily be faulty; but when a society in practice flouts its own ideals or badly compromises with them, education must not "follow suit." When the social situation is confused or is changing and the social ideals are not clearly defined, it is the duty of education to demand of society a clear statement of its guiding ideals. But this is quite different from having the school undertake the task of social reconstruction on its own responsibility.

Another point that must be made explicit is that education is by no means required to endorse the societal ideals as if their perfection were unquestionable. There is no such thing as a "perfect" ideal; every "perfect" ideal at some time gives way to one more "perfect." Pragmatic education must make it clear to the individuals whom it trains that human life is guided by human experience and by the interpretation of that experience. The ideals of a society must obtain loyalty and devotion from its members not because they are perfect but because, in the judgment of the individuals who have agreed to live together and to abide by common rules, they are the best so far available. Education, as a matter of fact, must make individuals, as members of the adult community, competent to change societal ideals. An intelligent education does not seek to hide imperfections. Loyalty to societal values must be taught at the same time that their shortcomings, as shown by experience, are pointed out. Especially must education do this with regard to values concerning which large doubts exist within society itself. Individuals must be given a sympathetic understanding of what society is trying to do, and that must be followed by a realistic appraisal of the manner in which these values have served in experience. It is true that, from the point of view of those who direct the educational process as well as from other points of view, such education is dangerous. But "education that is not dangerous is seldom important." [88] In the teaching of ideals, as in everything else, procedure must be governed by courage and skill and a large amount of common sense.

[88] T. H. Briggs, "Propaganda and the Curriculum," *Teachers College Record*, 34:470, March, 1933.

There is still a third implication that needs to be made clear. It is by no means intended that people who guide education, themselves students of society with a large insight into societal problems and needs, shall be prohibited from participating as citizens in the effort to bring about social improvement. More, probably, than any other single group these people have a disinterested concern in the welfare of the whole of society. It is their duty, on the basis of their study and conclusions, to formulate constructive proposals and bring them to the notice of the adult members of society, for discussion and for social action. "Those who advocate significant changes in our social or economic order have a primary responsibility to present their arguments to their fellow-citizens, who as partners in the great corporation of democracy must accept or reject their proposal." [39] That is the societal way of doing things. Education has no right, however, to inculcate any socially unaccepted beliefs in the minds of immature children who are not capable of truly evaluating them.

By application of the same social and pragmatic principles [40] the objectives of education in relation to the individual must be considered. It is improper to decide in any absolute manner whether education should or should not deal with vocational training. The purpose of education is to prepare individuals for competent living as that is conceived by society. Competent living demands a satisfactory solution of the vocational problem. When the vocational adjustment is a difficult one, when it presumes knowledge of special processes and skills which the individual cannot on his own easily acquire, then education must systematically provide for vocational competence. In the same way education must be governed, in the formulation of its other objectives, by the practical demands that good societal living makes upon the individual. The question "What knowledge is of most worth?" can be properly answered only by reference to this criterion. Education possesses no intrinsic character of its own; its character is imparted by society.

The problem of method must be approached in the same way. Whether education proceeds by way of the development of general intellectual powers or by way of training in performance of the par-

[39] *Ibid.*, p. 475.
[40] *Vide* pp. 249–251.

ticular life-activities depends upon which method has been proved more feasible and more effective in achieving the desired practical outcomes. Educational method is not intrinsically either a process of general "intellectual development" or of particularized training; it cannot properly be limited to the one or to the other.[41] Neither can it be said with justification that it is not dignified for education to "indoctrinate" the individual with the desired social ideals, attitudes, and modes of living. Education does not possess an inherent dignity; it gains dignity by serving society. Whether indoctrination is entirely proper and necessary depends upon whether there are available other and better means for securing in the individual all those modes of behavior that constitute good citizenship. As will be seen later, indoctrination by education is entirely necessary. Common sense and the pragmatic evidence of results rebel against the conclusions of the rationalist that there is no truth but one and that man is such a perfectly-intellectual being that knowing the truth will lead inevitably to living it. The evidence of experience suggests that the problem of knowledge is a complicated one, and that acceptance of knowledge as truth and application of it in living are greatly affected by the emotions.[42] Education must develop good citizenship. This is no easy task; selfish interests in society are at work influencing the individual—indoctrinating him—in special ways that lead away from rather than toward good citizenship. Education must counter these efforts with an indoctrination of its own, an indoctrination that is far more effective and that leads to the attainment of those qualities that society has agreed are desirable in the individual citizen.[43]

What has been said so far may be summed up briefly as follows: Education must be considered in the nature of an investment that society makes in its own future—an investment, indeed, that society cannot afford not to make. The returns on this investment are in the form of an improved society; society becomes a better place in which to live. By this general purpose education is governed; its character

[41] *Vide* Chapter II, pp. 172 ff.

[42] On this point, *vide Issues of Secondary Education,* p. 24.

[43] For a discussion of this question, *vide* T. H. Briggs, "Should Education Indoctrinate?" *Educational Administration and Supervision,* 22:561–593, November, 1936, and "Indoctrination in Education," *Educational Forum,* 1:133–142, January, 1937.

is determined by reference to this criterion. It is wrong to make rules as to what education should do, as to what education is or is not, except by reference to this criterion. Conversely it may be said that everything that contributes to this social purpose, provided that it is regardful also of the capacities, aptitudes, and interests of individuals and consistent with the facts of psychology, is appropriate to education.[44]

It is necessary now to apply the general principles to a consideration of the objectives of education in contemporary American society. The general purpose of education is to enable the individual to live in a democratic, practically-effective manner within his society, and to contribute in his own way to the common efforts to make society better. Definitely, the objectives of education can be stated only in terms of the governing conditions and needs of the American society.

The nature of these conditions and needs has already been described at some length.[45] A brief review may serve the present purpose. The primary governing principle of American society is the principle of democracy; the American people are definitely committed to the democratic way of life with all, in terms of method as well as content, that it implies. In recent years the American culture has undergone changes of a fundamental character; at the basis of these changes has been the very great development of science and technology. The changes have been not only of an industrial-economic nature but have penetrated into every area of life-experience. They have affected fundamentally our ways of living as well as of making a living. The development of mechanical processes of production has given industry capacity for a tremendous output; the lack of social planning and the resultant reckless, opportunistic individualism have brought about very great overproduction and consequent waste, cut-throat competition, unemployment, and general economic unbalance. Technology has brought about a decreased need for human labor, has made work-opportunities relatively scarce, has multiplied and specialized and routinized work-processes, and has made them subject to almost continuous change. As a result of industrialization, and of the invention of means of rapid communication and locomotion, society has grown tremendously in

[44] This thesis is presented and developed in T. H. Briggs, *The Great Investment.* 1930.
[45] *Vide* Chapter I, pp. 103 ff.

physical area and in internal complexity. The extent of human inter-relationship is greater; special interests are more numerous and more involved; the problem of maintaining intelligent awareness of social events much more difficult. If general living has become more difficult, living in the democratic way has become infinitely more so. Certain events are themselves unfavorable to the continuance of the demo-cratic way: individualistic and monopolistic economic practices have produced glaring inequities in essential material possessions; equality of economic opportunity can no longer properly be said to exist. In addition, conflicting interests of men and of nations have been instru-mental in releasing a flood of anti-democratic propaganda; democracy is being actively threatened by the aggression of totalitarian ideologies. The exercise of competent democratic citizenship in such a situation becomes acutely difficult. But as a producer too, and as consumer, as husband and as father, as friend and as neighbor, as a human being generally, the individual is beset with greater problems than have ever before challenged human competence.

With reference to this situation, education must formulate its ob-jectives. While an education that deals in eternal and unchangeable values can perhaps afford to disregard the "ephemeral present," a prag-matic education must squarely face these problems, and, in terms of the situation confronting him in his own time and place, make of the individual a socially-competent person. Each of the important life-needs emerging from the societal picture becomes an objective which education must recognize.

Judged by societal need, probably the most important objective of education is that of democratic citizenship. Of course the problem of citizenship cannot be divorced from the problem of effective social and economic living. The school, however, must specifically inculcate in each individual a loyalty to democratic ideals and processes and must establish him in democratic ways of living, at the same time as it equips him with the specific competences that he needs to solve effectively his social and economic problems. Democratic values stand out as the highest and most permanent to which American society as a whole is committed. In training for democratic living education realizes the primary function which it is meant to serve; the school "is a social in-stitution having for its primary and unique purpose such education of the citizenry as will enable our democratic society to progress and to solve intelligently its economic, social, and political problems."[46] For education to fail to train for democracy is unthinkable; and that this training may be effective, education must indoctrinate in democratic values. "Lacking faith that they can develop minds so trained that they will be competent to adjudicate all issues equally well, the schools must accept the responsibility of propaganda for the democratic way of life."[47] Training for democratic citizenship, however, does not involve merely inculcating the simple conception of democracy that served an earlier agrarian society. Modern complex conditions call for a redefinition of democracy and a clarification of its social and economic implications; new meaning must be given to equality of opportunity, to the rights of man, to the rights of government, to private property and public wealth. Society must make this redefinition; until it does, training for democracy calls not merely for the formation of generally approving attitudes, but for an understanding of the inadequacies of the present situation and a discriminating intelligence in making and in continuing to make the needed changes. Teaching for democracy is one of the great and abiding purposes of education.

Out of the analysis of the present situation there impresses itself the enormous and critical importance, in the life of almost every person, of the vocational adjustment. Because of its difficulty, the vocational adjustment has become pivotal: on it depends the general well-being of the individual—not only his economic status, but his physical and mental well-being, his standing in his own eyes and in those of society, his marriage and subsequent family life. In the vocational problem, education faces its most difficult objective. A mechanized economy has greatly reduced the need for human labor; increasingly adolescents, at one end, and older adults, at the other, are becoming unacceptable for employment. Steadily the work-day is being reduced and the period of potential idleness extended. The machine is constantly encroaching upon man; work-processes become routinized and call for progressively less operating intelligence. Vocations are highly

[46] H. R. Douglass, "Can We Revamp the High School Curriculum to Fit the Needs of Today?" *Baltimore Bulletin of Education*, 14:50, September, 1936.

[47] T. H. Briggs, "Propaganda and the Curriculum," *Teachers College Record*, 34:474, March, 1933.

specialized, and specialized vocational processes are continuously changing. In this situation education cannot possibly ignore its responsibility with respect to vocation; preparation for vocational competence is an indispensable part of the preparation for the larger social-competence. However difficult this task may be, and it is difficult, education must face it. That does not mean that education is to become vocational training of a kind that concerns itself with petty skills required by a specific job. Were this an effective way of offering vocational preparation (which it is not) it would still be undesirable. Education must keep its eye on the main goal, which is competence in performing all the important life-activities, rather than on vocational competence only. But among other things education must prepare the individual to make a right start in his vocation and to grow in it and through it.

Training for democratic citizenship and for vocational adjustment emerge as the two most immediately compelling objectives of education. But they are by no means the only important ones. The changing social world has created other problems which individuals find difficult of solution, and, true to its social purpose, education must help the individual to solve them. The development of technology has greatly extended man's opportunity for leisure-time pursuits. The machine has released man from labor and given him more time for his own use. The mechanization and routinization of work-processes have made it doubly important that leisure time be used not only for recreation and harmless amusement but for intellectual and personal growth and development, for *work* of an other-than-financially-remunerative kind. At the same time, technology has provided man with a large number of mechanical amusements which, though they may be in themselves harmless, are not intellectually stimulating and deprive man of the opportunity of developing his own talents and powers. The growth of mechanical amusement devices as well as the restriction of the area of the home have driven man into commercial places of amusement, often with undesirable results. Teaching for the effective use of leisure time has become a very great educational problem.

A direct outcome of the overproduction of goods beyond consumer needs has been a very great competition among products for the attention and favor of the consumer. The individual is from all sides assailed by high-pressure advertising that succeeds, at the same time that it impresses its product upon his attention, in withholding actual pertinent information regarding its true merit. Education has the problem of training for intelligent consumership. Other problems of the modern world which must serve as educational objectives are individual and social health, the establishment of desirable relationships in the home and in the community, effective homemaking, the application of science and methods of science in the solution of the numerous problems of practical living.

Effective living involves, however, more than the acquirement of fixed attitudes, habits, knowledges, and skills, more than learning how to do the things that are currently being done. Human experience is a changing thing; new life-activities are constantly evolving, new problems emerging to be solved. Especially in our time has change become rapid. Social-competence implies more than knowing how to adjust to existent situations. Education must prepare the individual to continue to learn and to develop, to acquire new competences in a changing world, to help to make society *a better place* in which to live. In addition to mastering the processes needed in every important type of adjustment, the individual must develop strong interests. Interests are the dynamics of learning. Having developed true interests in his activities as a citizen, in his vocation, in nature, in science, in art, the individual will continue to set for himself new purposes and to expend the effort needed for their realization. The possession of deep and varied interests is truly the mark of the liberally-educated man. Education that does not culminate in the development of enduring interests is incomplete. "The school may provide much of vocational utility, but unless it succeeds in finding, creating, and developing interest in the most permanently satisfying phenomena of the world, interests that set up favoring attitudes and persistent activity after all compulsions are removed, it fails in the important field of liberal education." [48] In addition to the establishment of deep and varied interests, education must also result in the acquisition of power to carry on independent study and to employ needed elementary methods of research, and in the possession of systematized knowledge that makes for greater effectiveness and economy in use.

[48] T. H. Briggs, *Secondary Education*, p. 521. 1933. Quoted with permission of The Macmillan Company, publishers.

It has already been said [49] that education is not only preparation for competent living in the adult world. The best way to serve society is through the development of proper individuals. Education cannot properly perform its social functions if, in its desire to give the individual mastery in the performance of the needed life-processes, it neglects him as a person. Education must satisfy important immediate needs (though it is true that increasingly, in the course of development, emphasis is placed upon deferred values). It is very largely by satisfying the continuously changing immediate needs of the learner that there are developed the interests, the aptitudes, the capacities that operate in making living effective.

In this respect the present social situation presents grave difficulties to the developing youth and to the education that seeks to satisfy his needs. The problem is one that acutely affects the older adolescent (this is not a reference to the normal psychological needs of adolescence). Conditions in society at the present time make it difficult for him to find employment and, with the vocation as a center, to continue normal development. Industry no longer offers adequate opportunity for youth. The age for assuming adult responsibilities, for taking one's place in the community, for satisfying normal urges for marriage and for a home of one's own, has been very definitely set ahead. There is no assurance of finding work even after a long period of waiting. The situation is destructive in its effect upon the morale of youth. Society is faced with a difficult youth problem; it must in some way compensate for the things that the youth requires and cannot himself obtain. It must find a way to restore his self-confidence, to give normal expression to his desire to do useful and gainful work, to give him standing as an adult in a community of adults. This is a social problem, and it is a problem of education. That this need can be satisfied through the agency of any school that now exists may well be questioned; it will probably be necessary to establish a new social agency working cooperatively with the school and with the community in carrying out this task, or perhaps a new kind of school different from anything that we now possess.

In the light of all this, not really very much needs to be said in defense of the obvious fact that education for competent living in our society

[49] *Vide* p. 249.

calls for an extended educational process. "Because of the greatly increased degree and importance of interdependence, and because of the very nature of democracy, the necessity for much greater effort toward economic and political intelligence is inescapable."[50] The difficult problems that education must help the youth to solve are a challenge even to adult society. There is not much doubt, under these circumstances, that common education must be carried on through the secondary period; that all may have a chance to acquire the social-competence necessary for satisfactory living, education must extend through the period of adolescence. But societal responsibility does not end there; society must concern itself with the older adolescent and even with the post-adolescent youth until such a time as the adult world is ready to receive them in economic and social partnership. Society must extend its guardianship of youth; it cannot, after seeing them through thus far, abandon them at the most critical time of their existence. To leave youth to shift for themselves would be to permit adverse social conditions to nullify what education may already have done toward making them socially-effective persons. Whether the job that society must do is to be regarded as part of secondary education is a matter of definition, and relatively unimportant. Probably it will be better for all concerned to separate this function from the secondary school, and to assign it to a new social agency which will work out its objectives as it goes along.

It is necessary to keep in mind, however, that education must justify itself in terms of the returns that it makes to society. Education is a societal investment and not a societal benevolence. Every extension upward of the compulsory school age must carry with it the promise of corresponding social returns. It cannot be said, at the present time, that we are meeting satisfactorily the educational needs of the students who are now in the secondary school. Another extension of the compulsory school age does not promise to render social returns of value equivalent to the social effort expended. Until we have devised an education that is appropriate to the capacities of all students, to suggest that we keep raising the compulsory level up to the age of 18 or 20 is to be guilty of superficial thinking. The school is not a custodial institution. How

[50] H. R. Douglass, *Secondary Education for Youth in Modern America*, p. 47. 1937.

can we provide adequate education for all youth beyond the present school age when we are not yet able to educate satisfactorily or even to hold all those students now in the secondary school?

The solution must be somewhat as follows. It is to be understood that ultimately (when we have developed an education appropriate to all) education through the secondary period will have to be universal. In the meantime, education, as far as it goes, must be socially productive: the student, having once acquired the fundamentals indispensable for social living, should not be kept in school beyond the point of diminishing returns. For the present the compulsory age limit may well rest at 16, with an effort made to retain all on a full-time basis until the end of the secondary school period (at 18 or thereabouts) provided that their continued education promises to bear personal and social results. For those who are forced to leave school prior to the latter age, society should establish agencies of a quasi-educational character to provide suitable work and suitable educational activity that the present school is unable to provide. When the secondary school is able to work out an educational program through which these young people may be trained for social competence, they will be retained there. For the older youth (beyond the present secondary-school age) who have not yet found employment and who are not in higher institutions, society should provide optional, part-time education, or possibly a full-time education on a work-instruction-recreation basis, through which they will be enabled to contribute to the work of society and to build themselves into responsible, participating members of the adult community. This education, however, should be kept distinct from secondary education, being something in addition to what is required for minimum social competence. (In other words, should economic conditions again permit it, these young people would be much better off working at regular jobs in industry than under societal tutelage.) But even this added service that society offers should bring social returns.

Such is the character of the education that must obtain for all individuals. Regardless of individual differences, all must acquire the competence necessary for effective social living. Individual differences affect greatly the manner in which that competence is to be exercised, and the particular talents that a person will bring to the common social enterprise. Each person must be trained in terms of his individual capacities, aptitudes, and interests. But individual differences cannot be allowed to determine whether or not the person is to become socially-competent, at least not in normal people. All normal individuals must be made socially-competent; whatever their special talents, these talents must become centers of their general development as well as the special means by which these individuals make their contributions to society.

The educational process is a "gradual, continuous, unitary process" [51] that persists until the educational objectives have been achieved. There is no real break in this process: it begins in infancy and extends almost into adulthood, to the point where the individual becomes capable of taking his place in society and continuing independently his own development. But the very extent of this process serves to make necessary a recognition of smaller divisions within it. Education must, in the course of training for social-competence, satisfy the important immediate needs of the learner. At the different stages of development, human needs vary greatly; the needs of adolescents differ greatly from the needs of younger children. Moreover, the nature of the educational process is such as to require different emphases at different times. While in the early stages of development there must be emphasis on social integration, on the learning of common things, on the inculcation of common fundamental ideals, attitudes, and practices, in the later stages there is added also emphasis on specialized training in accordance with individual interests, aptitudes, and capacities. It is advantageous to recognize within the unitary educational process a primary and a secondary stage.

The primary school is the school for children. Emphasis is on "developing the fundamental understandings and skills which should be common to all citizens," [52] on social integration, on satisfaction of immediate needs (of children), on building the foundations, in terms of interest and attitude, for continued development. The secondary school is, generally speaking, the school for adolescents. "One obvious advantage of segregated schools that minister particularly to the adolescent is that this segregation makes possible emphases that are peculiarly

[51] *Issues of Secondary Education*, p. 350.
[52] *Ibid.*, p. 27.

fitting to the adolescent stage of growth.[53] Secondary education "finds its goal in carrying forward the educational process which the elementary school has begun to a point at which that process has been completed for some individuals or at which it can advantageously be taken over for others at higher institutions." [54] Continuing and building upon the integrative work of the primary school, satisfying now the needs of adolescents rather than of children, the secondary school also "assumes responsibility for discovering and fostering the differentiated abilities of individual pupils." [55]

In the present situation, however, secondary education must be defined in flexible terms. It can neither be limited to a single age group (viz., adolescents, although adolescents do greatly predominate), nor to a single technical function.[56] By secondary education is meant "the education provided by schools for the purpose of guiding and promoting the development of normal individuals for whom on the one hand the elementary school no longer constitutes a satisfactory environment, and who on the other are either not yet prepared to participate effectively in society unguided by the school, or are not ready for the specialized work of the professional schools or the upper division of the liberal-arts college." [57] Such education does not of course deal with one type of individual, nor can it be provided by one type of school. Of the "twilight zone" that exists between the end of the secondary-school period and the point at which the young adult can take his place as a full-fledged member of the community, something has already been said; it is best, for the present, that such agencies as society institutes for the guidance and care of these young people be considered as distinct from the secondary school.

II

Growing out of the social and economic conditions of the present century, out of the development of a pragmatic attitude of life, out of

[53] *Ibid.*, p. 358.
[54] *Ibid.*, p. 27.
[55] *Ibid.*
[56] Cf. Social Evolutionism, pp. 236 ff.
[57] *Issues of Secondary Education*, p. 25. The functions of the secondary school from a methodological point of view will be discussed in the following chapter.

the development of a scientific psychology that has succeeded in implanting sound fact in place of unsound theory, there have been great changes in American secondary education. In many important respects the American secondary school has departed from tradition; a great many more students have been admitted than are accepted in any other country; vague guiding concepts such as "education for culture" have been given up in favor of objectives reflecting the needs of real living; the fact of individual differences has been recognized at least in theory, and even in practice some opportunity is afforded for discovering and fostering the aptitudes and interests of students; the junior high school has been established and has already proved its value in laying the basis for differentiated education. "As a matter of fact, there is much justification for pride. Not only have the privileges of secondary education been extended beyond the dreams or even the desires of any other people, but by and large the social atmosphere is more wholesome for youth than can be found elsewhere in the communities, the behavior problems are infinitely fewer than a generation ago, the administration compares favorably with that in industry and is superior to that in professional offices and most homes, the teaching is reasonably good, and the curricular offerings have been steadily extended. It is no exaggeration to say that the courses of study even in the traditional subjects—such as English, foreign languages, history, mathematics, and the sciences—are better than have ever before been known, a statement that will be borne out by comparison of old and new textbooks." [58] To the extent that they have been made, these changes are gratifying. Secondary education has undoubtedly been moving in the right direction, and the strides it has made in recent years have been considerable.

It is true, nevertheless, that American secondary education has not been changed in a comprehensive way according to definite design, but has evolved, rather, through a succession of small changes. "At no time, from the beginning to the present, has there been fundamental thinking that has materially affected secondary education. The history of American education is chiefly a history of tradition modified slowly, and usually by factors other than a clear vision of what it should

[58] T. H. Briggs, "Indoctrination in Education," *Educational Forum*, 1:133. January, 1937.

contribute to the social order." [59] As a result, we are at the present time not operating under anything like a single clear conception of secondary education. While verbally we commit ourselves to certain principles, there remains in our thinking and even more in our practice a large residue of traditional beliefs. We have not on the whole been successful in realizing those objectives that express the needs for competent living in our society. Some of these objectives we have not realized because of the looseness and ineffectiveness of our method; other of the objectives we have not yet fully faced.

Secondary education has been extended to a great many youth. A large percentage of them, however, are still without that education. The welfare of a democratic society demands that all possess the competence necessary to carry on effective social living. Even more serious is the fact that, of those at present in the school, not all or even a large majority are getting an education appropriate to their needs and one that promises therefore to render large returns to society. The present secondary school is still better suited to the relatively smaller number of academically-minded students. It is paradoxical but true that many of the young people who, through lack of interest or satisfactory achievement have dropped out of school, are potentially more capable than many of those who have remained; the latter, lacking the initiative to leave school and to seek a job, have, in spite of small success, persisted in school beyond the point where their education promises to make a comparable return to society. For them the school has become a custodial institution. They are held to no accounting in terms of social-pragmatic values; and the school does not really know to what extent it is being successful with them and to what extent it is failing.

The situation represents a danger to democracy and to our effectiveness as a society. Moreover, the school, unless it can give more convincing evidence of its practical worth to society, runs the immediate risk of losing some of the financial support that is needed if educational opportunity is to be extended to all. While theorists clamor for further extension of the compulsory school period (without considering whether we can immediately put the additional time to socially worth-

[59] T. H. Briggs, "A Vision of Secondary Education," *Teachers College Record,* 34:2. October, 1932.

while uses), taxpayers are demanding elimination of "fads and frills" (in some of which true educational values lie) and further limitation of the opportunity for secondary education.

True equality of opportunity in education does not yet exist. Secondary education still holds much more opportunity for the academically bright students than for students whose capacities and aptitudes and interests are non-academic. Society has not yet provided equality of opportunity for those who cannot go to school because they lack adequate transportation or clothing or because their parents cannot spare them from wage-earning employment. The whole problem of universal secondary education is one with which society and the school will have to deal comprehensively. It is a curious fact, apropos of this, that society as a whole has not focused widespread attention on the needs of those young people who have left the secondary school but who have not yet been placed in a vocation. It is hard to believe that society would so concern itself with youth up to the time that they reach the critical point in their life-experience, and at this point abandon them. Educational guidance has not gone beyond the secondary school itself. Society has not made a comprehensive effort to enlist industry in the cause of youth and to have it cooperate in the care of youth. It has not made a strenuous effort—although a beginning, with very definite limitations,[60] has been made in the establishment of the Civilian Conservation Corps—to create agencies to provide opportunities for youth to do necessary and important work of a kind that would have great educative value. It has undertaken no comprehensive measures to restore and maintain the morale of youth. The failure of society and of education to do this represents a real threat to democracy.

Secondary education (and education as a whole) is not yet conceived as a social investment from which there must be returns to society. We are not yet stressing sufficiently those values for the sake of which society expends so much effort and time and money upon education. We have not been successful in educating for democratic citizenship, social events bear out the validity of this charge. Educational theorists with considerable influence upon practice are, in fact, still gravitating between the extremes of advocating a policy of non-

[60] *Vide Issues of Secondary Education*, p. 113 ff.

indoctrination in any ideals and principles (as if that were possible) and advocating a policy of indoctrination in the principles and ideals of the particular social order that they have visualized, without benefit of social consent. They fail to see that neither proposal is feasible or defensible. The function of education is to indoctrinate—in the ideals and modes of living that society accepts, not in social ideals that have not yet been accepted or that have been considered and judged unacceptable. It is evidence of our general confusion that we make rules and regulations about education without reference to the social ends which education serves.

Secondary education has not fully carried out the implications of its pragmatic philosophy. Although it has become generally more practical in its outlook, it has not faced squarely all the problems that are implicit in educating for social-efficiency. There seems to have remained a strong strain of the disciplinary tradition that regarded competence in specific life-activities as an outcome of general training. Education has not undertaken with energy and realism the task of training for vocational competence. What we have done in the way of vocational education has been done hesitantly and incompletely. Society has given some assistance to those aspiring to the professions; for those preparing to enter the world of business there have been offered a few and not very effective commercial courses; for the rest, not very much has been done. Lately some schools have entered very much more completely into the problem of preparing for vocations, but the nature of the preparation has been unrealistic: students have been taught the specific skills needed in a specific job, in spite of the fact that the specific job may not be obtainable and the needed skills may very quickly change. On the whole, students leave school not prepared to make intelligent adjustment to the vocational problem.[61] Other of the important life-needs are similarly neglected. Training for the effective use of leisure time has not been given the importance that it deserves. "Unfortunately the prevailing conception, even among educators, of leisure-time activities is that they are primarily hiking, games of various kinds, creative work that is more or less artistic, and improved association with one's fellows. These are, of course, all good, common in the lives of all people and improvable by education. What

[61] F. T. Spaulding, *High School and Life,* Chapter IV. 1938.

has been unfortunately overlooked is that the most common and the most satisfying of all activities are those of the intellect." [62] Specific training for intelligent consumership, specific training for effective homemaking, have not been given to all. Secondary education is still too largely of an academic cast, relying to an unjustifiable degree upon the probability of transfer.

It cannot be justly maintained that the secondary school has been very successful in helping students to form deep and enduring interests in worth-while activities that they have carried on in school. There is, in fact, some evidence to the contrary, that there has been "complete abandonment by the boys and girls who do not go on to higher schools of many of the activities on which the secondary schools commonly lay great emphasis. Left to their own devices, most of these young people cease to read serious books and articles or good fiction; they seldom listen to the best music; they study as a means of preparing for a vocation, rather than for fun or to add to their general education." [63] Nor can it be said that secondary education has done enough to encourage students to develop special aptitudes that they may possess; unusual talent in music, in the arts, in technics has, on the whole, been neglected.

III

Not only education but society at large must become more sensitive to its full responsibility for youth. In part, society can be blamed for the imperfection of the present education. There is need for a reformulation of societal ideals, a redefinition of democracy in the light of the important changes that have taken place. The school requires of society a chart stating explicitly its aims and ideals. Possessing this, the school will know how to steer its course; without this, the school must founder. But this is not the only obligation of society. Society must come to the aid of the school by creating new agencies which will be able to satisfy the important needs of youth for whom the school, as it is at present constituted, cannot effectively care. It

[62] T. H. Briggs, "The Philosophy Which Must Guide Secondary Education," Department of Secondary School Principals, National Education Association, *Official Report*, 1935, p. 102.

[63] Spaulding, *op. cit.*, p. 52.

must, at least for the time being, establish agencies to guide and train the youth who have found the present secondary curriculum inappropriate, and who have therefore dropped out of school; it must help the youth who have completed the secondary course make safely the transition to satisfactory adult living. Finally, society is responsible for effecting better coordination among the principal social agencies, both public and private, which exercise a strong educative influence.

Given direction, assistance, and backing by society, the secondary school can proceed more capably to live up to its defined purpose. That purpose will come to be generally understood as the training of all youth for effective social living. The work of the school will be wholly governed by that purpose. Education will cease to be regarded as an independent enterprise which, irrespective of its societal setting, can be governed by its own general laws. It will be regarded as an investment by society which must be so managed that it ultimately brings the largest returns in social benefits. The school will thereupon take on the characteristics of the society it is serving. Its work will be evaluated pragmatically in terms of changes-for-the-better that it helps to effect in society, and not in terms of credits amassed or knowledge gained by the student.

Guided by the ideals to which society has committed itself, the school will analyze the activities, conditions, and factors that characterize societal living, and in terms of these formulate its objectives. The objectives toward which the school will strive will be the types of competence that effective living in modern American society demands— good personal health, the effective exercise of democratic citizenship, vocational competence, the pleasurable and educative use of leisure time, the maintenance of wholesome and pleasurable human relationships, intelligent consumership, the utilization of science for the improvement of daily living. The school will accept as its responsibility the training of every normal person so that he becomes competent in these respects. But the school will not attempt to mold every individual according to a common pattern. In terms of the capacities, aptitudes, and interests that each individual shows, it will help him to understand his social environment, live desirably and efficiently within it, and contribute his share toward making it better. And the school will be mindful of the fact that deep and varied interests serve best to guarantee that a person's development will continue after his formal schooling has ceased.

Having formulated its objectives, the school will move to attain them with the greatest efficiency and economy. It will not be swayed from its course by such emotion-charged words as "indoctrination" and "training." It will use every sound means at its disposal to inculcate in the student those ideals, those attitudes, those knowledges, and those habits and skills that he needs for good living in society. And concern whether what the school is doing constitutes "training" or "intellectual development" will be a distinctly secondary concern, a problem of method and not of aim.

But in striving to prepare the young person for effective living in adult society, the school will not overlook the fact that it is necessary, in the course of the process, to satisfy his important *immediate* needs, whatever they happen to be. The school will not neglect to attend to such needs, in children and in adolescents.

The school will recognize that education is a "gradual, continuous, unitary process." The secondary school will succeed the primary school as a stage in common education. The secondary school will satisfy the important needs of youth who are predominantly in the adolescent period; it will continue, in diminishing degree but on an increasingly high intellectual level, the social integration of students; it will explore and discover the capacities, aptitudes, and interests of students, and on the basis of its discoveries guide the students into increasingly differentiated activity.

EXPERIMENTALISM

I

The Good Life of man is to be defined in terms of a flexible, adaptable method of living rather than in terms of adherence to fixed goals. The Good Life consists in the continuous direction of experience so as to realize, within a social culture and through the sharing of experiences, values that advance individual living. In a sense the Good Life is not something that can be attained—it is conative, prospective, progressive. To live the Good Life is to be moving forward, constantly realizing new values out of experience, constantly becoming more adept at controlling and guiding one's own living while advancing the living of others.

The Good Life is essentially individual. Experience is "one's own affair," and while particular experiences can and should be shared, the control of that totality of experiences that constitutes a person's *life* can be shared with no one. Man inherits a culture and, with it, its values. Most of these values he takes over and uses in his own living, but not indiscriminately and mechanically—rather in ways that are appropriate to the particular experiences that he has. Other values he develops for himself in the course of his living. In its entirety, his life is unique, different from the life of any other individual. Its underlying circumstances, its needs, its purposes are different; hence, the precise direction that it takes must be different. Each individual life must be evaluated in its own terms.

The Good Life is in acting and behaving, not in contemplating. Goodness must be related to the biological function of the human organism. Living is establishing, pursuing, and realizing purposes that are instrumental in maintaining the life-process. Intelligence is instrumental in the maintenance of this process; to be intelligent is to act in such a way as to advance the life functions of the organism. Goodness lies therefore in the intelligent exercise of living. Reflection, analysis, the gathering of ideas are medial in this process; they are a means to an end, not an end in themselves. Mind is evident in the attainment of consequences that foster right living.

Learning to live the Good Life is learning to deal properly with experience. The secret is in knowing what is going on—what is affecting the life-process and in what manner. It is in being able to distinguish the variety of meanings implicit in situations, in being able to use these meanings inventively in setting up and in realizing ends. Essential for living the Good Life are a method and an attitude—a method of entering into experience, taking hold of it, analyzing it, and changing factors in it so as to make it more suited to the satisfaction of life-needs, and an attitude of willingness-to-try, of open-mindedness, and of honest regard for results, whatever they are. Essential also is a personality which, while acting out of regard for its own genuine needs, is mindful also of the fact that the life-purposes of human beings often cross one another, that situations often must be shared, that, however, the needs of every individual must be respected. Both these essentials are implied by the term "the intelligent person"; intelligence implies individuality, socialization, continuous integrating activity, and an effective method of dealing with experience. One does not become once and for all an intelligent person, but one can be assisted to reach a point from which it is possible to carry on independently.

To a certain extent, a person developing naturally in society acquires the attributes necessary for intelligent living. He experiences, and his experiences are within a social culture. To an extent, experience does its own teaching: through the process of experiencing, one obtains meanings and a method of using meanings effectively in the direction of living. The fact that this experiencing takes place in society means (1) that one's stock of meanings as well as one's power of using them is immeasurably increased, and (2) that one's development obtains social direction. In the course of development there are acquired patterns of behavior, methods of thinking, attitudes toward things, based on prevailing social values; these the individual learns to use as well as he can in the guidance of his own living, gradually discarding those that prove unavailing, and substituting others out of his own experience. To a degree, then, a person developing naturally in society acquires an aptness for living the Good Life. But such development alone is not maximally conducive to intelligent living. For one thing, there is tremendous difference in the potential value of experiences for immediate and future living. Some experiences are replete with vital meanings, others yield meanings of much less relative significance. To realize fully his possibilities for intelligent living, a person must enter into those experiences the effect of which is most educative. For another thing, "natural" experiencing, without added systematic guidance, is not conducive to the development of a sufficiently effective *method* of dealing with experience. A person can profit greatly from guidance, both in the matter of economy of learning and of potential desirability of outcome. Experiences not infrequently prove too much for the single individual; and in these cases their effect is likely to be mis-educative rather than educative. Finally, while in a general way, natural development in society does obtain the benefit of social direction, that direction is not likely to be the most desirable nor is it likely to follow the shortest line.

While, of course, life is educative, the life that is likely to be most fruitful in its returns to the individual and to others is that which, at least in its earlier stages,[64] received systematic guidance in experiencing. The young person especially needs guidance; through such guidance he becomes better able to conduct his living in the present and in the future. It is to such guided learning from experience that the designation "education" is generally given (perhaps the term "intentional education"[65] is more appropriate, to distinguish it from the education which is an inherent part of all experiencing). Society long ago recognized the necessity of this when it organized agencies of education such as the school, and enforced a period of education upon every individual. It is in the special sense of "intentional education" that the term education will here be used—representing the manner in which society assists in the development of the individual by guiding his experiencing toward the end of rendering him better able to live the Good Life.

"The only justification for the existence of a school is that it can through intentional effort produce an environment in which the experiences of youth will be more truly educative than they otherwise would be."[66] The principal purposes of education are (1) to incline the individual in the direction of significant experiences (and that implies that education has a task of selection), and (2) to help him work his way through these experiences, and *all others that he is having,* so that he understands them, sees their import or significance, and can use the meanings distilled from them in the directing of his immediate and future living. The function of education is to assist the individual in getting more power and better direction than he otherwise would have. Education implies influencing the individual; there is no doubt of that.[67] A certain amount of influencing is as inevitable as it is essential. Education must incline the individual toward an acceptance of those values which human beings have come

[64] This is not to be interpreted to mean that education is for children only. *Vide* p. 278 ff.

[65] J. L. Childs, *Education and the Philosophy of Experimentalism,* p. 135. 1931.

[66] *Ibid.,* p. 80.

[67] For the extent of influencing that is permissible, *vide* pp. 279 ff.

to cherish—peace, justice, the rule of law, cooperation, democracy, and the validity, in the conduct of living, of the scientific method and the experimental attitude.

Though education, as defined, is something "in addition to" the process of natural experiencing, it is by no means distinct from it or independent of it. Education is not something that is carried on separately from the life that the individual lives. To be effective, education must make itself an integral part of life itself. In the period of education every significant experience that a person has comes under systematic scrutiny, so that such potential educative values as are inherent in the experience may be realized; every additional experience that the school presents has for the individual interest-compelling value. The guidance that is implicit in education encompasses the whole life that an individual lives; the selection that is implied is so carried out that nothing is introduced except what is germane to the needs and purposes of the individual. In thinking about education it must be remembered that the human being is a unity, that his purposes and activities are integrated. While it is true that the school provides educative experiences supplementing the natural life-experiences, it cannot in so doing counteract entirely the harmful effects that may be suffered in the course of the life-process. When values that the school is sponsoring conflict with the values supported by the surrounding culture, individual personality is adversely affected; there is discord, confusion, disintegration. Education cannot exist apart from the individual's life-experience; it must enter into every phase of that life-experience, and help the individual more effectively to deal with it.

The same may be said of educational method. Learning is not something distinct from or added to the experiencing process. It is an intrinsic part of this process. When one experiences, one learns; unless there is experience there is no learning. Experiencing implies facing situations, purposing, analyzing situations and extracting meaning, and "turning back" meanings into new situations. Learning takes place in that way and in no other. It is futile to think of the method of education as the "assimilation" of meanings—extracted from context, stored, and piped into the individual—the acquisition of habits and skills by a special drill process, or the memorization of facts. Meanings, habits, and skills are an essential part of the equipment of an intelligently-behaving person, but the only way to obtain them is within a context in which they actually operate.

Education has been defined as the transmission of culture. So it is, in part. The cultural heritage—the sum total of meanings that human beings have found of value in shaping their experiences—must be transmitted (through appropriate experiential context and not as disembodied forms). But essentially this transmission is a means to an end. The end is to enable the individual to deal more intelligently with his own experience. And to that end, the "transmitted" culture is not the only means; another very important means is the experiences that the individual himself has. Through these experiences, and with inherited meanings as accessories, the individual must be helped to become capable of dealing intelligently with life in all its aspects. An education that stops with the transmission of culture performs only one part of the task with which it is charged.

To educate effectively is to take into consideration the entire experiencing of the individual, to help him meet his every situation intelligently. This presumes that education must be made to extend to wherever the learner is and to whatever he does. It further presumes a concern about the life-experiences themselves and the social environment in which they take place; and it foreshadows at least an attempt to coordinate and make more harmonious these experiences (and possibly also, when it is necessary, an attempt to discover and root out the causes that give rise to educationally-harmful experiences).[68] The task of education propels it beyond the individual himself into the social environment in which experiencing takes place. Its concern with the individual serves to bring education into an active critical and constructive role in society.

It follows that education is not confined to participation in activities furnished by the school and taking place within the school. Education must penetrate (in its effects) every phase of human experience, it must be carried on in all areas of living into which the guidance of the school can reach. The school serves a very important purpose within the total educational process. The ideal school is a planning

---

[68] This statement represents the view of one wing of Experimentalism, *vide* pp. 281 ff.

center, where ways of coordinating, supplementing, enriching the learner's experiences are devised, and where direct assistance is given to the learner in the analysis and reconstruction of his own experience. The ideal school reaches out into the home and the community and wherever influences are at work in shaping the development of personality. To say that the school must cooperate as an equal with other social agencies is not enough: the school has a function, as coordinator, to seek as far as possible to influence every other social agency so that it fosters the highest development of the individual.

Repudiation of the traditional conception of education as something that takes place within the school leads also to a rejection of the idea that education is an affair of children and teachers. Education draws in everyone in the community—children, parents, citizens, teachers. The teachers (and among them must be included the physician, the psychologist, and the social worker) are the principal planners and coordinators of the educational enterprise. But the community as a whole has an important role as educator; ultimately it is the community that shapes the experiences a person is to have.

Similarly education must cease to be regarded as a social enterprise that is intended for children exclusively. "The idea that a dozen years more or less of schooling toward the beginning of life could, in a world so at sea and still always changing, supply sufficient education to last for the rest of life has become absurd even for those who try to conceive education in this inadequate preparatory fashion." [69] The situation requires that education be extended to all whenever in the course of their living they require it. Education can hardly be defined as participation in academic activities preparatory to going out into the world. Even the school must be conceived as a general community center to which all citizens may go for expert and sympathetic guidance in the solution of their problems.

The function of education is primarily in relation to the individual, but the nature of society and the conditions prevailing within it are of utmost concern to education. Education cannot operate except in terms of social-individual interrelationships; its task may be defined as the guidance of these relationships for the ultimate benefit of the individual. Generally speaking, the school seeks to extend and to

[69] W. H. Kilpatrick, in *The Educational Frontier*, p. 123. 1933.

coordinate the social experiences of the learner, and to make these experiences the basis of his continuous development. But how the school must conduct itself in the execution of this task and what else, if circumstances demand, it must do, depend upon the nature of the conditions prevailing in society.

Our present social order is characterized by tremendous complexity and an increasing rate of change of the conditions vital to the maintenance of life. Capacity for intelligent living in this culture calls for adaptability, for flexibility in thought and in action, for an understanding of the forces that act upon us, for creative ability to discover the meanings of new situations, to establish ends and devise means, for a devotion to the sharing of experience and the cooperative solution of problems, for faith in the individual and the democratic way of life. The experiences which the culture affords, however, do not operate to promote these ends; rather the conditions within society at the present time tend to make genuinely intelligent living very difficult to attain, not so much because of the intrinsic complexity of the culture as because of its disjointedness and inner conflict. The difficulty of educating for socialized living and the cooperative solution of life-problems is greatly aggravated if at the same time there exists in society a condition of highly competitive individualism; the problem of educating for faith in the democratic way of life is made enormous where equality of opportunity does not exist except as a slogan. Without question the prevailing conditions in American society tend to hurt personality development. To educate the individual at this time is inevitably to be deeply concerned about the state of society.

In what manner shall the concern of the school for society be expressed? In what manner shall the present societal situation influence the school in mapping out the lines along which to guide the experiencing of the individual? Two general answers to these questions are available, based on differing convictions as to the degree to which it is ethically proper for the school to influence the individual in the direction of a theory of social reconstruction, and (incidentally, but very important) on differing convictions as to the capacity of the individual to attain to wholesome personality and intelligent living, in spite of the unfavorable social conditions, and to work out intelligent remedies for these conditions when the time comes.

One answer is [70] that, however deplorable the present situation and however much of a handicap it is to the development of wholesome personality, the duty of the school is to orient the individual as best it can to the prevailing culture, to point out to him its defects, and to set him on the road toward working out his own solution in a democratic way. Integration of personality must take place around purposing, around the formulation of needs that ultimately will have to be satisfied. It is necessary to have faith in the ability of the individual to work out experimentally the solutions of the important problems that face him. The imposition of any plan of a social-order-to-be is incompatible with democracy and the experimental way of life, and is further

[70] This answer is offered by Bode, Hopkins, Thayer, and Cox. Within this general answer there are further differences in degree. The point of view of each may be summarized as follows.

Bode: The school is an agency maintained by society for its own progressive reconstruction; it prepares the way for social changes in the future. The school, however, does not lead in making social changes. Education must point out the areas that require reconstruction and help to make individuals intellectually capable of effecting this reconstruction. The directions in which individuals are to be inclined is that of greater socialization, but any more definite adjustments must be left to them. (*Vide* "Education and Social Reconstruction," *Social Frontier*, Vol. I, No. 4, pp. 18–22, January, 1935; also *Progressive Education at the Crossroads*. 1938.)

Thayer and Hopkins take virtually a common stand: Our society needs reconstruction. The fact that it does is obvious in the experience of every person. If we begin at the point where society seems to the developing learner to be inadequate, that is, with a need felt by the learner, then by exploring the causes of this need and the nature of its possible resolution, we can orient the learner properly. If we then teach him how to proceed, and induce him to operate in a democratic way, he will in time re-create society in a manner as to resolve the present tensions and retain and strengthen democracy at the same time. (Thayer, "Orientation to Life as a Function of Education," *Occupations*, 13:677–686, May, 1935; and elsewhere. Hopkins, "The Current Educational Awakening," *Democracy and the Curriculum*, Chapter IX. 1939.)

Cox: Collectivism is inevitable and a new social order is already in process. The ultimate arrangements will have to be worked out democratically. A voluntary collectivism such as is characteristic to some extent of the Scandinavian countries is the only one suitable to a democracy. Students should not, however, be indoctrinated. Once they become aware of their needs, they will do what is right "almost instinctively." Individual experience may be trusted. (Cox, "The Middle Ground in Education: A Rejoinder to the Plea," *Educational Forum*, 1:169–188, January, 1937; and "Youth's Response to his World," *Educational Forum*, 3:96–98, November, 1938.)

precluded by the fact that the movement of events is so rapid as to make unworkable any present scheme for the future.

The other answer is [71] that, in order truly to orient the individual to the present culture, the school must show that economic individualism is no longer compatible with democracy. To indicate the only possible resolution of the present conflict that is compatible with democracy, the school must actively foster the establishment of an economy that is intended for the common welfare of all individuals—a completely socialized and, necessarily, a planned and planning economy. It is not desirable nor is it possible to offer what can be called precisely a "blueprint" of the new social order, but it is necessary

[71] This is the point of view of Kilpatrick, Childs, and Counts (and is also represented in secondary education—*vide* "The Function of the Curriculum," in *The Changing Curriculum,* Chapter III, 1937, by Laura Zirbes). Again a range in degree of emphasis is noticeable.

Kilpatrick: The present situation is hostile to the development of personality. The basis of social maladjustment is economic. Teachers must do all they can as citizens to bring about a reconstruction in the economic basis of society. In addition, however, they must lead the students to see the need for a fundamental change in the present social order in the direction of much greater socialization, not by unreasoning imposition of their convictions, but by democratic discussion and cooperative working out of values in which individual deviations will be respected. (Kilpatrick, "The Social Philosophy of Progressive Education," *Progressive Education,* 12:289–293, May, 1935.)

Childs: Education is the selection of experiences through which the individual learner may develop in power and direction. There is no such thing as neutrality by the school. By the selection of experiences it reveals its particular biases. The school must present the child with the significant, realistic situations that present the world as it is. These experiences will almost speak for themselves. Reaction to them will lead to the search for solutions. The school must help to search out the forces and patterns which, if they were promoted, would on the one hand remake society and on the other hand enable individuals to find themselves. (*Vide* especially Review of Bode's *Education at the Crossroads,* in *Social Frontier,* 4:267–268, May, 1938.)

Counts: The school must face the fact that a new economic order has already come into existence and if it wishes to reconcile this collective order with democracy, it must act. The school must lead the way to a refoundation of democracy on the basis of a collective economy, and it must influence individuals to seek the social changes necessary to effect a democratic rearrangement of society. This does not mean that it must indoctrinate in the specific arrangements that shall exist; no one really knows what they are. But to teach for a realistic conception of democracy in the present situation is its sacred duty. (Counts, "Dare Progressive Education Be Progressive?" *Progressive Education,* 9:57–63, April, 1932; also, "Education for What?" *New Republic,* 71:12–16, 38–41, May 18 and 25, 1932, etc.)

to inculcate the idea that greater (indeed, extreme) socialization of economic resources and activities is the only solution to our present difficulties. For the school to neglect to do this is to fail in its duty to the individual and to stand by idly while democracy is being destroyed. Intelligent living cannot exist except in an environment of democracy and individual freedom; the experimental life presumes the democratic life. The present social situation does not allow true democracy and individual freedom, and makes impossible therefore the attainment of intelligent living. If the school is to carry out its obligation to the individual it must take its stand on behalf of real democracy. Beside this obligation, any "ethical" obligation it may have to be "neutral," that is, to help maintain the existing inequities and injustices, is childish. The obligations of the school can hardly be defined on a contractual basis. The school is an agency of social intelligence that serves all of society, not the special elements that happen at any particular time to be in control.[72] It is entrusted by society with the social duty of assisting all its individuals to attain to the Good Life. It cannot do its duty by withholding from individuals the solutions that they must inevitably apply if they would aspire to that Life.

Whatever the role that the school is to play in social reconstruction (whether direct or indirect), it is obvious that it must in the meantime help the individuals under its direction to overcome, as far as possible, the hurtful effects upon personality of the prevailing social conflicts. This duty the school cannot escape. In a period when the essential human relationships are by no means democratically governed, the school must all the more exert itself in fostering democratic ideals and attitudes. The activities that the school itself fosters must be permeated with the spirit of democracy. In a period when youth can see no immediate opportunity for employment and for participation in the

[72] "It is assumed here that in American democracy the ultimate loyalty of the teacher is neither to political administrations nor to state forms, but to the processes of democracy and science and to the ideal of the welfare of society." (G. S. Counts in "The School and the State in American Democracy," a paper presented before a meeting of the National Council of Education, Cleveland, Ohio, February 27, 1939.) This group of Experimentalists bases its view in large part on the distinction that must be made in a democracy between "society" and "the state." When the state ceases to express the will of society as a whole, it cannot be relied upon to effect needed social changes. Cf. p. 113, footnote.

normal adult activities of the community, the school must provide opportunities for the expression and utilization of work-energies; it must foster the participation of youth in adult activities; and must, in general, provide compensatory experiences to prevent the personality frustration that would otherwise result. The "Youth Studies" of the American Youth Commission reveal sufficiently the lamentable consequences that follow when the school neglects its duty in this respect.

The proposition that in the present state of our society universal education must extend through the period of adolescence and possibly beyond that, can hardly provoke disagreement. Not only do the requirements for developing power in dealing with experience call for an extended educational process, but the requirements for personal mental well-being as well. The period of adolescence is at present a critical stage in the development of the individual. The hardships with which the adolescent is confronted—the confusion in ethical perspectives, the demoralization that comes from delay of employment opportunities, the feeling of being unneeded and unwanted—are problems that make essential a sympathetic educational guidance. Though in the past the primary school may have been adequate for "furthering the effective participation in the essential relationships of life" of most men and women, that is no longer true. The secondary school must become the school for all adolescents, and must "take its character from the urgent needs that grow out of the characteristics of adolescent youth and the impact of contemporary life and conditions upon them." [73]

The new materials of education are experiences—the experiences that the young person has naturally in the course of his living, and the experiences which the school adds on the ground that they possess significant meanings which he should acquire. The educand is first of all a living, growing being who has needs that must be satisfied. The needs grow out of his experiences, and differ with the different stages of development. With reference to the same needs, the school selects and presents those additional experiences which it regards as educative; for these, too, the individual must have need, although the need may not be consciously expressed or awareness of it lie close to the surface. What must be regarded as education at the different stages of the life-process

[73] Quoted from H. O. Rugg in *Democracy and the Curriculum,* p. 284. 1939.

is guidance in dealing with the experiences—the individual's own and those additionally furnished by the school—that are related to individual needs. This is essentially the basis for distinguishing between the primary and the secondary school: while the primary school helps children to deal with the experiences natural to children and also with those, presented by the school, which bear upon the developing needs of children, the secondary school *deals with adolescents,* helps them to cope with the experiences that in the course of this period rapidly progress toward an adult level, and provides added experiences that help adolescents to satisfy their developing needs in a complex world. "The supreme mission of secondary education at this time is to help young people realize upon the significant possibilities implicit in their changing status—to help them find themselves anew in their personal, social, and economic relationships, and to develop a working philosophy of values which will give meaning, zest, and purpose to their living. This is in large part the responsibility of the school: life outside provides too little opportunity for participation and affords too little direction toward establishing young people in a rightful place of their own." [74]

Among the needs of adolescents the most cogent are those of an economic nature, and those related to employment and vocation. It can hardly be doubted that the school should legitimately concern itself with satisfying these needs. The function of the school is to guide the individual in his experiencing to the point where he becomes capable of intelligent self-direction. Vocational concerns and the economic problems that center around them are an inherent, unavoidable part of the life-experience. "No child in an American family escapes the inquiry, 'What are you going to do when you grow up?' " [75] and the question is hardly a routine one. Economic conditions are now far less favorable to youth than ever before, and "young people suffer the insecurity of all those who have no sure place in the world. With others who are baffled by this helplessness in the face of economic conditions, they readily give up the effort to understand and control them. Without guidance American adolescents may easily follow their youthful fellows abroad into fantastic movements which make promises of bread at the

    [74] V. T. Thayer, C. B. Zachry, and R. Kotinsky, *Reorganizing Secondary Education*, p. 6. 1939.
    [75] *Ibid.*, p. 242.

cost of democracy, and provide young people with an early sense of their own crucial importance in the adult world. For these reasons, all adolescents, irrespective of their economic circumstances, need assurance of the significance and responsibility of their present and future roles as producers and consumers. And, as an essential concomitant of this, they need understanding of the economic organization of the society in which they live. Meeting these needs is the school's obligation. Young people now find their contact with their complex economic environment primarily through the school, and it is chiefly the school that can help them comprehend it and their own roles as workers, consumers, and citizens." [76]

It has been a mistake of the traditional education, with its atomistic view of world and man, to balance the practical (including the economic and the vocational) against other types of experience called cultural. All experience is cultural provided that it is wholesomely educative. The individual who wishes to acquire the personality equipment that will enable him to deal intelligently with the wide variety of life-experiences that must be his, must undergo a wide variety of experiences during the period when he is being guided by the school. A person cannot become intelligent by avoiding contact with the real problems of practical living and of work. It hardly requires explicit statement that the education of adolescents must include orientation to the economic-industrial problems of our society and participation, to the extent to which adolescents are able, in planning their solutions,[77] and, moreover, exploration and development of individual vocational interest and talent to the point where the learner feels himself capable of taking intelligent part in vocational activity. (It must be stressed again that any experience is a means of general personality development; realistic participation in work-experiences is a means of developing the meanings, the attitudes, the power to cope intelligently with all experience.) Moreover, the education of adolescents must include participation in adult community activities, in the planning and execution of community projects, that will direct the currently unused work-energies of youth into channels of community improvement or reconstruction.

In the past the school has been mistaken in the manner in which it

---

[76] *Ibid.,* p. 244.
[77] This is to be understood in the light of the discussion on pp. 279 ff.

conceived "vocational training." The appeal has been to the motives of personal interest and profit that prevail in the industrial world; emphasis has been on the inculcation of fixed habits and skills that copied the current processes of industry. When vocational training was opposed to academic training, it was not unnatural that vocational activities should tend to be lacking in intellectual substance and depth. Interest in these activities was probably, as much as anything else, an escape from the meaninglessness of the academic routine. The school must revise its attitude toward vocational training and the role of work-experiences in the development of the adolescent. At present vocational preparedness requires a flexible intelligence and a deep social consciousness, as well as some technical proficiency in a trade. The school should give more emphasis to these at the expense of training in what may, on the surface, appear to be more immediately utilitarian skills. Moreover, the work-experiences offered by the school must not be confined to those which have only gainful vocational value. There is no sound purpose in having the work-interests and energies of youth completely absorbed in activities leading to a vocation that is still a good many years distant. There is danger that in the meantime, denied a chance to practice what has been learned and an opportunity otherwise to participate in the constructive work of the world, youth will become despairing. Some of the energies of youth must be channeled into constructive activities that are real, that can be immediately undertaken, that are socially useful and personally educative—into social projects of the kind that are generally carried on in a progressive community. Youth must be helped to participate in community life, to participate in the planning and management of community affairs and in the improvement (and, where necessary, in the rehabilitation) of community services and functions. The means of doing this the secondary school is only now beginning to work out, and it is evident that each community will have its peculiar requirements. Whether the community will ultimately reimburse youth for its labor, or in what other realistic way society will recognize the value of the contribution of youth still remains to be specifically considered.

The full meaning of education for adolescents cannot yet be stated; it is a meaning that must be experimentally elaborated. It is obvious, however, that the modern conception of secondary education is far more comprehensive than the traditional, and that the traditional secondary school as it exists today is wholly unsatisfactory. A new type of secondary education will have to be achieved—one that will be based on the wide and developing needs and interests of youth and will orient them realistically to their culture. The form that the school will ultimately take is not yet known; whether it is called a secondary or high school is unimportant.[78] The chances are that the latter name will not survive since it is associated with an educational tradition that is foreign to the present conception, and since it tends to emphasize the present discontinuous nature of the school.[79]

One more fact needs to be made explicit. The secondary school, whatever it is, is the school for all adolescents. All adolescents require guidance in experiencing, all need to learn how intelligently to direct the course of their life. There is very little doubt that all physically normal individuals can learn to do this. Intelligence is not an innate power; it is a capacity developed in the process of experiencing. Individual differences distinguish human beings from one another, but they do not serve to brand a person as intelligent or unintelligent. In place of the atomistic, deterministic conception of individual differences that has characterized in recent years the activities of the secondary school, the new secondary school must develop another. Each adolescent is an individual, different as a total personality from every other; the experience-process that he undergoes and in which he must be guided is, as a whole, different from that of every other person. The problem of providing for the development of full individuality is not quite as simple as to be solved, for example, by the formation of "homogeneous" groups. (For that matter, satisfactory individualization may very well be realized in common learning situations, without recourse to artificial "ability" grouping.) What is important is that the essential equality of each person as a human being, his inherent potentiality of becoming an intelligent person, his inherent individuality as a complete person with experiences, needs, purposes, values of his own, be recognized and suitably provided for.

[78] Some of the terms now used by Experimentalists are: Institute, Folk School, Community School, etc. (*Vide* especially *The Community School*, S. Everett, editor. 1938.)

[79] *Vide* P. R. Hanna, "The School Looking Forward," in *Democracy and the Curriculum*, Chapter XIV. 1939.

II

Recent years have seen a beginning in the development of education along Experimentalist lines. A good start has been made in breaking away from the sterile educational conception of tradition; there is reason to believe that the future will see much greater growth. The primary school has in this respect made greater progress than the secondary; in spite of the many promising beginnings here and there, it must be said that by and large the secondary school still is a traditional institution.

The principal defects of the prevailing secondary school arise from the conceptions of education under which it operates. Whatever conceptions it does represent (and it must be understood that it does not follow out consistently any one educational theory), this secondary school does not represent education as guidance of adolescents in the reconstruction of their experiences toward the end of intelligent living in an industrial-democratic society. Education seems to be academic, detached from the world of real events; the school operates as if it were a separable institution, within society but not really an integral part of it, not sharing in its immediate life-experiences. In the midst of dynamic social forces creating a new world, the school pursues its academic activities—it teaches courses and sets up subject-matter to be learned. When the school does descend into the social arena and engages in activities that have bearing upon present living, it operates in an unrealistic manner; presumably preparing individuals for practical living in a changing world, it labors to equip them with fixed habits and skills. The secondary school is handicapped not only by its adherence to a traditional conception of the educational function but also by its reliance upon an unsound mechanistic psychology.

Some years ago the secondary school placed itself on record as seeking to help individuals to become socially-efficient.[80] But the statement of objectives that was issued did not offer clear evidence that the school was aware of the character of the culture in which it was operating.

[80] The reference is to the Report of the Commission on the Reorganization of Secondary Education, *Cardinal Principles of Education,* Bulletin No. 35. Bureau of Education, Department of the Interior, Washington, D. C., 1918.

What was issued was a pallid statement of good intentions that would have served anywhere; it seemed to be notably lacking in a social philosophy.[81] Now to fail to admit that a school is a function of a culture and reflects that culture, and to refuse to define an orienting social philosophy is not to ensure that the school is without social biases. By failing to take a stand against the existing inequities in society, the secondary school has tacitly aligned itself with these; by failing to incorporate a strong social philosophy into its conception of its function, the secondary school by default lends itself to the preservation of the *status quo* with its internally contradictory and chaotic "social philosophy."

In some respects the secondary school has been well-intentioned. There has been in recent years an extension of the opportunity for secondary education to a great many adolescents. More youth are in secondary school today than ever before. This in itself seems a commendable step toward real democracy. But actually the cause of democracy has not been greatly served by this extension of educational opportunity. It cannot be said that the school has fostered an active and abiding loyalty to democracy. The reason is to be found mainly in the unrealistic and ineffectual manner in which the school performs its task of orienting its youth to their culture and in its failure to help them to understand and solve their immediate problems and needs.

The school has not succeeded in giving youth a realistic understanding of the currents and undercurrents in our modern society. The implications of a high-powered technological economic order for social living have not been made clear to them. They do not know the true meaning of democracy in the present day. The school has been content to hand down the social concepts and the slogans of an earlier era; individualism, the laissez-faire principle, poverty, struggle, inequality are taken for granted. "There is a subtle suggestion running through our whole philosophy of life that the ideal society is not one in which there is no exploitation of man by man but rather one in which the privilege of exploitation is merely reserved to the strong and the gifted. The high school seems to have accepted this philosophy." [82] It disregards or tones down the tensions, the conflicts, and the inequities that prevail today.

---

[81] *Vide* G. S. Counts, *Secondary Education and Industrialism.* 1929.
[82] G. S. Counts, *The Prospects of American Democracy*, p. 342. 1938.

It seems to radiate a kind of general good-will; it supports also a kind of general, vague, disembodied spirit of democracy. The result is not conducive to an intelligent understanding of society or to an abiding faith in democracy. Youth do not know where they are. Coming into contact with many of the forceful pressures of modern living, they are much more influenced by them than they have been by the insipid activities in the school. Many of these social influences are not favorable to the ideals of democracy, and others are completely hostile; but they exercise a compelling attraction upon youth.

The frustration of youth is increased by the failure of the school to help them in the satisfaction of their immediate needs and the solution of their personal problems. The present economic situation—the lack of employment opportunity, the lack of prospect for ultimate economic stability and security—is discouraging in its effect upon youth; studies of adolescents show that they are facing the world with a demoralized spirit. Society has "let them down," and the school has neither proffered them the prospect of a better society around which their energies might be centered, nor has it offered them activities that would even temporarily compensate them for their other wants. The school has not used the ambitions and the energies of youth in the direction of improving themselves and society. Instead it has continued to offer them academic palliatives. Small wonder is it, then, that youth are suspicious of adult society and all that it represents. Youth have become skeptical of democracy, too, and in that lies the great danger to the American way of life.

There is little doubt that the so-called "scientific education," under whose influence the school has fallen, is to a large degree responsible for many of the school's present difficulties. Allied with the Newtonian concept of a mechanistic world-system now abandoned by modern science, this "scientific education," by the "objective" attitude that it displays toward the present social order, by its inadequate grasp of the demands of the modern dynamic world, by its mechanical and over-simplified view of experience, human nature, and the educational process, has contributed to many of the school's shortcomings. It has already been stated that "objectivity" or "neutrality" within an unbalanced and inequitable social order amounts to tacit support of things-as-they-are. This is characteristic of the attitude of educational "scientists": while a prohibition has been placed upon the right of the school to intervene in social controversy, while the school is kept from its obligation to offer social criticism, it is considered to be perfectly proper for the school unthinkingly to continue to perpetuate traditional modes of thought and of action in social matters, however unsuited some of them may be to modern living, simply because they have the sanction of long usage.

Ours is an environment that is complex and dynamic, and that is increasing all the time in complexity and rate of change. An alert and active intelligence finds it difficult to keep abreast of the movement of events. In such a world, "scientific education" has decided that proper orientation of youth is obtainable through the learning of traditionally accepted attitudes, and fixed habits and skills. Since the concept of mind or intelligence is large and complex, and its total manifestation does not lend itself easily to analysis and measurement, "scientific education" has decided not to rely upon it. Accordingly human behavior is viewed in terms of specific acts; intelligent behavior means making the right responses to the right stimuli. Preparation of youth for intelligent living in the present world means assembling those responses which are judged by present society to be "right," and helping the students to learn them. The school makes a thorough canvass of the current life-activities (meaning adult activities), prepares lists of these activities, and each activity becomes an educational objective. The world of experience viewed statically is thus analyzed into its constituent elements, and each element is treated individually; there is no limit to analysis, and, as objectives become more and more specific, the learnings of the school become more atomistic. By summating later the individual atoms, an effective personality is supposed to result. Such a procedure cannot possibly produce the intelligent person that the modern world requires.

"Scientific education" does not recognize the unity of personality and the need for its wholesome, continuous integration. Personality is defined as "the sum total of the specific traits possessed by an individual"; personality is built by cumulating specific traits. "Scientific education" therefore never succeeds in gaining an insight into the needs and problems of youth; as long as the social situation produces tensions and discords in the life of youth, the activities offered by the "scientific" school can never satisfy its students. The failure of the school to recognize the concept of integration accounts, in large part, for the aloofness of the school in the face of a social situation that should challenge its greatest concern.

One of the most serious mistakes that the secondary school, under the influence of "scientific education," has made has been its misinterpretation and misapplication of the concept of individual differences. Here especially the "objectivity" of "scientific education" has been consciously or unconsciously made to serve the demands of the *status quo*. Essentially the concept of individual differences implies a recognition of the individuality of each human being; differences in specific traits also exist, of course, but they are of secondary importance. It is the true function of the secondary school to treat each adolescent as an individual, with his own needs, purposes, and preferences, and to help him become, in his own way, an intelligent person. Instead of interpreting the implications of individual differences in this way, the school has chosen to regard them atomistically and deterministically. On the basis of a partial criterion students are differentiated and labelled in one way or another. The most common basis of differentiation seems to be "mental ability" or "intelligence" (as it is unwarrantedly called). The testers and measurers and classifiers have gone to work and they have succeeded in setting up what appear to them to be inclusive and comparable categories of intelligence. Students are designated bright, average, or dull. Moreover, it is assumed that intelligence is an innate capacity, that students who are average or dull are destined to remain so. Students are segregated in "homogeneous" groups and provided with separate and often special activities "appropriate to their capacities." The inequalities of the existing social order are reflected in the unequal treatment of children in the school, and this, in turn, helps to perpetuate them. "Scientific" education is blind to the fact that the meaning of individual differences is much more fundamental than it has yet recognized, and that the true educational solution is quite different from that which is at present being tried.

III

What is needed, first of all, is the reconstruction of the educational theory that underlies the secondary school. The reconstructed theory must contain two essential elements: a social philosophy that is in accord with democratic values and that grows realistically out of the present culture; and a psychology that recognizes the purposive, integrating nature of human behavior, the instrumental function of intelligence, and the need for an intellectual method that squares with the dynamic quality of experience. This theory must further recognize that the function of education cannot be defined entirely with respect to the individual but must be conceived in terms of an individual living within a culture; that the school, therefore, has a "stake in society," that it cannot hold itself aloof from the troubles of society but is, in fact, deeply involved in them. Such a theory of education must be accepted before the reform of the secondary school itself can be achieved. Merely to tinker with the curriculum or with the organization and administration of education is insufficient; what is needed is a comprehensive re-examination of the basic problem. The Experimentalist philosophy offers a basis upon which American education can be reconstructed.

Given such an underlying theory of education, there must follow a reform of the existing educational institutions and the establishment of a school that carries out the fundamental purpose of education—to guide the learner in the conduct of his experience so that he becomes an intelligently self-directing person. Such a school must be established for all the young. Precisely how the school may be organized for instruction in terms of smaller units can be decided later. Consistent with the change in substance of secondary education, it is likely that considerable alteration will be made in the organization and form of the present secondary school.

A condition of discontinuity exists today among the various units of the school. It must be recognized that the educational process as a whole has a single character—that the function of general education as it has been called is to orient the individual to his culture in such a way that he can participate in it effectively as a social human being. In accordance with this aim, the educative experiences of the learner, insofar as they can be controlled by the school, should constantly reflect the progressive development of the learner advancing toward the status of intelligent adult. The distinguishing feature of the secondary school is that it is a school for adolescents. The secondary school, in the form in which it ultimately emerges, will carry out its orienting function with regard to adolescents; it will help them to meet their adolescent needs and cope successfully with their adolescent problems; and it will induct them realistically into the adult life of their society. Unlike the present secondary school, this secondary school will enter into the intimate thought-life of the adolescent and will see him through in his troubles and conflicts. This school will do for the adolescent and even for the older youth what today the intelligent Progressive primary school tries to do for the child.

Such a school, of course, will hardly retain the "scholastic" character of the present institution. It will, in the first place, be a community institution, not only in the physical sense but in the sense that it will concern itself with everything that is of importance to the community. The community experiences will be the matrix of the curriculum. The school will bring together adults and adolescents in activities that touch upon the community's welfare. It will cooperate with all necessary social agencies and educative influences. It will be the "community's organ of social sensitivity," [88] an instrument of social intelligence the function of which will be to integrate the life of the community for the benefit of all its individuals.

Such a school will approximate more nearly a "college for all youth" than does the secondary school of today, which, despite considerable gains made in enrollment, still excludes many youth. And it will be truly democratic. In the first place, society will take measures to render assistance to those young people who, because of financial need, cannot today enter the secondary school or long remain in it. In the second place, the school itself, replacing the present feeble "democratic" institution (the democraticness of which lies chiefly in allowing students to enter and to get what they can in the way of "training"), will assume a positive and vigorous role in educating for democracy—by not only providing equality of opportunity but by fostering in its own surroundings a democratic way of life.

The activities of the secondary school will not be circumscribed by tradition or authority, but will remain flexible and consistent with the final purpose of education, which is to guide individuals in the process of living to the point from which they can themselves operate intelligently. The present secondary school is preoccupied with its intellectual tasks, and seems to regard other tasks as outside its province. It appar-

[88] P. R. Hanna, in *Democracy and the Curriculum*, p. 393. 1939.

ently is unwilling to assume an active role in helping youth in the solution of their problems. The new secondary school will extend its activities through the whole range of adolescent living; it will seek to satisfy adolescent needs of whatever nature. And that means that the new school will most actively concern itself with the economic problems of youth, and with the many personal problems that arise from them. By impressing into its service society as a whole, the school will seek to eliminate or lessen the economic difficulties that confront youth, and, where that cannot be satisfactorily done, it will provide compensating activities. It will provide opportunity for the wholesome and educative expression of the physical energies of its young people in useful community work-projects. It will help youth to win the approval of their elders and to gain satisfactory status in the adult society.

It is, further, not to be overlooked that the school will, on its own initiative, furnish the student with experiences of great educational significance. That is required. The school function is not confined merely to helping the student resolve his immediate difficulties. The school must, in addition, select important experiences upon which the student may focus his critical and creative intelligence, and from which he may extract important meaning for the conduct of his own living. These experiences, however, must not be merely such as are renowned for their antiquity or traditional respectability, but must be relevant to the individual's own purposes and to the values which are dominant in his culture.

The new secondary school will deal with each student as a unique personality, operating in terms of his own background of experience and in terms of his own purposes. Education will be individualized with respect to both outcomes and process. But that does not mean that the school will segregate individuals and try to provide them with educative experiences that are theirs alone. The social environment provides a common matrix of educative experience. Out of this each individual will draw what he requires—understandings and skills that will help him to satisfy his needs and realize his purposes. Individuality will be respected, but socialization will be encouraged; the new school will not set up students in competition with one another. Nor will one factor—"mental ability" (deterministically conceived)—be taken out of the whole complex of personality, and made the basis of a partitioning of the school community. Needless to say, all the attitudes and the devices that have come in with educational determinism will be abandoned.

The new secondary school will not be an authoritarian institution either in its human relationships or in its attitudes toward knowledge. It will not accept dictation from authority either in the past or among those forces that at any particular time happen to control society. It will be a flexible, experimental, social, democratic institution, that will at all times seek to advance the welfare of each of its individuals.

4: The Method of Secondary Education

HUMANISM

I *

Eᴅᴜᴄᴀᴛɪᴏɴ ᴍᴇᴀɴꜱ guidance of the personal development of the individual along lines that mankind has marked out. Human development was made possible by human mind, and fundamentally education attempts to realize the possibilities of mind in all aspects of human living. These possibilities have been expressed not merely in the attainment of great power in the world of nature, but in the modification, the refinement, the *humanization* of man himself—in self-conduct based upon ethics rather than motivated by instinct, in the refinement and sublimation of natural emotions, in the development of esthetic tastes. Education seeks therefore to assist the individual, in the process of his development, to attain all these attributes of humanness. Since mind itself is a quality that is possessed by human beings in varying degrees, education is bound to realize these attributes in individuals in a varying manner. Justice to human beings requires that each individual be assisted in the realization of the Good Life that his capacity makes possible. Left to individuals themselves, human development would be fortuitous and uncertain, and it would assuredly be most uneven. Societal living presumes a degree of commonness, and the need for such living requires a common minimal level of development in all individuals. The higher this common minimal level, the better for individual and social living. The extent of the common development that is desirable and obtainable cannot be set absolutely, but must

* The Roman numerals used in this study to mark off sections have the following significance: I—General Principles, II—Evaluation of the Existent Situation in Terms of These Principles, III—Nature of Constructive Proposals.

be determined in the light of the societal status already reached, and in the light of the possibilities of human nature to make further and increased advances.

In the United States, common education under present conditions should extend through adolescence:[1] a number of important factors—democracy, high industrial development, social and economic complexity, change, the advancing age of employability—all combine to lead irresistibly to this conclusion. Secondary education therefore is no longer exclusive and selective, but part of the common education of youth. The principle of societal need for commonness must not, however, be allowed to obscure the fact of the essential inequality of human beings and the principle that every individual is to be assisted to develop to the limit of his capacity. Beyond the common level of living, each individual should be encouraged to go as far as his capacity allows and in directions in which his special talents, interests, or opportunities incline him. Within a given educational period, individuals can develop to different extents. Secondary education should be so differentiated as to make this possible. Beyond this period, for the ablest individuals, continued public higher education should be provided.

The central factor in education is intelligence. The good man is possessed, of course, not only of high intellectual qualities; he is distinguished also by the possession of spiritual, moral, emotional traits of a high order of merit. But these traits in the individual human being are made possible by intellect. Intellectual development may not lead automatically to spiritual, moral, emotional refinement of corresponding degree, but the latter is impossible without some intellectual basis. Without, therefore, discounting the importance of the other human attributes, it is necessary to emphasize in education the development of intellectual power. The nature of intellect and the method of intellectual development, the relation between intellectual and emotional development, between intellect and character, determine educational method. The extent of the intellectual capacity possessed by a person determines the extent of his educability, and helps to decide the manner in which he is to be educated.

Intelligence is the capacity to deal with meanings, that is, to apprehend or to conceive them, to relate them, to translate them into action.

[1] Not accepted by Foerster. *Vide* Chapter III, p. 213, footnote 5.

The greater a person's intellectual capacity, the more completely can he utilize meanings in all phases of good living—ethical as well as material —and the more can he be relied upon to do so. But, except possibly in the advanced education of the most capable individuals,[2] intellectual training, in and of itself, cannot be relied upon unfailingly to produce concomitant wholesome moral and emotional effects. For the most part, a process of deliberate moral and emotional training must accompany the process of intellectual training. The lower a person's intelligence, the greater is the emphasis that must be placed in his education on moral and emotional training as supplementary to the intellectual. Toward the end of the educational period, contingent upon the satisfactory intellectual progress of the learner, all types of training should be unified and placed under the rational control and guidance of the individual himself. Discipline must become self-discipline; intellect must regulate emotion and rule moral conduct. Similarly, meanings acquired by a person find expression in the material effectiveness that is implied in the concept of the Good Life. The higher a person's intelligence, the more capable is he of translating general meanings into the effective management of the countless specific situations comprising his life-experience, and the more can he be depended upon to allow reason to govern his actions. With individuals of other-than-superior intelligence, education must, according to individual capacity, concern itself with the "follow through," with the application of general meanings to specific situations. Emphasis in education is still to be on intellectual training, but (1) training in the acquirement of general meanings and general intellectual methods must be supplemented by the inculcation of habits and skills of a practical and specific nature, (2) even training for general intellectual power will be effected through materials that are themselves rather concrete.

Basic, then, in the educational process is the acquirement and use of meanings. Meanings underlie all of what is truly *human* living. Man develops into humanness as he comes into possession of them and ways of using them. Man does not begin by creating or by conceiving meanings entirely his own; his early development consists, rather, in receiving those made available or transmitted to him. In time, on the basis of the reserve he has accumulated, man is able to add meanings of his own, to

[2] *Vide* Chapter II, pp. 137 ff.

refine those already in his possession, independently to apply them in the understanding and control of situations, independently to modify them as the need for that is revealed. This is the state of being intellectually mature, and this is the goal at which education aims. Human progress, of the individual and of the race, requires that each person add to the common conception of the Good Life, and further refine it. This he can do *after* he has obtained a large fund of accredited meanings, and has acquired the technique of using them. It is with the accomplishment of this task that education is primarily concerned. In the early stages of the educational process, the learner does not analyze meanings out of the context of his own experience; rather, he begins by taking over those which mankind has analyzed out of *its* total experience and judged most necessary for the conduct of living. These he adopts as his own, weaves into his way of life, and expresses in his own conduct. In the process, the life about him—his culture—takes on intelligibility. He becomes capable of intelligent living; he acquires techniques making possible continued development under his own direction. From this point, self-education may well follow.

What is the source of the meanings that are effective in human development? They are, to a great extent, embodied concretely in the world as man has re-created it. They are present in the human environment—in our personal and social ways of living, in our societal organization, in our institutions, in our economic activities, in religion, in our artistic and recreational activities. The meanings are a key to the understanding of this environment; without possessing them it is impossible to understand the environment. One way to obtain possession of them is by ordinary, daily living in the environment, and every normal person does through personal experience, by a trial-and-error process, obtain for himself a fund of such meanings. But a person cannot in this way obtain a sufficient number of them, or grasp the significance of those he has obtained sufficiently well so that they may be of maximum service in his development toward the Good Life. In the first place, the immediate environment in which a person lives, however ideal may be his cultural surroundings, does not embody all the meanings that mankind has judged to be necessary and valuable. In their entirety, they are to be found in that great tradition of knowledge which is the human inheritance—knowledge that not only describes the present but sums up all that is worthy in the past as well. The great source of educative meanings is the whole of human experience, and the meanings themselves are to be found in the heritage of human wisdom that has been preserved. In the second place, the method of obtaining meanings by analysis of the concrete situations that comprise the natural life-experience is slow, imperfect in its results, and sometimes painful in its consequences. The method is too slow for human requirements. In the relatively short period of childhood and early youth, the individual must come abreast of the progress of mankind. There is a great deal to be learned. Always, learning by personal experience alone is a wasteful, uneconomical process; sometimes it produces effects that are lastingly harmful to the individual. And there is nothing to insure that, even then, learning will take place perfectly. Optimum human development requires both selection and concentration of meanings. Development in a desired direction proceeds most effectively when meanings are communicated *directly as such*. That is the reason that special educational agencies such as the school were instituted.

The purpose of education is to help the individual to obtain swiftly, economically, and efficiently those meanings which have been judged to be of highest value in human living, and to obtain many of them in a relatively short time. This can be done much better if, whenever possible, meanings are communicated in abstract, condensed, systematized form. To realize this purpose, materials of education have been developed, harboring the meanings that represent the best in every element of the human heritage, and organized in such a way as to make more evident their functions, relations, and uses. It is hardly necessary to state that not all educationally-needed meanings have been so organized (for example, there are great independent moral truths), or that in some cases very significant meanings are missing from the school subjects in which they ought to be. But it may be said with much truth that "organized subject-matter constitutes that map and compass which race experience has sifted out as the most valued for its own continued progress." [3]

The direct, systematic imparting of important meanings and training in the technique of using them are inherent in what is meant by educa-

---

[3] I. L. Kandel, "Is the New Education Progressive?" *Educational Administration and Supervision*, 22:86, February, 1936.

tion. And, of all educational agencies, the school is the agency best qualified to perform these functions. The school is the institution notable for providing guided, concentrated learning. Though schooling is not the whole of education, by means of school instruction a youth is enabled to secure, most efficiently and most economically, a large fund of important meanings and to learn methods of dealing with them intellectually. He is also assisted in the application of meanings to the orderly solution of practical life-problems, to the development of standards of ethical conduct, to the formation of tastes and appreciations. The chief, though not the sole, vehicle of school instruction is a well-organized curriculum of important subject-matter. The function of the curriculum is formative rather than instrumental; it is to assist in the general cultivation of mind and character rather than to prepare for specific practical ends. All things that possess meaning are to some extent potentially educative; but school materials differ very greatly with respect to their educative possibilities. Other things being equal, that subject-matter is best which is possessed of the largest number of important meanings, which is best organized for the purpose of facilitating understanding and learning, which best trains in the use of intellectual methods, and which calls forth the most sustained and comprehensive effort. Desirable as it would be to utilize such educative materials in the instruction of all students, that is not possible. Subject-matter must be appropriate to individual capacity. An inferior intellect cannot master abstract, highly condensed materials. In such case it becomes necessary, without surrendering the general aims of education, to differentiate among individuals with respect to the specific approaches they are to try and the specific materials they are to use.

It must not be supposed, however, that the school is the only institution of systematic education, even in the strict sense in which education has been defined.[4] The family and the church, among other institutions, though not primarily established for the systematic instruction of the young, also possess important educational functions. Historically, the special province of the home and of the church has been moral and religious training, while the school centered upon intellectual training and the rationalization of moral habits. At the present time, with the character of the home and of family life under-

[4] *Vide* Chapter III, pp. 209–210.

going important modifications that may possibly be permanent and that tend greatly to lessen their unity and influence, and with the influence of the church considerably weakened, a great burden has been placed upon the school. It is doubtful whether the school alone can support this burden, especially in the face of so many deleterious social influences. If education is to be totally effective, the home must continue to exert some influence upon formation of good character, and there must be a revival of the religious influence of the church.

The secondary school cooperates with the primary school in providing common education. The general aim of common education is, minimally, to develop in each individual those attributes of character and that practical effectiveness which are common to all other good men in society and which are necessary to make effective a common Good Life; maximally, to develop the individual of high personal character and effective intellect who, in the fullest sense, will conceive and lead the Good Life and assist others toward it. With the latter person it is not expected that the common school shall alone complete the educational process; he will most likely continue his education in a higher institution. It is to be noticed that even the general aim of common education must be differentiated, at least in terms of degree, according to the capacity of the individual.

Stated in specific terms, the objectives of common education must be further differentiated *in kind*. The superior student can independently apply general intelligence in the satisfactory solution of specific problems. Such a student must, in the popular expression, be taught not so much "what to think" as "how to think"; that is, a large fund of important general ideas, a high degree of skill in the use of intellectual techniques, and high intellectual ideals will suffice to prepare him to live, in all its many and varied particulars, the Good Life. Ethical living will grow out of reason. Taste and discrimination, with some little guidance, can easily follow from keenness of thought. Citizenship will develop out of intelligence, not only because the intelligent man is likely to be social, but also because true citizenship can come only with intelligence. Vocational success will grow out of a knowledge of the world, out of willingness and ability to learn, out of a high degree of adaptability, out of courage, and patience, and self-discipline. A trained mind will result in a happy and useful life. It will result in benefit to the individual and to the community. It will facilitate social change and make it more intelligent.[5] For the other type of individual, common education, leading in the direction of the same general ends, must be stated in somewhat different specific terms. Such a person cannot be expected to develop an equally high degree of adaptability, sensitiveness to situations, interpretative insight, and mastery of technique. With such a person there must be greater emphasis upon specific knowledge, upon routine techniques, upon the *application* of principles. Where adaptability and inventiveness are lacking there must be as compensation the comfort that comes with definiteness and certainty. There must be in the specific objectives of common education a greater emphasis upon vocation, upon citizenship in the narrow sense, upon the important actual situations that constitute the routine of living.

In its processes, the secondary school builds upon the achievements of the primary school and in the light of the changing nature of adolescence. It is the function of the primary school to provide the simpler and fundamental attitudes, knowledges, habits, and skills needed for immediate living and for continued development. Upon these foundations the secondary school must build, turning its effort to the task of continuing the training in character and practical effectiveness that helps each person to become, to the best of his ability, the good man. It must take cognizance of the increased readiness of the individual to gain more significant knowledges, master more difficult techniques, more satisfactorily solve practical life-problems. It must take some cognizance of the nature and needs of adolescence. Through all, the secondary school must accept and deal with each student as a separate educational problem. It must know the student as a person, his potentialities and the extent to which they have been realized, his special aptitudes and intellectual interests. "Learning students is a prerequisite to teaching them,"[6] and the school must make every effort to obtain about the student the kind of information that can serve it in educational guidance. On the basis of this knowledge, the school must provide the student with a curriculum which is for him educative. Differentiation is an indispensable feature of secondary-school instruction.

[5] *Vide* R. M. Hutchins, *No Friendly Voice*, p. 130. 1936.

[6] I. L. Kandel, "Examinations and the Improvement of Education," *Tests and Measurements in Higher Education*, Proceedings of the Institute of Administrative Officers of Higher Institutions, 8:223. 1936.

What has been stated so far pertains, in general, to Humanism as a whole. It is impossible, however, either to pursue further the discussion of the principle of differentiation or to enter upon a description of the school curriculum in terms of specific content, without being affected by the consequences of the difference in point of view existing among Humanists on the issue of formal as against non-formal discipline (an issue which, as has been shown,[7] arises from a yet more fundamental difference in theory of mind). Being a central psychological concept, formal discipline has important bearings upon educational method. In terms of this issue, the content of the curriculum and its organization for instruction will be described.

For formal discipline,[8] the general aims of secondary education are best attained through a curriculum that provides, *first,* training in the acquisition of the necessary intellectual tools and techniques along with inculcation of ideals and desirable habits of conduct, *second,* opportunity for the rapid and intensive assimilation of ideas of universal importance to man. The general principle followed is that a person who has been intellectually well-trained is capable of applying himself with success to any life-activity in which he, in the future, engages. It is the primary function of the curriculum to teach the student how to think, that is, to equip him with the tools of thought and to train him in the ways of their effective use. For a considerable period in the educational process, the gaining of a thought-content is subordinated to the systematic cultivation of intellectual method. When the student to some extent has the use of tools and techniques that make good thinking possible, he can begin to assimilate, with relative intellectual efficiency and economy, a content of the ideas that have made a lasting mark on civilization.

It becomes irrelevant, then, to inquire whether the school curriculum is up-to-date, whether its materials are drawn from the culture in which the school exists. The materials of the curriculum are chosen not on these bases. They are selected for their value as disciplinary instruments or because they contribute ideas of great permanent significance. Necessarily, the subject matter of such a curriculum at its best is largely abstract. "It is paradoxical but true that the most practical curriculum is

---

[7] *Vide* Chapter II, pp. 139 ff.
[8] The reference is to Hutchins and Foerster.

the most theoretical one." [9] First come the formal subjects, the object of which is to equip the student with the required intellectual tools, to train him in their use, and, incidentally, to help him develop ideals and good habits of intellectual work. Following are the liberal studies, within which the ideas that constitute the great inheritance of mankind exist and within the areas of which these ideas operate—philosophy, the arts, literature, pure mathematics, the social sciences, the natural sciences. Especially are the important ideas to be gained within the context of the works (books) in which they originally appeared, works which have since become recognized as classic.

With the rules of curriculum so strictly defined, the problem of providing for individual differences in native ability becomes difficult, and on its solution in secondary education formal discipline is divided within itself. According to Hutchins,[10] the formal studies to be given in the first three or four years of the secondary period (in an institution which Hutchins calls "the secondary school"[11]) are intended for all students. These studies are primarily linguistic, and include the study of mathematics (Euclidean geometry) and some formal training in scientific method. The curriculum may in certain respects be modified for individual students (for instance, not all students need to learn Latin), but all are to learn the subjects which will enable them "to read, write, and speak" and to use the tools of thought effectively. The work of this period is to be in all cases preparatory. At the end of it, a differentiation in type of curriculum is to take place. The more literately-able students are to proceed to obtain a "general education" in a "college" during a period of three or four years. Central in the curriculum of this "college"[12] is the pursuit of the liberal studies, carried on in conjunction with the reading of the classics in which they are obtainable. The latter activity is an extremely important phase of liberal education. "These books are

[9] R. M. Hutchins, *No Friendly Voice*, p. 126. 1936.

[10] *Ibid.*, pp. 109–110. Also, by the same author, "The Organization and Subject-Matter of General Education," Department of Secondary School Principals, National Education Association, *Bulletin*, 22:6–14, March, 1938.

[11] For the special significance of the use of secondary in quotation marks, *Vide* Introduction of this study, p. 4.

[12] The "college" is for the general education of youth of approximately the age of sixteen to twenty (R. M. Hutchins, *No Friendly Voice*, pp. 109–110. 1936). It is in this study regarded as coming within the period of secondary education.

essential because it is impossible to understand any subject or comprehend the contemporary world without them. . . . Four years spent partly in reading, discussing, and digesting these books will make an experience that will help the pupil to understand the world." [13] Prominent also in the curriculum is to be the study of grammar, rhetoric, logic, and mathematics. For those who cannot cope with this curriculum, who are "hand-minded" and not "book-minded," there is to be worked out a parallel course that will present through concrete materials the ideas that comprise the great Human Tradition. This differentiation in type is to be regarded primarily as differentiation in method rather than in educational aim. The purpose in the case of the latter curriculum, is to provide a "general education" through technical and practical rather than through literary and cultural materials. To distinguish it from the "college," the educational unit offering this curriculum is to be known as the "institute."

The problem of differentiating among students, as Foerster sees it, [14] is considerably simpler. Secondary education is not to be given to all, but only to those who, at the age of twelve, have proved themselves to be educable. Of these, the less superior are to be "trained in preparation for some activities of citizenship and some types of instruction. Receptive of authoritarian instruction, they can be indoctrinated in a set of ideas, habits, and attitudes approved by the adult society of which they will presently be a part, and at the same time they can learn how to do some of the things done in the useful vocations." [15] For the others, the curriculum of "the secondary school" is to be disciplinary and preparatory for college. [16] The purpose is to give mental training, to equip the student with the necessary intellectual tools and techniques, and at the same time to prepare him for the higher liberal studies to be pursued in the college. The curriculum of the high school is to be the traditional one emphasizing the study of languages, mathematics, and

[13] R. M. Hutchins, *The Higher Learning in America*, p. 81. 1936.

[14] N. Foerster, *The American State University*, p. 179. 1937.

[15] *Ibid.*

[16] Foerster is thinking in terms of the conventional arrangement of a high-school followed by a college education. He would not, as Hutchins would, alter the institutional forms of the present education.

Note that Foerster comes closer than Hutchins to typifying classical Humanism, except for his rather extreme pronouncements regarding ineducability and the need for educational segregation.

science, purged of the utilitarian and undisciplining activities that have lately come in. The liberal studies themselves would be part of higher and not of "secondary" education. They are to be studies embodying "the permanent sense of mankind"—religion, philosophy, literature, art, mathematics, and history. Naturally an important feature of this education would be the reading of the great books.

According to the thought of the Humanists who do not accept *formal* discipline,[17] the intellectual training that forms the general end of secondary education is effected not through a specified set of studies, progressing from formal and linguistic materials to materials possessing ideational substance, but through intellectual application to any meaningful content that is suited to the capacity of the learner. To learn "how to think" is much more important than to acquire any particular facts of knowledge, but development of power is a result of dealing intelligently with a significant content. Intellectual power is achieved in the course of obtaining meanings, organizing them, and applying them. Mind is not a passive instrument that can wait to assimilate ideas until it has been properly prepared. Man is getting ideas all the time from the world in which he lives. If the ideas are important enough, if a person keeps applying himself to them sufficiently, if he is taught how to utilize them, the attainment of intellectual power will inevitably follow. No subjects can make claim to special distinction as disciplinary instruments, and no books can claim to constitute the sole appropriate context for important ideas. All subjects have disciplinary potentialities, provided they are rich in meaning, are well organized, and provoke precise and systematic thinking. It is, therefore, better to use educative materials which are, to some extent, drawn from the culture in which education takes place. It is not desirable that the source of subject-matter be limited entirely to the contemporary setting; it is much better to make judicious selection from the whole of the human heritage of wisdom, of the past and of the present. A curriculum must not be static; it should be subject to continuous growth as well as to constant refinement. The modern world has, for example, made advances in science that leave far behind the contributions of the past in this respect; these need to be represented in the curriculum. Moreover, it has been demonstrated that important elements of the traditional curriculum, however appropriate they may

[17] Butler, Kandel, and Learned.

have been once, are today not well suited to all students in the secondary school. The essential principles in constructing a curriculum of secondary education are that every major area of human achievement be represented, that the ideas embodied in the subject-matter be big ideas, that the materials be organized in orderly, logical fashion, and that the pursuit of any study be sufficiently sustained to allow the student to mature in it and to profit by it intellectually.

Differentiation does not require as drastic provision as is necessary in the case of formal discipline. Beginning with a common body of studies representing every important element of the human heritage—"scientific, literary and linguistic, esthetic, institutional, and religious," [18] it is easy to introduce modification of these materials in fine, continuous gradation to suit every type of capacity represented by the students. Modification may be made by means of introducing or withdrawing or adapting content, enriching or simplifying subjects, varying the organization, the presentation, or the modes of learning procedure. Between the two extremes—the curriculum given to the most capable and the curriculum given to the least capable student—there will surely be a great difference. One will be intellectual, abstract, logical, systematic; the other will be concrete, specific, involving practical knowledges and skills, relying upon obvious motivations, and looking toward practical ends. But between the two extremes there will be almost infinite gradation, and within these extremes by far the large majority of the students will be accommodated. It is not desirable that there be too much differentiation in *type* of school program in common education.[19] Such differentiation may foster specialization not in means but in ends.

The classical curriculum of the past is no longer suited to serve as *the* curriculum of the secondary school. It was in the first place intended for an intellectually select group; the student body at present in the secondary school is highly heterogeneous, and soon may widen its range to include the entire eligible population. Moreover, the study of classical languages, with emphasis in instruction on the philological rather than the cultural, has very properly fallen into disfavor. It is necessary to organize a new and broader core of studies for secondary

[18] N. M. Butler, *The Meaning of Education*, p. 26. Revised edition. 1915.
[19] Learned does not commit himself on this point. He may possibly not be in agreement.

education. Possessing disciplinary value, these studies must also be appropriate to the abilities of students. No single inflexible curriculum for all can serve this purpose, nor even several well-differentiated types of curricula. Furthermore, provision must be made for more than merely intellectual training; training of the emotions, character training, physical education must be provided for as well.[20] From a common body of important studies, in language and literature, the social studies, mathematics, science, music, and art, there must be drawn in varying proportions the elements that suit the intellectual needs of the individual student. Variation for individual differences there must be, though only between extremes of superior and inferior should the difference in type of curriculum content be great. The problem of vocational training will have to be considered anew, and perhaps for some students a degree of vocational specialization will have to be introduced. For the superior student a broadened and enriched classical curriculum may be satisfactory, while for less capable students the general principle may be followed of placing less emphasis upon linguistic and symbolic materials and more upon concrete. Whatever the materials they must be systematically organized, if their developmental value is to be realized.

No choice of subject-matter can itself serve as a guarantee that effective education will take place. Whether it will or not, depends upon whether the student will assimilate the ideas the subjects embody, incorporate them into a body of permanent knowledge that shall be his own, and develop in the process worthy intellectual interests and desirable intellectual habits. Effective education presumes careful educational guidance. Throughout the educational period, every valid device must be used to take soundings of the extent to which learning is taking place. Examinations, whether used to test progress or final mastery, whether used in guidance or in appraisal, have an important place in the educational scheme. The educational process cannot be aimless and haphazard; it must possess definite direction and system. It is necessary periodically to ascertain whether educational movement is in the right direction and to what extent purpose is being realized. Examinations serve this function. It is necessary, however, to take care that not only the obvious, superficial educational outcomes are meas-

[20] Butler and Kandel only. Learned does not admit the need for specific training of this kind. *Vide* p. 139 of this study.

ured. Examinations must be as comprehensive as are educational objectives. However subtle are some of the qualities of mind and character that education is to develop, however elusive and difficult of precise evaluation, forms of examinations must be worked out which adequately represent them all.

II

That the secondary school has not operated in a manner which, by humanistic standards, can be regarded as creditable is primarily the fault of the values governing present-day American society. Educationally, these have expressed themselves in the philosophies and psychologies that dominate present school practice. Working within this milieu, the secondary school has necessarily suffered from its defects. Specifically, how have these defects been revealed in terms of educational method?

Educational method, in the first place, has not been based upon a realistic understanding of the meaning of individual differences. Naturalistic psychology has in general attached much importance to the fact of individual differences, but in practice it has greatly misinterpreted this fact. Taking its direction from the naturalistic psychology, the secondary school has also badly applied this doctrine. The school has become involved in complicated attempts to provide for small, specific differences among individuals, but it has failed to provide for the largest and most important difference—in intellectual capacity. Intellectual capacity is not one trait among many, all of them of similar or comparable importance; it is *the* trait that distinguishes men as human beings, that determines the extent of possible human development. Despite the introduction of large numbers of students of greatly varied ability, the secondary school has never really provided educative materials and instruction adapted to difference in capacity. Its several policies with regard to individual differences have been, all of them, inadequate. A large common reservoir of studies is made available to all. Within it are several differentiated "curricula," created in advance on the basis of the practical purpose which they serve. A student may enroll in any curriculum he chooses, regardless of whether it is suited to his educational need. Since considerable election of studies is allowed within a curriculum, a student may choose the subjects to which, for one reason or another, he is attracted. All students are on a par and receive like treatment. Programs of study are not graded in difficulty. A common level of instruction prevails in all subjects, and the standard of achievement is geared to the average. Bright and dull students may pursue the same studies, take the same examinations, and satisfy the same requirements. In recent years, the school has made some amends by applying more industriously the principle of homogeneous grouping within subjects; individual schools have begun to carry the logic of individual differences even further. This, of course, is a movement in the right direction; but it may be balanced by the fact that a number of schools, influenced by modern pedagogical theory, have lately recognized *interests* of students as governing factors in the selection of subject-matter, as if interests were not themselves in need of educative guidance.

The harm done naturally by this inadequate and confused treatment of individual differences has been augmented by the application in educational method of a pragmatic, mechanistic attitude toward mind and intelligence. The S—R psychology, in its several variations, has succeeded in banishing from education the concept of mind and the ideal of human development as growth in mind. Judged by its present influence, the conception of culture and liberal-mindedness may be said to have disappeared from secondary education. It is unfashionable these days even to use the terms. The place of liberal education has been taken by specialized training, by "conditioning" in specific knowledges and skills. Psychology has influenced secondary education to become utilitarian preparation for a multiplicity of things. With the influx of new students, the number of "practical needs" was greatly increased. To meet these "needs" the secondary curriculum had to be expanded. The original compact curriculum, the elements of which complemented each other in forming a curriculum that was an educative whole, gave way to the present curriculum of about 250 subjects.[21]

Earlier, the Committee of Ten had unfortunately given currency to the notion that, with respect to educative possibilities, subjects are equal. The influence of this idea helped to give educational respectability to

[21] I. L. Kandel, "Our Adolescent Education," *Educational Administration and Supervision,* 18:565, November, 1932.

the practice of curriculum expansion. The principle of election, primarily created for mature college students, was introduced into the high school, and soon the high-school student was threading his way through a labyrinthine curriculum by "electing" subjects. An ingenious system of credits was devised to help keep the count; a certain number of credits certified the student as "educated" and entitled to graduation. Secondary education lost its unity, comprehensiveness, thoroughness. With the multiplication of subjects came specialization; and, while specialization as a means of reaching common ends is to a degree necessary in educational method, in a curriculum instrumentally conceived it becomes a means for leading men not toward a common understanding of each other but away from that. Specialization that does not rest upon a common base of ethical character and intellectual effectiveness defeats the ends of education. With the introduction of credits and half-credits, it became possible to nibble at this and at that. The inestimable educational gain that comes with continuity of learning, with the slow maturing of ideas in a confined field of study, was lost. Education became a hit-and-run affair. Even such educative values as remained were further dissipated by the low standards of achievement that were erected.

The curriculum of the secondary school is a "rope of sand, without texture or organization. Effective education through related ideas is sacrificed to the mere registering of information."[22] The curriculum lacks intellectual dignity. It is scrappy; there are too many subjects pursued for too short a time. There has been developed an elaborate machinery of administration, guidance, grading, and crediting, and we are misled by the sound of the machinery into thinking that it is educationally productive. Secondary education has not even succeeded in obtaining the variety that it seemed to be after. A humanistic education, though bringing men together, also makes them true individuals. The present superficial diversity of curriculum makes men more individualistic, more self-centered, but in all important positive respects more conventional and ordinary. The commonplace has become the ideal, and the mediocre has become the universal. The brightest minds

[22] W. S. Learned, *The Quality of the Educational Process in the United States and in Europe,* Carnegie Foundation for the Advancement of Teaching, Bulletin No. 20, p. 5. 1927.

have been swallowed up in the phenomenon of mass performance. We no longer aim at ideals; we "analyze activities" and set them up as masterpieces for others to imitate.

In foreswearing the principle that education is for character and intellectual development in favor of the concept that education is for immediate "efficiency" in "practical" things, the secondary school has exchanged a curriculum rich in training value for one that offers factual information and mechanical skills. Emphasis is today on information, on current events. The loosely organized, inexact social studies have gained popularity at the expense of subjects possessing better organization, more developmental value, and calling for much more precise and rigorous thinking. Preparation for good citizenship has come to mean learning facts from the social studies. Foreign languages, where they are still taught, are taught not for the insight they offer into human culture nor as preparation for the reading of great literature, nor purely for their formative value, but for their possible utility as spoken languages. Emphasis on culture and discipline in language study has given way to the inanities of the "direct method." The classical languages that have been shunted from the curriculum would very likely be unsuited to the capacities of most students in school today, but nothing of equivalent value has been found to take their place.

The weakness of the school curriculum is not especially compensated for by other aspects of educational method. Instruction has not been such as to overcome the handicaps of inferior educative materials. Teachers themselves are, in most cases, lacking in liberal learning. In the training of teachers, emphasis on character, knowledge, and intellectual power has been replaced by emphasis on "personality" and teaching techniques. The effects of bad training are further aggravated by the fact that a teacher is often required to teach several subjects. "Progressive" education has not helped any, since it has counseled teachers against the need for preparing and planning lessons or even of "knowing" subjects. In testing the results of learning, the secondary school is caught between the "objectivity" of educational science and the obscurantism of "progressive" education. On the one hand there are being developed and applied tests increasingly factual, increasingly minute, increasingly dry and unimportant, increasingly "objective"; on the other hand, there is a barrage of sentimental and unintellectual argument to the effect that children's "growth" cannot be measured, that it should not be measured, that "pencil-and-paper" tests are inadequate in any case, and so forth. That is not to say, however, that educational science, at least, has been altogether unsuccessful in producing worthwhile testing devices. It has not. But the extent to which these devices have been carried is not sound nor is their use altogether judicious.

It is possible to add to these instances of weakness and confusion. They extend to every aspect of the educational process—content, organization, instruction, administration. Our method is bad and ineffectual not because American teachers lack ability or American students intelligence, but because we have been misled into accepting erroneous conceptions of the meaning of education and of the Good Life toward which it is to lead.

III

Where process is obviously faulty, it is not sufficient to begin its reconstruction without opening up for examination its basic assumptions and major guiding principles. It is not to be questioned that a radical reconstruction of the present method of secondary education is called for. No minor changes, no mere tampering with curriculum, with organization, with tests, with instruction, will serve. In effecting such reconstruction, it would be necessary to rebuild some of the foundations upon which the secondary school rests, and these foundations are a part of the present American temper.

An educational renaissance is necessary if secondary education is to perform well its function in common education of helping all individuals to live the Good Life as mankind has conceived it and to help, in turn, to elevate the collective Good Life of society. Preceding even this renaissance, there must be communicated to all men the true conception of the Good Life—a conception in which there is no place for the over-materialistic, the aggressive, the predatory, the crude, the envious, but one in which are operative all the ideals that men have recognized as distinguishing them as *human* beings. A life of refinement, of self-respect, of self-discipline, of voluntary sharing—yet of reserve, of recognition of the rights of the individual and of the privileges of society, of the cultivation of the human spirit and of things of the spirit must be set up as the supreme end of education. There must further be recognized the true status of mind in human affairs, the cosmic mind as well as the individual—mind as the creator of the good, as arbiter of human values, as the source and fountainhead of all humanness. Thus launched and accepted by all men, the true conception of the Good Life will be effective in restoring to education its true significance—not that of training men to become carpenters or mechanics, stamp collectors or amateur photographers, Democrats or Republicans, but that of helping them, in terms of commonly accepted ideals, to become the very best human beings they are capable of becoming. A theory of education will be developed which will seek to materialize this educational ideal in terms of the conditions of modern life. It will recognize that the high social-economic status of modern American culture dictates a need for an extensive common education, one that will offer to all equal opportunity but one that will also recognize the superior claim of the superior individual. Of this common education, secondary education will be a part. The secondary school will be a common school, providing for the needs of perhaps the entire youth population. It will seek to assist all in the attainment of the Good Life, insofar as individual ability allows.

For the good secondary education is based upon a realization that all men are different, that man is primarily an individual being, and develops as such. Secondary education will be in accord with individual possibilities; it will not disregard them or go contrary to them. In terms of his possibilities, each individual will be assisted to develop the attributes of the good man. The good secondary school will take care, however, that all individuals are brought up to the highest common level of which they are capable.

The return of a true perspective of the meaning of humanness will once more reveal to secondary education the psychology that is to guide its processes. If human mind makes man what he is and helps him to visualize directions in which he wants to go, then it is in terms of mind that man must be helped to develop. Mind will be studied and defined in all its aspects—in what it is, in what it brings, in how it proceeds. Secondary education will become training in the development of human qualities primarily through the medium of mind, and the method of the secondary school will be formulated in accordance with the processes of mind, and the manner in which these processes operate in human living.

The secondary school will then seek to determine its function in relation to the whole educational undertaking as carried out by the home, the church, the living community, and the other educational agencies. Without trying to assume any responsibilities that more properly belong to the others, the secondary school will define its responsibility. If the other agencies of education properly assume their responsibility, the function of the secondary school will be conceived as the higher training of the intellect and the emotions required of the ethically good and materially effective individual. Knowing its responsibility, the secondary school will marshal its resources in order to carry it out.

The resources of the secondary school are chiefly its educative materials. These materials will be selected with a view to forming the mind and to inducting the individual into the life of mankind. This will be their primary purpose—to make a man human, to make him good, to make him intellectually effective. The school will not lose its perspective and come to regard vocation or nationalism or the inculcation of political ideology as the governing factor in its selection of materials. It will not set up society as its end and as its shining example. It will take its ends from humanity, and will attempt to realize these ends in the individual through appropriate materials that are suitable also to the individual capacities of the learner. The educative materials will be unified by a common principle—the end at which they aim. They will not be merely an assortment of activities. They will be coherent, systematic, dignified. And they will be taught in a manner worthy of their content.

The secondary school will not deceive itself into accepting appearances as realities. It will not be tricked by devices such as credits, elective schemes, a streamlined mass efficiency. Education will be a simple affair of bringing a student into contact with an appropriate curriculum. From that point on, the process will be activated by the student himself, with the school offering firm but sympathetic direction. Guidance will be an essential part of the school's task, guidance and periodic re-direction. The school will restore to the student a certain amount of independence in procedure, a certain degree of self-reliance which belongs to him by right of developing self-control and intellectual maturity. The curriculum itself, if it is properly chosen, will induce in the student a sustained application to the work before him, many and varied intellectual interests, a system of enduring knowledge which he can translate into proper action, and ethical and intellectual traits which stamp him as the good person.

SOCIAL EVOLUTIONISM

I

The aim of education is to help each individual to develop the social, adaptable personality that will enable him to make successful adjustment within his social environment, and through such individuals, to enable the race to make continuous progress toward higher levels of living. Education is not "natural growth," nor is it systematic development of the child's "inner potentialities." The method of education is not merely the method of "natural experiencing." The educational process is a systematic process in the course of which the individual learns to make all those adaptations that render him increasingly capable of effective living. The adaptations are learnings that have been gained in the course of the racial experience and made available to him. The individual develops as he assimilates these learnings and makes them part of his adjustive equipment. In the process he becomes a changed being, a new kind of person who knows how to live, intellectually and morally, in a civilized world. The higher the civilization into which one is born, the more difficult is adjustment within it, and the more education is therefore needed. Effective living in our complex changing world calls for a high order of adaptability. That high order of adaptability the educational process must enable every individual to attain.

Education is a necessity for all. Differences in native capacity are hardly sufficient justification for denying anyone the right to acquire all the learnings that he needs for successful life-adjustment. For education is not merely a process of "realizing native capacity"; it is rather the process of creating adjustive capacity with reference to a particular environment. Education begins with the adjustive capacity that the individual possesses as a gift of inheritance, and *increases that through learnings.* For learnings, when assimilated into personality, have it in their power to add very greatly to adjustive capacity. The naturally "brighter" individual, equipped with but few learnings, cannot match in adjustive capacity the normal individual equipped with many learnings. The purpose of education is thus to raise every individual (unless, owing to some pathological condition of the organism or of the nervous system, the person is definitely subnormal) to the point where he can, in an independent way, operate satisfactorily in his environment. This may require different emphases with different individuals. Of course, education does not erase individual differences; quantitative and qualitative differences in adjustive capacity still remain. But regardless of differences every individual becomes capable of satisfactory living. And as a result of education new kinds of differences are created—differences in intellectual interests, in acquired knowledges and skills; these are the differences that promote the ends of adjustment in a common environment.

The conditions of adjustment in our environment make necessary a period of general education that extends through adolescence almost to adulthood. Secondary education, previously selective and with aims rather different from those that governed common education, has become therefore part of a common educational process intended for all individuals. Following primary education, it takes up the responsibility for helping the individual to achieve adaptability in his present environment. Primary and secondary education together make up a continuous, unitary process. But experience has shown that some sort of line of demarcation must be drawn between them. The principle on which the demarcation is based should be psychological. The primary school deals with immature children who have not yet acquired the primary learnings that they need for proper immediate living as well as for further development to the point where they can become adaptable individuals. The secondary school deals with adolescents who, on the basis of adaptations which they already possess (and in particular the language adaptation), can proceed more quickly and with increasing self-dependence to acquire the learnings that will stamp them as intellectually, morally, and volitionally mature. Secondary education must possess a content of learnings more advanced, more difficult to assimilate, presuming a certain amount of progress already made toward maturity. It is to be characterized by a method of learning that stresses the use of language as a tool for the acquirement of further learnings, and by independent individual study. It must in general recognize the greater self-reliance of the learner in guiding his continued development and his own immediate living.[23] That is not all, however. The mental processes on higher developmental levels are qualitatively different from those on the lower; they are more conceptual in character, they are more highly organized, they involve transfer of learning. Secondary education needs to be qualitatively different in general method from primary education. It has to concern itself with the cultivation of the *higher mental processes;* it must increasingly emphasize generalization, the organization of ideas; and, to a much greater degree than the primary school, it must emphasize application and develop transfer ability. Secondary education should culminate in the attainment of the independent effectively-adjusting person.

Education is of course provided not only by the school. Not to speak of the normal life-experiences that are highly educative, there are other agencies—the home and the church—which cooperate in the task of making man capable of civilized living. But the problem of human development (that is, the need for absorbing a tremendously large number of learnings in a relatively short time) is such as to make the influence of systematic instruction paramount in education.[24] In recent years the school has more and more assumed what formerly was the responsibility of the home and the church. Without overlooking or minimizing the continuing educative influence of these agencies, and the very great educative influence of natural living in civilized society, the fact remains that the school is by far the most important agency of education. Whether the objective of adaptable personality is realized depends very greatly on the manner in which the school performs its function. It is of no use for the school to attempt to shift some of its responsibility to other societal agencies or to society in general. To the best of its ability, the school must cooperate with all other social institutions, and it must attempt to realize to the full the potential educa-

[23] The points that follow are made explicitly by Judd and Bagley. *Vide* pp. 160 ff.

[24] *Vide* W. C. Bagley, *Determinism in Education,* pp. 156 ff. 1925. Judd and Morrison are in agreement.

tional values that all possess, but ultimately the responsibility for training the individual devolves upon it.[25] The secondary school therefore
becomes by far the most important agency for training youth of adolescent age for intellectual independence and social and volitional maturity.
And the method of the secondary school becomes a matter of decisive
importance.

It must be admitted at the outset that it is not yet possible to state,
with the completeness and definiteness that is desirable, the manner in
which the secondary school is to proceed to carry out its responsibility.[26]
It is easier to show what is not an adequate method. Certainly the
secondary process as it was traditionally carried on in the high school
and as it is at present carried on in some European secondary schools
is not suited to the present purpose of secondary education. Neither an
education that offers a pre-professional education to the few, nor a
process of intellectual training through formal discipline, will do; what
is needed is a general education on a higher level, suitable for all, that
will prepare for effective living in the present complex social environment. Largely on an empirical basis, such a method of secondary education appropriate to the present situation can be described, but its
formulation must still be in somewhat general terms. Many of the
large details of content, organization, and method still elude us. It
will be the task of educational science eventually to supply them. We
require additional information about needed learnings on higher adjustment levels, about the nature of the higher mental processes, about
procedure in instruction on the secondary level. When these facts are
in, it will be possible to present with much more precision and comprehensiveness the method of secondary education.

The learnings that the secondary school is to transmit and the individual is to incorporate into his own adjustive behavior are the
adaptations which the race has made and which it judges to have been
most serviceable in human adjustment. Generally speaking, many of
these adaptations are found in our society at the present time—in the
mores, in the social institutions, in our language, in technical economic
and social processes, in our religions, in our arts and sciences. The

[25] It is of interest to compare the emphasis on the role of the school in the various educational theories. Cf. in particular, pp. 302–303.

[26] From what follows it will be seen that Morrison has a more explicitly formulated theory of secondary education than have Bagley and Judd. *Vide* pp. 327 ff.

adaptations are expressed as ideals, attitudes, ethical and moral practices, techniques, intellectual and mechanical tools, methods of thinking. For various reasons,[27] however, the school cannot assume that its particular society possesses the full complement of needed adaptations, and realizes them, with the proper proportionate emphasis, in its social behavior. The ideal source of needed adaptations is the racial history; an analytical and comparative study of past and contemporary societies would very well reveal the learnings that contribute to human progress and are applicable in our present situation, and those negative, restrictive learnings that we would do well to heed.

Pending such knowledge, however, there is available a ready source of learnings, which, though not scientific in the manner of its compilation, is reliable. That source is the school studies as we know them. The school studies represent an empirical but well-considered and systematic effort to bring together the important racial learnings and to integrate them in a way to make them effectively and economically presentable. The school studies are not so much learnings themselves as they are the subject-matter through which learnings may be effectively communicated. They are the product of long social evolution, and thus have amply proved themselves in experience. It need hardly be said that the school studies, in their present form, are not a perfect instrument. Important elements are undoubtedly missing; some of the subject-matter is without present educative value; some of the school studies are badly organized for purposes of instruction. But to say that the school studies constitute an immediate reliable medium of racial learnings is not to imply that they will be accepted and used as *they have been,* without considerable change and improvement.

The purpose of the primary school is to help the pupil to acquire those learnings that are needed for proper immediate living and those which are fundamental to further development. Many of these learnings are obtained in the home, prior even to entrance into the primary school, such learnings as care of self, use of spoken language, health habits and knowledges, proper habits of conduct. They are acquired by imitation, and as a result of direct instruction, admonition, correction. In the primary school, these and other learnings are communicated more formally through language study, number study, the social

[27] *Vide* pp. 157 ff.

studies, elementary science, health education, art, and music. Generally speaking the secondary-school learnings are to be found within the same subject categories—in the study of language and literature, in the social studies, in science, in mathematics, in the fine arts and the practical arts. These are the general categories of studies which should constitute the secondary-school curriculum. It is a fact that most of the important adaptations needed for adjustment in our environment can be conveyed through much of the subject-matter that has empirically found its way into the secondary-school curriculum. At the present time, however, the specific content and the organization of these subjects leave much to be desired; and most of the subjects are not so taught that their *adaptive* and *socializing* values are to any considerable degree realized.

It must be understood that the studies of the secondary-school curriculum are not chosen with primary regard for their practical value. They are chosen for the reason that they embody the learnings which build social, adaptable personality. The learnings are, so to speak, dissolved within the medium of the subject. Assimilated by the individual, the subject yields up the learnings that it holds.[28] Even the learnings thus released do not have an immediate cash value; they become fused with the structure of the organism and ultimately create the social, adaptable personality. Subjects do not all have the same educative value. To possess such value, a subject must in the first place possess important learnings that contribute to proper personality development. It must be so organized that it is effectively and easily presentable and assimilable. It must be so graded that it keeps pace with the psychological development of the learner. (Mathematics, for example, is at the present time badly organized for instructional purposes because it follows the logic of the creative mathematician rather than the developmental process of the learner.) Subject-matter is most educative when it is systematically organized, when the interrelations within it are logical and discernible, when it provokes such sustained thinking. But in the final analysis every subject, however well-organized to begin with, must also be well-taught if its educative values are to be realized.

[28] A good example of this is the equation in mathematics the mastery of which yields "the inward personality accretion in terms of which the individual's thought processes take the form of the equation in appropriate situations." (Morrison, *The Practice of Teaching in the Secondary School*, p. 23. Revised Edition, 1931.)

A number of important questions arise in relation to the content of the secondary-school curriculum. Should the curriculum of general education on the secondary level be common to all or should it be a differentiated curriculum? If differentiated, should any of the studies be elective? Should vocational studies be included in addition to the general subjects enumerated? The questions are intrinsically related, and therefore may be considered and answered from a common point of view.

Two such points of view, however, exist within Social Evolutionism. According to one,[29] "the curriculum of general education is a common school curriculum, and not one of special interests and individual tastes. . . . The notion of a differentiated curriculum or the elective system is archaic in principle and antiquated in social evolution. It is archaic in principle because it rested upon the gymnastic theory of mental training. . . . It is historically antiquated because it could be justified socially on the theory that there are as many worlds as there are local communities. . . ."[30] The subject-matter of secondary education is to be common. Individual differences constitute a problem of teaching rather than a problem of curriculum; they call for differentiation in learning procedure and perhaps in scope of the content rather than in type of content. Bright students will learn more easily, more quickly, and they will learn more. But to say that the curriculum is to be common is not to imply that the curriculum is to be regarded as a rigid thing, that there are to be no adjustments occasionally when individual need requires. By the same principle, in a curriculum of general education, the attitude toward vocational training must be negative. "A great deal of space is occupied by 'vocational subjects' which have little reference to vocational needs or effective vocational training. Some of it is related to the fundamental adjustments which constitute education. The rest of it ought to be organized with reference to the capacity of the community to take up its product, and then be assigned to special vocational schools. . . . In general, the special vocational school should follow, rather than precede or parallel, the school program which is devoted to general education."[31] It follows that from this

---

[29] That of Morrison (*School and Commonwealth*, pp. 68–79. 1937).
[30] *Ibid.*, pp. 69–70.
[31] *Ibid.*, pp. 90–91.

point of view the curriculum of the secondary school consists of a small number of well-organized general studies.

According to a second point of view,[82] some differentiation and some election of studies are desirable, though, in regard to the place of the vocational studies in general education, there is disagreement. Common education does not necessarily presume the same subject-matter. Subjects are not in themselves learnings; they are only the means through which learnings are conveyed. Educational means may be varied if the capacity of the learner requires it. A common curriculum has been found to be unsuitable to all the students. It is necessary to devise or develop materials that will be suitable to the types of mind that have found the general and liberal subjects of the former curriculum beyond their abilities or alien to their interests. This does not mean, however, that there are to be fully differentiated curricula. It means rather that there is to be some differentiation along each of several lines—some enrichment or simplification of subject-matter, some differentiation in method of instruction, some differentiation also *in kind* of subject-matter. The process of differentiation must, however, be cautiously entered upon; no hard-and-fast differentiation such as is characteristic of some post-primary education in Europe is desirable.[83] Choice of specialized activity must be on the basis of exploration. Specialization must be with respect to peripheral rather than central subjects. The matter of election of studies is a troublesome one, but it may be assumed that some election can be permitted, particularly in the marginal activities.

[82] Judd and Bagley. C. H. Judd, "What Is General Education?" Department of Secondary School Principals, National Education Association, *Bulletin,* 68:5–16, October, 1937. See also: W. C. Bagley, *Education and Emergent Man,* p. 117. 1934.

[83] Compare this with the general readiness of several Humanists to provide for radical differentiation (p. 306 to p. 308). Judd, while favoring some differentiation, is very critical of the manner in which it is being done in other countries, notably in France. ("The Eastbourne Conference," *Proceedings of the Institute for Administrative Officers of Higher Institutions,* pp. 179–189. 1931.) He sees value in the elective system in that it allows for an adequate test of interest and ability in various subjects. Bagley is very skeptical of the use of tests as a basis for differentiation, favoring the proposal of Briggs for exploration through materials "otherwise justifiable." (W. C. Bagley, "The Task of Education in a Period of Rapid Social Change," *Educational Administration and Supervision,* 19:561–570, November, 1933.)

It is agreed that vocational training, in the manner in which it has been carried on in the past, is not compatible with the purposes of secondary education. On the larger question, however, of whether it is desirable at all to include vocational activities in the secondary school, there is difference of opinion. Judd's position may be summed up as follows: "There must be invented and installed a new kind of general education, and the relation of general to vocational education must be made clear. . . . There ought to be no conflict between general and vocational education. General education is aimed at the perfection of the individual. Some kind of vocational education should be administered to every pupil. . . . General and vocational education are not antagonistic." [34] It is Bagley's view, on the other hand, that although it has lately been judged proper to institute vocational courses and establish vocational schools on the secondary level, preparation for artisan trades is better accomplished through some form of apprentice training. He foresees in the future an increasing limitation of secondary education to general and liberal studies.[35]

The subject-matter of the school is, however, a means to an end—a means to the end of transmitting learnings that serve to create the social, adaptable person. Subjects themselves, by their general content, do not assure the attainment of desired ends. All the subjects that have been mentioned so far have long been present in the secondary curriculum, but their presence there has not been attended by marked educational success. What is extremely important is the precise selection of content within the subjects, the manner in which this content is to be organized, and the method of instruction. Each of these is definitely influenced not only by the character of the learnings to be transmitted but, even more, by the conception of the *method by which adaptable personality is achieved*. Since there exist among the Social Evolutionists under discussion two somewhat different conceptions of the method of human development,[36] there are to be found also two theories concerning the exact make-up of the subject-matter, its organization for instruction, and the desirable method of instruction.

[34] C. H. Judd, "What Is General Education?" Department of Secondary School Principals, National Education Association, *Bulletin*, 68:13, 14, 15, October, 1937.
[35] W. C. Bagley, *Education and Emergent Man*, pp. 50–57. 1934.
[36] *Vide* pp. 159 ff.

In the view of Morrison, development of personality takes place through the acquisition by the organism of successive, unit learnings. By a process of continuous, small accretions to and modifications in original organism, the social, adaptable personality is finally produced. The learnings are adaptations which are expressed in behavior as attitudes or acquired abilities. (Skills are learnings of a sort. They are not true adaptations, since they do not become a permanent part of the human structure. Many skills are, however, acquired in the course of the developmental process.) These learnings have by long empirical process found their way into what we know at the present time as the subject fields. The curriculum of the secondary school properly should contain these subjects: language and literature (this would include general language, but not foreign languages; the latter do not contribute much to adjustment), the social studies, science, mathematics, and the arts.

Traditionally, however, these studies have been regarded as ends-in-themselves, and have been organized for instruction from that point of view. A student was offered mathematics organized for comprehensive mastery of the mathematical field, and not for the purpose of helping him to develop methods of precise, quantitative thinking about the facts of his environment. The subjects, in general, have been laid out in blocks of pedagogically convenient "lessons" and taught as such, rather than organized and presented as arrays of meaningful learnings. There is required, in the first place, systematic and exact identification of the learnings that the race has in the course of its history acquired and which individuals need to serve them in adjustment. The learnings are obtainable in the school subjects, but they need to be clearly distinguished. The next problem is to discover within the realm of the subjects the appropriate contexts or materials through which each of the learnings may be conveyed to the student. For every learning there is obtainable a suitable context or allotment of subject-matter through which that learning may be realized. This allotment may be called a unit of subject-matter, a unit of study, or a learning unit. Learning units are, of course, not confined by definition to actual school subjects. "A serviceable learning unit is a comprehensive and significant aspect of the environment, of an organized science, of an art, or of

conduct, which being learned results in an adaptation of personality." [37]
Each of the subjects of the secondary-school curriculum is to be organized in terms of comprehensive learning units, each unit to result in
one or a number of personality adaptations.

True personality adaptation takes place when learnings are assimilated from the subject-matter into the human organism. This does not
necessarily occur when subject-matter is "learned" merely to the point
of recall or perhaps successful application. Complete mastery is required. The object of study, therefore, is mastery; the aim of instruction
is to make mastery possible. Since important adaptations are needed
equally by all people, the important learning units must be mastered
equally by all students. The variables are the technique of presentation,
the time and effort required for mastery, and the extent to which study
is continued beyond the mastery of minimal essentials.

Once the needed learnings have been catalogued and appropriate
units of subject-matter blocked out, it is necessary to develop pedagogical techniques which will bring about assimilation of learnings.
Instruction must be carried to the point where mastery of subject-matter is complete. To achieve this, it is necessary rigorously to apply this
general formula: pre-test, teach, test results, adapt procedure, test again,
and continue the procedure to the point where actual learning has
taken place. One of the mistakes made in the past was to assume that
all learnings could be acquired by means of the same instructional
procedure. Procedure must be adapted to the type of learning represented in the subject-matter. Five types of subject-matter, according to
the learnings they embody and the procedures needed for their assimilation, are distinguishable: the science type, the appreciation type, the
practical-arts type, the language-arts type, and the pure practice type.
Each calls for a somewhat different emphasis in instructional procedure.

The subjects comprising the secondary curriculum, in sum, are to be
organized in terms of learning units, each of them intended to achieve
certain needed personality adaptations. Within each subject, the learning units are to be arranged so that there is progression in difficulty,
so that there is demanded an increasingly greater background of knowledge, more exact and more systematic thinking, greater self-application

[37] H. C. Morrison, *The Practice of Teaching in the Secondary School*, pp. 24–25.
Revised edition, 1931.

and expenditure of effort. With reference to each unit, the object of study is complete mastery. The method of instruction is (1) to vary according to the types of learnings that each unit of subject-matter represents, the formula for mastery being in general followed, and (2) to be adapted to the ability of the individual student. The essential learnings are the same for all students; variation with respect to learnings not in the same degree essential is permissible. Re-teaching is to be considered a necessary step in instructional procedure when students have fallen short of mastery. Testing is to be used constantly in measuring the approach to mastery. Throughout the secondary period the direction is toward greater student self-dependence in study.

The theory of human development held by Judd and Bagley does not as yet allow the formulation of a program as explicit and specific as Morrison's.[88] Human intellectual development is not by continuous, single accretions; it is rather by a series of integrations on progressively higher levels. At different levels mental operations take on qualitatively different aspects. Secondary education has as one of its objectives the development of the higher mental processes. Unfortunately we do not know much, at present, about the operation of these processes. Until science comes to our aid, it will be difficult to formulate in detail a program of general education on the secondary level, even if we know the general results, in terms of learnings, that we wish to obtain.

Certain general principles of curriculum-content, organization, and method of instruction can, however, be stated. In the first place, the content of all the studies must possess *socializing* as well as intellectually constructive value. To be truly adaptable, personality must also be social. "We are not producing, as a result of our educational effort, those results in social understandings which we ought to be producing."[89] The content of the secondary-school studies must be reorgan-

[88] Judd comes closer than Bagley toward offering the outlines of a complete secondary-school program. Strictly speaking, the following account is descriptive of Judd. Bagley, as far as he goes, is in agreement with the main principles. Two probable (but as yet unexpressed) points of difference might arise out of (1) Bagley's preference for "exact and exacting studies" as against the less "exact and exacting" social studies, (2) Bagley's failure to emphasize broad survey courses.

[89] C. H. Judd, "The Scientific Development and Evaluation of the Curriculum," National Education Association, Department of Superintendence, *Official Report*, p. 182. 1933.

ized so that the social learnings that they potentially offer will be more fully realized. It must not be assumed that the only studies capable of making contributions to the socialization of the individual are those which have been labeled the "social studies." Language and number are fundamental social arts, and they should be taught as such. "There is no subject of instruction in either the elementary or the secondary curriculum as at present constituted that cannot be made to realize a rich socializing value." [40]

The curriculum of secondary education should consist of a relatively small number of well-organized subjects, broad in scope and rich in content. Adaptability presumes an ability to operate in terms of (1) concepts, (2) relationships. The possession of ordered systems of important ideas is the indispensable basis of adaptable behavior. Each subject is to cover a large area. "One of the most important functions of education is to develop breadth in systems of experience, but comprehensive systems of ideas are built first by constructing comparatively simple systems." [41] The formula should be: "Begin with young pupils and require, first, concentration. Proceed, then, to develop broader and broader combinations of ideas." [42] A good beginning on the lower end of the secondary level has already been made with the organization of courses in general science, general mathematics, general language, general history. But breadth is not all. Within, the subjects must be organized not in terms of the logic according to which they were created but in a manner that provides most opportunity for the development of the learner. The gradation in difficulty must be consistent with the continuous psychological progress made by the learner.

The method of instruction must aim at the objective of intellectual independence. Intellectual independence presumes the power of analysis and comparison, the power of generalization, the power to carry over generalized learnings into a great variety of situations. Instruction on the secondary level must concern itself, therefore, with the cultivation of these kinds of power. Secondary education is incomplete unless

[40] W. C. Bagley, *Educational Values*, p. 153. 1911. Quoted with permission of The Macmillan Company, publishers.
[41] C. H. Judd, "How Shall the Enriched Curriculum Be Made Systematic?" *Elementary School Journal*, 37:660–661, May, 1937.
[42] *Ibid.*

the individual has developed a method of dealing successfully with the world through the effective use of intellect. Such a method does not develop of itself but must be deliberately cultivated. In addition to being provided with broad, well-organized fields of subject-matter, the student must be given increasing opportunity to obtain the information himself, to make his own analyses and syntheses, to develop the power of independently applying learnings to the solution of his own problems. Secondary education is more than a matter of presenting unitary learnings for assimilation by the student; the organization and application of learnings become matters of increasing importance.

Human development is, in the final analysis, an individual affair, and no uniformity is possible when each person is required to think for himself, to organize his own content, to apply his ideas, and to evaluate his results. There is no need to worry excessively about "providing for individual differences." The process of learning must, of course, be adapted to individual ability, and such adaptation has been greatly facilitated by the utilization of individual materials and study-devices. It is questionable whether recourse should be had to such an arrangement as homogeneous grouping. In the course of the learning process individual differences in capacity are invariably reduced, while truly needed and desired differences—in intellectual interests and aptitudes, in technical knowledges and skills, for example—are formed.

On the matter of the institutional organization of secondary education, Social Evolutionism is once more in accord. The several units of the secondary school now in existence are badly coordinated. It is premature at this time to make definite prescription concerning the plan of reorganization to be followed, but it is extremely desirable that the arrangements of school units parallel the progress of the learner in psychological development. Each school unit ought to have its proper place in a common scheme of secondary education. The junior high school and the junior college have established themselves as important and needed features of the secondary system, but are not yet sufficiently well-articulated with the high school to operate with the needed efficiency. Very likely secondary education would profit from the consolidation of the existing three institutions into two.[43]

[43] This is specifically Judd's opinion. *Vide* C. H. Judd, *Education and Social Progress*, pp. 256–257. 1934.

II

As has been stated previously,[44] secondary education is to be lauded more for some of its praiseworthy intentions than for its actual achievements thus far. To the extent that the secondary school has sought to break away from the aristocratic pattern of the past and to fashion itself in a manner consistent with the principles of American life, to the extent that it has increased educational opportunity and tried to raise the level of effective intelligence of almost the entire nation, to the extent that it has experimented with curriculum, it is to be praised. The source, however, which has imparted to American secondary education its strength has also imparted to it many serious weaknesses. In its positive aims, secondary education suffers from having mirrored too accurately the values and conditions of the existing society. It has come under the influence of educational theories, reflecting these values and conditions, which in the long run cannot but be harmful to the individual and to society. On the whole it cannot be said that secondary education has adequately fulfilled its responsibilities. The learnings that it must transmit to all its students to enable them to make proper adjustment in their present environment have not been effectively given. The educational opportunity that has been extended to so many individuals has not been utilized to sufficiently great advantage.

Method cannot be evaluated completely apart from the aim which dominates it, and when aims are misleading, method can never be accounted wholly satisfactory. Many of the criticisms which must be made of the secondary school, therefore, stem primarily from the aims which it has seen fit to accept.[45] It is a fact, however, that the method of secondary education is, in some respects, quite as reprehensible as are the aims which govern it, and must be criticized with as much severity. To state this in another way, no improvement in American secondary education is likely until certain misconceptions germane *to method* are removed.

[44] *Vide* pp. 240 ff. of this study.
[45] For the manner in which Social Evolutionists differ individually in their critical attitudes toward the present secondary education, *vide* footnotes on pp. 22, 85, 164.

In a sense, it is not surprising that deficiencies should exist in our educational method. A system of education such as ours, that has broken with tradition and pioneered in new directions, is bound in time to develop practices that are discontinuous and sometimes inconsistent. Of these, the American school system has its share. The several school units are not altogether in harmony; the high school, the junior high school, and the junior college developed at different times in response to different needs. Each unit is influenced by its special background and purposes, and these purposes do not always form a common coherent pattern of education. Similarly, the curriculum in any of these school units is far from being the compact, well-ordered body of important studies that it should be. While some studies were dropped probably too hurriedly, many other studies were introduced in response to social pressures that sometimes reflected either temporary or only supposed needs. The curriculum is a sprawling affair, containing much material that cannot truly be called educative. On the other hand, there have survived from the traditional high school certain studies for which no very good justification can be offered at present. Similarly, method of instruction has suffered. At the present time, on the secondary level it lacks psychological purpose; it does not differ very much from method on the primary level.

But defects resulting from the evolutionary development of the school system are not catastrophic; rather, they would not be, if they were not at the same time aggravated by more serious flaws in the substance of education itself. It is, however, unfortunately true of American education that many of the surface defects resulting from lack of functional integration are combined with much more serious defects growing out of the fact that secondary education is accepting methodological guidance from an unsound and misleading mechanistic psychology and a "soft" pedagogy. This psychology and this pedagogy are primarily responsible for the present misconception regarding the function of secondary education, the educationally defective curriculum, the excessive specialization and particularization of activities, the undemocratic and indefensible stigma that has attached itself to the slow student, and the low levels of attainment.

The goal of secondary education is the production of the adaptable person. Adaptability is a general capacity of personality which a person either has or does not have. Adaptability does not lie in the mastery of a bag of tricks; it is not possible to make a person adaptable by training him in correct responses to fixed situations. By definition, adaptability is the capacity to invent the proper responses to any new situation that may arise. The character of the social environment within which adjustment is to take place makes training for adaptability a necessity. Yet, an education that to so large an extent repudiates the theory of transfer cannot train for adaptability. On the basis of small evidence a mechanistic psychology surrendered belief in the likelihood of any considerable transfer. Education has come to mean training for performance of specific activities; the curriculum has been expanded to include many such activities. Subject-matter has come to be regarded as instrumental in purpose. The great racial learnings which are needed by the individual if he is to succeed in making adjustment to his environment have been neglected in favor of "practical" activities. The curriculum has tended to assume a local character, to duplicate community activities. A new profession of "curriculum making" has been developed—curriculum making by a technique of activity analysis, job analysis, etc. Various types of analysis are used except, apparently, a cold-blooded analysis of the factors that have entered into man's long climb to the top. Along with this, the curriculum learnings have tended to become more highly individualized. A large degree of differentiation has been introduced. At a time when more than ever emphasis should be placed on those learnings that help to keep society together as a cooperating unit, emphasis has been shifted to the "needs" of the individual.

After the theory of transfer was largely abandoned, psychology ceased to concern itself greatly with the special study of the nature of the higher mental processes. It was assumed that such processes were, in the manner of their operation, qualitatively no different from the lower, only more complex and advanced in degree. It was overlooked entirely that man, in the course of self-development, was capable of becoming progressively a different being, different in the *quality* of his behavior. Out of a study of the characteristics of behavior of animals and very young children there were formulated laws of learning purporting to be descriptive also of advanced human behavior. Neither volitionally nor intellectually were the laws of learning justly representative of human behavior on the higher levels. Volitionally, they depicted man as a creature actuated in behavior by physical pleasure-pain incentives; they overlooked the fact that, though man may be such a creature prior to the process of systematic development, in the course of such a process he can develop a very different set of conduct dynamics. Intellectually, the laws of learning served to picture man as a rather simple-minded creature of habit, who was "conditioned" into proper behavior, who operated according to previously established "connections." On the secondary level instruction became no different in its general method from what it was on the primary level. Such a method, of course, did nothing to compensate for the shortcomings of the curriculum-content in the matter of training for adaptability. What the intellectual result has been is reflected in our inadequacy in dealing successfully with the major problems of our society.

In a period of social transition it is more than ever necessary that education act as a stabilizing influence, that it exert particular effort to impart to all individuals those qualities that make for strength of character and intellect. As an influence to this end, the mechanistic psychology has, of course, been negative. But intensifying this negative influence is a pedagogy advancing a theory of human development which both volitionally and intellectually would serve to degrade man rather than to elevate him. As a theory of education, it maintains that satisfactory human development will result from allowing the student "freedom" and "self-expression," from following his "interests" in learning and using the content of his own experiences as the principal subject-matter. It inveighs against moral and intellectual discipline, against effort, against setting out subject-matter-to-be-learned even when that happens to embody the important learnings obtained out of human experience, against system in organization, study, and instruction. Its doctrines being naturally attractive, this theory has "caught on." Its general effect has been to intensify some of the defects arising out of the mechanistic psychology, and to weaken still further the influence of the secondary school as an agency for producing social, adaptable personality.

The mechanistic psychology has further been instrumental in propagating false and harmful notions regarding the nature of intelligence. Refusing to recognize general intelligence as the joint product of heredity and training, it has insisted on regarding it as purely a product of heredity, determined at birth. (The function of education with respect to the *creation of mind conceived as adaptability* has been overlooked altogether.) The effect has been to misconstrue the meaning of individual differences and to exaggerate their significance. Instead of conceiving inherited adaptive capacity as the raw material out of which is to be made, in the case of almost every individual, an intelligence capable of effective adjustment in its social environment, education has been induced to accept inherited capacity as the decisive limiting factor in development. Education, it is thought, must work within the framework of inherited individual differences; it cannot alter that framework. This determinism has gone far to undo the effect of the great extension of opportunity for secondary education. The prevailing concept of I. Q. has contributed to the adulteration of the secondary-school curriculum, and it has served as well as a kind of universal excuse for the inadequacies of educational achievement. Basing itself on the prevailing notions regarding the significance of individual differences, the secondary school has come to offer, in place of a general, largely common curriculum, a series of differentiated curricula. Quite apart from the fact that they are not suitable for purposes of common education, it is a fact that many of the activities contained in these curricula can only by the sheerest stretch of imagination be called educative. Moreover, students are excused for failure to render a satisfactory account of themselves on the ground that they are "dull" or "dull-normal," and therefore incapable of much learning.

Determinism has brought into the secondary school a number of devices and practices of questionable validity. One of these is the practice of homogeneous grouping, generally on the basis of intelligence-test scores. The "homogeneous" groups are, of course, not homogeneous at all, and it is to be questioned whether it is desirable that they should be. Generally speaking there is over-classification and over-grading of students. A guidance machinery has been introduced with a great many shortcut devices for the sorting and differentiation of students; aptitude tests, for example, are sometimes used as a means of influencing student choices of vocations. In instruction, some of the emphasis has been taken from teaching and placed upon guidance; the teacher at times seems to be more concerned with materials and devices than with values. Altogether the influence of determinism, from the point of view of both aim and method, has been bad.

III

What American secondary education needs most of all is a basic reorientation. It will not suffice to make minor changes here and there. Certain of its general tendencies the secondary school must retain: to extend common educational opportunity to all, to attempt to offer practical preparation for effective living in our social environment, to move in directions away from aristocratic privilege, whether social or intellectual. The school needs also to acquire certain new conceptions. First of all, it must clarify for itself the meaning of adjustment, and determine how adjustment can be achieved in a complex, changing environment. The inevitable result will be to set up adaptability as the goal of secondary education. The school must then proceed to study the implications for adjustment of societal living. The quality of being social will be recognized as an indispensable element of adaptability, and the training of the social person—particularly so, in view of modern world conditions—will emerge as one of the objectives of secondary education.

On the basis of sound objectives, it will be possible to plan an appropriate method. The method must recognize, first of all, that the human being is capable of very great self-development, that of decisive importance of education is what man is *capable of becoming* rather than what he is "naturally." Educational science must contribute an understanding of what takes place in human development, and how instruction can render human development more effective. On the basis of empirical knowledge and of scientific studies already made, it may be agreed that mental development takes place through a process of successive integrations, that on higher levels mind is qualitatively different from what it is on lower, that on higher levels mental operation is not a simple affair of conditioned reflexes and bonds, but that conceptualization, organization, transfer, are all involved. On the basis of common-sense experience it cannot be denied that man is capable of a degree of volitional and moral development so that his acts are no longer primarily motivated by fear or physical satisfaction or selfish interests. Educational method must be governed by understanding of these things before it can proceed adequately to formulate a plan of secondary education.

In the light of the knowledge of method of human development that experience and science can furnish, it will be possible systematically to construct a curriculum for general education on the secondary level. The great racial learnings that must be incorporated within individual personality to make it adaptable in a societal environment need to be accurately catalogued. The subjects that we have inherited must then be revised and refined so that only the subject-matter capable of conveying the desired learnings is included. The curriculum will be cleared of the remains of the old secondary education which no longer serve a worthwhile educational purpose, as well as of the unworthy elements that have recently been introduced. What is retained will be simply and effectively organized for purposes of instruction. It will then be possible to effect such modifications in the common curriculum as must be made to meet the individual needs of students. Individual differences will still influence the content of secondary education, but not in the present manner.

The learnings of greatest importance in human living are gained as a result of sustained self-application; they must be achieved, they must be mastered. Education does not take place simply through long-time exposure to instructive materials. It must be the object of instruction to help every individual learner to master his curriculum. High standards of effort and achievement must be set for all; individual differences are to serve as a signal for adapting procedure, not as a reason for degrading standards. Instruction on the secondary level must be geared to the learner's growing intellectual capacity, and must aim toward eventual individual volitional and intellectual self-dependence. Not until each learner has achieved such self-dependence can the task of instruction be considered complete.

Individual differences will generally be seen in truer perspective. They will serve as a challenge to education, and not as a ready excuse for lowering standards. Regardless of inherited differences, it will be the recognized responsibility of education to raise all normal individuals to the point where they can operate with a high degree of effectiveness in adjusting to their environment. Adaptations to individual needs will be made in curriculum and in method, but they will be such adaptations in means as are necessary to achieve a common desired aim. Not that it is the task of education to produce individuals all of whom are alike.

That is undesirable and, fortunately, not possible. But differences in vital adjustive capacity will be reduced to make way for acquired differences of a kind that are necessary and desirable in society—differences in intellectual interests, in technical skills, and in vocational proficiency. There will be no need for many of the sorting devices that are used at present. Tests will be used to measure attainment and to stimulate progress, not to differentiate and classify and label individuals. Guidance will have primarily a developmental purpose, not a differentiating one.

When the aims and method of secondary education have been satisfactorily defined, it will be possible to proceed in the task of reorganizing the several school units and establishing them on a more efficient basis. Such a basis will be a psychological one. Each unit will then serve its own educational function, but all will be coordinated so as to contribute to a common educational aim.

SOCIAL REALISM

I

The object of education is the training of individuals for effective living in a highly industrialized, interdependent, democratic society. Education is in the nature of an investment by society, the purpose of which is to preserve society and progressively to improve it in the direction in which it has chosen to go. Society realizes on its investment as socially effective individuals make it "a better place in which to live." [46] The social ends for which it is intended dominate the educational process. Education is evaluated in terms of the consequences that it has for practical living—by the manner in which it improves the exercise of democratic citizenship, family life, vocation, and so forth. The educated person is the person who can perform with competence the manifold life-activities that society holds necessary and desirable, and who can do his share toward improving them and conceiving and developing better ones. Every normal individual must be helped to become such a person, or society as a whole suffers. Social integration and competence in living the common life do not, however, imply standardization of person-

[46] T. H. Briggs, *The Great Investment*, p. 19. 1930.

ality. Civilized society has need of many different talents, and each person, in terms of his own capacities, aptitudes, and interests, can contribute something of great need and worth. In terms of his individual capacities, aptitudes, and interests, each person must be helped to become socially-integrated and socially-competent.

A social-pragmatic education derives its objectives from the ideals and life-processes of the society which maintains it. On this basis, the leading objectives of American education are training for: (1) health and physical well-being; (2) competent democratic citizenship in a complex industrial society; (3) happy and effective family and social life; (4) vocational efficiency in a highly industrialized society; (5) the effective use of leisure time (in a society in which the trend is toward the mechanization and routinization of leisure activities); (6) intelligent consumership; (7) competence and skill in the performance of the many practical activities of daily living, and in particular of those involving science and technics; and (8) many, varied, enduring, developing interests that impel the individual to go on learning and growing as a person long after his formal schooling has ceased. Education must be so pointed and so activated that it results in the realization of these ends for every individual.

Education must not, however, lightly take on added responsibilities. Mindful of its societal origin, purpose, and responsibilities, a prolonged education must be prepared to make returns to society proportionate to the increased investment. A further extension of the educational period means the assumption of new social obligations. Education has not yet been able to provide appropriately for all the students in its charge at the present time. Until it does that, it should hardly be urged to extend its services. Society must create social agencies to take care of those young people whose needs the present secondary school cannot immediately satisfy—the youth who have left school without completing its course and the youth now in school who are ill-adapted to the present curriculum, *as well as* the young people who have completed the secondary-school program but who have not yet been able to find employment that would make it possible for them to take their proper place in the adult community. In the former case, the social agencies must experiment with educational activities, possibly of a work type, that will have developmental value for the students for whom they are intended, that will help to raise them to the level of social-competence. If a suitable program of activities is developed, it can ultimately be incorporated within the secondary school. In the case of those young people who have completed the school course but have not found employment, the social agencies must provide activities that compensate for this want and help to obviate the many personal difficulties that grow out of the lack of a job. These agencies need not be permanent; when economic conditions allow, they can be disbanded or turned into agencies of part-time instruction or recreational activity. In any event, it is well to think of them as distinct from the secondary school because their functions extend beyond training for social-competence as that is understood at the present time.

The educational agency that assumes the greatest responsibility in training for social-competence is the school. Education is, of course, not identical with schooling, and there are other agencies that participate in the work of conscious, systematic education (as defined).[47] But the school is the institution which society has created specifically for the training of the young, it is the institution that society can most easily control and adapt to its purpose, and it is the institution upon which devolves the major responsibility for training the young for effective social living. And "the school" consists of the primary and secondary schools.

It has been said [48] that education in the school is "a gradual, continuous, unitary process" in which there is no intrinsic break. Primary and secondary education are successive stages in the same process. It is necessary to have a secondary as distinct from a primary stage because (1) the needs of adolescents, which the school must satisfy, are different from the needs of younger children, and (2) the character of the educational process is such as to require different emphases at different points in the course of human development. While earlier in the child's training there must be emphasis on social integration, on learning fundamentals, and on building the common foundation upon which individual development takes place, in the later period the emphasis must be on the development of the special capacities, aptitudes, and interests that a person possesses and that make his type of social-com-

[47] *Vide* p. 248.
[48] *Vide* p. 264.

petence—his contribution to the common Good Life—somewhat different from that of every other person. These characteristics serve to distinguish the secondary from the elementary school. But the special functions of the secondary school in the common educational process are not merely the satisfaction of the immediate needs of its (for the most part) adolescent students, and differentiation of learning activities in terms of special talents and interests. It is not as simple as this. Aptitudes and interests are not ready-made in people; they are formed and become known as a result of participating in different activities, of taking note of the possibilities in the various fields of human endeavor, and of testing oneself in a number of them. Actual differentiation of learning activities is not made until the process of secondary education has been well under way.

The special functions of secondary education, in more complete and systematic form, may be stated as follows: [49] Building on the work of the primary school, *to continue,* in gradually diminishing degree though on an increasingly intellectual level, the integration of students "until the desired common knowledge, appreciations, ideals, attitudes, and practices are firmly fixed"; *to satisfy* "important immediate and probable future needs" of adolescent students and to guide their behavior "in the light of increasingly remote, but always clearly perceived and appreciated, social and personal values"; "*to reveal* higher activities of an increasingly differentiated type in the major fields of the racial heritage of experience and culture," their values and implications for social living, and to make them desired and attainable by those whose capacities and aptitudes show them to be gifted in these directions; "*to explore* higher and increasingly specialized interests, aptitudes, and capacities of students," and, on the basis of this exploration, to begin and gradually to increase differentiated education taking care at the same time to provide a balanced program of general education; *to guide* students very carefully into advanced study and vocation as well as into wholesome social relationship and maximum personality adjustment; *to help* students to systematize knowledge gained and perceive its significance, and to acquire independence in thinking and knowledge of

[49] What follows has been adapted from the *Functions of Secondary Education,* Report of the Committee on the Orientation of Secondary Education, pp. 5–7 (January, 1937). The quoted phrases and sentences are from the same source.

the elementary principles of research; "*to establish* and develop interests in the major fields of human activity as means to happiness, to social progress, and to continued growth"; and "*to retain* each student until the law of diminishing returns begins to operate, or until he is ready for more independent study in a higher institution," and, if it is necessary to eliminate him, to do so promptly, "if possible, directing him into some other school or into work for which he seems most fit."

The principles of educational method which are implicit in this formulation of the special functions of the secondary school, and which must be followed if these functions are to be realized, derive from a basis of data relating to the nature of human development which we have gained from empirical experience, enriched by the findings of scientific research. A brief summary of the basic facts is necessary before proceeding to describe the specific steps in the method of secondary education.

On the whole, we are not as yet sufficiently familiar with what takes place in human mental behavior to formulate reliable generalized, economical, and indirect methods for bringing about desired specific results. Effective human living consists in being able successfully to carry on definite and specific life-activities—the care of self, the care of home, the exercise of citizenship, the activities of the vocation, etc. Science has substantiated the suspicion long entertained by common sense that mind cannot be trained in a general way so that transfer takes place automatically to a wide variety of specific situations. Transfer of training does take place in moderate degree to situations that possess identical or similar elements when the individual is aware of the identity or similarity and has a conscious purpose for making the transfer. To the greatest extent that science deems possible, education should rely upon transfer to take place, but in general (until science has greatly extended our knowledge of the nature of mind) *the surest way to learn to do something is to practice doing it under skilled direction.* Competence in democratic living is best assured by carrying on democratic living in a wide variety of situations; vocational competence is best assured by being well-informed in advance about vocational activities and possibilities, by possessing proper attitudes toward the problem of vocation, by thinking and planning and learning about vocations. To make practice effective in achieving desired results, psychological science has developed "laws of learning" or descriptions of the conditions under which learning takes place most effectively. Probably the most important of the conditions that science has thus brought to light are those embodied in the "law of effect."

As experience has always indicated and the idealistic philosophy as consistently denied, man is first of all a behaving rather than a rational being. The distinction must not be misunderstood, since thinking does operate in a most important way in *illuminating* behavior. But thinking is instrumental to doing, to the carrying on of the life-functions. The urge to action, especially that which has a vital influence, is more basic than the urge to reason. As dynamics of conduct, desire and emotion are more inherent and more potent than reason. Reason is often a means of rationalizing desire and emotion; the latter also often affect receptivity to intellectual facts and interpretation of them. By the same token, habit is an important factor in human behavior because it telescopes activity. Man is regarded as "good" by society if he *carries on* in an effective and desirable way his life-activities, and if in his *mode of living* he displays the socially approved traits. Education undertakes to produce *such a behaving person* rather than merely the person who *knows* what to do. It is not enough to impart information and develop the intellectual processes. Democratic living cannot be relied upon to follow inevitably from a knowledge of democratic principles and procedures. Education must equip the individual with the emotionalized attitudes, and with the habits and modes of living that make him a democratically-behaving person. Proper education implies much more than intellectual training.

Science has confirmed and extended our empirical knowledge of the fact of individual differences. Individuals differ from one another in a great many particular respects; most significant for education are differences in capacities, aptitudes, and interests. Capacities are inherited, but they become actualized in the course of experience. Capacity is not a general trait but a complex of specific traits. Although a general factor is present, making it possible for some individuals to be called generally bright, others generally average, others generally dull, it must be remembered that an individual does not possess every type of capacity to the same degree—an individual who possesses high abstract verbal intelligence may not possess an equally high mechanical intelligence.

This is not to be interpreted to mean that "nature" compensates for withholding a high degree of one type of capacity by always endowing the individual with a high degree of another; the rule, as has been implied above, is correlation rather than compensation. But every individual possesses more capacity to learn some things than to learn others, and in that lies the key to the special talents that education must help him to develop. Although every type of capacity in the individual should be developed as far as possible to give him general social-competence, the capacity that he has to the highest degree must become the basis of his special development. In terms of that, he must develop special competence, that is, learn to do some things much better than others do them. Education must cooperate with nature by helping the individual to make the most of such talent as he naturally possesses. Aptitudes, moreover, can be the means not only of specialized development but of all-round development as well, bringing the individual closer to the general social-competence that he needs to possess.

Irrespective of individual differences, all normal [50] persons must be trained for social-competence. Individual capacities, aptitudes, and interests indicate *the method* by which the educational objectives are to be pursued, and the *particular respects* in which the individual is to make his special contribution to society. Every individual possesses some natural talent which society can use to advantage. Education must discover this talent and make it a means of continued social integration as well as of specialized accomplishment. This talent is not, however, fully formed prior to training; it is developed in the course of activity. Education must provide the activities through which an individual's special aptitudes are revealed and developed.

Special mention must be made of interests. Interests are the dynamics of learning; learning cannot take place without purpose, and learning is assured and intensified as purposes are embodied in permanent interests. In the educational process interests operate as means and as ends. If a person is to continue to learn and to develop after the compulsions of the school have ceased (and he has to, since the changing world requires continuous adjustment to new situations), education must succeed in helping him to establish deep and enduring interests in many of the life-activities that naturally engage him.

[50] For a definition of "normal," *vide* p. 181.

It is now possible to explain more fully the special functions of the secondary school in the larger educational process. Training for competent living implies the inculcation of common ideals, attitudes, knowledges, practices, and interests that society has judged to be essential for the common Good Life, and it implies the development of special aptitudes and interests and attendant knowledges and skills by virtue of which the individual makes his particular contribution to the common Good Life, and by virtue of which he becomes distinguished as an individual. (It must not be supposed at this point that objectives of common ideals, attitudes, etc., presume an identical subject-matter for all students. As will be seen later, that is not essential.) The special aptitudes and interests that an individual is to develop are to be in terms of activities that society holds to be necessary and desirable.

Continuing to foster the common learning activities through which the fundamental common elements of social integration are to be obtained, the secondary school begins very early to provide activities, in themselves worth-while and educationally justifiable, through which the student may obtain a growing and increasingly specialized understanding of the possibilities available in the various fields of human achievement. These possibilities he studies from the point of view of continued learning as well as from the point of view of future vocation. Through these revealing activities the student develops interests which, however short-lived they may be, have for him developmental value as long as they are present; through these activities he becomes aware of the capacities and the special aptitudes that he possesses. Even if no special aptitudes are revealed by the student in one or another of these activities, the effort and time have not been wasted; indeed, considerable has been gained because the student has, in the course of learning, acquired some important knowledges and skills.

Although the revealing activities serve also important functions of integration, the peculiar values that they possess are those of revealing the opportunities that exist for continuing specialized development. The next task of the secondary school is to help the students discover their aptitudes and form their special interests. "The secondary school is the important social agency for ascertaining the peculiar interests, aptitudes, and capacities that each individual adolescent has so that it can direct, encourage, and help him toward future endeavor that promises most success and happiness to him and most profit to the social unit that provides the education." [51] These are to be discovered on the basis of the student's experience with the revealing activities already mentioned, and through additional exploratory activities organized and provided for the purpose. Exploration must be along many lines— academic, artistic, vocational, recreational. Results of exploration must be positive, not negative. It is not enough for the school to know what the student cannot do; it must know what he can do, and, moreover, what he can do especially well. It must be emphasized that exploration is not only for the purpose of disclosing vocational opportunities and aptitudes and interests; it is primarily for the purpose of discovering aptitudes and interests that would be effective in the specialized development of the entire personality. But exploration must concern itself with vocational fitness as well. "It is a great social economy if secondary education is able to ascertain in what major type of vocation each individual is most likely to succeed and be happy—and not merely the type of vocation, but the highest type for which he is competent. There is tragic evidence of failure when after years of study the 'educated' individual does not know for what he is fit and the school is not competent to advise him. Exploration, then, should be wide and varied. It will not cease after the major field of academic and vocational fitness is found, but will continue with gradually increasing specialization." [52]

Continued integration, revelation of higher activities, exploration of special aptitudes and interests go on concurrently. The time for this is predominantly in the junior-high-school stage of the secondary process. Each individual is perfecting the common ideals, attitudes, modes of behavior, and knowledge that society deems necessary for all. At the same time, he is studying opportunities in higher fields of learning and vocation, seeing their values, drawing from them interests, and testing his own capabilities in relation to them. With the assistance of certain other somewhat more specialized activities, introduced for exploratory (try-out) purposes, he tests his mettle, discovers the areas that have for him the greatest appeal and in which his talents lie. Toward the end of this period, he is ready to begin specialization.

[51] T. H. Briggs, *Secondary Education*, p. 268. 1933. Quoted with permission of The Macmillan Company, publishers.
[52] *Ibid.*, p. 270.

On the accumulated evidence of interests, aptitudes, and capacities demonstrated in previous activities, differentiation begins and is progressively increased. Differentiation must not be immediately narrowing and it must not be along a single line. Moreover, it must again be emphasized that, along with differentiation and balancing it, there is to be as broad and extended a program of general education as possible. Even toward the end of the secondary period the differentiating activities should attain a maximum of not more than three-fifths of the curriculum.[53] (For exceptional cases more differentiation can be provided.) Differentiation should begin earlier for those students of fewer interests and aptitudes and more limited capacities who want to leave school earlier, later for those students who can go on exploring with profit a larger number of fields of learning. The school is responsible for providing those varied differentiated activities through which each individual can develop social-competence.

This, in general, is the scheme by which the secondary school can contribute to the training of the socially-competent person in terms of his own interests, aptitudes, and capacities. It must be remembered, however, that simultaneously in the process of secondary education other purposes are to be realized. The secondary school cannot neglect the student himself, his personal needs of the moment. The individual must be helped to become a well-rounded, wholesome, happy person. Also, to the extent that general methods of thinking may be developed through practice in a great many specific situations, that must be done; to the extent that facts may be reduced to principles and laws, and knowledge systematized for future application, and mastery be acquired in the use of tools of learning that are important for later development, these things too should be done. And from all activities, common and differentiated, there must come a rich store of interests that will stimulate the individual and help him to keep growing and developing intellectually throughout life.

The purposes of secondary education are realized through the activities that the secondary school provides, through that body of activities and materials that have come to be called the curriculum and the extracurriculum. "The curriculum of any school, public or private, is essentially the means by which those responsible for establishing the

---

[53] Briggs, *op. cit.*, p. 282.

school and those responsible for sending children to it provide for these children what is considered to be an appropriate and desirable education." [54] The curriculum cannot be appraised except with reference to the objectives of the school; principles of curriculum are formulated in terms of educational purposes. Whatever contributes most effectively or as effectively as possible to the realization of educational ends and is in accord with the facts of psychological development is legitimate curriculum material. Negatively, whatever, inherited from tradition, does not contribute very much to the realization of these ends, even if it does not go contrary to them, is so much curricular excess baggage. Not only curricular content but the organization of that content and the manner in which it is imparted in instruction must be dictated by what the ends of education require and psychology says is feasible.

The invalidation of the neat theories of mental discipline place a very great importance on the selection of proper curricular activities. It cannot be said that we know, as yet, what the optimum curriculum (including the different types of specialized "curricula") should be. Much comprehensive experimentation and research are needed to ascertain the needed learning activities and to determine in what form they could best be organized and presented in instruction. Experimentation and research must be undertaken on a grand scale, properly coordinated, and carried out under expert rather than under lay direction; the results must be systematized and made available to all the secondary schools. It is certain that the curriculum or curricula as at present constituted are inadequate. They do not sufficiently reflect the conditions of the changing world; they do not provide for training in many of the important life-activities; they include materials which yield the kind of knowledge that can only be valued for its own sake; and they are not so organized as to yield maximally the educational values which they do possess, except to the most academic-minded students.

The studies which comprise the school curriculum must be regarded instrumentally: only those activities which, in the judgment of experience and soundly supported theory, contribute to the effective performance of the important life-activities and to effective growth should

[54] Committee on the Orientation of Secondary Education, *Issues of Secondary Education*, Department of Secondary School Principals, *Bulletin*, No. 59, p. 260. January, 1936.

be retained. In the absence of further scientific data regarding the exact nature of the higher mental processes, application must be made, in curriculum building, of the principle, that the best way to learn to do a thing is to practice doing it under skilled direction. Every learning activity in the curriculum must be picked on these bases, and must be valid in its own right. The curriculum is the sum total of these activities, each of which has been validated. It is absurd first to choose or to accept a curriculum as a whole, then to analyze out its important learning activities. "The absurdity of developing curricula first of all and then developing teaching units, that is, courses of study, inevitably perpetuates traditional subject-matter, inhibits the introduction of new materials that may be manifestly better, and makes difficult, if not impossible, a justifiable redistribution of time." [55]

The task of determining the studies of the curriculum of the secondary school must begin with a canvass of the traits, abilities, ideals, knowledges, and skills that characterize the "good" person in the effective performance of his life-activities in our democratic society. The first step is getting a "blueprint" of the ideal person to be produced by education. The range of the canvass to be made must include all the fundamental categories of human living. The categories, such as citizenship, vocation, family life, must then be broken down into lower terms, into the component ideals, attitudes, abilities, etc. The canvass should be made on a nation-wide basis, and should have at its disposal all the experience, technical efficiency, and data that have been accumulated by educational science in recent years. Primary emphasis must be given to those elements which are common on a national scale, secondary emphasis to those which are common on a local scale; abilities, knowledges, and skills that are specialized with individuals or groups must not be neglected. The items thus obtained constitute in highly specific terms the objectives toward which the secondary school must direct itself.

Once obtained, it is necessary that the specific objectives be collected and systematized. It will then be possible to decide which of them the school cannot for some reason deal with, which of them may safely be left to be realized through informal social experience, which of them

[55] T. H. Briggs, "If There Were Millions," *Teachers College Record*, 35:659, May, 1934.

(for example, religion) should be assigned to other educational agencies. Those that remain become the specific objectives of the school; to realize these objectives the school bends its every effort. To correspond to these objectives, the school must devise learning activities or learning units through which they may be effectively realized.

In the past the secondary school assumed that the traditional subjects corresponded as educative material to the categories of human experience, having been developed empirically over the course of many years. This assumption can no longer be maintained; we can say with truth that many of the life-activities are not educationally represented in the traditional subjects. The subject categories (as will be seen below) still have very definite uses, but not as *determinants* of what the curriculum shall contain. (They are, rather, pedagogically convenient ways of arranging and presenting the units of learning.) For a determination of what the curriculum shall contain it is necessary to identify the important needs in real living, and then by experiment and empirical trial to invent learning activities through which these needs may be met.

The second step, therefore, in the construction of the secondary-school curriculum is to devise appropriate learning activities which will enable the individual to acquire the desired ideals, attitudes, abilities, and modes of living. The governing principle is to be the rule of pragmatic psychology that the best way to learn anything is to practice doing it under skilled direction in a setting that as closely as possible approximates the natural. The method of the disciplinary tradition has been to try to gain the desired objectives by requiring students to assimilate abstract, intellectualized subject-matter. In the pragmatic secondary school, the objective of good citizenship is sought not by subjecting the mind to formal discipline, but by providing the student with the opportunity to develop ideals and habits of good citizenship in a wide variety of real life-situations. Ideals of community health and community hygiene are not left to be formed by the student himself after his mind has been adequately "trained," but are directly fostered by the school through learning situations in which consideration of these ideals and training in them are involved.

The learning activity or unit of learning in the curriculum is a functional unit of experience—a problem, a challenge, a real situation—in which are inherent those outcomes which the secondary school is endeavoring to achieve. For every specific objective that the school recognizes as important and assumes as a responsibility, appropriate learning units must be found. In an ideal situation, the units of learning would be worked out not locally by teachers limited in time and training and in opportunity and means for experimentation, but centrally, by experts, having available all the means of coordinated research, devising units of learning and testing them under a variety of teaching conditions. The units of learning—a larger number of them than any school would require—would then be made available to the particular schools, to be selected for use by the schools with such adaptations as local conditions make necessary.

The units of learning that would thus become available to the schools would constitute the immediate source of their curricula. The range of such learnings would be much greater than the present, and they would much more truly be intended to meet real life-needs. On the principle that "the first duty of the school is to teach pupils to do better the desirable things that they are likely to do anyway," [56] each school would select those units of learning which correspond to the life-activities that the community regards as desirable and necessary for its individuals, and would give them primary emphasis. The secondary school, as distinct from the primary, would remember in each case to "continue, in gradually diminishing degree though on an increasingly intellectual level, the integration of students" especially in the ideals, attitudes, knowledges, and skills that they were too immature to grasp earlier. On this basis the units of learning serving the purposes of integration would be distributed throughout the grades. On the principle that the school must also "reveal higher activities and make them both desired and to a maximum extent possible," [57] that it must help students to explore higher and increasingly specialized interests, aptitudes, and capacities, and that it must provide increasingly differentiated activities, it will select and assign to appropriate grades available units of learning. Throughout, units of learning leading to the ideals, attitudes, knowledges, and skills common to all individuals would be given prominence, but units of learning leading to socially desired specialized knowledges

[56] T. H. Briggs, *Secondary Education*, p. 258. 1933. Quoted with permisson of The Macmillan Company, publishers.
[57] *Ibid.*, p. 263.

and skills would not be neglected. Among the latter the knowledges and skills relating to vocation must loom large.

The curriculum of a school represents a summation of deliberate acts of selection. Every learning activity must serve a recognized and justifiable purpose. Every learning activity should, so far as possible, be valuable to the extent that it is pursued. The relative emphasis given to learning activities must correspond to the relative value of the objectives to which they lead. Every required social outcome must be represented, but care must be taken to see to it that no objective gets more emphasis than it merits. Activities leading to the gaining of knowledge must balance with activities leading to the formation of ideals and attitudes and modes of conduct. Learning activities must be adapted to individual capacity; it must be kept in mind that it is not necessary to employ identical learning activities with all students to obtain common outcomes.

The third large step in curriculum making is to arrange the learning units under common categories for teaching purposes. (The conventional subject-names will serve.) This step is necessary, although "it is even conceivable that secondary schools would in some instances have curricula made up of no such 'subjects' as are now universal, but would organize activities of all sorts around some important central themes that would produce a truly fused curriculum." [58] Assuming, however, that the subject organization is to be used, its values are: it makes possible sound psychological gradation in learning, and that is very important; it helps the student increasingly throughout his secondary-school course to discover and note relationships among units, to discover and formulate principles and generalizations; it makes for economy in learning and in instruction; and, finally, it makes possible the maintenance of higher standards of scholarship in teaching. There is needed, however, a new orientation in thinking about subjects. It has been the general tendency not to question their value, to regard them as fundamental categories of educational experience, to accept their claims at face value. That must be changed. In the course of time, many of the subjects have become abstract systems of knowledge without anchorage in the world of actual things. In their present form they are

[58] T. H. Briggs, "If There Were Millions," *Teachers College Record*, 35:652, May, 1934.

probably of some value to the academically-bright students who can elicit the general principles involved in these subjects and translate them into concrete activity, but even for those students they are far from being altogether adequate. For the large heterogeneous population of the present secondary school in general, they are incapable of serving as means to the desired educational ends.

The principal categories around which the learning activities would be organized, then, might be such categories as English, the social studies, science, mathematics, the practical arts, the fine arts, foreign languages, and vocational subjects, but the *learning activities* within these categories (and the boundary lines would not necessarily be respected) would be indeed very different from the present. Important units of learning in practical citizenship, homemaking, vocation, recreation, reading on higher levels, would be brought in, while much material, inherited from the past, that no longer has any but eruditional value would be eliminated. Activities, whether formally incorporated into the curriculum or less formally included in the extra-curriculum, leading to the development of wholesome attitudes and interests, would be added.

The purpose of the secondary-school curriculum is to enable individuals in terms of their capacities, aptitudes, and interests to become socially-effective persons. No single set of learning activities, organized into a curriculum, can therefore serve all individuals—no better in integration than in differentiation. The secondary school must offer a great many diverse learning activities suitable to the individual talents and needs of its students. No one curriculum will do. Starting on the broad base of the more or less common activities of the primary school, the secondary school must gradually lead off its students into differentiated curricula—academic or scientific or technical or commercial or fine-arts. Not only in the specialized activities but in the integrative activities there must be adaptation to individual differences. It is not possible as yet to offer a complete plan as to how this may be done. Such a plan must be worked out experimentally when once we have made a serious attempt to provide an appropriate secondary education for all. Two considerations of a practical nature must loom very large: the financial investment that society can afford to make, and the practical workability of the curricular arrangement. There is no use in proposing either an ideal arrangement that society could not afford to finance or an arrangement that would on paper seem ideal but would in practice prove cumbersome.

In sum, it may be said that "courses of study should be developed and so organized that they will provide all students with a balanced program for the various principal objectives of education—citizenship, home-leadership, leisure, vocation, health, and continued effective study. All programs should therefore include instruction in social studies, biological and natural sciences, literature, physical and health education, and aesthetic studies and arts. . . . In schools large enough to permit it to be done economically, a sufficient variety of courses should be offered to provide an orientation in all the principal fields of human knowledge. . . ." [59] Beyond this, course offerings should be of a type intended progressively for smaller groups of individuals. There is need for "sufficient variation in lines of study so that students with peculiar talents and disabilities, interests, or antipathies along literary, musical, artistic, manual, domestic, agricultural, scientific or social lines may not only have opportunity for study in appropriate directions but may be freed from discouraging and unpleasant failures in non-essential fields." [60] Within the subjects themselves adaptations must be made to individual needs by such administrative devices as homogeneous grouping (where numbers permit it) when once we are able to discover on what basis or bases such grouping can best be made, and by adaptation of learning materials and instructional techniques.

The secondary school must provide effective training for vocational life. "Social welfare . . . demands that every individual be prepared by some means to render specific vocational services to society. The welfare of the individual also demands it. Most people must turn to some work for livelihood, health, companionship, and for a central purpose in life to which they may relate their experience." [61] Through its curriculum, therefore, the secondary school must lead every individual into the initial competence that is required for obtaining a job, holding it, and growing within it and through it. Some vocational

[59] H. R. Douglass, *Secondary Education for Youth in Modern America*, pp. 91–92. 1937.
[60] *Ibid.*, p. 96.
[61] *Issues of Secondary Education*, p. 185.

instruction must be given to all; especially must the school concern itself with the students who will need to continue formal education beyond the secondary period. "For every pupil who is to complete his formal education in that school, each secondary school ought to provide a necessary minimum of definite preparation for a vocation." [62]

The objectives of vocational instruction are by no means limited to learning the particular skills needed for working at a specific job. Indeed that is one of the last things for the school to provide. For most students, vocational education "ought properly to include experience with the basic operations of various kinds of jobs, through which these pupils may become used to adapting themselves to differing requirements and accustomed to learning on the job; experience in getting along with fellow workers and superiors under job conditions; and enough specific training in a salable vocational skill to give each leaving pupil the chance for a foothold at the bottom of a recognized occupation. In addition the high school ought to provide young people with some fundamental understanding of the social problems inherent in vocational employment. No boy or girl ought to leave school without knowing, for example, about organized labor and the part which it plays in various occupations, or about the working conditions created by the growth of large-scale corporations and combinations of employers. With respect to skills and understandings both, the high school curriculum ought to furnish each boy and girl who is going immediately to work with the background which is clearly necessary for every beginning worker who is to be in any sense a master of his own vocational fate. High schools ought not, however, to try to make boys and girls who have never had vocational experience into highly skilled craftsmen. . . . Moreover, the school needs to recognize that, for beginners particularly, vocational adaptability is likely to be more important than highly developed specialized skill." [63]

Though the problem of providing a suitable vocational education for all has not yet been solved, a tentative plan of vocational training may be offered. It is to be remembered that vocational training is an

[62] F. T. Spaulding, *High School and Life,* Report of the Regents' Inquiry into the Character and Cost of Public Education in the State of New York, p. 269. 1938.
[63] *Ibid.,* p. 270.

integral part of training for social-competence. In some measure it is to be given to all; in every case it must proceed on the basis of explored and revealed capacities, aptitudes, and interests of students. The program may well begin with an extended survey by all students of the major fields of human service in our society, made perhaps first from a social, then from a vocational point of view. The number of such fields of service is not unlimited, though the number of specific vocations within them is very large. The object of this survey would be to reveal "the major needs and values of our society and the resources, equipment, personnel, and technology available to meet them." [64] Following this, on the basis of further exploratory activities provided by the school, the student may be asked to make a tentative choice of one broad field of service for further special study. This choice does not at all commit the student to a particular vocation, or even to this general field; it must be regarded merely as an expression of interest. The time for making this choice should not be prior to the beginning of the senior-high-school period, but it is obvious that it cannot very well be postponed beyond that time.

In the course of intensive study of his special field of service, the student will become acquainted with the major conditions and problems characterizing this field; with its social functions and with the conditions that operate to advance and to hinder the realization of these functions; with the social responsibilities of workers in this field; with the history, status, and conditions of labor, and with the opportunities of advancement; and with the ideals, attitudes, knowledges, and techniques that are required of successful workers in this field. If the student's interest still persists, and if the results of exploration of his personal capacities, aptitudes, and interests warrant it, the student, with competent guidance, should map out for himself a program of activity through which the ideals, attitudes, knowledges, and techniques could be attained. Emphasis even in this must be on the basic knowledges and on the basic techniques rather than on the little skills specific to one job; in the case of those students, however, intending to enter employment immediately upon leaving school, the latter should not be neglected. In the case of any student, it may be said that "no program of secondary education should be regarded as acceptable unless it makes

[64] *Issues of Secondary Education*, p. 203.

some provision for specialized vocational education and for the vocational aspects of general education previously discussed." [65]

In training for the vocational as well as for every other aspect of social-competence, careful guidance is necessary. In education which depends for effectiveness upon adaptation to individual capacities, aptitudes, and interests, systematic guidance must be an inherent part of the instructional process. Generally speaking, guidance should be based upon accumulated evidence resulting from demonstrated ability in the various fields of learning and of work rather than upon the results of aptitude testing. It was to help provide such a basis that the junior high school was founded, and it has already proved its worth. On the basis of demonstrated ability in previous work, the student is to make needed educational and vocational choices. Since a societal investment is at stake, the school has a right to intervene when the student is about to make a patently unwise choice. Skillful guidance, however, consists of much more than helping the student to elect school studies. A great deal of skill is required in guiding the day-to-day learning of the students, helping them to formulate for themselves or accept from others the worthy, definite purposes through which alone learning takes place, and which ultimately develop into strong and abiding interests. The teacher as well as the personnel officer plays a responsible role in the guidance function.

Guidance cannot cease with the completion of the secondary-school period. It is, indeed, at this point that the need for guidance becomes most acute. Brought up to the point of initial social-competence, the individual must be inducted into his role as a member of adult society. The school (or some other social agency) must step in and help the young person to make his initial adjustments to the adult world. If for any reason entrance into a responsible role in the adult world is delayed, the school or another social agency must help to tide him over the period of delay. It was with this thought in mind that it was urged that society establish additional agencies to take care of the older youth for whom jobs are not available at present and whose entrance as adults into society must therefore be postponed.

It is necessary to speak briefly of the role of extra-curricular activities in secondary education. The present extra-curriculum is in part an out-

[65] *Ibid.*, p. 210.

growth of the failure of the curriculum to meet the needs of students. Even with an ideal curriculum, however, extra-curricular activities would serve certain very important purposes. They provide an opportunity to experiment with new activities that ultimately may become curricular; they encourage the development and cultivation of student interests in a great variety of worth-while things; they help to develop the social life of the school; and they foster certain desired ideals, attitudes, and practices much better than can any corresponding studies of the more formal curricular type. Extra-curricular activities, it must be remembered, are governed by the same educational criteria as govern the curricular activities, and their ultimate worth is appraised in terms of what they contribute to social-competence.

II

The American secondary school has within the present century made very substantial gains. For these gains several things have been responsible: the pressure of social-economic changes that placed great numbers of students in the school and compelled a revision of the curriculum along more practical lines; a growing pragmatic attitude that expressed itself in an interpretation of education in terms of social efficiency; the influence of the developing science of psychology which operated to discredit unsound theories of mind and mental development long held and to substitute for them hard fact and plausible theory. The secondary school has become more democratic, more cognizant of its social function, more realistic in its approach to its acknowledged task, more willing to provide for the needs—both immediate and assured—of the students whom it serves. To society the school has become a more valuable and effective agency; to the students it has become a better means of wholesome development and, in general, a happier place in which to be.

It is also true that the secondary school has important weaknesses. It is democratic but not democratic enough: when nearly one out of every two students of secondary-school age is not in school in a democratic society that demands a high order of efficiency of every citizen, that is a serious failing. The school is probably more sensitive to its social purpose than ever before, but it has not yet recognized the full implications of the social investment principle. There is still a great tendency for education to regard itself as a kind of social benevolence; there is still a tendency to regard education as if it were possessed of an independent character apart from society. The school has become more realistic in its approach to its problems, but it has by no means freed itself from tradition. There are in the curriculum many studies that cannot be accounted for at all except as remains of the past, while many of the important activities of present living are not represented at all. The school has become more sensitive to the immediate needs of students, but it is far from providing effectively for their needs, from the point of view of both the immediate present and the assured future.

A systematic criticism of the method of secondary education must take as its point of departure the most striking fact about American education as a whole. The fact is that American education has not developed according to comprehensive and systematic plan, but has grown up through numberless small accretions, each accretion responding to a separate social impulse. As a result there is no very clear idea as to what, in social-pragmatic terms, the secondary school is doing, nor is there a widespread idea as to what the secondary school should do. Perhaps the reason for this condition lies outside the secondary school and within society itself. Perhaps society has no clear plan of direction and of method. In any event, under these circumstances, method—viewed comprehensively—must inevitably be faulty; it cannot possibly be satisfactory. And the method of American secondary education, for precisely this reason, possesses large faults.

Of course, there have been made in recent years a great many improvements in the secondary school: such studies as general science, art, music, health education, home economics—flesh-and-blood studies that represent needs in practical living—have been introduced into the curriculum; extra-curricular activities have been developed and so widely extended and so enthusiastically received that many of the most important values in education now come out of the extra-curriculum; numerous provisions for individual differences have been made—differentiated curricula, homogeneous grouping, enrichment and simplification of subject-matter, special provisions for bright students, etc.; the junior high school has been established to serve as a sorting school while continuing necessary integration, and not only has it stamped itself as a success but it has influenced favorably the other school units; guidance procedures are being systematically worked out; instruction has grown in quality and improved in efficiency; organization and administration have become more efficient; and, generally speaking, there is a growing tendency to rely upon science and research for needed information rather than upon introspection or upon authority. But these improvements must not obscure the fact of the existence of large weaknesses.

Probably the most fundamental weakness is that we have not yet freed ourselves from tradition, and, accepting the mandate of society, gone on to devise means of reaching directly our social objectives. Almost in spite of ourselves we have been forced by social-economic events, by the discoveries of psychological science, by a growing pragmatic attitude on the part of the supporting public, to extend the curriculum, to include practical activities, to discontinue many of the old offerings. But it appears that we still cling to many of the old notions associated with mental discipline and the faculty psychology that we superficially reject. How else can we account for the fact that most of our school studies are still bookish and academic, that for many of the objectives which we have ourselves set up we have failed to provide suitable learning activities? Training for effective citizenship, in the broad sense of the term, is the most important function that the school has. Yet the training in citizenship that we offer to youth is not satisfactory. We do not directly provide sufficient training in the principles and practices of democratic living; the time that we ought to spend on this we spend in teaching other more "intellectual" subject-matter. We seem almost unintentionally to fall back on the principle that good democratic citizenship is an outcome of the general training of the "intellect." The vocational training that we offer is in most respects half-hearted, in some respects zealous but unwise. For most students in general high schools little is done in the way of vocational instruction; for a relatively few students in the vocational high school we provide much training of the wrong kind—in place of large understandings and techniques we offer mastery in the skills specific to a single job. Training for leisure has not yet (apparently) gained academic respectability; it is still associated more with extra-curricular than with curricular activities, and more with recreation and superficial hobbies than with serious intellectual interests and activities. Some attention is being given to health education, to training in effective homemaking, but in each case not enough. Not enough is being done to promote development in practical skills of a non-vocational kind (useful in daily living); very little is being done in the way of training for intelligent consumership. A pragmatic education does not rely upon these important adjustments to follow automatically from general training. The answer is, of course, that the present secondary school is only partly pragmatic.

The chief sufferers from our failure thoroughly to pragmatize the secondary school have been those who can least afford to go into society without adequate preparation for effective social living—the slow students. The academic curriculum is most suited to the academic-minded students who can draw out such educative values as it possesses and translate them into effective performance of life-activities. But such students are in the minority. "The typical non-vocational curriculum of the school today is pitched for children of I. Q. 105 or above. Youth, particularly boys, with an I. Q. of less than 95 have very little chance of learning enough of algebra and Latin to receive a passing grade, modest criterion though that may be, and those with an I. Q. less than 90 have little chance of passing or doing reasonably well in these two groups of subjects, which require on the average a minimum I. Q. of 105 and 100 respectively. Appreciation of the significance of these statements is heightened when one recalls that only 35% of all children have I. Q.'s as high as 105. . . ." [66] The curriculum of the secondary school is therefore inappropriate for the larger part of the students now in it. It is impossible through such a curriculum to train for social-competence the very many students who have great potential talent to contribute to social living but whose capacities, aptitudes, and interests do not lie in academic things. And failure to train all students for social-competence is a danger to democratic society.

Much of the traditional subject-matter still remains. For the most part (although some reorganization has taken place), studies are still organized in terms of logically-related, abstract subjects. Even some of the newer studies that have been introduced—general science, home

[66] H. R. Douglass, *Secondary Education for Youth in Modern America,* p. 29. 1937.

economics—have succumbed to the deadly organization. Perhaps to offset the dryness and lack of interest in the curriculum, there has developed the large enthusiasm for the extra-curriculum, but even this is sometimes spoiled by introduction of some of the pedantic methods of the curriculum.

What is worth doing is worth doing well. Were the school efficient in doing whatever it has tried to do, it could still hold claim to a large degree of public confidence. But there is no reason to believe that the school is successful in getting students to master whatever it does teach them. Admittedly the percentage of school failures is high. Even those students who do not fail show on objective tests that they are far from being masters of what has been taught to them. Many leave school because they have become discouraged by repeated failure in studies. It cannot be said that the school is successful in imparting its subject-matter. Year after year there are discharged into society students who have not been properly trained for social-efficiency and who have not obtained such values as are latent in the subject-matter that the school has offered them.

It is true that the school has become more sensitive to the needs of its students. But in the upper reaches, at least, of organized education, provision for satisfying their needs is still inadequate. "Youth" studies have established the fact that the greatest needs of the older youth at the present time are an appreciation by adults of their worth, a feeling of assurance that society needs them, an opportunity to participate in the worth-while activities of the community. Satisfying these needs would go far toward compensating youth for the apprehension they feel concerning their economic future, for the lack of confidence concerning their ability ultimately to find a good job and establish a good home. The learning activities, however, that the curriculum of the school offers them are academic in nature, more of the same thing to which in their earlier years they had become accustomed. What these young people require are school activities resembling more nearly the actual activities of adults, to which they are by normal interests attracted.

The school has not handled well the problem of the leaving students. It does not generally take the initiative with respect to the students who have failed to profit from the curriculum offerings. They are allowed to linger until they manage somehow to get through or until, discouraged by failures, they drop out. The student who leaves school, whether by graduation or through withdrawal, ceases to be the subject of its concern. The school has no means of knowing whether society realizes on its investment; guidance does not generally extend beyond the end of the school period. On the whole the school does much more for the capable student than for the backward student, although the latter is the one who needs help more.

Much headway has been made in the course of the present century in obtaining sound information founded upon experiment and research. A great deal of research has been done in many areas of secondary education. But it cannot be said that the research has been conducted in the most effective manner possible or that the results have been used to greatest advantage. In the first place, educational research has often been carried on without much guidance from philosophy. Fact-finding that is undirected by principles can never be productive. Much of the statistical research that has been done is for this reason unusable. In the second place, much of the research that has been done has been concerned with petty problems of only local significance. There are a great many problems left to be studied by the methods of science, but the study of them must be centralized, coordinated, conducted efficiently by people expert at their task. In the third place, only a very small fraction of the information thus acquired has been used or is even available for use. Findings have not been assembled, systematized, and applied. With larger vision and a clear understanding of its purpose, the secondary school might seek to coordinate its research activities and integrate its findings; science would in this way contribute much more to secondary education than it now contributes.

III

It must not be supposed that the current situation in secondary education is cause for despair. The American secondary school is moving, though ever so slowly, in the right direction; when balanced against the secondary school of tradition its achievements stand out as not inconsiderable. What is needed is an acceleration of the change already begun, and the carrying of it to completion. We have modified our conception of the aim of education so that we now regard it as social-efficiency; we must continue to change our method of education so that it becomes consistent with this aim and with the facts of psychology as experience and science have made them available to us.

The critical problem in educational method is the problem of curriculum. Our present curriculum is about half way between the traditional academic and the curriculum of realistic learning activities that is to be. We must hasten the process of curriculum reform, discarding the worthless elements in the curriculum as we have it (that does not mean, however, that it is necessary to discard everything that has come down from the past), and replacing them with learning activities that (1) are capable of serving as instruments in the attainment of the present objectives of education, (2) are appropriate to the varied capacities, aptitudes, and interests of students. The making of such a curriculum is no easy task; no single school and no single community alone can do it. To work out units of learning, to test them under various teaching conditions, to make them available to particular schools in such numbers as they require, will call for the service of a central guiding agency, having at its disposal expert educational talent and the coordinated resources of educational science.

The problem of devising a suitable method of vocational education is so important as to require special mention. The secondary school must assume as one of its chief responsibilities training for vocational competence. The present efforts to provide vocational training are unsatisfactory. The secondary school must work out a way (1) of giving some vocational training to every student, varying the amount of training according to the needs of the individual, (2) of giving this training in a way to render a person competent to accept a job and work at it successfully without at the same time encumbering him with specific skills that are expensive to acquire and soon become outmoded, (3) of providing training in such a way that the larger social values are not sacrificed to the acquirement of technical skills. It cannot be said that at the present time we precisely know how to do this; if we once agree, however, that it is to be done, suitable plans will be worked out by trial and experimentation.

The reform of the curriculum is the key to the solution of many large problems of secondary education. Once this reform is under way, it will be possible to take up consideration of questions contingent upon it. That will be the time to consider proposals for extending common education and for making the longer school period compulsory to all. It will then be pertinent to study various optional arrangements of school units and reorganizations within the system.

Another critical problem in secondary education, comparable in importance to the problem of curriculum, is the problem of increasing educational results. The secondary school must succeed in training students so that they *actually are socially-competent* and give society a full return on its investment. No half-way measures are acceptable. The school has not been accustomed to a realistic appraisal of its accomplishment: it has generally evaluated itself in terms of its own processes; and even in these, it has accepted a good deal less than satisfactory achievement. It must be remembered that the school is not a "good" in itself; it is good only to the extent that it serves society. The processes of the school are a means to the end of social-competence; it is in terms of how the individual lives in society and serves it that educational success or failure must be determined.

Exacting a certain amount of accomplishment from students is not sufficient. The school must bend its every effort to see to it that every individual becomes a socially-competent person. All its resources—administrative, curricular, extra-curricular, instructional—must be organized to that end. Guidance must be continuous and must extend beyond the end of the secondary school; the school must see the individual safely inducted into society. Especially with the student who is having difficulty, who is failing, who has dropped out, must the school concern itself. In the proper guidance and direction of such a student, other agencies may have to be called upon to assist, but that is as it should be. The school is only one of the agencies carrying out a societal purpose.

EXPERIMENTALISM

I

Secondary education is a continuation of that guided process of experiencing through which an individual becomes capable of intelligent living in society. With respect to essential educational method, it is not different from the earlier educative process, "secondary" being a term of convenience to designate that stage in the larger period which is concerned with the adolescent. All youth must be educated to the point where they become capable of intelligently managing their life-experiences within their social environment. Owing to the complexity of this environment, the length of the needed educational period has been increased. It is too soon to establish the optimum terminal point of secondary education, but it may be assumed that the period of secondary education extends through the whole of adolescence.

The method of secondary education is precisely that of natural living —learning by experience. The medium in which education takes place is the individual's continuum of experiences; in terms of physical place, education occurs in the home, the school, the community—wherever the individual is. All that the individual experiences is the concern of the school, for all that is the subject-matter of education. The materials of education are, therefore, much more than the studies provided by the school. The school guides the student through his own significant life-experiences, helping him to interpret them and to learn to control them; as far as possible it seeks to harmonize and coordinate these experiences and to shape them so that their total effect upon the individual is integrative and satisfying of needs. In addition, the secondary school provides significant educative activities through which the individual may gain meanings and values necessary for intelligent living within his culture; these it selects from the sum total of activities which comprise the life of that culture. The secondary school is not so much the place where instruction is given, as it is the educational planning center and the center from which guidance issues—for adults as well as for youth; for the school is a community center of guidance rather than a place intended exclusively for children.

The end-product of secondary education, as of any extended experiencing process, is a person who, though he shares values, meanings, patterns of conduct common to all others, is, as a total human being, an individual. He is that by virtue of the peculiarly personal nature of the experiencing process that he undergoes. The school can help him to become a *social-minded* individual, but it cannot keep him from developing a personality that is essentially his own. The duty of the secondary school is to guide the student in the development of a personality which is characterized by effective individuality at the same time that it maintains wholesome, friendly working relationships with the other individuals in the common culture. Such personality is the goal of education; it is such personality that makes possible living the Good Life.

It is in that, rather than in anything else, that the implication of the fact of individual differences lies. Human beings are each of them different from all others, qualitatively so different in total make-up as to make comparison impossible. Each student constitutes a separate educational problem, and offers a personality to be assisted in its own way to intelligent self-direction. Personalities are not commensurable; the secondary school need not resort to artificial means of separating students and of providing them with "suitably" specialized learning activities. If it provides each student with educative activities suited to his needs and interests (whether or not these be situations in which others participate on apparently equal terms), it *is* providing for individual differences. The manner in which each student engages in these activities will be his own, the outcomes in terms of changes in himself and in his surroundings will be individual. The secondary school is working with individuals all the time; its task is to make them more effective in the conduct of their experiences within a common environment.

The secondary school must further be guided by the fact that man is a purposefully-behaving organism, whose wholesome development depends upon the continuous achievement of his purposes. A situation does not become an experience until a person enters into it for the satisfaction of some end intimately related to his living. The effort to understand a situation, to influence the factors in it, to re-create it, is induced by the desire to achieve certain consequences. In the light of these consequences learning takes place—meanings and values are acquired, new behavior patterns formed, new attitudes gained. The experiences with which the secondary school helps the student to deal—whether they are his own, or those that the school has helped to provide—are such as must lead to the satisfaction of his needs.

Needs are not innate, they do not develop from within; rather they are outcomes of the experiencing process. At the point where the culture impinges upon the life-process of the individual, a need develops. The individual acts to satisfy it; and if the need is real and important enough he must satisfy it or suffer some hurtful effect upon personality. The task of the secondary school is to help the adolescent to satisfy his genuine needs. Its task is also, in the process of doing this, to reveal to him areas of experience by means of which new needs will be uncovered and new means of satisfying them achieved. The need of the individual (the actual conflict in his experience, the disturbing element in the equilibrial relationship which he maintains with his environment, not any "manufactured" need) is the starting point of the educative process.

Needs are growing, developing, changing things. They are a function of a developing personality interacting with a changing environment. In the nature of things the needs of adolescents are different from those of younger children. But needs take their character also from the surrounding culture. Adolescence is always accompanied by certain strains and conflicts—some growing out of the physical "coming-of-age" during this period and the adaptations that have to be made in the transition from childhood to adulthood,[67] other needs arising out of particular conditions prevailing in the culture which may be especially disturbing to adolescents. Needs, however, do not emerge only as problems requiring emotional adjustment. They emerge also as intellectual problems: the adolescent seeks to understand his world, to create his own values, to form his own judgments and regulate his own behavior, to function in healthy independence of his parents and of others. Needs must not be understood as being in any sense pathological, as calling for curative treatment. They are the normal characteristics of healthy, developing young people; they touch upon every aspect of living.[68] By satisfying needs as they develop, the individual grows in wholesome personality and in intellectual power, and becomes better able to deal with future needs. The secondary school must help the adolescent to secure the insights from experience, the meanings and methods and attitudes, that enable him to satisfy his needs.

The conditions of modern society have made difficult this task by

[67] For a discussion of the meaning of adolescence, *vide* Chapter IV, "The Developing Personality of the Adolescent" in *Reorganizing Secondary Education*. Report of the Commission on Secondary School Curriculum, Progressive Education Association, 1939.

[68] For an explanation of the concept of needs as an intrinsic element in the life-process, *vide* Chapter II, p. 190.

intensifying needs and creating many new ones. The discouraging outlook for gainful employment facing youth, the feeling that they are unneeded and unwanted in occupational fields, the feeling that personal independence and the fulfillment of normal adult desires are far away, have had a very depressing effect on adolescent development. What makes the task even more difficult is that in the present conflict of social values and social practices, it is hard to "understand" the world, to form intelligent and consistent personal values and to live by them. The effect of mutually conflicting experiences is harmful to personality. The secondary school is hard pressed to coordinate educational agencies and activities when they are themselves in conflict. Within such a situation must the school "help young people realize upon the significant possibilities implicit in their changing status—to help them find themselves anew in their personal, social, and economic relationships, and to develop a working philosophy of values which will give meaning, zest, and purpose to their living." [69] It is no longer enough merely to prepare individuals to face changing ways of living. "This might foredoom them to accept their fortune as it comes—to abandon their fate to chance. The time is ripe to set a new goal—to plan social and cultural change and give it desirable direction, rather than merely accept it. But for young people to take a creative part in shaping the conditions under which they live, they must be able to relate themselves effectively to complex and intangible social groups, to formulate cultural standards appropriate to their times, and to choose their allegiances with intelligent discrimination." [70]

Thus helping the individual to grow within and through the process of satisfying his needs,[71] secondary education must deal with every area of the life-experience. A human being in action is a single integrating whole; every experience has its educating effect for the whole of personality. The secondary school cannot afford to ignore any experience, especially if its effect is of a disturbing nature. The curriculum of the

[69] *Reorganizing Secondary Education*, p. 6.

[70] *Ibid.*, p. 12. This statement would be acceptable to all Experimentalists. The second sentence in the quotation would be differently interpreted by various Experimentalists. Some would go much farther than others in "planning social and cultural change and giving it desirable direction." *Vide* Chapter III, pp. 279 ff.

[71] With the differing emphases as to social direction implied in the footnote above.

secondary school must be reflective of the comprehensiveness of life itself. As with increasing growth and development the life-experiences of the adolescent reach further into the community, and beyond the community out into the world, the curriculum must be prepared to follow. This does not mean that the curriculum is to be an indiscriminate assemblage of the current experiences of youth, and that every one of these experiences is brought under critical scrutiny. The school must naturally (1) select from the current experiences of youth those which are most significant, and (2) it must add to them significant experiences which it regards as necessary. But it must select and add and it must guide in such a way that the youth's total living is affected—clarified, made meaningful, made amenable to direction, and influenced in the right direction. Whatever the school does must influence the life of youth in its entirety, and school activities, by whatever other criteria they are also chosen, must be germane to the life-experiences of youth in their progressive development.[72]

For convenience in the arrangement of an educational plan, the total life-process of a person may be analyzed and classified under its broad categories or areas of experience. Such a step makes it easier to ensure that the curriculum will be representative of the entire range of life-activities. The precise terms in which these categories are formulated (whether in terms of large clusters of activities similar in purpose—such as "protecting life and health," "getting a living," "making a home," "expressing religious impulses," etc.,[73] or in terms of dynamic social relationships—such as "immediate social relationships," "wider social

[72] The term "curriculum" will here be used to denote the educative experiences (drawn from the life of the adolescent and from the broader culture) with which the school actively deals (that is, which it subjects to scrutiny, analysis, evaluation) and through which it guides, as distinguished from those other experiences in the life of the adolescent which it only *affects* but does not actively deal with.

This distinction is made by the writer on his own responsibility. Experimentalists are sometimes inclined to use the term "curriculum" in different senses, referring to it in some places as "composed of all the activities or aspects of living of all learners which are directly influenced by the school" or as "something that goes on in the experience of the child twenty-four hours a day," and speaking in other places of "organizing a curriculum," "making a curriculum," "creating a curriculum pattern" that shall have internal coherence, continuity, etc. The two uses of the word "curriculum" are obviously not identical.

[73] *Vide* Chapter IV, "The Organization of the Curriculum" by Henry Harap in *The Changing Curriculum*, 1937.

relationships," "economic relationships," and "personal living"[74]) are not in themselves important. What is important, though, is that these categories allow for the inclusion of the basic human experiences, that they be broad enough to allow the inclusion of entire experiences and not merely limited and partial activities, that they be functional and not academic centers of learning. The use of such categories makes it possible to define in more specific terms the function of the secondary school: it is to help the individual manage intelligently his experiences within each of the categories, and through the total process become increasingly an intelligently self-directing, wholesome, social-minded person.

Within a curriculum so outlined, the unit of learning is a unit of experience. Learning is a natural result of an experiencing process. Not all obtainable significant outcomes of this process may be immediately realized and incorporated into personality; some re-experiencing (systematic repetition and remedial work) may be necessary. But such additional learning is essentially supplementary. Even skills are best learned in connection with the actual situations in which they are utilized. The unit of the secondary-school curriculum is an experience. A curriculum of such experiences may require some supplementation in the form of systematic drill for the purpose of mastering necessary skills, but it must be remembered that the unit of learning normally is "not a specified lesson of subject matter to be learned, as was formerly held, but a person facing an actual situation." [75]

The rejection of a subject-matter unit of learning does not lessen the need for a pattern of organization for the curriculum. A curriculum design must be worked out that provides for both horizontal and vertical sequence. Horizontally the curriculum organization must reflect the unity and relatedness of human experience. (The traditional subjects, aside from their un-psychological internal organization, were also unrelated to one another.) To achieve this unity and relatedness within the curriculum organization, various devices are possible—the use of "centers of interest" or of "integrative themes," etc.[76] Again the precise

---

[74] *Reorganizing Secondary Education,* p. 44.

[75] W. H. Kilpatrick, *Remaking the Curriculum,* p. 48. 1936.

[76] For discussion of the ways in which such a pattern may be achieved, refer to Chapter IV, "The Organization of the Curriculum" by Henry Harap in *The Changing Curriculum,* 1937.

type of unifying device employed is not important; what is important is that unity be achieved. Vertically the design of the curriculum must be arranged so that the educative experiences will have psychological continuity, that is, will keep pace with the progressive development of the individual, his growth in insight and ability as well as his changing needs and interests. (The traditional school did not provide the continuity of learning activity that would enable the individual to develop deeper insights consonant with growing experience, nor was it well-adapted to the individual's changing needs. The principle of organization was academic: the relevance of subject-matter to subject-matter only was considered.) The secondary school must be prepared to keep pace with the pupil's changing experience, and must follow where this leads.

In the case of the adolescent, this normally leads away from the schoolroom and toward the activities of the adult community. The experiences, the needs, the interests, become less those of children, centering around play, and become more those of adults, centering around work. To satisfy these needs and interests, and to foster continued development of wholesome personality, the secondary school must provide for adolescents increasing opportunity to participate in adult activities, and must do its utmost to compensate for those restrictions that modern cultural conditions place upon adolescent participation in the serious activities of adult life.

The curriculum of the school—those experiences which it directly helps the learner to examine, to analyze, to reconstruct, those through which it actively guides him—is necessarily a sampling, a selection. The purpose of the secondary school is to bring under the intelligent self-direction of the adolescent every experience that he has, to make him generally an intelligent person; and to realize this purpose the school must make its influence felt in every part of the human experience. But it is manifestly impossible for the school critically to deal with, actively to guide the reconstruction of every one of these experiences, in other words, to have a curriculum as replete as life itself. Selection is unavoidable. The school selects for critical examination by the student those experiences which promise to have the greatest educative value, those most heavily weighted with the meanings which make intelligible the life-experience within the culture. Experiences are not of equal value for purposes of education. One criterion of value is the meanings that the experiences possess for living within the culture; another criterion is their relevance to the intrinsic needs of the learner. On the basis of these criteria, experiences are selected from every area of living previously mentioned, and become the "content" of the curriculum.

"We look at the curriculum as the succession of educative experiences for which the school accepts responsibility. As the unit element of the old curriculum was an assigned lesson, so the unit element of what we call the new is an educative experience." [77] The curriculum is constantly in the making. Within the relatively permanent categories of the life-process, experiences are changing. Relationships change; a new culture, new activities are constantly in process of development. Even for the same student an advancing curriculum must be continuously planned. It is impossible, therefore, to set down with finality, except in terms of generalizations, what experiences should make up the school curriculum. This must be a function of the culture in which the school exists and more particularly of the community in which it is located, of the experiential backgrounds and needs of the children with whom it deals, of the current and perhaps unexpected happenings which affect it. In the continuous curriculum-planning enterprise, students must participate. The opportunity of the students to share in the selection of educatively valuable experiences is perhaps as important as the subsequent analysis and reconstruction of these experiences. The experiential substance of the curriculum, therefore, must be an outcome of cooperative student- and teacher-effort.

Whatever the particular categories under which school activities are assembled, and whatever the precise nature of the activities ultimately chosen, the secondary school must concern itself with guiding personality in the following directions: toward a democratic way of life—with all that this implies in the matter of regard for the dignity and worth of the individual common man, reciprocal individual and group responsibility for promoting common concerns, and the free play of intelligence in the solution of common problems; toward an understanding of the culture, its values, its strength and its weakness, and toward developing the desire and the ability to work for the advancement of this

[77] H. L. Caswell, in *Democracy and the Curriculum*, p. 414. 1939.

culture; [78] toward knowledge of oneself—one's privileges, duties and obligations, the essential relationships one has to maintain, the essential attitudes and abilities one is required to possess, one's special aptitudes, interests and needs; toward becoming better able to participate effectively in the activities of the community—social, economic, political, artistic—in such a way as constantly to promote a common Good Life by Experimentalist standards.

A statement of these directions points to the nature of the experiences which the school is to offer (in addition to guiding the adolescent in his personal living [79]): experiences in discovering the meaning of democratic living, and its social, economic, and political implications; in exploring the present culture—its historical foundations, its guiding principles, its practices, its problems, in testing various aspects of this culture by democratic values, and in planning improvements; in exploring the world of science—its achievements, its dynamic relationship with the modern culture, its bearing upon democratic living; in studying human relationships, past and present, to discover the values men live by; in appreciating and creating literature, music, and art; in exploring man's world of work; and so forth. And these experiences must be so organized that they have horizontal interrelatedness, that they have vertical continuity, that they respond to progressively changing needs, that they keep pace with youth in his development from the interests and behaviors of early adolescence progressively into the broadening concerns and activities of the adult community and larger society.

The nature of the work-experiences that the secondary school needs to offer must be specifically considered. The importance of including in the curriculum of the modern secondary school such experiences, both those of a gainful, vocational nature and those which are non-gainful but socially and educatively important, has already been discussed. [80] The life-process is an active process: experience generally ends in activity, not in reflection. The offering of activities that call for constructive accomplishment is a necessary part of the educative process. But these activities must be selected by the same educational criteria as

[78] *Vide* p. 370, footnote 70.
[79] *Vide* pp. 380 ff.
[80] *Vide* Chapter III, pp. 285 ff.

are the others—their intrinsic educative value and their relevance to the needs of the learner. Consistent with these needs, the work-experiences provided by the school will necessarily vary according to the stage of development reached by the learner. There are work-experiences adapted to the needs of children, to the needs of adolescents, to the needs of older boys and girls, to the needs of young adults. Those provided by the secondary school must have educational relevance to the needs of adolescents in the varying stages of their development. Admittedly among these experiences there must be some which look toward preparation of students for participation in a remunerative vocation. But not all work-experiences can be or should be of this type, nor should even participation in vocational activities consist in learning specific habits and skills incidental to working upon a particular job, but without broader developmental value.

Vocational activities should be regarded as falling within the larger vocational-economic category of experience. Training for a vocation must be related to the larger problem of understanding intelligently the economic character of society. The secondary school must help every student to understand the complexities of the modern industrial-economic situation, its possibilities and its requirements; in terms of this understanding to develop interests in vocational activities consistent with individual aptitudes; to implement these interests by developing broad knowledges and abilities in a field of vocational endeavor through active work-experiences. But these work-experiences must be introduced gradually. They must be of a nature adapted to the needs and interests of adolescents rather than of mature adults. They must be progressive in character rather than static. And, whenever that is possible, they should lead to the opportunity to apply the creative abilities of students in actual work-situations *under expert school guidance.*

Lacking, however, sufficient opportunity for the expression of their vocational abilities in remunerative occupations, secondary-school students must also be helped to develop and to apply their abilities in financially non-remunerative but socially useful community projects. Whatever disadvantage participation in such projects may have for the adolescent in terms of financial returns is sometimes more than compensated for by the genuine *educativeness* of the projects, by the feeling of confidence and by the faith in himself that the youth develops, by the status that he acquires in the community. The returns are not only to the learner himself but to the entire community. Precisely how such participation in community work-experiences is to be managed cannot yet be set down in detail; the chances are that a variety of procedures not only is possible, but ultimately will be necessary, each adapted to the needs of the students and of the community.[81]

It may be worth while to repeat that work-experiences are of tremendous educative value and that they need to be regarded in that way; that work-experiences are not necessarily "vocational training"; that they constitute an integral part of the secondary-school curriculum; that they need to be organized so as to meet the progressive needs of the students; that some work-experiences should lead out into the community and provide for student participation in community enterprises; that concurrently with these (in some cases it is possible for vocational activities of the students to serve non-vocationally a community purpose) there should be vocational work-experiences which will help to develop interests, disclose aptitudes, give a realistic insight into at least a portion of the world of work, and develop general attitudes and abilities that will enable the youth to adapt himself to a job; that, whenever possible, the school should provide opportunities for the student to utilize his vocational abilities in a real occupation (for at least part of the time), and in a remunerative way, under its careful guidance; that the whole problem of learning in vocational situations be treated as education and not as training, and that such learning be evaluated in terms of growth in attitudes, understandings, creative abilities that mark the intelligently self-directing person.

The curriculum of the new secondary school does not minimize the essential importance of knowledge, even of knowledge organized as school subjects. But it regards knowledge as instrumental in function; its proper place is within the context of experience. The experience

[81] For a discussion of the manner in which youth participate in community activities, *vide:* P. R. Hanna, *Youth Serves the Community,* 1936; Chapter VII, "Meeting the Needs of Adolescents in Their Economic Relationships" in *Reorganizing Secondary Education,* 1939; Chapter XIV, "The School Looking Forward," especially pp. 392 ff., in *Democracy and the Curriculum,* 1939; Myles Horton, Chapter VII, "The Community Folk School" in *The Community School* (edited by S. Everett), 1938.

curriculum makes wide use of knowledge in the organized fields of the social studies, the natural sciences, mathematics, literature, and the fine arts. But this knowledge is not the starting point. The starting point is the experiences to which a youth is impelled by his needs and his interests, with which he must deal intelligently in every area of his living. The broadly organized subject-matter fields furnish the meanings and the techniques necessary for dealing with these experiences. For this purpose, the subject-matter fields must be canvassed so as to disclose the knowledges that can be brought to bear on a particular situation. For each major experience, several broad fields of subject-matter will contribute that knowledge which each distinctively has to offer.[82]

For several reasons, it is advantageous to retain the distinctions between the various fields of subject-matter. In the first place, these fields are "representative of categories of learning derived from the experience of the race. Foreign languages are the tongues of alien peoples; science and the social studies, mathematics and English, art and language were not taken out of the thin air. They represent the methods of approach used by scholars and scientists, and have proved their worth on the advance line of inquiry into the unknown."[83] In the second place, "each field contributes a unique set of intellectual tools: the methods, data, findings, and area of exploration are not the same in the natural and in the social sciences; language and mathematics represent quite distinctive methodologies in logic and analysis of experience; the art approach is still different from any of these. Stressing these differences in the curriculum enables the student to identify his own particular type of interest and ability, and puts him in a position to begin developing his capacities as natural scientist and not as artist, as mathematician and not as social scientist. . . . Each set of tools equips the student in a different way for independent participation in a democratic society."[84] But retaining these broad-fields categories is not the same as retaining the narrow disciplines, the conventional subjects of the traditional secondary school. There are numerous reasons

[82] For a discussion of the place of organized subject-matter in the experience curriculum, refer to, *Reorganizing Secondary Education*, pp. 421 ff. 1939.
[83] *Ibid.*, pp. 423–424.
[84] *Ibid.*, pp. 424–425.

for abandoning the conventional organization by subjects. "Primary among them is the fact that the subject—algebra, or geometry, or trigonometry, for example—is not so good a resource for meeting student needs as is the whole field or area of mathematics. The separate subject tends to become an abstraction, with certain conventional sequences and limits that are irrelevant both to the on-going life of the student and evolving structure of mathematics itself." [85]

But it must be repeated that the primary educative unit is the experience itself. It is in the analysis and reconstruction of experiences that the resources of all the subject-matter areas are utilized. "Conventional subject-matter is introduced as it is needed in the study of the many aspects of living." [86] What logic or system such subject-matter is to have must be determined in the light of the nature of the educative experience. The learning of subject-matter does not become an end in itself. Within the learning experience, however, there may be systematic drill for the purpose of assuring the incorporation of learnings into the personality makeup of the individual. Subject reviews may be supplementary to the functional study of areas of living,[87] and the school may provide sequential work in the subject-matter fields for those whose interests incline them to these studies or who need added systematic study in preparation for college.

In general, the curricular offerings on any level of learning are to be common experiences. What each student brings to a situation is, of course, an individual thing, and what he takes from it, in terms of attitudes, understandings, techniques, patterns of conduct, is also specific to himself. The school curriculum does not need to be specialized in order to provide for individual differences. Facing a common situation, learners react to the situation in their own ways, and at the same time profit from the experience of working together. Of course, some differentiation is desirable. While the core of the curriculum is to consist of common situations which each learner faces in his own way, additional learning experiences are to be provided to meet special needs and interests. (And to this is to be added the fact that the school offers to each student individual guidance in the problems of personal liv-

[85] *Ibid.*, pp. 422–423.
[86] Henry Harap, *The Changing Curriculum*, p. 97. 1937.
[87] *Ibid.*, p. 98.

ing.) [88] Such learning experiences may be of a work type, or college-preparatory type, or remedial type, or a follow-up of a special interest. It is the task of skillful guidance so to direct the student that he is at all times working as an individual. The artificial and spurious device of homogeneous grouping on the basis of "ability" need not be resorted to; the only kind of homogeneous grouping that is justifiable is that based on interests and special needs, and that kind of grouping, in the nature of things, is temporary, being maintained only until it has served its purpose.

The curriculum, of course, does not consist only of the experiences provided or made available by the school. A large part of the curricular activity of the school consists in guiding the adolescent in his personal living, in the experiences that affect him as an individual most of all. The secondary school must influence the entire life-experiencing of the learner: unless curricular activity has a beneficent effect on all of life-activity, the school cannot be said to be successful. The experiences which the school makes available must of necessity be selected, and they must of necessity be social experiences common in the culture; on the other hand, the student needs guidance, too, in the much wider range of his own life-experience, and such guidance the school must directly provide. Personal integration demands that the adolescent be as effective in dealing with the problems of his own life-experience as he is in reconstructing the social experiences presented by the school. Through its staff—physicians, psychologists, sociologists, teachers—and in the course of its normal student-school relationships, the secondary school must help its students to become better men and women in all respects. The school will be successful in doing this to the extent that it gains the confidence and good-will of students, parents, and community.

The fundamental concept inherent in "intentional" education is guidance.[89] Natural experiencing is inherently educative, but without a basis of valid meanings, values, techniques, it is not educative enough. For the individual to possess such a basis on which to operate, "intentional" education is necessary. "Intentional" education means guidance in experiencing. Providing students with educative experiences is a

[88] Note the paragraphs that follow.
[89] *Vide* Chapter III, pp. 275 ff.

form of guidance; helping them to analyze these experiences and to draw from them values serviceable in living is another; helping them to deal better with their personal problems is another. The school and all its activities are a manifestation of the guidance process. Without guidance, experiencing alone would not make most individuals intelligently self-directing. Also, without guidance "it is unlikely that the individual student will meet his needs in ways that lead toward democratic living or in the process form a personality which moves of itself in the direction of democratic ideals." [90]

Guidance is the heart of the educational process: it is what the school —everyone and everything in it—does. Instruction is guidance, pure and simple. But guidance goes beyond mere instruction; in helping the student to solve his personal problems, in fostering wholesome student-community relationships, in helping to solve community problems, the school is administering guidance. The administering of guidance should not involve setting up special school machinery beyond what the school already has for the achievement of its stated objectives. The guidance function must be performed in the course of the ordinary learner-school relationships: it relies not so much upon mechanical contrivances, upon "intelligence" tests and "vocational aptitude" tests, and upon self-conscious guidance "experts," as upon the normal, wholesome relationships of the individual with his school companions, his teachers and the school staff, and the community, upon the discovery of needs and awakening of interests, upon cooperative tentative arrangements for meeting these needs and interests through educative experiences, upon testing and evaluation in which the student himself plays an active part.

The meanings inherent in the concept of guidance also clarify the nature of the instructional process. Instruction is a means of carrying on one of the functions for which the school has been established: the function of making available to students the experiences which hold for them the most significant educational values, and of helping them to reconstruct these experiences so that their values for immediate and future living are fully realized. The activities involved in the performance of this function are collectively called instruction. The principles of instruction are governed by the general nature of the learning process

[90] *Reorganizing Secondary Education*, p. 359.

and by the particular needs of the learner at his stage of development. The general nature of the learning process has already been indicated: [91] it begins with a need which may have already been defined by the learner in his own mind, or which may exist as a yet undefined and inarticulate tension or conflict in experience; learning thereupon takes place through experiencing, and, to the extent that the experience enables the individual to satisfy his need, to that extent does the experience result in wholesome, integrating behavior, in desirable attitudes, in growth in power of dealing with experience. All this demands that the learner rather than the teacher and his knowledge must be in the foreground of learning; skill in instruction is skill in stimulating learning activity on the part of the learner rather than skill in imparting information.

The developing abilities of the learner during the adolescent period require a continuous adaptation of teaching techniques to learner-needs. As the learner matures, develops, he becomes more competent to direct himself, that is, to take greater part in the selection of the educative experiences that hold out greatest promise to him, and to guide himself through them. The guidance of the teacher, therefore, steadily becomes less decisive and less prominent. As the student acquires greater intelligence, he acquires greater freedom to direct himself. The technique of instruction must be formulated with a view to the developing independence of the learner.

The educative effect of experiences is all-pervasive: the school cannot either cancel or discount the educative effect of an experience simply by refusing to accord it official recognition. The learnings which are concomitant to the "intentional" learning process are of great importance. In the past, the school taught democracy without itself practicing it. The relations between individuals in the school—administrative staff, teachers, students—were carried on in an authoritarian manner, while "the moral of the lesson" always pointed to democracy. The secondary school must recognize the fact that students will accept democracy, will acquire democratic meanings and develop democratic attitudes and modes of behavior, to the extent that *all* their experiences incline them toward democracy. The experiences within the school and within the community, so far as the school can control or influence

[91] *Vide* Chapter II, pp. 198 ff.

them, must be such experiences. The secondary school must practice democratic living in all its relationships.

Evaluation is a vital part of the educative process. It is of necessity the culmination of experience, when the forces that have generated activity are either disbanded or marshalled for renewed effort. But traditional education has helped to simplify and at the same time to distort the meaning of evaluation so that it is commonly regarded as equivalent to "measuring results" after "learning has taken place." Evaluation is an inherent part of the act of learning itself; in a sense, learning is through continuous evaluation. Evaluation is not in terms of knowledge, which is instrumental, but in terms of less measurable, less tangible, more subtle, and much more important changes in personality, and in power of dealing with experience. There is no objection to the use of the testing devices provided they do not divert the educational process to mechanical ends, or place emphasis upon instrumental rather than terminal values. Testing is an extremely important part of the evaluational process, but it is not the whole of it; moreover, there must be worked out more valid means of testing than are at present available. Periodic testing must be subordinated to the continuous evaluation of adolescent development, and evaluation made, not in terms of "achievement" detachable from the personality of the student and the situation within which he operates, but in the light of the experiences, interests, needs, and the thus far developed personality of the learner. To be able to effect that kind of evaluation, the secondary school must get to "know" the student, and must avail itself of every device through which it may learn about him. A valuable device that has been developed for this purpose in the last few years is the cumulative record; but, in compiling this record, far more important than the symbols that tend to classify the student in atomistic ways are the accounts that throw light on his total behavior in various situations.

The form that the secondary school is to take will be determined experimentally in the light of the knowledge of its function. At present it is too early to deal with form. The secondary-school curriculum is in process of development. Beginnings have been made at different points in the secondary period, and at points traditionally considered removed from the secondary school, as exemplified by the formation of the Civilian Conservation Corps for out-of-school youth, and by some of the projects of the National Youth Administration. The present schematic arrangement, with a junior high school, a senior high school, a junior college, and independent organizations dealing with youth not in any of the formal schools, is good enough for the purpose of the experimentation that must be carried on. Ultimately the form of the secondary school will be reorganized as the curriculum is being reorganized today. Very likely there will result no uniform organization, but a flexible organization appropriate to the functions which the secondary school is to perform in the community. Such sub-units of the secondary school as will then be formed will be formed not primarily to promote administrative efficiency, but for psychological advantages that will redound to the benefit of the learner.

II

Reference has been made to beginnings in the reconstruction of secondary education that will ultimately bring it into accord with the needs of individual living in our modern democratic-industrial society and with the facts of modern dynamic, organismic psychology. That such a beginning has been made is undeniable; that the movement toward reconstruction has made considerable headway is also undeniable. It is to be hoped that the movement will spread and become accelerated until American secondary education at last becomes an effective means of assisting individuals to attain the intelligent life in terms of our culture.

Of the present, however, it must be said that secondary education is still very far from satisfactory. Of course, the fault is not primarily in the method; that the method of secondary education should be weak in fundamental ways is unavoidable. The weaknesses stem out of more basic weaknesses in social orientation, in conception of functions, and in psychological background. In a divided society, the school possesses no positive social philosophy—rather, it is under the spell of an "objective" scientific movement which, by refusing to take sides, tacitly aligns itself with the controlling elements in society; the social functions of education in a dynamic society are misunderstood and education is treated as if it were a timeless and spaceless affair; the underlying educational psychology is mechanistic in its conception both of world and of human behavior in it.

It is necessary to point out how these more fundamental misconceptions have exercised an undesirable influence on the method of the secondary school. The weaknesses in method are many; perhaps the following are the most notable. In place of adequate, real, educative experiences, the secondary school still offers, for the most part, abstract subject-matter, arrayed in logical fashion, having little functional relationship to the life that the student is leading. Most of this subject-matter has been inherited from the past, and it is taken for granted that it is the function of education to "transmit knowledge." The school accordingly busies itself with its own affairs and leaves the more important business of teaching life-values to the uncontrollable and unpredictable experiences, forces, and agencies of society. Except for the fact that it is supported by the community, the school has only a slight functional relationship with it.

Instead of helping adolescent youth to satisfy their most compelling needs and grow through the reconstruction of significant experiences, the school is very largely ignoring these needs, and creating artificial "motivations" to make its subject-matter more palatable. The experiences that engage youth and sometimes prove too large for them to cope with are not taken up and dealt with by the school; they thus are permitted to operate toward the disaffection of adolescent personality. The social conflicts and stresses which are at present evident in society, the unpromising employment situation and the prospect of long idleness that it produces, the personal distress that comes with being unable to make proper adjustment, all serve to create personality conflicts in youth which it is vitally necessary to resolve. In its attitude toward the problem, the traditional secondary school is hopelessly academic.

In many quarters where attempts have been made to change the secondary school from the classical mold and to make it more realistically serve life-needs, these attempts have led to the reorganization of the curriculum on a mechanical plan that recognizes habit formation as the underlying purpose of educational method. The influence of the connectionist psychology has been expressed in a conception which identifies the educative process with learning to make fixed responses to given stimuli, as if the world of human life were a static world of events that could be prepared for in advance. The "scientific" attitude to which this psychology aspires has led to the advancement of the propositions that the school cannot strive toward any higher ideals than those which society recognizes, and that the outlook of the school cannot have an organic unity not possessed by society itself. As a result there has developed great curricular activity that consists of canvassing the important "life-activities," analyzing them into their constituent abilities, and setting up curriculum counterparts, unrelated to one another, by which these abilities may be achieved. The secondary-school curriculum thus becomes an aggregation of discrete elements among which are activities leading to "character development," "effective use of leisure time," "vocational ability," etc. The curriculum possesses no organic unity and no immediate bearing upon the needs of the learner. The school offerings become an elaborate arrangement of specialized curricula, with ingenious devices for attaching the student to one set of learning activities rather than to another. Although these schools come somewhat closer than the traditional in realizing a functional education, the spirit throughout is that of mechanism rather than organism; and, because education is regarded as preparation for an adult living that is static and apparently perfect, the ultimate purposes of the school are not realized.

In rejecting the patently faulty conceptions of mind that dominated the older traditional schools, these schools go to an unjustifiable extreme when they reject the reality of mind. The basis of learning seems to be conditioning. Thus, vocational education logically becomes the acquisition of skills needed at a particular job; in practice such training has disastrous results. Vocational education is separated from general education, to which are assigned other "objectives." In the same way, general education becomes training in citizenship, training in intelligent family-living, etc.—training meaning, in each case, conditioning in specific attitudes, skills, and facts of knowledge. The curriculum of the school is compartmentalized to accord with a compartmentalized view of personality. There is no relatedness in learning and no continuity in learning experience. The divided and subdivided curriculum calls for an elaborate administrative machinery the main function of which seems to be matching the student with the school offering.

The mechanistic attitude is also responsible for the mistaken interpretation of the meaning of individual differences. A student is regarded not as a unified organism, with unique tendencies and purposes and needs, but as a complex of specific factors each of which must be "catered to" individually. Providing for individual differences, therefore, requires specialization of studies, leading to different types of curricula and ultimately to different types of schools. The fact of individual differences also seems to demand a segregation of students according to ability. Students are subjected to a sorting process—tested, labeled bright, average, or dull, and sorted out into classes ("homogeneous" groups) where instruction is "adapted to their needs," that is, "enriched" or "simplified." Such guidance as a school offers usually expends itself in this process—in the process of testing and sorting; true guidance in the solution of problems that are of great concern to the learner is not given to any appreciable extent. Also, as if learning effects could be balanced as are entries on an accounting sheet, there are "socializing" activities to balance the "individual" activities. The whole point of the meaning of individuality seems to be lost.

The "scientific" attitude also serves to beget a considerable confusion between evaluation and measurement. Emphasis in evaluation is placed upon the definite and the measurable; in method, evaluation becomes "objective." Intangible attitudes and interests and growth in creative power are neglected in favor of those outcomes that can be objectified. Evaluation tends to be separated from the learning experience, and placed in a separate category: one is tested after he has "learned," and if the results of the test seem to demand it, he "re-learns." Often evaluation serves purposes removed from learning itself: test results are used to appraise efficacy of method, or teaching efficiency. Little of the evaluating is generally done by the student. He is the one who is evalua*ted*. The movement to test and to measure has spread until it dominates many schools.

Instruction itself, in these schools, tends to become mechanical. Teachers are "specialists" in their fields rather than well-rounded, social-minded, educated men and women who understand and can satisfy the intellectual-emotional needs of adolescents. Knowledge in almost every case is treated as thoroughly authenticated and final. Learning becomes mastery: acquisition of knowledges and skills, not the formation of wholesome attitudes, interests, meanings, creative abilities. The "progressive development of intellectual independence" means either progressive skill in academic procedures or progressive self-reliance in the performance of fixed activities.

Somewhat more than the older classical schools, those schools based upon the "scientific" psychology attempt to deal with some of the immediate needs of adolescents. But their efforts do not avail much. The schools do not go out into the community and identify themselves with the community activities, needs, and problems. Their very "objectivity" and "lack of social biases" operate against them; they do not therefore really penetrate into the social causes of many of the problems that now concern youth. The schools are better adapted to the needs of children than to those of older adolescents; the closer a youth comes to adulthood, the more do the schools fail to satisfy him in the solution of his immediate problems and in his preparation for adult living. On the other hand, it must be admitted that the student social life in these schools has been greatly improved, and that the extra-curricular activities have sometimes managed to draw more genuine interest and satisfy more genuine needs than the curricular activities.

III

The modern secondary school, as has been indicated, cannot be reconstructed in terms of method alone. Logically antecedent to the reconstruction of method [92] there must be a revision of some of the fundamental attitudes that affect men's thinking in education. There must be a complete change in conception of the social function of education: education must be granted the right to share in the most critical cultural experiences, to partake in social debates, to hold opinions on controversial social questions. Beyond this education must formulate for itself a positive social philosophy, holding individual good to be the end of all living, and everything else a means to this end. Finally education must be securely based upon a psychology that recognizes the dynamic nature of world, that recognizes the organismic nature of man and of human behavior, that sees intelligence as a tre-

[92] It is not to be inferred that this revision of fundamental attitudes must necessarily come first *in time;* what is meant is that all this *is involved* in the reform of secondary education.

mendously important factor in human living, that defines intelligence in terms of meanings continuously acquired from experience. It will then be possible to define education as it should be defined: as a process of helping individuals, through the continuous reconstruction of experiences, to become intelligent in their living in a complex, industrial, changing culture. Secondary education will be seen as the phase of this process dealing with young people in the adolescent stage of development—inducting them, in terms of the experiences that they have and in terms of other significant experiences that satisfy their life-needs, into a life-time process of intelligently self-directive experiencing.

When the function of secondary education is thus identified, it will be possible for the secondary school (the agency or agencies charged with the task of carrying on secondary education) to plan its method. The medium within which education takes place will be seen as the social environment: the school will become a living, functional, integral part of the environment. It will be recognized that growth, development, education, take place within a social culture; that within this culture every experience is educative; that the school, therefore, is not a "dispenser of education," but, as far as possible, a coordinator and harmonizer of the educative influences within society, a planning agency that seeks to make the utmost and best possible use of the resources of education, a guide that seeks out the most educative experiences, makes them available to its learners, and assists in their intelligent analysis and reconstruction. Such a school will establish and maintain a close working relationship with the community. It will keep itself apprized of community needs, assist in planning and in executing community undertakings, and place itself in readiness to serve the community in whatever way it can.

It will be recognized that the subject-matter of education are experiences, that intelligent living is possible only through the continuous analysis and reconstruction of experiences, that the essential service of the school is guidance in this. The curriculum of the school will consist of dealing with those experiences of the student which are significant in his personal living, and those, in addition, which the school has made available. The curriculum will reflect the comprehensiveness of life itself; especially will those experiences which are exercising a dominant effect on the living of all individuals within the culture be represented. The curriculum at any one time will have unity; progressing with the development of the individual it will also have continuity. It will be continuously reconstructing itself to keep pace with the changing needs of its students and the changing events within society. In the continuous reconstruction of the curriculum the students will have a large role.

The curriculum of the school will not be insensitive to the tremendous usefulness of systematized knowledge in the development of human intelligence. The broad fields of knowledge and intellectual and artistic activity will be brought into the curriculum, and used to resolve those difficulties in the learner's experiences in which only the most important and accurate knowledge and skills can serve. Indeed, there will be no lack in the learner's mastery of knowledge; but the knowledge will be pertinent to his own living, and therefore real and important. The learner will develop skills, attitudes, ideals, habits of behavior, but they will be part of the total pattern of his personality, interacting with the culture for the satisfaction of life-needs.

For the learner will be regarded as an organic unity, operating as a whole to satisfy needs that affect the whole organism. The secondary school will be very much concerned to see that the learner's needs are continuously being satisfied; when conditions in society make satisfaction of needs difficult, the school will take either remedial or compensatory action. The experiences of the personal living of every individual student will fall within the province of the school's responsibility. The individuality of each student will be respected; though he partakes in common learning situations, it will be understood that he is carrying away those meanings and values which most suit him as an individual, living in continuous and harmonious cooperation with others. The true meaning of individual differences will be recognized; the differentiation of learning activities will be a regular feature of the curriculum, but learners will not be segregated in any artificial way, nor will specialized curricular activities draw the attention of the learner away from those central understandings that people living together intelligently in a common culture must have.

Evaluation will be an important part of the learning process, but it will be an aspect of the learning experience rather than an aftermath of learning. Evaluation will be continuous; it will be carried on primarily by the learner himself, in terms of his own needs and purposes; it will not overlook the more subtle educational values for those that prominently obtrude themselves in consciousness. Testing will be part of the larger evaluational activity, but it will be considerate of the full purpose of the learning process rather than merely of those results that lend themselves to objective treatment. The results of evaluation will be used to throw light upon the needs of the individuals rather than to sort out individuals for purposes of segregation.

Teaching will be interpreted as guidance in experiencing. In the center of the educational process will be the learner, not the teacher. The guidance of the teacher will be directed not so much at helping students to acquire knowledge and skills as at the solution of their human problems. The teacher himself will be primarily an intelligently self-directing person, capable of dealing with the personal problems and intellectual needs of adolescents.

5: Critical Summary

THE WRITER approaches the task of criticism from a certain point of view. He is not altogether "unbiased," nor completely unpartisan. He favors the theory of secondary education here designated as Social Realism. But his preference has been determined by intellectual considerations, rather than in an irresponsible a priori manner or by a vague and indefinable temperamental "affinity." He is impressed by the reasonableness of the basic premises of Social Realism: that the first and foremost problem of man is how to live in the world; that the most important criterion of the reality and meaning of things is the Pragmatic Rule; that human intelligence must be defined with reference to the problem of human living, and that the sole source of intelligence is experience; that individual experience is not a reliable guide to intelligent living, that the pooled experiences of many individuals constitute a much more reliable guide; that society is to be valued tremendously because, among other things, society is an agency which enlarges the human intelligence; that society must be recognized as an entity, that its integrity and its continuity must be assured, that its general principles of operation must be respected; that it is necessary to distinguish, in degree if not in kind, between objectively verifiable knowledge whether of physical nature or of biological and social life and the much less objectively verifiable assumptions concerning the meaning of experience which it is necessary to make in order to carry on life-activity, and to which we give the name of "beliefs"; that society is much more of an authority on the validity of beliefs than is the individual. Correspondingly, the writer is intellectually alienated by some of the patent characteristics or tendencies of the other theories. Humanism seems

392

to him to emphasize beyond justification the differences between man and biological nature, between man and man, and to understate and underestimate the likenesses; its tendencies are, accordingly, toward exclusiveness and aristocraticness, and it must be charged at times with turning its back upon the facts which common sense bids us to recognize. Social Evolutionism, on the other hand, still sees life too largely in terms of "struggle for survival"; its values seem to reflect excessive preoccupation with that, and an insufficient concern for the amenities of human living. It is inherently cautious and conservative, and too inclined to look to the past for guidance in present living. Experimentalism, at times contrary to what its name denotes, tends to be prematurely dogmatic in its stand on certain debatable matters. It suffers inherently from a subjectivistic tendency to place too much reliance on individual interpretation of experience.

But preference for a theory of secondary education does not mean complete partisanship. In the judgment of the writer, Social Realism is not without some weaknesses. Correspondingly, he can see some merits in each of the theories presented in the study. It is not to be doubted that Humanism is urging American education on to higher levels of effort and performance. Its attacks on the low standards of value that do exist in contemporary American education, its exposure of the intellectual limitedness that characterizes a good deal of modern educational science, are already producing results. Its criticism of the trivialities that have crept into the school curriculum and of the disorganized state of that curriculum has been a timely warning to American education. Social Evolutionism must be admired for its warm and uncompromising democratic spirit, for its persistent battle against the fallacies and inadequacies of the mechanistic psychology, for its vigorous impatience with those principles of "progressive education" that play upon the weaknesses of human beings rather than capitalize their strength. And Experimentalism—one must admire its idealism, its resolution to give us redress from our present deep troubles, its understanding of the nature of many of the economic and social problems that afflict our era. The writer holds that the goal toward which Experimentalism aims, the kind of life that it envisions ultimately for each individual human being, may well serve the American people as the common objective toward which to chart their course. Further, Experimentalism offers a new and valuable insight into the nature of intelligence, into the workings of "the mind," and should enable us on that basis to build a new and better educational method. In some degree, Experimentalism has already liberated American education from its ancient stuffiness; it has brought the school closer to life, and in the areas of both elementary and secondary education it is making important curriculum inventions.

It is in this spirit that the task of offering a critical summary of the theories of secondary education is approached.

HUMANISM

Humanism is not a single theory of secondary education; it does not move or operate as one. Rather it is a complex of theories held together by a more or less common conception of the Good Life, of the good man, of the good society. Though it is heir to an ancient heritage, it is not a static theory in the sense that it has made no progress. In varying degrees, Humanism has advanced. But that advance is not an even one; it extends in range from the relative reactionism of Hutchins and Foerster, who see in the movement of the last several centuries a departure from the Human Tradition—from the spirituality, from closeness to God and the whole of mankind which characterized man in the later Middle Ages and immediately after—and who would bring man back to that spiritual state in the material setting of the twentieth century, to the relative modernism of Kandel, who sees twentieth-century industrial America as necessarily giving expression to a changed world-spirit, which however, must continue to cherish the dominant Humanist values. In some respects the principles of Humanism as a whole can be summarized and criticized; in other respects, reference must be made to particular Humanists.

Humanism regards the present world as essentially continuous with the past. In some respects we are distinctive. In the utilization of nature for the advancement of material life, great strides have been made. We have, too, speeded up our general tempo of living. But human nature has not changed essentially. The highest human values have not changed; the meanings that human intelligence brings to the interpretation of its own experience are in large part not new. The ancient wisdom of mankind is still applicable to an understanding of the world today; what Plato wrote has yet considerably more import for human living than the most recent conclusions of the latest sociologist. Humanism, therefore, is unable to understand why modern man is so impressed by the newness of his own situation, why he is so willing to turn his back upon the accumulated wisdom of mankind.

According to Humanism, the present unhappy world-situation has been brought on not so much by inherent economic difficulties as by a general lapse and breakdown in the morale of people. Economic difficulties may be in the background of the present strife, but human beings of intelligence, courage, and moral integrity can overcome such difficulties. The fact that they have not done so is testimony to their weakness. It is not too late; it is never too late. Men of courage and good-will do not succumb in the struggle with material things.

The machine has been a factor in inducing the present crisis; there has been a temporary disturbance in the economic situation—in production, labor, distribution. In this emergency many people have found an opportunity to strike a blow at the humanistic tradition of mankind. Two groups of people have done so. There are the people who lack courage and human dignity and faith in themselves as individuals: these have turned to Communism as a panacea, and have wrought mischief by breeding class hatreds, by setting one group against another, by making man lose faith in himself, by setting up materialism as God. On the other hand there are those who, in pride of physical power, have turned savagely against the spiritual values of civilization which it has taken mankind many centuries to build—liberty, justice, peace, lawful living, tolerance. These would revert to a kind of barbarism and barbaric mode of living. In some cases they have created myths of a super-race or a super-state to help them gain their ends. Each in its own way, Communism and Fascism would brutalize man and degrade him.

Humanism sponsors or supports no special social program by which the present situation could be improved. It distrusts all made-to-order social formulas as panaceas. The present crisis is acute, but in the past there have been acute crises, too. The way to emerge from a crisis successfully is to "keep your head" and to do the very best thinking of which you are capable. Do not refrain from taking action, but remember that he is wisest who "makes haste slowly," who does not break with the good in order to eradicate the bad, who conforms to the principle that social improvement cannot of necessity be rapid. Beyond this, Humanism offers no specific suggestions. It is, indeed, likely to be irritated by those who would act in a hurry, and who would seek "overnight" to make things better, who offer utopian schemes to banish poverty forever, to make toil unnecessary, and so forth. It is vexed by the rampant social disorder of our age, by the inadequate concern shown for the moral and spiritual lapses of mankind, by the extreme preoccupation with material difficulties. It feels that, in many cases, there is a tendency to exaggerate the difficulty of enduring material hardships; that, on the whole, we have overpainted the picture of lack of economic opportunity, of the difficulty of securing employment, of the misfortunes of the rising generation. And it decries the tendency to condone moral wrongs on the ground that their roots are economic.

On the whole, Humanism does not offer much consolation or much hope to those who are victims of the present social-economic situation. It takes the long-time, historical view, and, while in general terms it may be sound, it is not adapted to human living and thinking in terms of each man's life-span. Humanism tends to forget that its generalizations, while very likely valid as historical generalizations, lose a great deal of their force when transferred to particular situations. It may be true that no specific formulas for social betterment are completely good; but such social betterment as is realizable can be realized only by the incessant application of these formulas, though each is imperfect. Human intelligence does not operate in a vague, general way, but in terms of specific plans, applied one after another. While no one plan may be perfect, these plans possess an accumulated validity that far surpasses their individual validity. Even when viewed historically, human betterment must be said to have been attained, not merely through moral fortitude and physical endurance and a vague trust in the ultimate triumph of the human spirit, but through intelligence applying itself vigorously to the mastery of specific and particular situations, buttressed by moral faith and physical fortitude. And such active application of intelligence on the part of many different individuals itself militates against the maintenance of the perfect order that

Humanism desires so much. Human beings clash because human intelligences clash, and the only way to avoid some resultant disorder is to command human intelligence to desist from activity. It is inevitable that human difficulties produce social movement and social unrest or, as the Humanists see it, disorder. It is hardly possible to live in a difficult economic period without upsetting even some rightfully cherished values. In the first place, values do not declare themselves to be invalid or in need of important modification: such values have to be discovered, and until the "guilty" ones are isolated, a great many others are suspect. In the second place, values do not operate in discrete ways. They belong together in a certain way of life. Turn against some of the values and you disturb the entire way of life. The continuous order which the Humanists crave is, therefore, impossible of maintenance; any difficulty, and the corresponding social action taken to resolve it, upsets the social equilibrium.

Humanist values tend to emphasize man's differentness in nature. The highest good lies in those things to which there is no parallel in the rest of living nature, and which, in their ends, distinguish man from other living things. Thus, Humanism would rate the ability to read and enjoy books above the power to provide for bodily comforts (assuming that a man did both), the skill involved in carrying on abstract mathematical processes above the skill in foraging for food, building a fire, and devising and using tools, the art involved in painting a picture above the art involved in designing and erecting a simple dwelling. The highest life of man is conceived in terms of its differentness from nature, and human worth is so estimated.

It is evident that human beings differ greatly in their ability to live on these terms. Since such are the criteria of human worth, however, men must be regarded as greatly unequal in their essential worth as human beings. Humanism recognizes an aristocracy in human life. By the same token, the Good Life of man is essentially an individual thing. Human beings must be regarded as individuals, and evaluated in two ways—according to their potentiality to live the Good Life, and according to the degree to which they realize this potentiality.

Unlike Experimentalism, Humanism does not regard individuality as a qualitatively unique product of a social experiencing process, expressing essentially common tendencies in unique configurations. Individuality emerges essentially from the degree of intelligence a person possesses; quantitative differences in intellectual capacity result in qualitatively different kinds of living. Humanism does not hesitate to pronounce some individuals inferior to others. The Humanist society is not a closely welded thing; it is a congregation of individuals. Individuals live together in harmony because to live in that way expresses a human attribute. Cooperation in social living is not, however, on the basis of unlimited "give-and-take": man remembers that he is first of all an individual with an intelligence, standards, tastes of his own. But the good man is undoubtedly also the social man, who contributes to the well-being of society as Humanism conceives it.

The Humanist concept of intelligence places a correspondingly great emphasis on the exclusiveness of man, on the differentness from nature that man is supposed to represent. The intelligent man is not only effective in material things, but—more important—he can aspire to live a life of the mind, and express his humanness in ethical and spiritual ways. Intelligence consists not primarily in an aptitude for mastering material nature, but in an ability to rise above material things and to live independently of nature according to values created by man himself (or intuitively apprehended by man). The Humanist conception of the Good Life places great emphasis on non-material aspects of living; the Humanist conception of intelligence unites with this conception of the Good Life in fostering an aristocratic view of human society.

Democracy consists in a recognition of the integrity of the individual, his rights as a free human being, and of the fact also that the individual is prior to society in importance. The Humanist regards democracy as a necessary compromise in a society of essentially unequal individuals— a compromise that assures each person of a certain dignity to which he as a human being is entitled, and which recognizes his integrity as an individual even when he lives in society. The alternative to democracy would be rule by force (either by the *aristoi* or by the masses) or anarchy, both of which alternatives Humanism finds repugnant. But democracy must be reconciled with the fact of human inequality. The best kind of democracy is that in which the course of social action is constantly influenced by the judgment of the most intelligent. Humanism, therefore, regards democracy that identifies political equality with general equality as an evil—an unnatural thing—that in time is bound either to despoil the individual of his natural rights or to uproot society itself.

Humanism sets a high standard of living for each individual human being. He must be effective in the mastery of material things, but that is only the starting point. He must have a mind of his own—a private life of the mind into which the world is not allowed to intrude—and spiritual resources of his own. He must be emotionally a refined, esthetically a sensitive person. He must be meticulous in person and in dress, distinguished in manner and speech, particular in his tastes, discriminating in his choice of friends. The Humanist individual has dignity, forbearance, and restraint. He is a sympathetic, socially-cooperative person, without at the same time being a person who regards all things as subject to his concern. He is not a "hail-fellow-well-met." He has sympathy for human beings but never allows it to degenerate into sentimentalism. He is not likely to forget at any time that he is a person in his own right.

The Humanist concept of the good man stands or falls on the fundamental Humanist postulate that the essence of humanness is in man's distinctiveness or differentness in nature. In making this postulate Humanism goes further than is justifiable; it seems to overlook that man is in the important respects continuous with nature, that the respects in which he is different, although they stand out very prominently, are the lesser. Man is born, lives, matures, ages, dies. Birth and death are the two greatest events in human life, and in these respects man is alike with nature. Man must have air and light and nourishment and rest and freedom from disease, and in these respects man is alike with nature. Humanism tends also to emphasize too much the differences among human beings and to ignore the fact that human beings are more essentially alike than they are unlike. They are members of a single biological species, and resemble each other in their most dominant characteristics. Moreover, each is endowed by nature with a life which is his to be lived, and in that respect each is the equal of all others. Beside this paramount equality, such inequalities as even those in quality of thinking that people can achieve, in emotional refinement, in esthetic sensitiveness, are relatively minor. Consequently the Humanist conception of the good, its conception of intelligence, tend to emphasize the esoteric qualities in man, the exclusiveness of mankind as a class and of man as an individual. One must grant the Humanist doctrine that man's living should aspire above the material, but Humanism seems to slough off material existence as if it were no problem.[1] (Even a quick look about should suffice to convince Humanism that if a little intelligence could be spared from the "finer things in life" and put to work in aiding man in his material problems, it would be worthily employed.) Material living (which cannot be separated from ethical and spiritual living, contrary to what Humanism seems to imply) calls for the exercise of man's greatest intelligence, and it calls for the exercise of a great many abilities. It is difficult to set up a hierarchy of human abilities when so many types of abilities are required for the maintenance of life.

The fact that human beings are unequal with respect to abstract thinking ability, emotional refinement, and moral and esthetic sensitivity, has been known to man probably since the beginning of his social existence. But along with the recognition of human inequality in these respects, there has come to be recognized a much greater and more important kind of equality—the essential equality of all men as human beings. The element of inequality cannot be ignored, but the main fact of essential equality also cannot be set aside (as Humanism tries to do). The Humanist seems to disregard the greater equality for the lesser inequalities. (It must be remembered that human beings are unequal in a great many particular respects—in height, weight, vigor, physical beauty, sex appeal, etc., but the Humanist would not dream of setting up these as criteria of human goodness.)

The Humanists' conception of democracy is, in their own terms, untenable. Maintaining at all times the general principle of human inequality, they cannot also recognize the principle of political equality, and accord it any respect. How can a person who persists in believing that his neighbor is inferior to himself in all the essential qualities that go to make up a human being, still respect the latter's political judgment, and happily abide by his decisions? Especially vulnerable is the Humanist who persists in maintaining that a sizable portion of humanity is altogether ineducable. Indeed, the assurance offered by this

[1] The reader will recall that this fallacy may be traced back to Plato, who would have used the least intelligent to create a class of workers for his ideal society.

person of his regard for the principle of political equality must be viewed with suspicion. Such assurance places too large a strain upon human credulity. To regard people as utterly incapable of attaining true humanness, and at the same time to agree to extend to them the privilege of an equal share in the government of society is to effect a reconciliation of mutually incompatible ideas that is truly heroic.

We come now to the educational theory of Humanism. The criticisms that Humanism levels at American education are harsh and sweeping; yet they do not seem to be without foundation. Humanism charges American education with being shallow, Philistine, utilitarian. Education caters to the mass, and adopts the standards of the mass. It ignores the fact of human individuality, the fact of the inequality of man; and the people who suffer chiefly are those whom society can least afford to neglect—the bright. It seems to possess no character of its own, and allows itself to drift with the tide: at a time of moral laxity, when true values have become obscured, education registers no protest, but reflects the very qualities that are so weakening American civilization.

The secondary school has been guilty of all these mistakes. It admits all individuals on a uniform basis, making little distinction among them. The mediocre set the tone of its work. The curriculum is a sprawling affair having no inner consistency or intellectual gradation. It is parcelled out in small allotments called subjects, each pursued for a short period of time. Many courses lack real intellectual content. The quality of the teaching is, on the whole, poor. And dominating the entire structure is a ridiculous system of credits which often obscures the fact that no true education is taking place. The main function of the school, which is to bring the student into intellectual contact with a worthwhile, educative curriculum, and to help him to grow in it and through it, is not attained.

The validity of much of this criticism, even if it seems excessively strong in tone, is undeniable. Humanism renders a great service to education by consistently pointing out some of its shortcomings, and by constantly striving to induce it to elevate its standards. As a minority point of view, in recent years, Humanism has been an important factor in stimulating American education to examine itself, and it has been instrumental in getting under way some important educational experiments.² One cannot agree with all the criticisms made by Humanism (one is puzzled, for example, as to why Humanism so consistently singles out the bright student for its special concern when it is evident that not only the bright are neglected), but one must, in general, admit the force of the Humanist charges. The counter-proposals that Humanism makes, however, are most of them much less easy to accept. With regard to these proposals Humanism does not speak as one, and therefore it is necessary to refer to the several existing points of view.

Underlying all of them is the Humanist psychology, or, more accurately, the Humanist psychologies (for three of them are discernible). Humanist psychologies have this much in common—they are all empirical. Humanism distrusts the intrusion of science into human affairs; it is much more willing to trust its own insight into experience. Accordingly, Humanist psychologies consist (for the most part) of such facts and generalizations, gathered out of the past educational experience, as they consider valid.

There is, first, a psychology which (1) postulates a theory of formal discipline, and (2) assumes as a fact that there are people in considerable numbers who are inherently ineducable. (At this point, only this latter principle will be critically considered; the doctrine of formal discipline will be discussed presently.) The assumption of human ineducability is supposed to be substantiated by these two facts: (1) some people have in the past failed to profit from subject-matter that should have given them mental training; (2) countries that have put into effect a broad program of popular education have not, by virtue of that fact, become better. Judging by the facts that are offered as evidence, the assumption of ineducability is still, to put it very mildly, a daring assumption. From the evidence presented, one is quite justified in reaching very different conclusions: (1) that the doctrine of formal discipline is untenable; or (2) that the subject-matter presented was not appropriate for training the minds of the particular students who

² The reference here is to Learned's Pennsylvania Study, the reports of which stimulated anew discussion of the whole question of "credits," and from which several experiments in education have developed; the experiment sponsored by Hutchins at St. John's College; Kandel's forceful criticisms of Progressive education which undoubtedly stimulated the latter to remove some inconsistencies in its doctrines.

did not profit from it; or (3) that, in the countries which did not profit from a broad program of popular education, the people were misled by bad leaders, and it is the latter, therefore, who should be called ineducable. Furthermore, the case for ineducability is not made any better when the proponent of it (who, by the way, consistently denounces the intrusion of science into thinking about human affairs) points to the intelligence testing done during the World War as evidence of the fact that many adults are intellectually very limited. A better acquaintance with the scientific psychology which he so decries would have served to reveal to him that the early intelligence test is among the most vulnerable of the productions of educational science. In any event, so important a conclusion as that of ineducability should hardly be adduced from mere negative evidence. It needs to be established positively.

A second Humanist psychology accepts the theory of mental training by formal discipline, but veers away from the doctrine of ineducability. It does, however, emphasize the fact of great inequality in human abilities. It frankly states that verbal and symbolic materials do not serve to discipline intellectually-inferior people. These people require more concrete materials, perhaps of the general nature of work-activities, which, even if they do not train the mind very much, at least equip the learners with knowledges and skills they will need in the course of practical living.

The doctrine of formal discipline is very weakly supported. The theory that mind can be trained is, in the judgment of the writer, one that has sound foundation in experience. But the theory of formal discipline has not. Even if Humanists refuse to accept the verdict of educational science in rejecting formal discipline, they still need to justify their theory by offering positive empirical evidence for it. While their theory cannot be proved to have been unsuccessful with such intellectually-superior students as were not repelled by its content (and one must insist that even in these cases it has never positively been proved successful), it has almost invariably been proved unsuccessful with the less bright students. The Humanists would be among the first to maintain that schooling is not the whole of education, and that bright students are quite capable of educating themselves. It is quite possible, therefore, that with such students the formal studies of the school merely "streamlined" an education that was already taking place. One cannot merely make assertions; it is necessary to support assertions by evidence, if not scientific then empirical, that seems conclusive. The formal disciplinarians tend merely to repeat themselves; it is necessary to establish once and for all what validity their contention has. One can see the temptation occasionally to go back to formal discipline: disgust with intellectually-feeble, poorly-organized educational materials is almost enough to make one yearn for intellectually-challenging, well-ordered materials, such as formal discipline does provide. But to remain a reputable theory of educational development, formal discipline must explain itself in much more positive and acceptable terms than it has so far.

The third psychology evident in the Humanistic system, that which holds that mind is disciplined through working with a content of ideas rather than with formal materials, is on much more solid ground. One is compelled seriously to entertain it because of the difficulty of accepting the remaining alternative, that is, that mind cannot be disciplined at all. If a person, in the course of an educative process, cannot be trained to behave more intelligently in the future than he otherwise would, then of what educative value is experience? Is it merely to yield "learning results" which are usable only at the time and in the place in which they occur, and never again thereafter? In whatever terms training that results in more adequate dealing with future experience takes place, whether in terms of specific knowledges and skills with which an individual is equipped or in terms of broader ideas and more general methods, one is justified in saying that such training constitutes "mental discipline." The Humanist psychology at present under discussion maintains that mental discipline is in terms of systems of broad ideas and general methods of intellectual procedure rather than of particular knowledges and skills. The writer for his own reasons is inclined to concur in this belief. But beyond granting the soundness of this general premise of Humanism one may not go. Humanists make the mistake of regarding what seems to be a common-sense argument for the existence of mental discipline as the equivalent of an entire "psychology of mental discipline." They rest content with what may be regarded as a safe statement of fact, and fail to provide any coherent account or picture of the human mind in action.

In general, those Humanists who would offer valuable,[8] intellectually-stimulating activities to the bright students and who would then go to the other extreme and offer intellectually-meager work-activities to the un-bright, have much to answer for. Almost down to the present, secondary education has been selective; it has dealt with the intellectually-gifted. These have shown that they can respond to the abstract, verbal, academic studies (whether or not they are actually *educated* by them); those less gifted intellectually have shown that they cannot. But Humanists have not really bothered to prepare educative materials to which the latter can respond. Such young people are now being told that they must choose between the devil and the deep sea: on the one hand there are studies which they admittedly cannot master, on the other hand there are work-activities which they can master but in the educativeness of which Humanists do not greatly believe. It seems that Humanists display an altogether unwarranted lack of patience with human beings. The task to which they must address themselves is that of *educating* people, not of promoting or protecting their favorite subjects.

The Humanists least subject to criticism are those very few who refuse to commit themselves to any special array of subjects but who insist that whatever subject-matter is employed shall be taught with a view of disciplining the mind of the student for whom it is intended. These seek educational materials, important for intelligent living in our culture, that shall yet be appropriate to the intellectual abilities of each student, and insist that through such materials each must develop a large fund of important meanings and intellectual methods. It is more than likely that ultimately education will swing around to this position: that educational materials must be rich in ideas, that they must be selected with reference to the culture in which the learner lives, that they must be suited to the educational capacities, aptitudes, and needs of the learner, that they must be taught in such a way as permanently to influence the mind in the direction of more intelligent present and future living.

In the main, Humanism supports the principle of universal sec-

[8] That is, valuable in the judgment of these Humanists. The Humanists here referred to are Foerster, and to a lesser extent Hutchins and Learned. *Vide* pp. 306 ff.

ondary education. It insists, however, that secondary education be differentiated according to individual ability. Each individual must be educated to an extent that is proportionate to his ability, within the common limits of the secondary period. Up to a certain minimal level of educational achievement all must be raised; beyond this level each is to rise as far as he can. Each student is to be provided with materials that (presumably) are appropriate for him. Equality of opportunity is not to be interpreted as identity of opportunity; individuals are not to be treated in the same way. Beyond the point of secondary education rigorous selection must be exercised—only the more capable are to be admitted into institutions of higher learning to receive advanced training as individuals and future leaders of society.

While one must agree, in a general way, with this idea, one must also take exception to particular principles here involved. Humanism has put its finger on one of the chief weaknesses of American education when it points to the prevailing commonness or sameness in educational expectancy, and the general mediocrity which that fosters. But secondary education should be differentiated not alone according to capacity for abstract thinking, which is more or less what the Humanists mean by the term "ability," but as far as is possible according to whatever potentially valuable capacities and aptitudes the student possesses. Even the Humanists who recognize that education is more than an affair of training in abstract thinking power have not yet reached the point where they are willing to grant equality to bases of differentiation other than that which was traditionally expressed by the ability to "read, write, and reckon." One objects to the tendency manifest within Humanism to interpret differentiation as the separation of those it conceives to be the superior from the inferior. Humanism would do well to cease emphasizing the need for differentiating secondary education so as to afford the superior students all the advantages to which they are "entitled." Regardless of whether "brightness" alone actually stamps a person as a superior human being (and one must file a large reservation here), it is not seemly for Humanism (to judge it by its own criterion of modesty which it regards as an attribute of humanness) to display such special and unflagging concern for the superior person and such barely-concealed contempt for the inferior. One would be much more impressed by the Humanist demand for a differentiated secondary education if one did not have a sneaking suspicion that Humanism is primarily interested in separating the "sheep" from the "goats."

One is struck also by an apparent contradiction that persists in the thinking of some Humanists. Insisting that education to be genuine must be differentiated according to intellectual capacity, and maintaining also that there is wide variation in the intellectual capacities of students, several of the Humanists, in consideration of the demands made by our present complex civilization, propose that a common terminus be established for secondary education at the age of eighteen or twenty, and imply that education up to that point be made compulsory for all. If individuals do vary widely in intellectual capacity, and if education is to be truly differentiated according to this capacity, then it is reasonable to believe that the limits of the intellectual capacity of some students will be reached prior to the official end of the secondary-school period. Assuming that a student's intellectual limit is reached when he is fourteen years of age, what does he do in school up to the age of eighteen or twenty? Humanism maintains that education is essentially training for intellectual power, and that capacity for this power is not subject to growth but is inherited and already fixed in a person at birth. Of what value is "educational activity" in school when the limit of one's intellectual capacity has already been reached? (If the limit of one's capacity is never reached, and capacity can be, though ever so gradually, extended, then Humanism must surrender or greatly alter its aristocratic conception of individual differences, and admit that, given sufficient time for education, human beings can be brought to more nearly uniform intellectual levels.) There is no point, therefore, in proposing that the limit of education be raised for all to the age of eighteen or twenty. The school is not a custodial institution. It would indeed be a descent from the lofty educational principles of Humanism if it came to regard the provision of housing and guardianship as a large educational function. The uncompromising stand of Social Realism, in this connection, seems to be more logical: without postulating that there are definite limits beyond which intellectual development cannot go, Social Realism urges that a student be retained in school as long as he shows promise of making returns to society (the Social-Realist criterion of value) proportionate to its investment in him, and that when more individually-appropriate methods of secondary education are developed, all students shall be retained in school for a longer period.

As would be expected from the existence of differing Humanist psychologies, Humanism offers different plans for a secondary-school curriculum. A few common general principles of curriculum and method are the following: Educative materials must be well-organized for developmental purposes—they must have relatedness and continuity, they must progress in difficulty, in depth, and in importance of meaning; they must extend over a long enough period of time to allow the learner to mature through them. The best curriculum is a simple curriculum—one that brings the learner most directly into contact with the educative materials, and allows him to remain there. Educational machinery must be simplified as much as possible. Anything that obstructs the essential educative process is bad, and should be removed (and, of course, the prevailing credit system would fall within that category). Humanism is interested in preserving the integrity of the individual as a learner. It distrusts, therefore, mass education and all schemes and devices that may result in an individual's sinking his identity within a group—large schools, large classes, mass programming, mass promotion. Education is a simple affair between the learner and the curriculum. This does not mean that each learner is to get a special curriculum, but that out of a common large curriculum each learner must obtain especially those elements that most specifically fit his intellectual requirements. The individual learns better by himself or in small group conferences. Standards of attainment are to be high; education gets nowhere by coddling the learner. The best measure of attainment is not the periodic examination on a small "subject" area that has been thoroughly covered, but the general examination testing grasp of important and related ideas within a comprehensive area. In its conception of the teacher, Humanism emphasizes personal values. The teacher is the inspirational figure. The ideal teacher is the ideal Humanist person as well as the good scholar—the well-bred, cultivated man who, by personal worth as well as by the knowledge that he imparts, influences the learner toward education.

One could more readily embrace these generally admirable principles if they were not wedded to the typical Humanist subject-matter. For the Humanist preference for educative matter (even when it is non-formalistic) is inclined, like its preference for people, to be aristocratic. Humanism is partial to the abstract, the linguistic, and the symbolic. It prefers the rare to the common, the exacting to the manageable. It seems to be disdainful of the practical, often without educational justification. In recent years, when it became apparent that much of the older subject-matter was totally unsuited to the demands of those who were being educated, Humanism has broadened very greatly the area of studies to which it extends educational recognition. But it has not changed very much in its essential attitudes; it still regards the time-honored subjects as superior. For some reason the history of art still is more important than the history of technics, skill in a foreign language a more desirable attainment than skill in practical mechanics.

In summary, it may be said that the strength of Humanism lies particularly in its exposure of the many limitations of the recent American education. It brings to American education some of the respect for the intellectual, some of the regard for the individual taste, that have been notably lacking. It is admirable in its insistence upon raising the general standard of education, and, beyond that, the cultural level of the American people. It is sound in its attack upon Babbittry, upon provincialism, upon the native tendency to smugness and complacency. It is admirable in its attempt to elevate man's faith in the human spirit, man's faith in human possibilities. It is wholesome in its attempt to foster a regard for what is sound in tradition in an age that is possibly overconscious of its newness and differentness.

Humanism must be criticized for its undemocratic tendencies, for its condescending attitude toward human beings, for its tendency to overemphasize the fact of human inequality. One must ask Humanism, point-blank, precisely what good purpose this overemphasis is meant to serve (other, perhaps, than as a corrective to current tendencies to overlook the fact of human difference, and Humanism goes far beyond *that*). It must be criticized for its failure to commit itself to a definite, positive program of social improvement, and for sponsoring general remedies which sometimes remind one of Marie Antoinette's reputed answer to a complaint that the people had no bread. It must be criticized for its empirical stand with respect to its psychology—in that respect it is almost anti-rational. If Humanism wishes to obtain a real hearing from the American people, it must, in the next few years, produce a psychology founded upon more than a few generalizations from the past. It must be criticized for its failure to be more inventive with regard to educational materials. Instead of remaining as the apologist for the old educational curriculum, Humanism, with its genuinely high standards of life and of education, would do well to busy itself with the creation of a new one.

SOCIAL EVOLUTIONISM

Social Evolutionism regards the present social situation as one of those crises through which man, in his history, not infrequently has passed. It is an occurrence bound to happen periodically. In man's upward evolution the crises are continuously becoming more drastic and severe, since each new crisis finds man on a higher level of adjustment and involves the modification of more numerous and more difficult adaptations. But man has always weathered these crises, and the end of each has found him with new modes of living that have ultimately turned out to be to his advantage.

The basis of the current social crisis is economic, and it has been brought on by the emergence of a machine civilization. We have not yet oriented our ways of living and thinking to the machine. We have not yet become used to the possibilities of an economy of abundance. Naturally there are conflicts. But the bad situation is aggravated considerably by the fact that we seem to have unlearned many of the lessons of experience. We seem to have forgotten that man must at all times consider the welfare of society as well as his own, that people must pull together for the common good, and not strive against each other. We seem to have forgotten how necessary are the qualities of self-discipline, of balance, of moral strength, especially in emergencies such as the present one. These are lessons we should have learned from experience. Our society has long had within it seeds of weakness, and in recent years we have been further weakened by false prophets who, by preaching individualism and self-interest, have impaired our morale and sapped our strength. It is in this rather than in the inherent economic situation that the danger lies.

The present situation calls for a certain amount of economic readjustment. There is need for a more equitable distribution of the material benefits that have been made possible by the machine. Social Evolutionism is, on the whole, friendly to any social action that would serve to bring this about, provided that such action did not at the same time threaten further to weaken the moral fiber of the American people. In any such emergency as the present, a solution does not come all at once. It is not likely that any single plan or program would alleviate the difficulty. A considerable period of social experimentation will have to ensue. Social Evolutionism is distrustful, therefore, of any comprehensive program that might be used as a substitute for an evolutionary procedure. It is distrustful of schemes that would undermine self-reliance, the need and the desire for work. It is inherently conservative and fearful of introducing anything that upsets tried and familiar ways of doing things, if these ways have already been proved to possess some validity. Even if a new scheme were ultimately to prove successful, Social Evolutionism would regard it with caution all the way through until its ultimate success could no longer be questioned. Social Evolutionism is somewhat jealous of the treasures we have accumulated from the past and would not risk losing them. Insofar as it has a guide for the future, it is the record of yesterday.

Like Humanism, Social Evolutionism views human problems in cosmic terms. Its long acquaintance with history has served to temper its concern about the immediate future. It knows that man has worked himself out of difficulties in the past, and will again in the future. It is unsympathetic to social schemes that emphasize the newness of our situation, and the need for far-reaching but previously untried action. Like Humanism, therefore, it suffers from the fact that it has not oriented itself to human dimensions. It is hard to tell a starving, homeless person that he is starving and homeless because we are in a period of cosmic readjustment, and that we cannot hurry the process of readjustment because history shows that human progress has always been evolutionary; it is hard to tell this even to the housed and employed, who feel perpetual insecurity hovering over them, and frequently the pinch of real need. It may really be that history, which is a description of human affairs in the past, is inapplicable to the guidance of the future (not the understanding, but the guidance) because of the different scale and dimensions used; and that all those who look to history for guidance are bound to be misled. Theoretically there is no reason why the historian, looking back over the long sweep of time, should fail to see that individual lives are not dominated by majestic events but by the petty problems that crowd every hour. Social Evolutionism, however, has not done this. While its social attitudes are, therefore, positive in the main, it is likely to look askance at anyone who would "take time by the fore-lock." Most people worship God; many, however, worship science, and some worship history. When the last happens, and the "dead hand of the past" is allowed to paralyze thinking and action in the present, one is almost tempted to agree with the famous American who exclaimed that history was "bunk."

Unlike Humanism, however, Social Evolutionism is sympathetic to the tendency for an increasing socialization of human life. It is inherently social in its point of view, and sees nothing to fear in events that promise to bring people together in greater interdependence, provided again that such interdependence does not rob the individual of needed energy and initiative. Social Evolutionism regards society and not the individual as the unit of human life: man's life is, of course, his own, and he is born to live for himself, but except in society, man is pitifully incomplete. It is concerned, therefore, that in the immediate future the last traces of individualism of a kind that interferes with societal living be eliminated.

Social Evolutionism sees the good man as a product of social tendencies. It is not very much concerned with what dispositions, tendencies, or "capacities" the individual comes into the world, so long as he learns to get along in society. Of his chances of doing that (provided he is physiologically a normal person), it has not the slightest doubt. Intelligence is something with which society helps to equip the individual; when a person has learned all that society can tell him about how to live (or at least enough so that he can get along in it), he becomes intelligent. Society is the great equalizer of human beings. Social Evolutionism regards the good society as that which makes a strong effort to take systematic account of the learnings that it has to impart, and which imparts them to all its individuals. Society is, of course, the agency that makes possible man's progress by social evolution: a good society, performing its function well, makes possible a *more rapid* evolution and one that is consistently progressive. Social

Evolutionism, therefore, is inclined to be very impatient with anything that threatens to upset the societal equilibrium. Such an attitude makes it somewhat suspicious of the individual who "starts things," who breaks away from convention, even if in theory it is forced to acknowledge that this is the way in which progress is made.

What is admirable about Social Evolutionism is its genuine respect for each person as a human being, for the common man—whom, however, it does not condescendingly regard as "common." (In this respect Social Evolutionism, in the judgment of the writer, is superior to Experimentalism, which is inclined to become sentimental about the idea of "individuality" at the same time that it offers just cause for strong suspicion that it would give short shrift to any "individual" who held views contrary to its own fundamental convictions.) In this lies the democratic character of Social Evolutionism, and it is truly democratic, without reservations and without any sophistical constructions. Social Evolutionism is interested in each person in terms of what he becomes, and each person is, with the assistance of society, capable of reaching full stature as a human being. It disputes with Humanism the latter's interpretation of equality of opportunity as equity of opportunity. (It would soon become very apparent to Humanism that equity of opportunity is not equality of opportunity if someone decided to institute equity on the basis of race, religion, color of skin, etc., in place of its self-chosen intellectual basis.) Each person, by his inherent right as a human being, is deserving of every opportunity and every assistance to reach his full stature. Human beings are essentially equal. But Social Evolutionism, in emphasizing this essential equality, does not ignore the reality of individual differences. It does not subscribe to the doctrine of unlimited perfectibility of man, but it does uphold the principle that every man can be helped to live intelligently in his social environment (insofar as society as a whole is itself able to do so). It makes war upon that faction within scientific education that has exaggerated the significance of individual differences, and, on that basis, developed deterministic principles.

The meaning of democracy, according to Social Evolutionism, lies in faith in man and belief in human equality. In order that it may be possible to realize this theoretical equality, Social Evolutionism senses the need for a fairer distribution of economic opportunities and resources. Its inherent conservatism, however, coupled with the fact that it genuinely fears that man may be deprived of the necessity for self-reliance, personal initiative, and enterprise so essential for "survival," exercises a limiting influence on its campaign for the economic reform of society. Social Evolutionism does not go very far in pointing the way toward necessary economic rearrangement. And this is a great failing, because no amount of theorizing about human equality will itself effect this equality when economic handicaps are so great.

The ideal Social Evolutionist is a person of strength and character. He is self-reliant, self-disciplined, industrious, and socially-conscious. There is little about him that is aristocratic; in all likelihood, he is a self-made man. His intelligence is attracted to the common things of the world about him. He probably cannot quote from the classics, but he knows a good deal of what is of immediate import to his living. Because social living demands these, he is not without the social graces or personal refinement; but these are never allowed to become a fetish, nor to appear as an end in themselves. To a greater extent than Social Realism (which also places emphasis upon society as against the individual), Social Evolutionism emphasizes the need for a larger measure of personal independence in thought and action directed at common social ends. Its concept of socialness does not contain in like degree the implication of *commonness of movement* in thinking and in action. Society is the individual's source of strength and the thing into which he puts back his strength; but while that strength endures, it is primarily vested in the individual's own person and exercised by himself. In contrast with Experimentalism especially, Social Evolutionism seems to demand of its individual a quality of ruggedness, an ability to face and endure hardship, a willingness to undergo self-sacrifice.

Like the ideal individual, the ideal Social-Evolutionist society is marked by characteristics of self-discipline, of respect for law and orderly procedure, of regard for the welfare of all individuals, of ability to be relatively self-reliant and self-sufficient. This society is different from the aristocratic society of Humanism, with its classes of "betters" and "inferiors," and different, indeed, from the noisy crowd of "self-expressing" individuals which the Experimentalist ideal of society in truth tends to suggest. It is a society of dignified equals, each of whom is conscious alike of his dignity and of his equality. It is a society of men conscious of their power as individuals, and keenly aware of their debt and their responsibility to their society as the source of that power.

Reference to the values governing individual and social conduct brings us to the most important criticism that is to be made of Social Evolutionism, namely, the values which it especially singles out for emphasis. The fundamental tenets upon which Social Evolutionism builds its value-structure are suggested by the theory of human evolution which it postulates: the essential problem of man in cosmic evolution is maintenance of self and improvement under man's own direction; man learns from experience; learnings from experience are essentially acquired adaptations that serve man in his living; man accumulates and stores learnings, and draws upon them for use in the guidance of subsequent living; man transmits learnings, and oncoming generations are greatly the better for receiving them and utilizing them in the conduct of their own living. Values in human living, therefore, are based upon past learnings-from-experience.

One can accept every one of these underlying tenets, and still part company with Social Evolutionism when it begins to make its applications, that is, to identify the values that represent to it the greatest learnings. Thus, Social Evolutionism holds as unquestionable that self-discipline with its attendant implication of self-restraint and self-repression, that the necessity for working hard for whatever one seeks to obtain, that self-denial and the ability stoically to endure discomfort or hardship, are among the most valuable lessons that past experience has conveyed. Without denying that self-discipline is a much needed trait in the human character, one may question whether Social Evolutionism is justified in raising this purely neutral quality into a positive virtue of the highest order and in permitting it to stand by itself, without some proper complement. One can justifiably maintain that, while self-discipline is necessary, a degree of the self-expression which Social Evolutionism regards as the antithesis of self-discipline is also necessary; when self-discipline is carried to the extent that it interferes with the free play of intelligence and imagination, when it becomes obstructive to experimentation whether in science or art or social living, when it exercises an inhibiting effect upon thought or action designed to ameliorate conditions of social injustice, when it enforces adherence to prevailing patterns regardless of their goodness, it is bad. The Spartans were an impressively self-disciplined nation, but it is the easy-going, not very well-disciplined Athenians for whose existence posterity has been thankful. Similar exception may be taken to the other rugged virtues of Social Evolutionism, when they stand alone. If civilization does not mean a progressive easing up of the tension in living, a progressive refinement of some of the more rugged primitive virtues, what does it mean? Where, in the galaxy of Social-Evolutionist values, is provision made for this? A very important weakness of Social Evolutionism is its rather one-sided selection of values for emphasis.

Of course, Social Evolutionism can reply that it is mere common sense that the ability to exercise self-discipline, to sacrifice immediate desires in order to gain long-term ends, to endure severities, to be self-reliant, is more effectual in assuring human survival than many of the amenities, coupled with loss of hardihood and personal independence, that modern civilization has introduced. The reason that earlier civilizations have failed is that they did not possess, in sufficient degree, the hardier virtues. After all, even the Athenians failed to survive as a great culture because they became deficient in these qualities. If that is the line of argument pursued by Social Evolutionism, one must call into question its principal criterion of values. Is survival (in the cultural, not the biological sense) the chief criterion of human values, or even an important criterion? Even if one assumes that self-discipline, etc., assure survival (and in a world of emergents—to use a Social-Evolutionist concept—that is not easy to assume), one may reject survival as the chief criterion of values. Is not Social Evolutionism still indulging its habit of using a historical scale in planning the individual life? Survival in the individual sense is extremely important, but the survival of a culture (presumably until the end of time) is a much less important consideration. Human beings now have it in their power to ensure the biological survival of the individual to a respectable, though not yet biblical, old age through the cooperative planning and execution of what should be congenial tasks. One finds it difficult to become concerned about taking steps to preserve one's hardihood for the improbable benefit of one's remote descendants. The problem in living the individual life then becomes to develop values that complement purely survival values. The problem of our age is to direct our intelligence to the improvement of the conditions that now disturb us, rather than to sharpen by discipline our powers of endurance. The fact is that the values which Social Evolutionism selects for emphasis in guiding human living are, in the main, excessively harsh values. Historically its ideal society comes close to being represented by Rome in the earlier period of the Republic; and this is one of the drabbest cultural epochs for which any teacher ever had to stimulate enthusiasm. Also, one regards with consternation the idea that the Spartan culture might have survived until this day, if its members had continued to be sufficiently self-disciplining.

In justice to Social Evolutionism it must be pointed out that in all likelihood its overemphasis upon the "virile" virtues stems from a conviction that present-day society is suffering from a lack of them. It is also necessary to add that both Humanism and Experimentalism, each in its own way, would do well to adopt, in more moderate degree, some of the values which Social Evolutionism is sponsoring—Humanism in showing greater concern for the material well-being of individuals, Experimentalism in stressing more than it does the need for fortitude and the ability to "take it." But a philosophy of life cannot be accepted and evaluated merely as a corrective or as a complement to something elsewhere presented; it is responsible for designing a way of life which is itself balanced and normal. One feels that Social Evolutionism, preoccupied as it is with the failings of our time, does not offer a complete picture of the Good Life in the modern setting.

In its psychology, Social Evolutionism leans toward the organismic or Gestalt school, without accepting all of the latter's tenets (for example, the principle of closure). It is disturbed by the fact that as yet we know little about the workings of the higher mental processes, and fears that we shall not learn about them unless we depart from the conventional mechanistic thinking concerning the nature of mind. We seem to hold as axiomatic that the whole is equal to the sum of its parts. But we know that a chemical compound is not equal merely to the sum of its elements, and mathematics, and lately even psychology, have veered to the idea that the whole is not only the sum of its parts but has the character of a different entity. The mechanistic psychology has approached the study of mind as if that were a summation of simple activities such as we find to be characteristic of lower behavior levels. We have overlooked the fact that mind on higher levels of operation seems to be qualitatively different from that on the lower. No one can duplicate the *modus operandi* of the mind of the genius simply by cumulating the operations of a large number of little minds. The criticism that Social Evolutionism thus makes is so valid as to be unanswerable. The fact is that American psychology, laudably having set out to study the processes of mind from their beginnings, has not progressed very far from the lower levels, and on this basis it has made most of its generalizations.

Although Morrison goes considerably beyond Bagley and Judd in advancing a theory of mental development (and one that the others would not altogether accept), he does not succeed in filling this gap. His theory is based on the assumption that mental development takes place through a continuous and sequential assimilation of unit learnings. A picture of mental organization on higher levels is not given. In view of the absence of any substantial scientific data on the nature of learning on higher levels, one finds it difficult either to favor or to oppose his theory. As Experimentalists, however, have pointed out, his theory presumes a rather passive conception of mind. One must question, moreover, how much real meaning "learnings" conveyed through the kind of verbal subject matter that Morrison sponsors can have for the average student. Finally, the very simplicity and neatness of the picture that Morrison presents, unsubstantiated as it is by scientific data, renders it suspect.

Bagley and Judd are not fully ready to advance their own theory of the higher mental processes, but await the results of further research and study. They seek to stimulate scientific psychology to undertake such research. They feel some progress has been made in the last few years: at least we have become conscious of the need of knowing what takes place on the higher mental levels. For the present they are willing to offer some suggestions based upon experience. They are certain that, on higher levels, mind works in terms of patterns of ideas. Learnings are conceptualized—they exist in an abstract state. Man is able to apply general ideas in concrete ways to specific situations. On these levels, transfer is common or typical. Mind can be trained in the sense that it can be equipped with important ideas and with ways of obtaining them, relating them, releasing, and applying them. On higher levels moral behavior is conceptualized as well; self-discipline depends upon the establishment of intellectual foundations of moral acts. There is little doubt that Bagley and Judd are on the right track; and the appeal to science to substantiate and extend these principles or to refute them is a wholesome appeal.

According to Social Evolutionism mind is created in the course of a learning process. It grows out of the acquisition of learnings that have been gained in the course of human experience. The learnings relate to adjustment. When an individual has learned what the race has learned about making sound adjustment, he himself can adjust—he has achieved "mind." Every individual is capable of achieving mind; he needs only to acquire a sufficient number of learnings. Some individuals are slower than others in doing this, some will very likely never go as far as others, but all can achieve mind sufficiently to serve their life-needs. In this respect, Social Evolutionism is very close to Experimentalism, although it does not share the latter's conviction that learning is *active* experiencing, that a person just does not "assimilate" passively. Both these theories reveal a healthy point of view toward individual differences: without denying that there are differences among individuals (qualitatively and quantitatively), they at the same time reject the ill-advised and unhealthy determinism that has marred the thinking of some of the scientific psychologists. One feels that much of the existing confusion with regard to intelligence may be traced to a confusion of definitions. There are two capacities, in connection with both of which the term "intelligence" is used: a capacity for making adaptive responses as-yet-unknown (that is, prior to learning) with which one is born into the world, and a capacity for making adaptive responses after learning has taken place (that is, after one has had experiences, has acquired meanings, and so forth). The conventional scientific psychology assumes that the second capacity is a perfect realization of the first, that is, that the potential is merely made actual. Not being able to measure the first directly, it measures the second; then makes its conclusions with reference to the first. This ill-founded procedure has done a great deal to injure the morale of American education, and has provided teachers with a universal excuse for poor educational results—the low I. Q. of the pupil. It is to the great credit of Social Evolutionism that it has persistently fought the educational determinism that is the inevitable outgrowth of this procedure. Defining intelligence as a capacity which is the product of both heredity and learning, it is critical of the educational process rather than of the potentialities of the student.

Having done very well up to this point, Social Evolutionism now is guilty of a serious mistake. Having argued convincingly that education is a process of acquiring important learnings out of human experience of the past to help in the control and guidance of the future, Social Evolutionism falls into the error of assuming that the traditional school studies have in some fortunate way gained possession of these learnings, and have them in their keeping. The next step, one might reasonably expect, would be to make a comprehensive canvass of the past and present in human experience to see what learnings are indeed serviceable and necessary in present-day adjustment. And, though on the one hand Social Evolutionism counsels taking this step, it assumes on the other hand that the traditional subjects are, on the whole, what we have been looking for.[4] The result is that the curriculum which Social Evolutionism offers is very largely the curriculum which education has had for a long time, and that has not been notable for its success in educating all individuals.

In its criticism of American education, Social Evolutionism points out that the school has not set itself to combat the weakening tendencies observable in society itself. American society is in a period of confusion attendant upon a critical economic transition. Its morale has suffered badly; its standards have fallen; in many of its leading values and tendencies, it goes contrary to the lessons of experience. At such a time education has chosen to follow suit: it has itself adopted lower standards and adjusted itself to prevailing values. In this it has been aided and abetted by a mechanistic and over-naturalistic psychology, and by weak and misleading pedagogies. Nevertheless Social Evolutionism credits American education with trying to break away from the aristocratic pattern of the past, and with trying to adapt itself to the needs of a democratic people. It is inclined to be indulgent with secondary education for failing at once to proceed according to a pre-

---

[4] As has been pointed out all along, individual Social Evolutionists differ in the degree to which they accept the present curriculum. Judd goes much further than Bagley and Morrison in urging a study of "social trends" to reveal such units of learning as are needed but non-existent in the curriculum today.

arranged plan consistent with its democratic purpose because, to the Social-Evolutionist way of thinking, education must itself develop by an evolutionary pattern. It is pleased that education has looked to science for guidance, but chagrined that science, thus far, has tended to be mechanistic and deterministic. On the whole, its quarrel with American education is not that, according to the standards of the past, education has changed, but that it has submitted to the leadership of false doctrines to guide it in the present.

Social Evolutionism is eager to see removed the last traces of an aristocratic secondary education, both with respect to extension of educational opportunity and attitude toward curriculum materials. The secondary school must become truly a common school. Differences among individuals must be reckoned as differences in method, but not in fundamental educational purpose. The purpose must be the same for all: education for adaptable social living in a highly advanced culture. The curriculum needs to be purged of some of the remains of the aristocratic secondary education—foreign languages, for example. A real conception of general education on the secondary level must be formulated. The curriculum is to be common rather than differentiated, although marginal differentiation is to be permitted. For the most part, materials already existent in the present curriculum are to provide the raw materials of education, although these materials must be reassembled and far better organized for instructional purposes. It is necessary to keep in mind that we are not trying to teach subject-matter, but learnings implicit in subject-matter. Method of instruction must be adapted to the developing intellectual independence of students.

In the matter of vocational training Social Evolutionism is divided, and it is also, one is compelled to say, indecisive and unclear. One senses that Social Evolutionism is not entirely satisfied with the academic studies as a medium of preparing young people for their vocational activities, but (except for Judd) it is unwilling definitely to commit itself to vocational education. Judd emphasizes that there is no reason why vocational education should conflict with general education, why some of the same materials cannot be serviceable to both; but he does not go much beyond this point. Bagley and Morrison state that the secondary school should confine itself to a general (academic) education rather than include vocational education. Yet Morrison, at least, is quick to add that special vocational schools may follow the secondary school. While Bagley disapproves of vocational training as part of the secondary process, it is one's impression that he does not close the door to further discussion on this very important point. Social Evolutionism is undecided, and in conflict with itself. If the school studies really contain all the great learnings needed for successful adjustment (and if subject-matter is formative rather than instrumental in function), then Social Evolutionism should not hesitate to state that no special and direct vocational education is necessary. But Social Evolutionism is not sure of itself: apparently it feels that the vocational problem in modern society is so unique that the great racial learnings contained in the school studies may, perhaps, need to be supplemented by additional direct vocational training. If this is true of the vocational problem, is it also true of the problem of leisure time, of intelligent consumership, etc.?

The fact is that the weakest element in the Social-Evolutionist theory of secondary education is the subject-matter that it offers for the school curriculum, even if that is to be much better organized than formerly. Social Evolutionism offers the same academic studies, only very slightly less academic and bookish than before. Granting for the moment that these studies actually embody the great human learnings, one needs but to recall the recent educational past to wonder when, in the course of the learning process, the learnings really emerge. It is doubtful whether even Morrison's plan for perfect mastery would be of much help: the student might master the subject-matter, but would he also extract the genuine learnings within it? To use one of Morrison's own illustrations, how many algebraic equations does a student have to solve before he himself acquires the mental qualities of precision and balance that are inherent in the equations? One may, indeed, question whether learning to solve algebraic equations necessarily results in the acquisition of these qualities. And if this question has any merit, it points to the larger question of whether it would not be better to offer the important learnings in a more meaningful and immediate context.

In summary, it may be said that Social Evolutionism offers a very carefully considered theory of secondary education, at least up to the point when it begins to deal with the subject-matter of the secondary-school curriculum. Its outstanding merits are two. The first is its genuine democratic spirit, its general social-mindedness, its wholesome attitude toward the problem of individual differences. It regards education not as a luxury, but as a universal necessity; not as a means of dividing humanity further, but as a means of rendering all individuals capable of living the intelligent life. It regards individual differences as a challenge which education must take up, and not as something to which it must surrender. Social Evolutionism views with equanimity the continuous movement of individuals toward closer mutual relationships; it feels that society is but fulfilling its function. It castigates the existing society and the existing education for failing to live up to their obligations to maintain high standards of moral conduct and intellectual achievement.

Its second merit lies in its general psychological orientation—in its conception of intelligence, in its faith in a scientific approach to the study of mental and social behavior, in its dauntless opposition to educational determinism. It views mind as an outcome of an educational process—as something, therefore, that everyone can attain. It seeks to stimulate the scientific study of the higher mental processes, so that we can eventually achieve an effective method of secondary education. Its consistent attack upon an oversimplified, mechanistic psychology has already brought some results.

The defects of Social Evolutionism are, first, that it is one-sided in its choice of values upon which principal emphasis is to be placed. It tends to emphasize negative "goods." The picture it draws of individual and social life is rather forbidding. A second defect is that it does not take a sufficiently clear and strong stand on social issues, that it commits itself to no definite social program, and that it is inherently conservative enough to be suspicious of social programs advanced by others. A third defect is that the curriculum it sponsors is disappointingly traditional, especially in view of its advocacy of a secondary education that prepares all for intelligent living in our present complex civilization.

SOCIAL REALISM

Social Realism regards our present economic and social difficulties not especially as an inevitable or as a regular occurrence in any cosmic scheme of things, but rather as an outcome of a decidedly human failing to read, promptly and intelligently enough, the signs of changing experience. The acquisition of great scientific knowledge and the development of that creature of scientific knowledge, the machine, should have made men more alert and sensitive to the great changes that they portended. It should have been evident that anything that enabled man to extend so greatly the conquest of nature, to telescope time and space, to bring about revolutionary changes in methods of production and distribution of material goods, would have tremendous effects on the manner in which individuals would have to cooperate economically, socially, and politically in the problem of living and earning a living. But man was not sufficiently alert to anticipate these changes and to provide for them, or even to deal with them when they came.

Social Realism favors a program of social action that recognizes the basic economic facts that exist today and seeks to take measures to improve the status, not of a class or of a special group, but of all the people who are adversely affected by the prevailing social situation. It holds that such action would have to take the form of reducing work-hours so as to spread employment, of gearing production to need, of regulating industry in its labor and consumer relations, of eliminating ill-advised competition, of passing extensive legislation of a social-insurance type, and so forth. It recognizes as inevitable that there must be, through the agency of government, greater public control of natural resources, greater regulation and control of production, of capital, and of labor. It is unwilling to scrap the capitalistic structure, being convinced that resort to complete collectivism is for various reasons undesirable. It is willing to place its faith in the judgment of the people so far as to support the principle of a planning society. It feels that the people, knowing what is at stake and knowing what the governing factors are, will be bound to act intelligently. It trusts an *awakened* popular intelligence.

In its economic-social program, Social Realism, although in important particulars its thinking coincides with that of Experimentalism, yet reveals several notable differences. In the first place, it does not contemplate the drastic reconstruction of the economic foundations of society that is suggested in the social theory of several of the Experimentalists, nor does it go as far in the direction of fostering a collectivistic order as appears to be the trend within Experimentalism generally. To some extent this is due to a natural distrust, inherent in the basic philosophy of Social Realism, of prescriptions that would at once set into motion changes, comprehensive, thoroughgoing, and seemingly irrevocable, that do not have sufficient support in practical experience. Social Realism holds that it is unwise, in setting out to scout uncharted lands, to destroy the home base to which return might be made if necessity compelled. It is, therefore, committed to a policy of progressivism rather than radicalism. In spite of the large shortcomings of the private-enterprise order, as it operates at present, it would be unwise to abandon it in favor of an economic order that has not yet proved itself. It is far better to take such steps as will remove the shortcomings in the existing order and to follow where they lead, seeking always to maintain ourselves in the light of values already tried out and approved.

Furthermore, Social Realism has strong reservations regarding the desirability of a collectivistic order in view of the restrictions that this places upon individual liberty. Experimentalism, despite its advancement of individuality as a social and educational ideal, manages to reconcile individuality with an economic state of society closely approaching or approximating collectivism. This it does by distinguishing between two kinds of individuality, or, as it prefers to call them, between individuality and individualism. Individuality characterizes the behavior of a wholesomely integrating personality, acting in accordance with its ends in a socially wholesome manner. To be regarded as good, individuality must be socially beneficent. Individualism, on the other hand, is identified with the unrestrained freedom to pursue one's ends regardless of the potential effect upon others. Experimentalism accepts and elevates individuality as an ideal, and rejects individualism. The present capitalistic order it identifies with individualism in an economic sense. It maintains, therefore, that in the present situation it is necessary to curtail, even to a considerable extent, individual freedom in economic enterprise in order that there may be realized for all a higher personal freedom that comes with the assurance of a certain amount of material security. Granted this assurance, all people will be better disposed and better able to develop in their life-relations a mode of behavior that is wholesomely individual.

Social Realism is not greatly concerned with individuality as a concept or as an ideal, nor primarily with individual rights and liberties.

To its way of thinking, individual liberties are residual liberties, granted after the larger welfare of the group has been provided for. At the same time, it believes that no group can be strong and happy *as a group* if the individual members are restricted in ways that make social living irksome. It believes that a collectivistic society is bound to do just that, if present public sentiment is correctly read. Social Realism is, therefore, opposed to collectivism not *as* collectivism, but on the grounds that it seems to deprive the individual of certain rights that he wants and without which he cannot be happy in society, as, for example, the right of economic freedom, the right of *not being dictated to*. If, in some wonderful way, someone could think of a collectivistic society in which all individuals would welcome being dictated to, and would be genuinely happy despite the loss of a considerable degree of freedom which that would entail, Social Realism would be glad to sponsor it. If experience in the future serves to convince the American people, the whole of it or the majority of it, that collectivism is an acceptable way out of the present economic dilemma, Social Realism will raise no objection to it.

It appears, then, that Social Realism, which is not greatly concerned in principle with individuality, is in this instance inclined to extend to the individual a greater degree of total freedom than Experimentalism, which regards the ideal of individuality as a cornerstone of its philosophy. Experimentalism, moreover, is in a logical dilemma from which it cannot easily escape: it must reconcile its belief in individuality with its arbitrary definition of what individuality is. Presumably individuality also implies that the individual is free to decide where his individuality is to lie.

Another important respect in which the social thinking of Social Realism differs from that of at least one strong group within Experimentalism is in the matter of implementing the social program. Social Realism abides by its principle that the experience of a group is a sounder basis for making judgments than is the experience of an individual; that the judgments made by a group are, in the long run, wiser than the judgments of an individual; and that the larger the group, the wiser the judgment is likely to be. Social Realism finds in this assumption the basis of all societal living. It also regards social procedure as something that must be respected, as a *method* that is more important than the content it deals with at any particular time. Accordingly, though certain that its conclusions regarding the needs of the present social order are sound, it is insistent that these conclusions be first presented to society for its approval—to be debated upon, defended, and, if possible, ultimately accepted. It regards this procedure as the essence of democracy. It is certain, moreover, that society can be convinced of the soundness of its suggestions, that these suggestions are not peculiar to Social Realists, that they are widely held. On the other hand, a group within Experimentalism proposes that the school embody its suggestions and propagate them through the curriculum, without necessarily first obtaining society's approval. This group argues that impartial studies of social scientists have returned them, time and again, to these solutions as the only feasible ones for society. To submit these solutions to society would be to ask for a judgment, but an adverse judgment would not make the solutions incorrect. They would still be the only feasible ones.

One can recognize some validity in the contention of these Experimentalists that, in the present state of our society, their arguments may not get a fair hearing. Powerful forces might be set to work to influence people, by intimidation, to decide against their own best interests. (One still remembers that some years ago employees found little notices in their pay-envelopes carrying a "subtle" suggestion as to how they were to vote in the coming election.) Despite this, however, this faction within Experimentalism cannot defend its position, theoretically or practically. If commitment to a democratic way of life means anything, it means that we must take just such chances. Democracy is a faith in the common man, not only in his intelligence, but in his courage and moral integrity. Democracy assumes in advance that there will be no smooth sailing in anything, that a great deal of effort will frequently be expended in securing a recognition of propositions that are "self-evident." In the manner in which things are done lies the difference between democracy and benevolent despotism. Experimentalism is not true to its own commitment to democracy when it seeks to avoid a necessary conflict of judgments. It is not even faithful to its basic premise of pragmatism.

In this encounter with Experimentalism, the writer sides wholly with Social Realism. He finds that Experimentalism is too dogmatic in its interpretation of individuality and of democracy. Social Realism is probably not as idealistic as the other in its ultimate social theory, but it "cuts no corners" in its methods (and idealism is revealed almost as much in method as it is in aim). But in the practical application of its principles, Social Realism does not escape a dilemma. We live not in a single society but (1) in a number of overlapping societies, (2) in a number of concentric societies radiating out from each one of us as a center. Thus each of us is a member of a family group, a professional group, a circle of friends, a religious group, etc.; and each of us is a member of a community, a city, a state, a nation. If society legislates on questions of right and wrong, what if there is a conflict in legislation? A judgment made by the state may conflict with that made by a nation; a judgment made by a nation may conflict with a judgment made by larger civilized society. Suppose that a state law forbids the teaching of evolution in the schools at a time when larger civilized society regards it as a not improbable theory of human origins. What is the intelligent individual to do? Social Realism does not deny the reality of this dilemma. Its reasoning, however, would be as follows. In the first place, though it is true that a person is simultaneously a member of many groups, it is necessary to define society pragmatically. It is obvious that a family group, a circle of friends, a religious group are not separate societies but elements within a society. People have identified societies pragmatically by the very fact that they established cities, states, and nations, and empowered them to legislate for their inhabitants. A law is a judgment made by society which it has the right to enforce upon its members. People have gone further and selected the particular society which, by the pragmatic criterion, is *most* a society. In our country this is a state. Not only does the state legislate for its inhabitants, but it regulates the rights of smaller societies (for example, cities) to legislate, and it empowers certain smaller social units or groups to undertake legislation of a certain type. Thus a school board can legislate for the schools in a certain district, subject to the restriction of the state, and medical associations may set up standards for the practice of medicine which its members feel impelled to meet. Since the pragmatic necessity of a union of states has also been recognized, the state must share its jurisdiction over its inhabitants with the national government, and must submit to national arbitration whenever a state-with-state dispute cannot be settled satisfactorily by the states.

Thus, Social Realism would reply that law and the division of legal jurisdiction are outcomes of the need for arbitration among the judgments of the several societies of which the individual is simultaneously a member. The individual must respect the law of the particular society under the jurisdiction of which a particular judgment falls. That does not mean that laws are per se perfect: an individual may be convinced that a law which he must obey is wrong, and he may have the support of a considerable part of civilized humanity in this conviction. The individual must make every effort to get society to change its decision, but in the meantime he must abide by that decision. Increasingly society must be taught to base its laws not upon popular prejudice, but upon intelligent information; increasingly society must be taught to bring the judgments of other societies into its reckoning. Suppose, however, that certain prejudices are so ingrained in a community that the community can not reason intelligently where they are concerned. Social Realism feels that this is one of the sacrifices that man must make on behalf of societal living. It feels that stubbornness and failings in society are part and parcel of human life, that pragmatic living implies a gradual overcoming of these mistakes, that the problem is to make human beings progressively more intelligent so that they will, whenever possible, abide by the facts of science rather than by the prejudices of their ancestors. The unsatisfied idealistic reader will recognize in this argument some of the appeal to the time factor that is characteristic, in much larger degree, of Humanism and Social Evolutionism.

Consistent with its basic premises that human values are a function of changing experience, and that societal judgments antecede individual judgments in importance, Social Realism does not commit itself to a definition of *the* good man or *the* intelligent man in terms of fixed, absolute traits. Individual worth is socially defined: the good man is the man who does those things that society regards as good. The intelligent man is the man who lives in a way that society regards as intelligent (intelligence being an aspect of the larger quality of goodness). Reasoning in this way, Social Realism is enabled to accept (indeed to welcome) the fact of individual differences, and to use it to great advantage without diverting it toward undemocratic ends. Society has need of many different kinds of services, it has need of many talents; it has need, therefore, of many different kinds of men. Each man contributes some things of value to society, and in these respects he is a good man. There are many different kinds of good men. Social Realism stresses the fact of *differentness* among individuals, rather than of inequality. In the same way, Social Realism is quick to point out that, pragmatically speaking, intelligence is expressed in different kinds of ways; one is justified, therefore, in speaking of different kinds of intelligence, and of different kinds of intelligent men. Of course, all individuals do a great many common things, but even in these each man does some things better than he does others, Social Realism willingly recognizes each man's claim to intelligence, and seeks to discover the natural capacities and aptitudes by virtue of which he can make to society the greatest contribution of which he is capable.

The Social-Realist society is not equalitarian. Social Realism does not argue that since individuals are all different, they are all equal in their differentness. The estimate of human worth is an estimate made by society; in terms of its needs and its values, society may place different estimates upon individuals. The surgeon may be more highly regarded than the tax-collector. But society, aware of its needs and aware of the functions which each person performs in the community, is not likely to be indifferent to the value of the services of even the most menial worker. Social Realism was among the first of the present-day theories to point out that academic superiority is not the only kind of superiority that the school must recognize; that those students possessing superiority in mechanical, artistic, or social activities are entitled to as much regard as the academically superior. Though holding, as does Humanism, that capacities are innate, Social Realism avoids the great mistake of recognizing only a single type of capacity and of ignoring others.

It must be admitted that a large number of educational scientists who are inherently sympathetic to the Social-Realist point of view do incline toward determinism and its dangerous undemocratic tendencies. The Social-Realist doctrine that capacities are inherited is likely to foster such ideas in people who lack Social Realism's own strong social sense, and who overlook the fact that capacities are revealed in the course of activity and are not predictable prior to activity. Such people often make the mistake of measuring intelligence by a single criterion—usually one to which they are themselves attracted or with which they are familiar. Thus, school men are likely to judge intelligence by an academic criterion, which is the one they know best; and noting that some students, although they try, seem incapable of excelling in their school studies while others do so with ease, they are likely, in time, to begin to sort out students and consign them to different "intelligence" categories. There are undoubtedly engineers and technicians who would think similarly in terms of their own favorite criterion; and artists in terms of theirs. Unfortunately these people are not in charge of our education, else the popular meaning of intelligence might be somewhat different from what it is at present.

Whether or not Social Realism is justified in maintaining that the various types of intelligence are fixed by heredity is a moot point. No one would deny that capacities for *something* to *some degree* are inherited; the quarrel is whether these capacities can be extended or are merely actualized by learning. The writer has earlier stated his preference for a conception that holds intelligence to be an indissoluble product of heredity and learning (in the manner of Social Evolutionism and Experimentalism). As long, however, as Social Realism does not insist on trying to determine in advance what a student's capacity is (that is, before that capacity is given a chance to reveal itself in learning), no harm can be done. And Social Realism is careful not to do this: Briggs, for example, insists that exploration of capacities, aptitudes, and interests must take place through educative materials rather than through testing devices. In the meantime, the manner in which Social Realism has interpreted the fact of individual differences— namely, that each person is capable of contributing in an individual way to the advancement of the common life—is a valuable contribution to educational theory.

The good man, then, is one who, in society's own terms, is socially-competent, one who is not equally socially-competent in all things, but who does especially well those things which he is by nature best fitted to do. Such a person cooperates with society and does not operate against it: the disaffected, the socially maladjusted man is not the good man, however well-meaning his efforts may be, and however good he might have been judged at another time and place. As for the rest, Social Realism is willing that society do the prescribing. But when society does prescribe, the individual must fill the prescription. Thus, in our society, the good man must be, beyond all else, the democratic, social-minded, economically effective person.

It is the task of education to help produce such a person. If society expects an individual to be democratic, then education must teach him the art of democratic living; if society expects a person to be economically effective (and if he cannot be that without assistance), then that too becomes a function of education. Social Realism proposes that education attack its problems directly rather than indirectly. "The best way to learn to do something is to practice doing it under expert guidance." The way to educate for A is to teach A, rather than to teach B in the hope that A will eventually result. Education thereupon becomes transformed. The activities of the student in school are the activities of real life for which education is intended to prepare him. When he can perform them in a manner which society regards as satisfactory, he is declared socially-competent. And since social-competence is necessarily a dynamic thing, the student must be helped to establish interests in the life-activities that will impel him to continue to learn and to develop.

So straightforward a doctrine is not usual in education. Education has long been in the habit of trying to do things not in the most direct but in a roundabout manner. Plato, planning the education of the governors of his ideal state, that is, of men who presumably would direct foreign policies, manage fiscal affairs, plan public works, and so forth, decided that the very best preparation for their practical duties of state lay in extended and intensive studies of abstract sciences— arithmetic, geometry, astronomy, and music—as Plato understood them. Education has been following a similar formula ever since—not only for would-be-governors but for all others. Until recently, one of the ways in which the high-school student was almost invariably prepared to think straight in the context of modern life-experiences—in his social relationships, in business, in political affairs—was through a course in Euclidean geometry. Thinking in real life is done in situations that are alive, that do not stand still, that refuse to lend themselves to manipulation in the manner in which chessmen are moved on a board. Euclidean geometry, however much one may admire it as an intellectual achievement for the nicety and precision of logical thinking that it displays, offers problematic situations having not the slightest resemblance to those real-life situations in which good thinking is needed. One might understandably like to indulge in it as a pleasant intellectual exercise after essential learnings have been acquired. But decade after decade it has remained in the curriculum, not supplementing but occupying the place of the genuine life-problems for which one needed to be educated. Possibly its greatest value lay in that it served to mark the "good" students from the "bad." Most of the other subjects were, in their own way, no better. Except somewhat through the social studies, the complicated situations of the modern world, with their underlying mathematics, science, technics, economics, politics, ethics, and esthetics, were not dealt with directly. Education has, in recent years, improved a little; what contributed as much as anything else to this improvement was the fortunate fact that the schools were flooded with a great many students who were unable to learn the old subjects.

The point need not be labored. Social Realism does offer a fresh approach to the problem of educational method. It is necessary, however, to point out some ways in which Social Realism lends itself to misinterpretation, as much by its friends as by its enemies. In the first place, the doctrine of Social Realism at present under discussion is not for the simple-minded. It must be applied with intelligence and imagination rather than with literalness. The Social-Realist principle that it is the duty of the school to deal directly with the realities of life is a philosophic principle which, especially in view of the past history of education, points to a new conception of educational method. It does not mean, however, that the school is to be a pedestrian affair that does not rise above a faithful copy of things-as-they-are. It does not mean that the school is not to be selective: some things are much better learned in places other than the school. It is as unsound as it is unimaginative to draw up ponderous lists of life-activities, to try to get them all represented in the curriculum, and to give the student at least one chance at every activity.

In the second place, it must be understood that, though the school aims at developing competence in every important life-activity, and though the best test of educational success is the pragmatic test in living, the cause of failure to realize any aspect of social-competence cannot always be attributed solely or even principally to the school. To fail to see this is again to oversimplify the Social-Realist principles somewhat as follows: Education aims at social-competence; social-competence is appraised in a pragmatic manner in actual living in society; such an appraisal, today, reveals that a considerable number of individuals are lacking in certain aspects of social-competence; hence, the school is at fault. Society, wholly independent of the best efforts of the school, has a great deal to do with determining whether individuals can be made socially-competent. A pragmatic education is necessarily affected by conditions within society; given a serious maladjustment within society, and the best efforts of the school may come to naught. The Report of the New York State Regents' Inquiry has led some to criticize the school too harshly on the ground that, according to the survey made, a great many high-school graduates in the state, by a pragmatic criterion, do not possess vocational competence. The school is certainly to be criticized for not helping the students to become a little more intelligent about their vocational problems and for not preparing them more realistically to face the difficult task of finding employment following their graduation, but one doubts whether, under present conditions, anything that the school might do could possibly give students vocational competence, in the true sense of that term. Unless society arranges to cooperate fully in locating jobs, in helping the school to train for them, and in placing young people in them, the best that the school can do in the present circumstances is to give young people accurate information about the situation that does face them, knowledge regarding and some training for general opportunities that do exist, and some method of procedure that may render the task of establishing themselves in vocations a little more successful.

Finally, it is not always remembered, even by Social Realists, that the concept "social-competence" is a dynamic concept that must be defined in terms of what society expects of the individual at the particular stage of his development. Social-competence is one thing for a boy of fifteen years, another thing for a young man of twenty-five, quite another thing for a person of forty. There are many things that a person establishing his own home needs to know that would never have concerned him before. Social Realism in theory is always careful to point this out, by emphasizing that it is through immediate needs that the student is to be further led to provide for assured future needs; in practice, however, Social Realists are sometimes justifiably criticized because they want to propel the adolescent into an adult world in which he does not yet actually (psychologically) live.

We turn now to an examination of the psychology of Social Realism. It is typical of Social Realism that it is cautious in elaborating theories not wholly supported by soundly verified facts. In its view, education was badly fooled when it accepted such theories as the faculty psychology and formal discipline. Since the overthrow of these theories regarding mind, Social Realism feels that education must move warily in creating new ones: it must not assume anything for which science or solidly-supported empirical fact has not pointed the way. Social Realism is, therefore, attracted to the scientific psychology of Thorndike, the psychology of connectionism, which more than any other American psychology seems to follow a kind of "law of parsimony." Connectionism assumes that a response can be "vouched for" if it has been previously established by learning: for every stimulus, its own learned response. Transfer of training is limited: elements must be identical, the act of transfer must be consciously sought. To keep the individual learning continuously, interests must be established as drives to learning.

Without in any way challenging the principal theses of Social Realism—that one must practice doing those things in which he is expected to be competent, that the subject-matter of the school are life-activities —one may well question the scientific basis upon which it rules out the possibility of mental discipline. If the expression "learning by experience" means anything, it means that there is a carry-over of learning effects to succeeding situations. This carry-over (the degree of which is still to be established) may be called mental discipline, that is, if the word "mental" is not narrowly interpreted. The fact of mental discipline, so broadly interpreted, is an empirical fact: no one would seriously argue that there is no mental discipline. The theory of identical elements is a theory which purports to explain this fact, and to establish the degree to which a carry-over exists. Now the fact and the theory are on two different planes of knowledge. One may accept the fact and still reject the theory; indeed, one must accept the fact of mental discipline, yet question the assumptions and the data which led to the formulation of the theory of identical elements. One senses a tendency in education to think from theory to fact rather than from fact to theory: to doubt that much mental discipline takes place because the theory of identical elements so maintains, rather than to suspect the theory of identical elements as an inadequate explanation of the fact of mental discipline.

The theory of identical elements is not satisfactory. On the surface, it seems an apt explanation, but it conceals more than it reveals. What is an identical element? Are identical elements pre-existent in situations before these situations are known, or is it knowledge that makes elements in situations identical? How does the theory serve to explain that of two individuals viewing two situations, one may see identities and one may not? Is the identical element created by the individual, or is it inherent in the situation? How does the theory explain the fact that some individuals (with whom surely we are all acquainted) operate in similar ways in the most dissimilar situations? Are elements in real-life situations (not, for example, in languages reduced to grammatical principles) ever identical? If one deals with the identical elements in a situation by a recall of previous learning, how does one deal with the rest of the situation? Does one begin with the perfectly unknown, and proceed by the trial-and-error method? Are there degrees of identicalness, or is identity a "yes-no" affair?

One can hardly escape the conclusion that it is not the situation but the learner in whom the possibility of transfer exists. An individual is *affected by learning,* and he is never the same afterwards. The learning is incorporated into his being, and makes its presence felt in all succeeding behavior until it is modified by subsequent learnings. Learnings, moreover, are not carried around as elements: they fuse into the total personality structure. This is precisely what is meant by mental disciplining. Mental disciplining means affecting a person in ways that induce him consciously to keep changing his behavior as a result of previous learnings. How does this change take place, how are the previous learnings used? These are the important questions with regard to mental discipline, and answers are differently supplied by Social Evolutionism and by Experimentalism. In the present judgment of the writer, it is the latter that offers the more satisfactory explanation; but in any event, an improved scientific psychology will, in the near future, have to provide us with the data that will make possible more conclusive judgment.

The concept of discipline has fallen into disrepute. The old faculty psychology made possible the exploitation of a preposterous notion that mind is "automatically" disciplined by exercise with intellectually difficult and formalistic materials; the notion was not discredited sooner because for a long time the secondary school dealt with selected students with whom practically any theory of discipline would have "worked." The present revival of formal discipline is hardly less objectionable—it too assumes a gymnastic theory of mind. The conception of discipline of the non-formalistic Humanists is much better: it holds that the mind can be disciplined by the use of any *meaningful* materials into which the student intellectually enters. The weakness of these Humanists is that they cannot break away from the idea of subjects, and even of favorite subjects. Social Evolutionism goes beyond Humanism, and offers a plausible theory of how disciplining may actually take place. But the position of Social Evolutionism is also weakened by the fact that it falls back upon the traditional subjects. One begins to ask, with a little annoyance, just what meanings these traditional subjects possess that one can bring to bear upon his own immediate life-situation? Social Realism is immeasurably superior to both Humanism and Social Evolutionism in that it offers a curriculum of real life-activities—problems of youth behavior, of citizenship, of improving society, of health, of work, and of leisure. The mental discipline that the student can acquire in dealing with these problems is greatly superior to that which he can get in learning traditional subjects —if instruction is directed toward the end of discipline. Training in solving these problems can serve to give the learner an equipment of values, purposes, and methods which he could apply in his own immediate and future living. The techniques that he can evolve are those applicable to his life-situation. A proponent of the theory of identical elements might interject at this point that what has been said so far only proves the validity of his theory. One would reply that it does not prove anything of the sort. "Disciplining the mind" means enabling a person to use past learnings in dealing with present and future situations; it means providing a person with suitable ends and effective means of living. It is only sensible educational theory to maintain that ends and means of living come from the context of life itself, and not from a study of academic subjects. The proponent of the theory of identical elements takes advantage of this to promulgate an explanation in which he invents "identical elements in situations."

In sum, the proposition of Social Realism that the best way to learn to do anything is to practice doing it under expert guidance seems to be thoroughly sound educational theory. The possibilities for mental discipline inherent in it are greater than even the Social Realists have recognized. The writer believes that the most valuable kind of educational discipline can result from the application of this principle in school method.

Social Realism criticizes American secondary education chiefly on the ground that it has not followed this principle. It is glad to note that in the last few decades there has been considerable improvement: many of the old-line disciplinary subjects have been abandoned, many practical activities have been introduced. The curriculum has become a little better adapted to the needs of its highly heterogeneous body of students; we have begun to differentiate education in terms of student capacities, aptitudes, and interests. We have, however, fallen far short of the complete goal. The popular mind is still impressed with the idea of discipline (in the old sense), and the school is weighed down with subjects that can serve no other conceivable purpose. For a good many of the students the curriculum is inappropriate still: many of the more energetic and ambitious students, realizing this, have left school; those with less initiative have lingered on, wasting public funds and getting nothing very much in return for their stay in school. In providing for individual differences we have made but a beginning. Our efforts in the direction of vocational education have been half-hearted. On the whole, however, Social Realism views the situation not pessimistically; education must progress at a greatly accelerated pace in the same general direction in which it has been going.

Social Realism regards it as inevitable that secondary education for all must soon extend through adolescence. It urges the school, therefore, to do its utmost to make education appropriate for all its students —to make secondary education a paying investment to society. It fears, however, that secondary education will be expanded to take in the whole potential student population for a longer period of time before an adequate curriculum can be provided for all. The result of such a policy may be to make the public, at a critical time, lose confidence in the educational enterprise, or to influence the school to revert to its old ways of regarding itself not as a means of helping individuals toward social-competence, but as an academic institution concerned with teaching subjects. Social Realism advises, therefore, that the school delay, for the time being, its projected expansion, applying its efforts toward experimenting with curricula that would be appropriate to all; and that, until this is done, the school refrain from retaining students when it is obvious that they are not being educated. This does not mean that such students are to be abandoned by society, but that society must establish agencies which can care for them better than the school can. These suggestions seem to be so eminently sensible that it is difficult to see how anyone can take exception to them. It can hardly be argued that the school is in any way improving the morale of students when, after they have shown their inability to profit by the educative activities that it does offer, it shunts them into activities of doubtful educative value, and, by providing "busywork," creates an illusion of education.

The school curriculum is to be as common and as varied as life itself. Not all students are to engage in all activities—that is not true to life. For the most part, curricular activities must aim at common competences; and these activities may themselves be common or they may be differentiated according to student capacity. In addition, there must be activities aiming at the development of special competences; and these are to be based on disclosed aptitudes and interests. The immediate function of the school is threefold: to provide activities leading to the development of common competences; to provide activities that reveal to students possibilities in higher fields of study and of vocation, and also to help students to discover their own capacities, aptitudes, and interests; and to provide activities leading to special competences. Social Realism is strongly of the opinion that in the complex economic world of the present, the school must provide large vocational preparation and vocational guidance, extending beyond the school into the community. It wants the school to make the student intelligent and capable with respect to the world of work, and to help him develop interests compatible with the social needs. Moreover, the school must guide the individual not merely to the end of its course, but out into the job itself; it must help the student to find a job, it must advise him in it, it must cooperate with his employer.

The curriculum of the Social-Realist school would not dispense with subjects. But the unit within each subject would not be a topic of abstract subject-matter, but a life-activity—a problem, a challenge, a unit of experience, in the learning of which various kinds of subject-matter would be employed. In this respect, Social Realism stands very close to Experimentalism.

Finally, Social Realism recognizes that if the school is to be extended in the future to include older adolescents and young adults, it must provide activities more suited to their needs than would be the characteristic learning activities of the earlier school. Young men and women cannot be expected to be happy in pursuing studies wholly preparatory. They must be given adult work to do—work that will enable them to take their place with adults in the life of the community. How this is to be done must be worked out experimentally.

In summary, it may be said that Social Realism offers an original though essentially simple approach to the problem of education. The approach utilizes and develops the common-sense principle that since the aim of education is to help individuals to deal more intelligently with the problems of living, education should consist in being introduced to and learning to deal with these very problems. More, since society is the unit in terms of which human living is organized, and since society maintains education to preserve and better itself, the emphasis in education must be social. But Social Realism is much more than common sense in education: its philosophical basis is as sound as or sounder than the bases of its rival theories, and its logical structure is less vulnerable. Its basic premises are that what man knows, he knows only through experience, and that knowledge becomes truth when it has been verified in the experience of many individuals. On this basis, Social Realism establishes a theory of society, of mental life, and an excellently cohering structure of educational theory. At the point where its psychology suffers, it suffers from an excess of caution, rather than from reckless speculation. Social Realism, however, is in some danger from its friends, some of whom are inclined to oversimplify it, and interpret its letter rather than its spirit.

The special merits of Social Realism lie, first, in the social program that it sponsors to meet the present social-economic emergency. Describing the situation as accurately as the data obtained by social scientists make possible, it examines its causes, and points out the direction in which a solution lies. It then urges the American people to carry on from this point. The people must decide what is to be done; and the degree to which social reforms are to be radical and the pace at which they are to be made are both up to the people. It urges society to take action, insisting that the work of education is inextricably tied up with a definite social program, and that education is bound to be erratic until society knows once more where it wishes to go. Social Realism seeks to advance democratic aims, but not at the expense of democratic procedure.

A second merit of Social Realism is in its general interpretation of the function of the school in society. It regards the school as an agent of society, responsive to its wishes, and not as an independent agent, responsible only to its own conscience. It refuses, therefore, to extend to the school the privilege of setting up ultimate values and operating according to them, even in defiance of society. Yet it does not place the school precisely "under the thumb" of the groups that happen to be dominant at any time; the school can serve as society's conscience which, by repeated prodding, can stimulate it to live up to its responsibilities.

The deference to society's values that characterizes Social Realism is exhibited in its interpretation of individual differences. Undoubtedly, Social Realists as-individuals have their special preferences and biases regarding the precise attributes of the good man. But in setting up educational values, they prefer to be guided by society. The latter shows by its action that it is appreciative of many kinds of individuals possessing different abilities and talents. Social Realism, therefore, interprets individual differences from this point of view. It is stubborn in insisting that there are individual differences, and that something must be done with regard to them; but it does not consent to classifying students only from the standpoint of academic intelligence. Moreover, it goes on to develop a positive program for utilizing the special capacities, aptitudes, and interests of each person so as to give him value and standing in his own eyes and in the eyes of society.

Unlike earlier theories discussed, Social Realism does not shrink from the task of changing the curriculum. The patient is obviously very sick, but the other theories are unwilling to change the medicine which no doctor but long usage has prescribed. It is undeniable that some of the curriculum practices that many of the followers of Social Realism have initiated will not stand examination in the future, but such things are inevitable in the tremendous task of building a new curriculum. Social Realism must be given credit for not going to the extreme of discarding valuable subject-matter (as some of the Experimentalists were willing to do in earlier years), and for maintaining consistently that a reorganization from a functional point of view would make possible the realization of values inherent in some of the traditional subjects.

Social Realism must be given credit for taking an unpopular (with theorists) but thoroughly justifiable and consistent stand on the matter of extending educational activity at a time when education is in conflict with itself. This stand has brought upon it all sorts of undeserved charges; it has, for example, been called fascistic by those who are constitutionally resentful of being held to a sensible accounting of what they have done. It is hardly necessary to say that only as education is intelligent and realistic about itself, "knows itself"—its strength and its weakness—can it flourish as a great and growing national enterprise.

The weakness of Social Realism lies in its allegiance to a mechanistic psychology, and in the fact that its point of view is sometimes favored and exploited by "scientists" of limited educational vision. There are ample signs that the mechanistic psychology is losing ground. One hopes that the next few years will see Social Realism allying itself with some of the psychological principles characteristic of both Social Evolutionism and Experimentalism (without the former's partiality to an inert subject-matter and the latter's too exclusive preoccupation with "integration" and "purposing").

EXPERIMENTALISM

Like Social Realism, Experimentalism regards the present economic-social situation as a result, largely, of the failure of human intelligence and human action to keep pace with changing experience. It regards it, moreover, as an affirmation of its principal thesis that we live in a dynamic world, that human intelligence cannot legislate once and for all, that man must always be alert or face the possibility of disaster. Not that Experimentalism has in it either a note of the querulous or of an irritating "I told you so": it makes a point of emphasizing that the development of science and of technology are among the greatest events of human history; it stresses the completeness of the revolution they have caused, and the radicalness of the changes still to occur; and it does not believe, by any means, that it is too late for man to take hold of his situation and master it.

Experimentalism stresses certain elements or qualities in the present situation much more than does Social Realism. In the first place, it holds that the weaknesses of our economic-social situation reveal the need for a more drastic revision of many of our social concepts, arrangements, and practices than Social Realism is willing immediately to sanction. While Social Realism speaks of a planning economy with increased governmental control, making for a better equalization of economic opportunity and for extension of the idea of democracy in an economic sense, the general tendency within Experimentalism is to maintain that a much more thorough economic reconstruction is necessary. The laissez-faire system of economics is incompatible with the demands of the present situation, and in some way a socialization of the economic order will have to be achieved. (Some Experimentalists seem to go so far as to counsel the abandonment of the private enterprise order on any large scale.) In general the new situation would tend to approach a state of economic collectivism.[5] But, however thor-

[5] Not all Experimentalists are explicit in professing an economic creed, and it is impossible to say whether all would agree that a state of collectivism is the only way out of the present dilemma. To the writer's knowledge, Bode, Hopkins, and Thayer are certainly opposed to "indoctrinating for a collectivistic order," and are quite probably opposed to anything approximating complete collectivism. It may be that others are as well.

The situation may be summed up as follows: All Experimentalists agree that there is need for a drastic reconstruction of the economic order; in positive terms, that there is need for a much more broadly socialized economy. A few Experimentalists assert that relief can come only with the abandonment of the private enterprise order on any considerable scale. In general, it may be said correctly that the social orientation of Experimentalism is *in the direction of* economic collectivism.

oughly socialized the economy, it must be compatible with the essential democratic principles of individual freedom and equality, of government by the people and not by a dictatorship, of the individual and not the state as the end. Experimentalism is quick to agree that none of the forms of collectivism established thus far would serve the needs of the American people (although some of the voluntary collectivism now partially undertaken in the Scandinavian countries may point the way). Socialization may be carried on in many directions: in the direction of establishing a state or a class despotism, or in the direction of a genuine social control of economic resources and processes that would make possible real individual freedom and a Good Life for all.

Experimentalism emphasizes that our highly developed technology and the plentiful natural resources with which our country is fortunately favored, bring within reach a life almost beyond the dream of the Utopians: a life in which poverty and suffering because of material need would be non-existent, in which human energy would be released from its concern with material things to create a higher cultural life. It rests with human intelligence to do this; the direction in which the solution lies is obvious. And Experimentalism is correspondingly bitter because human intelligence has thus far failed to avail itself of its opportunity. It points ironically to the fact that we are more than ever preoccupied with material concerns, that human want and suffering are more widespread than ever. It points to the many contradictions in our social life as evidence of the fact that we are unwilling to face reality, that we are trying to squirm out of taking the decisive steps that we have to take.

In a positive way, Experimentalism points to the values of a socialized economy for the realization of human potentialities. Human potentialities do not lie, as some people seem to think, in the ability to "make" more money than the other fellow; they lie in the expression, by each person, of those powers which he acquires in the course of experiencing —powers that are his own, that are unique with him. The expression may be intellectual or artistic or mechanical or political. The good society, as Experimentalism sees it, is a highly colorful thing: it consists of individuals with personalities, each doing different things, each making his presence felt in a different way, yet all of them living happily together. It feels that a society in which individuals are always concerned with material self-aggrandizement is a drab society; that a society in which individuals are unsuccessful even in satisfying material wants has little excuse for being. Experimentalism aims at a Good Life for the individual, and it seems to be convinced that, in the circumstances that influence our living, the only society that makes possible such a life for all individuals is one that possesses a more highly socialized economy.

Another respect in which Experimentalism differs from Social Realism is in the greater emphasis that it places upon change as a factor in our living. The beat of our life is a quick beat. The rate of change is constantly increasing. Experimentalism warns that we may as well become accustomed to the idea that we shall never be able to "settle down." The present reconstruction of society is a prelude to the continuous reconstruction that is to come. It is necessary to impress this fact upon our generation, and to prepare our people to react to changing events much more quickly and decisively than we have done in the past. Experimentalism makes clear that any such plans as it suggests are not final plans. It, too, would have a *planning* society, and this planning society would be more active in continuously reworking and modifying its plans than would the Social-Realist society.

One must admire the social aims of the Experimentalist philosophy, the Good Life of man that it depicts, its genuine concern for the well-being of the individual. They are truly humanitarian, idealistic aims, much more so than those professed by "Idealistic" philosophies. And it surely is not beyond the reach of American civilization, with its own native idealism, its courage, its enterprise, and with the great natural wealth that it has at its disposal, to realize these aims. One admires, too, the courage of certain Experimentalists in setting themselves to the task of describing the means by which these ends can be achieved. They are in favorable contrast, in this respect, with those educational theorists who are constantly criticizing the social ideas of Experimentalism without offering anything better, or as good, in their place. These are likely to fall back on clichés that "time," "faith," "courage," etc., will work an improvement in things; in the meantime they are inclined to minimize our difficulties and to assume a things-are-not-as-bad-as-they-seem attitude. It is an important tenet of Experimentalism that human intelligence, and that alone, must operate in the direction of human affairs; it is true to this tenet when, during an impasse in human affairs, it tries to offer an intelligent suggestion of a way out. Its critics, while equally strong in affirming the need for the exercise of human intelligence, are inclined to check any bold, positive expression of that.

But one must be skeptical of the means by which the "collectivist" Experimentalists would proceed to attain these ends. (It is assumed that the term collectivism implies complete social control of basic economic resources and means of production. If it does not, then the following criticism loses point. These Experimentalists will then have to define, more explicitly than they have, the recurring term "collectivism.") One readily agrees that we must move in the direction of greater socialization of economic control; but one does not so easily agree that the drastic revision of the whole economic structure and some of the necessary consequences of that revision are either necessary or desirable. Recent events have shown that there is a dangerous tendency for collectivism to express itself in various forms of tyranny; the argument that economic collectivism (and the necessary restraints imposed thereby upon the individual) is but a step toward the true liberation of human beings was advanced also in the great Russian "experiment." Experimentalists, of course, insist that their collectivism would be in accord with the democratic spirit of this country; but they are not sufficiently definite about the form that this collectivism would take to enable us properly to judge. One feels, therefore, that while collectivism is a possibility, it is a possibility that should be tried last of all. Moreover, the Experimentalist argument that economic collectivism is desirable is not convincing on purely theoretical grounds: though Experimentalism very laudably distinguishes between freedom to acquire material possessions and freedom to live a higher life, one feels that it is improper for Experimentalism to limit human beings to a choice of one of the two kinds of freedom. It is doubtful whether freedom of the spirit can happily dwell in an atmosphere from which freedom of another kind has been rigidly excluded. If, as this element within Experimentalism maintains, true freedom is incompatible with struggle for economic existence, perhaps it is incompatible also with the existence of strong economic compulsions. The Social-Realist program for extension of social control within the present democratic scheme is more liberal and more truly experimental: it provides for reform measures incorporating some of the very suggestions made by Experimentalism; it advocates a planning society that will continue to make those changes that subsequent experience shows to be necessary; and it does not shut the door on collectivism, if society ultimately decides that it wants that.

What is disturbing is the tendency of these Experimentalists in this respect to depart from the very principle which gives Experimentalism its name. In its general philosophy, Experimentalism emphasizes the point (and properly) that meanings drawn from experience must be regarded and used as hypotheses. It is easy to understand that a person may have convictions about hypotheses, and may very much prefer one hypothesis to its alternative. But the concept of hypothesis implies that other hypotheses are possible (else there would be no need for the mental reservation imposed by the concept, nor for verification). By their general attitude, these Experimentalists suggest that they regard any other solution to the social crisis not only untenable but almost unthinkable. Granted that the *Experimentalist* concept of collectivism has never actually been tried, such forms of collectivism as have been tried have had, in democratic eyes, unfavorable consequences. It is enough to give one pause and to make one wonder whether collectivism does not inherently entail such consequences. The Experimentalist attitude, however, is characterized by the strong degree of assertiveness one ordinarily reserves for theories that have been tested and found to be true.

One must seriously take to task those Experimentalists [6] who would use education as an instrument for promoting their social doctrines without previously obtaining popular approval of them.[7] To have strong personal convictions (even when they exceed in strength the

[6] Again it must be emphasized that not all Experimentalists are so inclined. *Vide* Chapter III, pp. 279 ff.

[7] In fairness to the Experimentalists under discussion it must be repeated that they distinguish strongly between "society" on the one hand, and "government" and "the state" on the other. To them the state is at its best an expression of the will of the people, and government "the state in action at any given time." But even this stand does not make it possible for them to escape criticism. It seems to the writer that these Experimentalists insist upon regarding the school as an altogether independent agency of social intelligence—independent not only of government and the state, but of society itself.

conviction properly to be accorded to a hypothesis) is one thing; to use not merely a social instrument but *society's* instrument, set up for societal purposes, to propagate these convictions is another. It is the writer's belief that the ultimate ends of Experimentalism are unexcelled; he does not agree with those Experimentalists who are convinced that immediate collectivism is the means to these ends. But both ends and means—whatever ends and whatever means—must be approved and accepted by society; and the pace at which society moves, once it gets under way, must be of society's own choosing. This statement has been so often made that the Experimentalists under discussion probably regard it as trite. But its being trite does not detract from the fact of its being fundamentally sound. The justification that Experimentalists advance for urging education to lead society in new social directions cannot stand analysis. Granted that the new social program would probably not get a fair hearing in present society with great vested interests at stake and prejudice rampant, democracy must take its chances. The argument that fundamental changes in the social order must be consummated before individuals can have true equality has a great deal in it; but if these changes are to be consummated, the individuals, all of them, will have to do the consummating. Education cannot act for the individuals' good either contrary to their wishes or without their consent. That is the mark of benevolent despotism, not of democracy. Democratic rules cannot be suspended, even by the friends of democracy. One may very well agree that the democratic way is a desirable way of social living because it offers the greatest opportunities to the individual; that democracy is, after all, a means to an end. But if the individual is really the end, then his preferences hold first place. Experimentalism doesn't often descend to such statements as these, but to have done so even once is cause for alarm: "When education is made the tool of mass [8] control, it becomes responsible for blighted personal initiative, disintegrated personality, or hard-mindedness—all of which retard and frustrate the emergence of significant societal values in the interest of some transient or lesser good." [9] Reading such a statement one is assailed by the suspicion that some "Experimentalists" stand for

[8] Comment: the reader will remember that the "mass" is those individuals whose individualities Experimentalism would take special pains to foster.

[9] Laura Zirbes, in *The Changing Curriculum*, p. 68. 1939.

neither democracy nor the individual nor any principle, but are most interested in having their own way. That statement, however, is not typical of Experimentalism as a whole.

The argument offered by some Experimentalists that education necessarily implies selection, and that selection of significant social experiences (that is, those experiences that have greatest bearing on the welfare of the individual) will inevitably lead students in the direction of accepting the Experimentalist social philosophy is sound—to a degree. Selection there must be; and it is undoubted that a critical examination of the present social situation in its unpleasant reality will disincline young people from an acceptance of conditions as they are, and will influence them toward certain conclusions. Education must do its duty, which is to help young people toward an intelligent understanding of the world as it is, and to help them to become capable of improving it. Education would be faithless to its trust if it put anything in the way of young people's arriving at the only sound conclusions possible. But Experimentalism well knows that there is a subtle and fine and tremendously important distinction between helping young people to think through situations, see all the factors involved in them, formulate general and tentative and truly *experimental* conclusions to be tested in the light of their own subsequent experience, and, on the other hand, leading them along a straight and narrow path toward predetermined conclusions the merits of which they are not yet competent to examine. Selection does not necessarily force the issue. Experimentalism knows that, although some indoctrination is inevitable and desirable and necessary, education is not all indoctrination. Experimentalism must not hide behind the argument that either there is or there is not indoctrination; for a long time now virtue has been located somewhere near the mean between two extremes.

We turn to an examination of the Experimentalist conception of the individual. Experimentalism sees the individual as the end, society with all its arrangements as the means. In the sense that they are all human beings, in the sense that they are all of them different, individuals are equal. Experimentalism does not overlook the fact of individual differences; indeed, as Childs points out, Experimentalism was among the first to emphasize the educational importance of this fact. But the principal significance of individual differences does not lie in specific traits; rather it is in the total quality of the behaving personality. Each person as a complete human being is different from every other person, and in the fact of their differentness all individuals are equal. Experimentalism recognizes no aristocracy. It insists that personalities and intelligences are incommensurable, that they can be understood and evaluated only in the light of their experiences and in terms of their necessary life-purposes. Experimentalism fosters, therefore, a respect for individual personality, for what each person has become as a result of his experiences, for what each person is trying to do.

For individuality is a product of the experiencing process. Experimentalism repudiates any notion of individuality as something that is innate in the organism. Individuality is a personal product of social living, and true individuality, while it operates ultimately in terms of its own life-purposes, recognizes and cooperates with the life-purposes of others. The Experimentalist individual is easily recognized: he is quite different from his Humanist, Social-Evolutionist, and Social-Realist counterparts. While the Humanist individual is reserved, dignified, self-conscious, likely to be ill-at-ease in a crowd; while the Social-Evolutionist individual is the "strong, silent" fellow, conscious of the importance of being social, somewhat fearful of offending, but unable completely to unbend; while the Social-Realist is a gregarious fellow, at his best in a group, and likely to act and think as the others; the Experimentalist individual, at home in a crowd, nevertheless feels himself to be very much of a person in his own right. It is in company with others that he comes into his own; in the exchange of ideas, in the agreements and disputes, in the lending of his distinctive talents to the common enterprise, he finds his greatest enjoyment. He is not inclined to be easy to get along with, being too conscious of his own value, his rights, and the merits of his ideas. He is likely however, to be warm and sympathetic, and anxious to be helpful. The Experimentalist society is a collection of such individuals. It is unlikely to be a placid, settled community; in the Experimentalist society there is always "something doing."

The concept of intelligence that Experimentalism offers to education has great appeal. Intelligence is not aloof, nor does it restrict itself to the pursuit of the "higher life"; it does not lie in knowledge that is settled and permanent, and that can be transported from generation to generation in vehicles called subjects. It is a quality that characterizes man in every one of his waking, active moments. It is a quality inherent in living, revealed in every aspect of the life-process. The Experimentalist sees intelligence as something created by man out of his own experience and in the course of that experience. In this fact the Experimentalist takes great pride—and he finds in it also reason for the exercise of great caution; for man makes mistakes, and experience keeps changing. Intelligence presumes, therefore, constant alertness, constant creativeness.

To the writer, Experimentalism seems to offer a greater insight into what is meant by intelligence than do the other theories. Intelligence operates via meanings. Meanings arise out of experience, and are "read" in terms of the immediate or remote consequences of events for human living. To behave intelligently is to use meanings derived from past experiences to unlock situations so as to reveal their probable consequences, and so to guide one's self as to achieve desired and desirable effects. Since the organism in the various stages of its life-process is never the same, the situations in which it finds itself must be continuously read anew. Man uses meanings drawn from the past, but in understanding a situation confronting him, he creates something. And since man can never be certain that he is right, he must ever be watchful, ever active in testing, weighing meanings, ever creative in making new ones.

Experimentalism provides a plausible explanation of transfer of training without even employing the term. As was stated previously, there is no gainsaying that one does learn by experience; one must regard transfer of training as an empirical fact (even if science has not yet proved satisfactorily to what degree it does take place). The theory of "identical elements" oversimplifies the case and minimizes the degree of transfer; yet one feels uncomfortable in the presence of formal discipline and of other disciplinary principles that assert but do not explain. Experimentalism offers a key to the meaning of transfer of training and to the meaning, therefore, of mental discipline. What one obtains in learning are meanings; what are continuously being transferred are meanings. The mind that is disciplined is the mind that has meanings, that can obtain meanings, and that can apply meanings. But Experimentalism also teaches that transfer of training is not simply an application of old meanings to new situations (perhaps that is the reason that Experimentalism avoids using the term): what is demanded is a re-integration of meanings and a quality of creativeness. This explains why individuals apparently crammed full of knowledge do not necessarily act with intelligence in new situations. The contingency of transfer does not lie primarily either in the situation or in the meaning; it lies in the individual, in his alertness, in his insight, in his creativeness. But Experimentalism makes clear why transfer of training can never be perfect. Situations are constantly changing; the meanings inhering within them are ever new, never precisely what they were previously in another context. Transfer of training is, therefore, a misleading term. Nothing is precisely transferred. Every meaning withdrawn from its context immediately becomes something imperfect. Every situation demands a fresh start; but that does not mean that a person does not come to each situation bearing in mind a total accumulated product of previous experience.

The Experimentalist thesis that intelligence is a product of an experiencing process recalls the similar position taken by Social Evolutionism (which also, the reader will recall, assumes "transfer"). This thesis repudiates any attitude of intellectual determinism—that one is born with a predetermined capacity for a certain amount of intelligence, and repudiates as well many of the devices that have worked great harm in education. It provides a basis for the Experimentalist insistence that, in spite of variation in specific human traits and even of total quantitative differences in intelligence when different individuals are roughly equated, every physically normal human being can be rendered capable of guiding his own destiny. Experimentalism challenges the whole doctrine of ineducability and of partial educability. It is a needed challenge. It may bear repeating that until it is substantially disproved that every human being is capable of intelligent and responsible action, the dignity of all mankind demands that this be assumed.

The strategic role that Experimentalism assigns to the realization of "purposes" and "needs" in the development of human personality gives it penetrating insight into the personal problems of most individuals caught up in the conflicts of modern society, and especially into the personal problems of youth. More than any of the other theories (and only Social Realism rivals it in this respect) Experimentalism is sensitive to the difficulties of young people in our society; and one can judge from many signs that its concern is greatly justified. Experimentalism sees purpose as the dynamic of intelligent human behavior, and the satisfaction of purpose as a means of total integration. The lives of many of our older adolescents in society are characterized chiefly by a host of unrealized and unrealizable purposes. The central purpose to which all others are related is a desire for an economic place in society —a place that will afford some security, some economic well-being and status; denied the satisfaction of this purpose, youth suffer in their whole beings. The present widespread disaffection of youth is testimony of this fact. Along with Social Realism, Experimentalism regards the maladjustment of youth with sympathy and understanding; it attempts to offer a constructive education to reduce that maladjustment, and, if possible, to supplant it with wholesome adjustment.

One must credit Experimentalism, in this instance, with applying its doctrine of "purposiveness" and "integration" in a manner that "hits the nail on the head." The criticism that follows can in no way detract from this credit. The criticism, however, must be made. The writer is in no position to pass judgment on the extent to which the physiological data of integration actually support the theory of integration of personality as Experimentalism offers it. Examining the latter theory, on its own merits—comparing its implications with amply corroborated facts of empirical experience, and noting and weighing its own internal coherence and its completeness as an explanation—one is impressed by some of its shortcomings. Experimentalism holds that purpose is central in impelling and guiding intelligent behavior, that the origin of purpose is disturbance of equilibrium, noted and interpreted by the organism, that when purpose is realized there is (roughly speaking) a regaining of the equilibrium, that unless purpose is satisfied there is a more intensified disturbance, a more pronounced lack of integration, leading perhaps to a serious unfavorable effect upon personality. Experimentalism seems to be committing itself to an exclusive explanation of intelligent behavior and wholesome personality in terms of purpose, identifying realization of purpose with integration or personality development, and failure to realize purpose with lack of integration or disintegration or personality disarrangement.

This explanation does not square perfectly with what experience bears out. Empirically it appears that purposes are never fully realized, that life is a continuous series of compromises, and that such is a normal and not an abnormal state of affairs. The development of perfectly normal personality seems to take place on the basis of purpose only partially realized. We generally aim higher than we can reach; unable to reach what we want, we do not always retire in confusion. Sometimes we make the most of what we can get; other times we return to try again. Man sometimes sets ideals far ahead of him; he may never attain them, but there is a satisfaction in the striving. How does Experimentalism explain these things in terms of purpose and its single-track effect on integration? Are purposes shifting things? How is "balance" achieved when purposes are not realized? Assuming that it is a "good thing" to realize some purposes completely, to regain, at least for the moment, a perfect equilibrium in some matters, is it also good to realize one's purposes always? Isn't that conducive to lethargy, to a slackening of the spirit? Also, does it not sometimes happen that a person rises to greatest heights when he is utterly defeated in his quest for some object? Theoretically, he should be "disintegrated"; actually he is more integrated than ever. If the miracle is attributed to "sublimation" or "substitution," does this not weaken the force of the whole Experimentalist argument for the realization of purpose?

There occur also a number of questions that may sound somewhat Platonic, but which are far from being academic. Can it be assumed that every purpose, though actually conceived as a purpose and desired, is also desirable? People do sometimes sincerely crave the wrong things. Does satisfaction of purpose advance personality or set it back? Does one remain integrated if the act of becoming integrated establishes him in a hospital? What is the role of the human will in the creation of purpose? What is the reason that, of two people faced by the same temptation, one will succumb (that is, establish a positive purpose), and the other will not?

It is necessary to repeat: the doctrine of purposiveness seems to be essentially sound. Certainly not many would support those disciplinarians who assert that the way to develop character is not to realize desired purposes. But Experimentalism, in this respect, also seems one-sided; it seems to have omitted something vital from its explanation. It is likely that these questions, so self-suggestive are they, have not gone unanswered; but such answers have not been very noticeably incorporated into the Experimentalist theory of secondary education. Very evident is its consistent tendency to blame the social order for all the individual's ills, and its failure to emphasize the need of building within the individual a resiliency and strength of character that would enable him to resist some of the harmful social tendencies.

In its view of American education, Experimentalism is extremely critical of both the older classical tradition and the more recent "science"-dominated education. The former has suffered from delusions of universality—it has been aloof, academic, remote from the realities of American life. The latter is harnessed to a restrictive, mechanistic theory of universe and conception of man, and is devoted, on that account, to mistaken ideas regarding reality, truth, objectivity, human personality. Secondary education has suffered, successively, from the influence of each of these theories of education. The classical secondary school was exclusive, academic, unconcerned with the needs and problems of American life; the present-day secondary school, while it is very much less exclusive and has assumed much more responsibility for dealing with important current problems, has glaring inadequacies in objectives and methods. It oversimplifies both life and the educative process. It is training people for adjustment, as it were, to a static world: education is viewed as a kind of habituation of fixed responses to presumedly fixed stimuli. The approach to the study of personality is atomistic. Individual differences are not interpreted as lying essentially in the total qualities of personality. They are studied in terms of particular elements, and become therefore divisive factors in education and in human living. Using an unsound basis for grouping (the I. Q.), we differentiate learning activities, curricula, schools. We offer in the curriculum a great many unrelated activities, unrelated to each other and to the essential interests and needs of students. We do not adequately care for the needs which most concern youth.

Experimentalism believes that secondary education must devote itself whole-heartedly to the task of orienting students to the modern culture. The orientation must have as its starting point the needs that adolescents have and the needs that they develop as they come into contact with the wider and the more significant experiences presented by the school. The school must help students to become more intelligent in living their immediate lives, and to develop a method of intelligent living that will enable them to guide themselves in the future. This purpose will be realized as the school helps the students in the solution of their own problems, whatever they are, and as the school helps them to think through the problems that are of common concern in the culture. The school must work in the greatest intimacy with the learner (his experiences must be part of its subject-matter), and in the greatest intimacy with the community. From the community must come those social experiences which have bearing upon the life of all individuals. In the curriculum of the school every important area of life-experience must be represented, every important type of social relationship must be considered. Education must help each individual to enter into his own life-experiencing in an intelligent manner. The individuality of each person, as it emerges from the experiencing process, must be respected. The learning process must be conceived in terms of individual purposes and needs, and its outcomes must be evaluated in that way. It must not be thought that the curriculum of such a school will lack solid subject-matter of intellectual depth and systematic organization; this will be present in greater degree than ever before.

With the desire of Experimentalism to achieve an education that relates itself to the important problems of individual living, the writer is in complete concurrence. The Experimentalist interpretation of education as guidance in experiencing toward the end of making the individual intelligently self-directing is bound to have a vitalizing influence on the work of the school. One applauds the determination of Experimentalism to make the curriculum as real as life itself, and to make it representative of the entire round of life-activities in which guidance is needed. One of the most important contributions of Experimentalism to American education is the community-school idea, and it is an idea that gives purpose to the education of older youth that, under present conditions, would otherwise be lacking. And, in the judgment of the writer, the Experimentalist use of "subjects" realizes in full the purposes for which any kind of organized knowledge is intended.

The Experimentalist conception of curriculum is in many essential respects not different from the Social-Realist. American secondary education is already sufficiently divided by internal quarrels; as this study reveals, figuratively there are chasms separating the different points of view in educational theory. No good purpose can be served by creating a greater appearance of difference than the reality warrants. Experimentalism has frequently taken Social Realism to task for its method of curriculum building—for its tendency to canvass society to discover the dominant life-activities, and to base its curriculum upon these. It is true, as was pointed out, that those connected with Social Realism sometimes do not interpret its principles properly. There has been a tendency on the part of some Social-Realist curriculum builders: (1) to catalogue life-activities, without exercising the least personal judgment as to whether these activities were desirable, as to whether they represented social *ideals,* and (2) to be too minutely analytical, with the result that fairly staggering lists of life-activities are turned out. (To this latter tendency Social-Realist theory itself probably contributed, by its failure to emphasize transfer of training more than it has.) But essentially the Social-Realist and the Experimentalist approach to curriculum building are not dissimilar, nor are the curriculum activities dissimilar. Social Realism uses the term "life-activity," Experimentalism the term "area of experience"; if the former term is broadly defined, what essentially is the difference between it and an "area of experience"? Some of the Experimentalists who disapprove of the Cardinal Principles of Secondary Education as categories for curriculum building on the ground that they are lacking in dynamism, themselves use categories which may sound more dynamic, but which essentially are no different. What is a "dynamic" category? A category is a means of facilitating classification, a handle by which to take hold of something. What is much more important than the category is what appears within the category—the nature of the "life-activities" or the "experiences" introduced into the curriculum. And in this respect (except for the fact that some Experimentalists would use the experiences to give more explicit direction in terms of their own social ends and means) the curriculum-materials of Social Realism and Experimentalism would not be very dissimilar.

Experimentalism is at the present time testing a number of different approaches to curriculum making. Its technique has not become even relatively crystallized, and it would be unfair to criticize that technique, at this time, from the point of view of smoothness and working efficiency. But it does seem as if the whole curriculum-making procedure is somewhat overcomplicated. Experimentalists sometimes lose sight of the fact that what is important is the *experience* that is ultimately presented to the student for analysis and for educative effect. The identification of many of the potentially most educative experiences hardly requires the services of a curriculum expert; it can almost be done empirically by the intelligent "man-in-the-street." What is more difficult is to relate these experiences to the needs of youth in the various stages of development, and to tie them together in a way that will give the curriculum unity in breadth and depth. But even that does not make necessary the complicated "schemata" that Experimentalists have tended to give to the curriculum. The curriculum practices of the Social Realists are, in this respect, better because they are simpler.

The respects in which the Experimentalist curriculum seems to be superior are the following: Experimentalism strives for greater unity of curriculum materials, less partitioning of its subject-matter, better vertical organization of that subject-matter; it does not introduce as much actual differentiation in curriculum materials, although it takes steps to ensure that each student will carry away from the learning situation that which he most needs; it does not sort out students in groups according to any single criterion and keep the groups more or less permanently separated from each other. It is in these respects that the Experimentalist conception of the method of intellectual development operates at its best.

The writer is eager to see effected a reconciliation between what appear to him to be the two most promising theories of secondary education today—Social Realism and Experimentalism. Each has elements of superiority: Social Realism is thoroughly sound in its conception of the relation of education to society, in its entire social-pragmatic attitude toward the educational enterprise; Experimentalism seems to possess a helpful and revealing insight into the nature of the intellectual process. It was Socrates who maintained that human progress is achieved by continuously enlarging the sphere of human agreement: if such an enlargement could be created by a true synthesis of the best principles of Social Realism and Experimentalism, it would result in a great service to American education.

Bibliography

HUMANISM

BUTLER, NICHOLAS MURRAY.

"The Function of the Secondary School." *Academy*, April, 1890.

"Length of the Baccalaureate Course." *Proceedings of the National Education Association*, pp. 500–504. Washington, D. C.: The Association, 1903.

The Meaning of Education. New York: Charles Scribner's Sons, 1915 (Revised edition).

"Freedom, Responsibility, and Intelligence." *Journal of Adult Education*, 3:393–396, October, 1931.

"Vocational Courses and Colleges." *School and Society*, 36:858–860, December 31, 1932.

"Problems of Higher Education in America." *School and Society*, 39:15–17, January 6, 1934.

"The Challenge to Education." *School and Society*, 40:512–516, October 20, 1934.

"A Much Needed Prayer." *School and Society*, 41:759–761, June 8, 1935.

"The Schools and the Community." *Teachers College Record*, 37:577–587, April, 1936.

"The Paradox of Despotism." *School and Society*, 46:424–427, October 2, 1937.

Annual Report of the President to the Trustees of Columbia University. (Especially 1902, 1929, 1931, 1934, 1936.) New York: Columbia University Press.

FOERSTER, NORMAN.

The American Scholar. Chapel Hill, N. C.: University of North Carolina Press, 1929.

The American State University. Chapel Hill, N. C.: University of North Carolina Press, 1937.

The Future of the Liberal College. New York: D. Appleton-Century, 1938.

HUTCHINS, ROBERT M.

"Education and the Public Mind." *Proceedings of the National Education Association,* 71:163–167. Washington, D. C.: The Association, 1933.

No Friendly Voice. Chicago: The University of Chicago Press, 1936.

The Higher Learning in America. New Haven: Yale University Press, 1936.

"A Reply to Professor Whitehead." *Atlantic Monthly,* 158:182–188, March, 1936.

"Ideals in Education." *American Journal of Sociology,* 43:1–15, January, 1937.

"Grammar, Rhetoric, and Mr. Dewey." *Social Frontier,* 3:137–139, February, 1937.

"What Is the Job of Our Colleges?" *Sunday Times,* Section VIII, pp. 1–2, March 7, 1937.

"Tradition in Education." *Harvard Educational Review,* 7:301–313, May, 1937.

"We Are Getting No Brighter." *Saturday Evening Post,* 210:5–7, December 11, 1937.

"The Junior College." *The Educational Record,* 19:5–11, January, 1938.

"The Organization and Subject-Matter of General Education." Department of Secondary School Principals, National Education Association, *Bulletin* No. 22, pp. 6–14, March, 1938.

"The Philosophy of Education." *Proceedings of the William Rainey Harper Memorial Conference,* pp. 35–50. 1937.

"Too Many Colleges? No, Says Hutchins." *Sunday Times,* Section VII, pp. 1–2, June 12, 1938.

"Good and Bad Features of the American System of Education." *School and Society,* 49:775–776, June 17, 1939.

KANDEL, ISAAC L.

"The New School." *Teachers College Record,* 33:505–514, May, 1932.

"Our Adolescent Education." *Educational Administration and Supervision,* 18:561–572, November, 1932.

"Education and Social Disorder." *Teachers College Record,* 34:359–367, February, 1933.

Dilemma of Democracy. Cambridge: Harvard University Press, 1934.

"Academic Freedom for Teachers." *Teachers College Record,* 37:188–196, December, 1935.

"Is the New Education Progressive?" *Educational Administration and Supervision,* 22:81–87, February, 1936.

"Secondary Education and Social Change." *Kadelpian Review,* 15:347–355, May, 1936.

"Examinations and the Improvement of Education." *Tests and Measurements in Higher Education,* 8:216–229, *Proceedings of the Institute for Administrative Officers of Higher Institutions.* Chicago: University of Chicago Press, 1936.

"Promising Innovations in Secondary Education." *Educational Forum,* 1:29–38, November, 1936.

"Factors Which Contribute Toward a Philosophy of Secondary Education." *Teachers College Record,* 38:273–285, January, 1937.

"Liberalism and Education." *Educational Forum,* 1:261–270, March, 1937.

"Quis Custodiet?" *School and Society,* 47:676–678, May 21, 1938.

Conflicting Theories of Education. New York: The Macmillan Company, 1938.

"Prejudice the Garden Toward Roses." *American Scholar,* 8:72–82, January, 1939.

"Secondary Education." *Educational Forum,* 3:471–487, May, 1939.

LEARNED, WILLIAM S.

The Quality of the Educational Process in the United States and in Europe. Carnegie Foundation Bulletin No. 20. New York: Carnegie Foundation for the Advancement of Teaching, 1927.

"Study of the Relations of Secondary and Higher Education in Pennsylvania." *24th Annual Report of the Carnegie Foundation for the Advancement of Teaching,* pp. 81–89. 1929.

"The Purpose of an Educational Curriculum—Achievement or Transportation?" *Proceedings of the Association of Colleges and Secondary Schools of the Middle Atlantic States and Maryland,* pp. 63–79. 1930.

"Proposals for the Treatment of the Secondary Enquiry Group in the Senior High Schools." *26th Annual Report of the Carnegie Foundation for the Advancement of Teaching,* pp. 31–34. 1931.

Realism in American Education. Cambridge: Harvard University Press, 1932.

"Study of the Relations of Secondary and Higher Education in Pennsylvania: Admissions to College." *27th Annual Report of the Carnegie Foundation for the Advancement of Teaching,* pp. 65–81. 1932.

"Study of the Relations of Secondary and Higher Education in Pennsylvania: Knowledge as a Factor in Education." *28th Annual Report of the Carnegie Foundation for the Advancement of Teaching,* pp. 39–63. 1933.

"The Junior College, the University, and the Community." *29th Annual Report of the Carnegie Foundation for the Advancement of Teaching,* pp. 21–34. 1934.

LEARNED, WILLIAM S., AND WOOD, BEN D.

The Student and His Knowledge. Carnegie Foundation Bulletin No. 29. New York: Carnegie Foundation for the Advancement of Teaching, 1938.

NOCK, ALBERT J.

The Theory of Education in the United States. New York: Harcourt, Brace and Company, 1932.

WRISTON, HENRY M.

The Nature of a Liberal College. Appleton, Wisconsin: Lawrence College Press, 1937.

SOCIAL EVOLUTIONISM

BAGLEY, WILLIAM C.

The Educative Process. New York: The Macmillan Company, 1905.

Educational Values. New York: The Macmillan Company, 1911.

Determinism in Education. Baltimore: Warwick and York, 1925.

"Twenty Years of Progress in the Professionalization of Subject Matter for Normal Schools and Teachers Colleges." *Proceedings of the National Education Association,* pp. 906–912. Washington, D. C.: The Association, 1928.

"Some Handicaps of Character Education in the United States." *Proceedings of the National Education Association,* pp. 763–768. Washington, D. C.: The Association, 1929.

"The Future of Education in America." *Proceedings of the National Education Association,* pp. 218–225. Washington, D. C.: The Association, 1930.

Education, Crime and Social Progress. New York: The Macmillan Company, 1931.

"Modern Education Theories and Practical Considerations." *School and Society,* 37:409–414, April, 1933.

"The Task of Education Under the New Deal." *Educational Administration and Supervision,* 19:413–415, September, 1933.

"The Task of Education in a Period of Rapid Social Change." *Educational Administration and Supervision,* 19:561–570, November, 1933.

Education and Emergent Man. New York: T. Nelson and Sons, 1934.

"An Open Letter to Dr. Raup." *Educational Administration and Supervision,* 20:351–355, May, 1934.

"Is Subject-Matter Obsolete?" *Educational Administration and Supervision,* 21:401–412, September, 1935.

A Century of the Universal School. New York: The Macmillan Company, 1937.

BAGLEY, WILLIAM C., COLVIN, S. S., AND MACDONALD, M. E.

Human Behavior. New York: The Macmillan Company, 1929.

JUDD, CHARLES H.

The Evolution of a Democratic School System. New York: Houghton Mifflin Company, 1918.

Psychology of Social Institutions. New York: The Macmillan Company, 1926.

Psychology of Secondary Education. Boston: Ginn and Company, 1927.

The Unique Character of American Secondary Education. Cambridge: Harvard University Press, 1928.

"Materials for the Social Studies." *Educational Record,* 10:209–217, July, 1929.

"Adapting the Curriculum to the Psychological Characteristics of the Junior College." *Proceedings of the Institute for Administrative Officers of Higher Institutions,* pp. 1–13. 1929.

"Social Studies in the High School." *Junior-Senior High School Clearing House,* 4:572–574, June, 1930.

"The Eastbourne Conference." *Proceedings of the Institute for Administrative Officers of Higher Institutions,* 3:179–189. 1931.

"Application of the Psychological Doctrine of Individual Differences." *Proceedings of the Institute for Administrative Officers of Higher Institutions,* 4:13–20. 1932.

"Teaching Government in Public Schools." *School and Society,* 35:103–108, January 23, 1932.

"Various Forms of Organization of Elementary and Secondary Education." *American Association of College Registrars Proceedings,* pp. 329–335. 1932.

"Education, the Nation's Safeguard." *Addresses and Proceedings of the National Education Association,* pp. 560–568. Washington, D. C.: The Association, 1932.

"In Defense of American Secondary Schools." Department of Secondary School Principals, National Education Association, *Bulletin* No. 45, pp. 1–11, March, 1933.

"The Curriculum Revision Movement in American Education." *Proceedings of the National Education Association*, pp. 243–244. Washington, D. C.: The Association, 1935.

"Educational Trends and the General Social Order." *Proceedings of the National Education Association*, pp. 66–72. Washington, D. C.: The Association, 1933.

Problems of Education in the United States. New York: McGraw-Hill Company, 1933.

"The Reorganization and Coordination of Secondary and College Education." *Proceedings of the Institute for Administrative Officers of Higher Institutions*, 5:89–101. 1933.

"The Scientific Development and Evaluation of the Curriculum." *Official Report of the Department of Superintendents, National Education Association*, pp. 177–186. Washington, D. C.: The Association, 1933.

"What Constitutes a Good Secondary School and by What Standards Should It Be Evaluated?" *Proceedings of the National Education Association*, pp. 497–500. Washington, D. C.: The Association, 1934.

Education and Social Progress. New York: Harcourt, Brace and Company, 1934.

"The Historical Development of Secondary Education in America." *Official Report of the Department of Superintendents, National Education Association*, pp. 89–96. Washington, D. C.: The Association, 1935.

"Difficulties Involved in Introducing Socio-Economic Problems into the Curriculum." *Official Report of the Department of Superintendents, National Education Association*, pp. 261–266. Washington, D. C.: The Association, 1935.

Conference on Examinations, Folkestone, England. New York: Bureau of Publications, Teachers College, Columbia University, 1935.

"The Scientific Study of Social Trends as Background for the Interpretation of Educational Issues." *National Society of College Teachers of Education, 25th Yearbook*, pp. 142–162. 1937.

"Is Contact with Logically Organized Subject-Matter Sufficient for the Education of Children?" *Elementary School Journal*, 36:657–664, May, 1934.

"This Era of Uncertainty in Education." *School and Society*, 44:353–360, September 19, 1936.

Education as Cultivation of the Higher Mental Processes. New York: The Macmillan Company, 1936.

"Changing Conceptions of Secondary and Higher Education in America." *School Review,* 45:93–104, February, 1937.

"Can Divergent Views on Educational Theory and Practice Be Reconciled?" *Elementary School Journal,* 37:576–591, April, 1937.

"How Shall the Enriched Curriculum Be Made Systematic?" *Elementary School Journal,* 37:653–667, May, 1937.

"What Is General Education?" Department of Secondary School Principals, National Education Association, *Bulletin* No. 68, pp. 5–16, October, 1937.

"Specialization, the Bane of Secondary Education." Department of Secondary School Principals, National Education Association, *Bulletin* No. 22, pp. 14–20, March, 1938.

"Facing the Future." *Educational Record,* 19:125–140, April, 1938.

MORRISON, HENRY C.

"A Definition of the Secondary School and Its Implications." *High School Quarterly,* 17:111–116, April, 1929.

"Planning for the Whole School Period." *The English Journal,* 20:292–297, April, 1931.

The Practice of Teaching in the Secondary School. Chicago: University of Chicago Press, 1931 (Revised edition).

The Evolving Common School. Cambridge: Harvard University Press, 1933.

"Saving the Schools." *Educational Administration and Supervision,* 19:373–376, May, 1933.

Basic Principles of Education. New York: Houghton Mifflin Company, 1934.

School and Commonwealth. Chicago: University of Chicago Press, 1937.

SOCIAL REALISM

BRIGGS, THOMAS H.

"The Junior High School." *Classroom Teacher,* 10:3 80, 1927 1928.

The Great Investment. Cambridge: Harvard University Press, 1930.

"Jeremiah Was Right." *Teachers College Record,* 32:679–695, May, 1931.

"Caviling at Complacency." *Junior-Senior High School Clearing House,* 6:70–83, October, 1931.

"A Program for Secondary Education." Department of Secondary School Principals, National Education Association, *Bulletin* No. 40, pp. 1–12, March, 1932.

"A Vision of Secondary Education." *Teachers College Record*, 34:1–17, October, 1932.

"Propaganda and the Curriculum." *Teachers College Record*, 34:468–480, March, 1933.

Secondary Education. New York: The Macmillan Company, 1933.

"If There Were Millions." *Teachers College Record*, 35:633–666, May, 1934.

"What Constitutes a Good Secondary School and by What Standards Shall It Be Evaluated?" Department of Secondary School Principals, National Education Association, *Bulletin* No. 50, pp. 15–22, May, 1934.

"What the Emotions Do to Our Thinking." *Teachers College Record*, 36:372–379, February, 1935.

"The Philosophy that Must Guide Secondary Education." *Department of Superintendents Official Report, National Education Association*, pp. 96–103. Washington, D. C.: The Association, 1935.

"What Curriculum Organization for Secondary Schools?" *Educational Administration and Supervision*, 22:265–270, April, 1936.

"Should Education Indoctrinate?" *Educational Administration and Supervision*, 22:561–593, November, 1936.

"Indoctrination in Education." *Educational Forum*, 1:133–142, January, 1937.

"What Secondary Schools Should Do." *School and Society*, 45:312–318, March 6, 1937.

"Has the Junior High School Made Good?" *Educational Administration and Supervision*, 24:1–10, January, 1938.

"Articulation of the High School and College." *School and Society*, 47:649–656, May 21, 1938.

COMMITTEE ON THE ORIENTATION OF SECONDARY EDUCATION.

Issues of Secondary Education. Department of Secondary School Principals, National Education Association, *Bulletin* No. 59, January, 1936.

Functions of Secondary Education. Department of Secondary School Principals, National Education Association, *Bulletin* No. 64, January, 1937.

COX, PHILIP W. L. AND LONG, FORREST E.

Principles of Secondary Education. New York: D. C. Heath and Company, 1932.

Douglass, Harl R.

"Adapting the Curriculum of the Junior High School to the Needs of the Pupils." Department of Secondary School Principals, National Education Association, *Bulletin* No. 45, pp. 127–139, March, 1933.

"The Effects of the State and National Testing on the Secondary School." *School Review*, 42:497–509, September, 1934.

"The Next Step in Secondary Education." *Secondary Education*, 4:23–27, January, 1935.

"Can We Revamp the High-School Curriculum to Fit the Needs of Today?" *Baltimore Bulletin of Education*, 14:49–57, September, 1936.

Secondary Education for Youth in Modern America. A Report to the Youth Commission of the American Council on Education, Washington, D. C., 1937.

"The Problems of Youth." *North Central Association Quarterly*, 13:224–231, October, 1938.

Gulick, Luther H.

Education for American Life. General Report of the Regents' Inquiry into the Character and Cost of Public Education in the State of New York. New York: McGraw-Hill Company, 1938.

Spaulding, Francis T.

"What May the Senior High School Demand of the Junior High School?" Department of Secondary School Principals, National Education Association, *Bulletin* No. 25, pp. 286–299, March, 1929.

"What Extra-Curricular Activities Ought a Good School Not to Offer?" *Educational Method*, 9:140–151, December, 1929.

"Can the Small High School Improve Its Curriculum?" *School Review*, 39:423–438, June, 1931.

"The Small Six-year Secondary School." *Junior-Senior High School Clearing House*, 8:469–474, April, 1934.

"Graduation Without Equivocation." *Harvard Teachers Record*, 5:148–154, June, 1935.

"Whither Education in Evaluation of Pupil Growth?" *New York State Education*, 23:380–382, February, 1936.

"Education for Vocational Competence." Department of Secondary School Principals, National Education Association, *Bulletin* No. 60, pp. 88–98, March, 1936.

"The Evaluation of Secondary-School Curricula in the New York State Regents' Inquiry." *North Central Association Quarterly*, 12:26–33, July, 1937.

"Interest in Learning." Department of Secondary School Principals, National Education Association, *Bulletin* No. 74, pp. 52–54, April, 1938.

High School and Life. Report of the Regents' Inquiry into the Character and Cost of Public Education in the State of New York. New York: McGraw-Hill Company, 1938.

EXPERIMENTALISM

BODE, BOYD H.

Fundamentals of Education. New York: The Macmillan Company, 1921.

Modern Educational Theories. New York: The Macmillan Company, 1927.

"Education from a Pragmatic Point of View." Chapter XVI, in *Conflicting Psychologies of Learning.* New York: D. C. Heath and Company, 1929.

"The Problem of Liberal Education." *Educational Administration and Supervision,* 16:633–636, November, 1930.

"Currents and Cross Currents in Higher Education." *Journal of Higher Education,* 2:374–379, October, 1931.

"The Confusion in Present-Day Education." Chapter I, in *The Educational Frontier* (W. H. Kilpatrick, Editor). New York: D. Appleton-Century, 1933.

"Education and Social Reconstruction." *Social Frontier,* 1:18–22, 1935.

Progressive Education at the Crossroads. New York: Newson and Company, 1938.

"Democratic Education and Conflicting Culture Values." *Social Frontier,* 1:18–22, January, 1939.

CHILDS, JOHN L.

Education and the Philosophy of Experimentalism. New York: The Century Company, 1931.

"Bode at the Crossroads." *Social Frontier,* 4:267–268, May, 1938.

"Doctor Bode on Authentic Democracy." *Social Frontier,* 5:40–43, November, 1938.

"Progressive Education and the Secondary School." *Progressive Education,* 16:411–417, October, 1939.

COMMISSION ON SECONDARY SCHOOL CURRICULUM, PROGRESSIVE EDUCATION ASSOCIATION, V. T. THAYER, CHAIRMAN.

Science in General Education. New York: D. Appleton-Century, 1938.

Reorganizing Secondary Education. (Prepared by V. T. Thayer, C. B. Zachry, R. Kotinsky.) New York: D. Appleton-Century, 1939.

COUNTS, GEORGE S.

Secondary Education and Industrialism. Cambridge: Harvard University Press, 1929.

"Dare Progressive Education be Progressive?" *Progressive Education,* 9:57–63, April, 1932.

"Education for What?" *New Republic,* 71:12–16, May, 18, 25, 1932.

The Social Foundations of Education. Report of the Commission on the Social Studies, Part IX. New York: Charles Scribner's Sons, 1934.

"Three Hundred Years of the Secondary School Curriculum." Department of Secondary School Principals, National Education Association, *Bulletin* No. 55, pp. 111–122, March, 1935.

The Prospects of American Democracy. New York: The John Day Company, 1938.

COX, PHILIP W. L.

"Drift, Mastery, and the Zeitgeist." *Educational Method,* 11:193–196, 263–265, 326–329, 390–396, 477–484, January–May, 1932.

"Are the Conclusions and Recommendations of the Commission on the Social Studies 'Startling' or 'Alarming'?" *School and Society,* 40:554–557, October 27, 1934.

"Must the High School Survive?" *Educational Forum,* 2:25–39, November, 1937.

"The Middle Ground in Education: A Rejoinder to the Plea." *Educational Forum,* 1:169–188, January, 1937.

"Youth's Response to His World." *Educational Forum,* 3:96–98, November, 1938.

"Model T Examinations Lose Ground." *Clearing House,* 12:308–309, January, 1938.

DEWEY, JOHN.

Reconstruction in Philosophy. New York: Henry Holt and Company, 1920.

Experience and Nature. New York: The Open Court Publishing Company, 1929.

Experience and Education. New York: The Macmillan Company, 1938.

DEWEY, JOHN AND CHILDS, JOHN L.

"The Social-Economic Situation and Education," "The Underlying Philosophy of Education." Chapters II and IX, in *The Educational*

Frontier (W. H. Kilpatrick, Editor). New York: D. Appleton-Century, 1933.

EVERETT, SAMUEL (EDITOR).

A Challenge to Secondary Education. New York: D. Appleton-Century, 1935.

The Community School. Report of the Committee on the Community School of the Society for Curriculum Study. New York: D. Appleton-Century, 1938.

HANNA, PAUL R. AND OTHERS.

Youth Serves the Community. New York: D. Appleton-Century, 1936.

HOPKINS, THOMAS L.

Curriculum Principles and Practices. New York: Benjamin H. Sanborn Company, 1929.

"Creative Education." *Educational Method,* 11:1–8, October, 1931.

"Curriculum Development." *Teachers College Record,* 37:441–447, February, 1936.

"Differentiation of Curriculum Practices and Teaching Methods in High Schools." *35th Yearbook of the National Society for the Study of Education,* Part I, pp. 173–185. 1936.

Integration: Its Meaning and Application. New York: D. Appleton-Century, 1937.

"Emerging Emphases as to Learning." *Teachers College Record,* 40:119–128, November, 1938.

JOINT COMMITTEE ON CURRICULUM OF THE DEPARTMENT OF SUPERVISORS AND DIRECTORS OF INSTRUCTION AND THE SOCIETY FOR CURRICULUM STUDY, H. HARAP, CHAIRMAN.

The Changing Curriculum. New York: D. Appleton-Century, 1937.

KILPATRICK, WILLIAM H.

Education for a Changing Civilization. New York: The Macmillan Company, 1926.

(Editor). *The Educational Frontier.* New York: D. Appleton-Century, 1933.

"The Social Philosophy of Progressive Education." *Progressive Education,* 12:289–329, May, 1935.

Remaking the Curriculum. New York: Newson and Company, 1936.

RUGG HAROLD O. (EDITOR).

Democracy and the Curriculum. Third Yearbook of the John Dewey Society. New York: D. Appleton-Century, 1939.

THAYER, VIVIAN T.

"The Reorganization Movement and the Progressive Secondary School." *Progressive Education,* 6:127–131, April, 1929.

Supervision in the Secondary School (with H. B. Alberty). New York: D. C. Heath and Company, 1931.

"Wholesome Living and Preparation for College." *Junior-Senior High School Clearing House,* 5:595–601, June, 1931.

"High Schools—for Whom and for What?" *Our Children,* Chapter XXI, pp. 226–236. Child Study Association of America, 1932.

"The Report of the Commission on the Reorganization of Secondary Education." *Junior-Senior High School Clearing House,* 7:49–55, September, 1932.

"Adjusting the Curriculum to the Child." *Mental Hygiene,* 17:554–559, October, 1933.

"Integration of School and Community Resources in a Program of Secondary Education." *The New Deal in Education,* Bulletin, School of Education, University of Pennsylvania, pp. 150–157, 1934.

"The School in an Age of Transition." *School and Home,* 16:531–539, November, 1934.

"Orientation to Life as a Function of Education." *Occupations,* 13:677–686, May, 1935.

"The Scope and Aims of Secondary Education: The Program and Courses of Study Needed." *North Central Association Quarterly,* 11:308–313, January, 1937.

"An Approach to the Reconstruction of the Secondary School Curriculum." *Harvard Educational Review,* 7:27–35, January, 1937.

Index

(Whenever parallel references are given, *H., S. E., S. R.,* and *E.* refer to Humanism, Social Evolutionism, Social Realism, and Experimentalism respectively.)

473